LIVING on LESS

FROM THE EDITORS OF THE MOTHER EARTH NEWS®

The Mother Earth News
Books

The Mother Earth News, Inc.
Hendersonville, North Carolina

This book was produced by THE MOTHER EARTH NEWS BOOKS,
the book division of THE MOTHER EARTH NEWS, Inc.

EDITORIAL: Arthur T. Snell and Barbara S. Henderson (directors),
Lorna K. Loveless and Clark Center (associate editors).

DESIGN AND LAYOUT: Wendy Simons (director),
Jennifer Fisher Brock (associate artist).

With special appreciation to the following: Spanky Alexander, Ken Cross, Joy Davenport, Megan Davies,
Marsha Drake, Joanne Dufilho, Roselyn Edwards, William Finch, Ken Forsgren, Carolyn Frederick,
Michael Garner, Joni Gilmour, Jack Green, M. Grier, Mark Hillyer, Steve Keull, Gerald B. McMillan,
Diana Murdock, Pamela Phillips, Garry R. Ramo, Keith Roddy, Kathleen C. Seabe, Sherry Seagle,
Carolyn Dellinger Sizemore, Carol Wood, Mary Workman.

Published 1984
Printed in the United States of America
THE MOTHER EARTH NEWS, Inc.
105 Stoney Mountain Road
Hendersonville, North Carolina 28791

Library of Congress Catalog Card Number 84-60259
ISBN 0-938-43207-9

THE MOTHER EARTH NEWS

magazine is published at 105 Stoney Mountain Road, Hendersonville, North Carolina 28791. It is the bimonthly publication edited by, and for, today's turned-on people of all ages—the creative ones, the doers, the folks who make it all happen.

CONTENTS

INTRODUCTION

How can living on less improve the quality of your life? Living on less does not have to be a way of life born of necessity, only to be discarded when circumstances change for the better. As approached in these pages, living on less is an expression of the philosophy that people can live comfortable, complete, and fulfilling lives without depending on a large income. It is a way of life that is a manifestation of the desire to enhance the quality of life.

Living on Less is packed with ideas and methods for achieving greater independence, and it is filled with stories of how ordinary people all across North America have reduced their costs of living, increased their security and comfort, or otherwise improved their lives. These pages contain information on pursuing alternatives to conventional work patterns; finding and buying land and houses; homesteading in both the country and the city; growing, preserving, and storing, as well as foraging, food; raising livestock; cutting energy costs; creating clothing and housewares; using substitutes for commercial health and beauty aids; entertaining yourself and your family; and saving money through bartering, bargaining, and buying at auctions.

Many of the ideas contained in this book were developed to fit specific needs and situations. None of them will be suitable for every reader. It is the concept that is important—the belief that we can all exert a positive influence on our own lives and that we can fight back while living rewarding lives, even in uncertain economic times.

One of the greatest expenses any of us incur in our lifetimes is the cost of housing, and there are many ways that this enormous outlay of cash can be reduced substantially, simply by utilizing one of the many alternatives to the standard method of purchasing a ready-built house with a virtual lifetime of mortgage payments attached. Giving careful consideration to what kind of house to buy or build and to the methods of financing available can save a person literally years' of income that would otherwise be lost forever to repairs or interest rates. For instance, just the interest on a house bought by means of a conventional mortgage can amount to much more than the purchase price, and the cost would be substantially lower if only the cost of the interest could be cut in half. *Living on Less* tells you that it can!

Food is another major expense for the average household, and any reduction here would be more than welcome, especially by the member of the family who empties the checking account for just a week's worth of groceries. Gardening—even on a small scale—can help keep some of that money in the bank. However, you don't want to spend all your hours tilling the soil and tending crops, so high yields from a minimum amount of space and labor are important. Wild plants, too, can make a contribution, and there are few areas of the country where foraging cannot put natural, nutritious foods on the table. Both cultivated and wild plants that are not eaten while in season can be stored for future use. For people with a backyard, livestock can be an asset, providing them with meat, eggs, or dairy products.

Energy to heat, cool, and light our homes and to cook our meals is a third major expense of everyday living. Some people have completely cut their ties with the power grid, and others have turned to alternative sources of heat, while continuing to purchase electricity for cooking, lighting, and other functions. Installing insulation and taking advantage of the natural heat of the sun can also help cut down on the need for commercial fuels.

Clothes wear out, but that doesn't necessarily mean it's time to throw them away. With ingenuity and a little sewing practice, an enterprising homemaker can turn outgrown or discarded garments into useful or decorative items. The kitchen and the herb garden can provide cosmetics, hair colorings, and other toiletries. Skillful bartering and bargain hunting can stretch budgets considerably. Recreation can be found at fairs and other public gatherings rather than in theaters or amusement parks, and homemade games can provide diversions.

The successes of the people who have tried these and other ways of achieving more while spending less may well inspire you to similar accomplishments. By becoming more self-reliant, not only do you create your own peace of mind and find satisfaction in your own accomplishments, but you also help to conserve resources and demonstrate to the world that it really is possible to live better on less.

A MATTER
OF ECONOMY

CAN YOU AFFORD TO WORK NINE TO FIVE?

While many people yearn for a lovely and conventional suburban home with a predictable nine-to-five routine, that kind of security had lost its charm for at least one couple. Their dream was of a place in the country and of a way of life inextricably bound to the land. Both husband and wife were employed, but after each tightly scheduled and often unsatisfying day, their dream of a simpler existence had become ever more appealing.

One night the wife, armed with pen and paper, decided to analyze the economics of the job she held. She had been hoping that it was helping them to reach their back-to-the-land goal, but her computations indicated otherwise. The hard, cold figures showed that she was not only failing to save money toward the goal, but she was actually spending more money on job-related expenses than she had supposed. Her startling discovery was that she couldn't afford to keep her job!

Her salary as a teacher totaled $9,000 a year, yet her spendable income (consisting of net wages minus work-connected expenses) came to only $2,530 annually. The cost of working was quite amazing. Here is how her income was being distributed before any personal expenses:

Salary		$9,000
State and federal taxes	$1,500	
Car payment ($135/month)	1,620	
Gasoline for commuting ($160/month)	1,920	
Auto repair, tolls, miscellaneous	480	
Vehicle insurance and registration	350	
Working wardrobe, repair, cleaning	600	
Total work related expenses	$6,470	
Net spendable income		$2,530

She decided that if there was no greater benefit than that to be had from her nine-to-five routine, it was time to let go of it. So, with little hesitation, she did just that! From then on she managed to augment her husband's salary by cashing in on her love of horses. Years of training in riding, combined with her teaching experience, blended to produce a career—instructing young horsemen and -women—that provided not only an income but lots of outdoor activity as well. The new "job" also afforded her more leisure time to develop home and garden skills that helped to stretch what money she did bring home.

The new occupation eliminated the need for a second family vehicle, so they were able to barter their car for two acres of remote New Hampshire land. Once they acquired that property, they immediately wanted to relocate to it, and upon closer examination of the husband's earnings, they realized that the idea of simply packing up and trying to make do in a rural setting wasn't too farfetched at all!

The following figures demonstrate how much of his income was being used each year to do no more than maintain their suburban lifestyle:

Salary		$16,550
State and federal taxes	$1,800	
Mortgage payments ($235/month)	2,820	
Property taxes	1,200	
Electricity ($75/month)	900	
Telephone ($40/month)	480	
Oil heat	1,000	
Truck payment ($107/month)	1,284	
Gasoline ($100/month)	1,200	
Truck repair, miscellaneous	360	
Vehicle insurance and registration	350	
Food ($250/month)	3,000	
Dining, local travel, entertainment	1,200	
Clothing	480	
Total living expenses	$16,074	
Net spendable income		$476

Faced with those facts, the couple made the decision to abandon their suburban way of life. They sold their house and moved onto the two paid-for country acres, where they built a small, mortgage-free camp. They now cook with bottled gas for a mere $6.00 a month, and their light is produced by economical kerosene lanterns. A small barrel stove has taken the place of a costly oil furnace, and wood obtained through barter provides all their heat. A brook on the property supplies all the water they need.

The husband's financed pickup truck (and its accompanying payments) has been replaced by a used van (completely paid for) that has been converted into a camper. In a short time, the annual budget looked more like this:

Present combined income		$7,400
Rent/mortgage	$ 0	
Car payments	0	
Electricity	0	
Wood heat	0	
Income taxes	120	
Property taxes	75	
Telephone (occasional use of pay phone)	100	

Bottled gas and kerosene	120
Gasoline (errands and travel to seasonal work)	600
Vehicle insurance and registration	300
Food (to supplement the edibles they produce, hunt, or forage)	1,400
Clothing (leaving city jobs really cut this expense)	300
Total living expenses	$3,055
Net spendable income	$4,345

It's easy to see that their change of lifestyle has resulted in having more cash to spend than they did before. Because both are finally free of the 40-hour week, they can devote themselves full-time to gardening, foraging, fishing, hunting, free-lance writing (which helps to pay their bills), and traveling.

The couple's pleasure expenses have actually *increased* since their move to the country. For example, they rented out their camp (another source of income) while they spent a year exploring in Alaska. After three months on the road, with expenses totaling $2,900 for 12,000 miles of unforgettable experiences, they took jobs as caretakers of a remote cabin on the Alaskan coast. There they enjoyed the icy splendor of glaciers and snowcapped peaks while they continued to expand their knowledge and skills.

This man and woman are living their dream, but what it took was the conviction to free themselves from the life they thought they couldn't *afford* to leave. Until they faced the facts and figures, they never realized the astronomical costs involved in maintaining a suburban lifestyle.

It seems that the solution to money problems sometimes lies not in earning more, but rather in simplifying one's way of life and perhaps even earning less. Moving from a dwelling in an area with a high cost of living to a dream farm or camp in the country—to that place where you can garden, cut your own wood, and possibly even raise your own dairy or meat animals—may be the answer to your financial dilemma. In fact, you may be able to eliminate entirely that tedious 40-hour workweek and meet your reduced expenditures with a part-time or seasonal job, or a home business.

The transition from a life in suburbia to one on the farm does take time, thought, and money. How much of each *you'll* need will depend on your skills, level of determination, desired lifestyle, and current equities. You may have to cash in some assets and deplete your personal savings, devote extra time to honing a talent that will bring in the income you'll require, and learn the skills necessary to live in harmony with the earth. Whatever method you adopt to rid yourself of those Monday morning blues, rest assured it *can* be done. And the entire process can prove to be an exciting journey—one that may far exceed all of your original dreams.

HOW TO RETIRE SIX MONTHS A YEAR

Many people find the idea of working 40 hours a week 50 weeks a year until they reach retirement age less than appealing, but they feel trapped within a system that dictates that they take their leisure at the end of their lives. There are alternatives, however, such as gearing your life so that you have an annual, periodic retirement of six months or so.

Basically, periodic retirement involves working half the year and having the other half of the year to do with as one pleases, to devote totally to living. Being able to do this means, fundamentally, that expenses and income must be brought into balance so that the amount earned in six months equals the amount needed to live for the entire year. It means deciding what is required to live comfortably and what is not necessary. It means planning expenditures and sticking to that plan. It does not mean sacrificing one's sanity or subjecting oneself to severe privation.

Carrying out such a program is obviously easier for a single person, simply because there is only one individual involved in deciding what can be done without. A couple would find periodic retirement slightly more difficult, and though it could be done by a family, this larger group would certainly find it even more arduous. However, a periodic retirement plan doesn't necessarily have to be geared to a six-months-on, six-months-off cycle. It's entirely possible to set up a plan to work eight months a year and retire for four or to work out another schedule.

Gaining free time doesn't mean getting away from the city to a country homestead or retreat, where—ironically—a great deal of work can be required to provide oneself with the requirements of a comfortable life. As a matter of fact, the plan can work best in an urban setting where free or low-cost transportation, entertainment, and other facilities are available and where there is a range of housing from which to choose. This can mean some flexibility in the amount of rent one opts to pay and this expense can be held down without settling for quarters that lack an aura of comfort and cleanliness.

GETTING THERE: The first step in adjusting your lifestyle so you can take several months off a year is to look at your present budget, determine what various aspects of your life are costing, and decide which expenses can be reduced or eliminated.

You'll probably find that a few giant steps can be made by changing just a few aspects of your lifestyle. Supporting even a modest automobile can easily cost the equivalent of about three months' work a year, which means that about 25 percent of the work done in this country is done solely to support the family car. By simply doing without a car, then, a person can free nearly three months' salary a year.

In an urban environment where there is good public transportation, doing without a car may not be the hardship it might seem at first glance. Some adjustments will be necessary, though, to live comfortably without a private vehicle. Avoiding a long commute daily by bus might require that a person move to an apartment within a walking distance to work of no more than a couple of miles. To live without your own car, it's essential that you live close to a good shopping district.

The second major area where savings can be made is in housing. If, for instance, you're shelling out about a third of your take-home pay for rent each month, you might consider finding a smaller, less expensive place that would cost you closer to 20 percent of your monthly net income. This may not seem like a great amount, but it can mean a saving that is equivalent to several months' rent. It's entirely possible that an even greater dent could be made in housing costs without enduring a hardship. It is important to select housing that is suitable and in a location that is convenient to schools, libraries, churches, community centers, or whatever else the individual finds important. No drive for economy can work if the person involved cannot be comfortable and happy.

Controlling the food budget is also important, and the plan should include a combination of eating out at inexpensive restaurants and dining at home. Avoid instant meals such as TV dinners and pot pies, which are expensive and generally not as good as meals you fix yourself. When shopping for food, stick to inexpensive, reasonably priced items. Do not overlook salads, which can be low-cost meals by themselves. You also might consider foraging, hunting, and fishing to put food on the table, but be careful of hunting and fishing. If you spend $15 on an angling expedition and return home with a single one-pounder, it's going to be a mighty expensive meal.

When reducing living costs it's important to give consideration to entertainment and to avoid eliminating recreational funds from one's budget. However, when spending money on diversions, it's a good idea to choose those that don't require additional or continuing expenditures. Buying a camera, for instance, requires regular outlays for film and processing; golf clubs will demand buying balls and paying green fees; and a phonograph wants to be supplied with new records from time to time unless the owner is satisfied to listen to the same old ones forever. On the other hand, a radio requires only the initial purchase price and will provide years of musical entertainment with no more cost than the small amount of electricity it will use, and a night school course will remain with a person without any repetition of the payments for tuition and supplies. Community activities and groups are usually free or cost very little, and they can provide a great deal of enrichment. The public library offers literally (and literary) stacks of diversion.

A person should realize fully that discretionary spending competes directly with the amount of free time available each year, and this needs to be taken into account when planning and budgeting. For example, for an individual who has cut living expenses to $300 a month, spending just an additional $20 each month will mean less time available for periodic retirement, since more of the year must be spent working to earn the extra $240.

AN EXAMPLE: Suppose you are working at a full-time job that gives you a net salary of $130 a week. Working at that job all year round will produce $6,760 after deductions, or $565 a month. Assume that it is costing about $1,700 a year to operate your car, including insurance, gas and oil, licensing fees, tires, repair, and incidental expenses. This amounts to $141 a month. If you are living in a $175-a-month apartment, the cost of that and owning a car comes to $316 a month, leaving $246 of your monthly take-home pay to cover all your other living expenses: utilities, phone, food, clothing, entertainment, and miscellaneous items. All this is probably taking most of what you earn.

In order to retire for six months out of the year, you will need to reduce your expenses so that only half your annual salary will cover them all year; you'll need to develop a way of living on $3,380 a year, or about $281 a month, which means cutting your living costs to approximately half what they where when you were working year-round. It means cutting about $281 in regular monthly expenditures.

Doing without an automobile may be the first thing to consider, and cutting out the expense that owning one entails will put you just over halfway to your goal. Subtracting the $141 a month that a car is very likely costing you leaves only $140 in monthly living expenses to cut.

The next thing to look into is reducing your rent. You need to decide if you really must spend $175 a month for an apartment or whether you can live comfortably in smaller, less expensive quarters. If not, then it's unlikely that you'll be able to make enough cuts in the rest of your budget to reach the level at which you can retire for a full six months of the year. However, the more you can trim this expense, the easier it will be to reach your goal without incurring hardships or discomfort in other areas of your life. Finding a studio apartment or similar adequate housing for, say, $125 a month would cut $50 a month from your expenses, leaving $90 a month to cut to bring your cost of living down to a six-months-on, six-months-off level. This might seem like a lot, but it amounts to only about $20 a week, some of which will have already been taken care of by the banishment of automobile expenses.

Parking fees and bridge and highway tolls will automatically disappear, possibly saving you $5 a week, and the remaining $15 can probably be eliminated without even being felt. With only a small amount left to cut, it's time to take a look at the odds and ends such as movies, newspapers and magazines, smoking (if you do), and other smaller aspects of your life. If you're a moviegoer, cutting down from once a week to once a month will save five or six dollars a week. Not purchasing newspapers and magazines will mean a considerable savings for most people, and it need not result in a deprivation, because these can usually be found and read at the public library. Anyone who smokes can take care of the remaining cuts needed, and nonsmokers should be able to do so by keeping a close eye on other miscellaneous expenditures.

This demonstrates that you can cut down enough to live on only half a relatively modest income, but where does it leave you? Out of the $281 you will allow yourself to spend every month, $125 will go for rent, leaving $156 a month, or about $36 a week, for the rest of your expenses. This amount may seem low, and if you find it too low, you might want to consider a still less expensive dwelling, and a different ratio of work to leisure.

OTHER MATTERS: Security is a serious concern for most people and should be given consideration before the initiation of any periodic retirement plan that might affect a person's financial buffer or peace of mind. Feelings of insecurity are usually related to two types of possible situation: unforeseen disasters or events such as accidents and illness, and unemployment or other things, over which one has at least some control.

While some people may wish to adjust their budgets to include regular payments to maintain medical and other insurance, there is the alternative of developing a cash reserve to cover emergencies in this area. Before diving into a periodic employment plan, for instance, work long enough to set aside a fund containing $1,000, $2,000, or whatever you feel is adequate to meet unforeseen contingencies.

In the area over which one has a certain amount of control, the main problem is the fear of being unable to find work that pays enough. Finding employment for the months you choose to work should not be a large obstacle. There are several areas where work is seasonal because of the climate, and there are other job possibilities that are nicely geared to a work-half-the-year, retire-half-the-year life. Many short-term jobs are available in the resort industry and offer a sometimes welcome change from living in the city. These also enable a person to just about choose the season he or she wants to work, and some include room and board as part of the bargain.

EXTRA EXPENDITURES: Though a person might plan and budget carefully, unforeseen needs can occur. There will always be something extra that requires spending more than a strict periodic retirement plan will allow. These fall into the category of discretionary expenditures and still require extra work if the purchases are to be made. A decision must be made about whether the purchase is worth the extra work it will require. Though someone may be unwilling to work the extra three months a year it would take to support an automobile, that same individual might well consider it worthwhile to invest the four or five days it would take to earn enough money to buy a decent bicycle.

SPECIAL CONSIDERATIONS: When searching for a place to live, take careful note of the hundreds of small things that might make you want to flee the place an hour after moving in. Think about the things you like and dislike about your present lodgings and other places you've lived, and see which of these exist at any new location you are considering. Determine whether you're likely to hear the neighbors' parties, stereos, and arguments. Find out whether they are people you want to live next to. You should also pay particular attention to the apartment managers, for they will play a big role in determining how well the building is maintained and how quiet or noisy the place is. The neighborhood itself is vitally important, not only because it needs to be in a convenient location, but because you'll be relying heavily on your own resources and will need a supportive environment. Compromises will be necessary, of course, but be certain not to make any that will make living in the place you choose an unhappy experience.

FUTURE SECURITY: Anyone considering a periodic retirement plan must do what is needed for future security, and there are several options. One can continue to work, carrying on their plan into later years, or one can make financial provisions that might depend partly on working an extra month a year and setting that money aside and partly on a pension plan of some sort. The thing to keep in mind is that most people spend 40 years or so working at jobs they may not really like so they can enjoy about seven years that they can call their own. In addition to these seven or so years, they have been awarded a couple of weeks' vacation each year, which amounts to a whole year and a half off. A person following a periodic retirement plan, on the other hand, will, by the time retirement age is reached, have enjoyed 20 years of retirement—two decades of free, unstructured leisure time.

THE DIVIDENDS: There are unforeseen benefits to a periodic retirement plan. For example, walking puts a person in touch with the environment in ways that driving cannot, and it adds to a sense of independence. But the most important dividend is the fullfilment gained by pursuing one's interests for six months every year.

AFFORDABLE HOUSING

A LOW-COST, CIRCULAR EARTH SHELTER

Is it possible to achieve self-sufficiency and independence on a single acre without spending a fortune on developing the land and building a home? Probably so, with imagination, planning, hard work, and the right acreage. Of course, providing a family's food and energy from such a small plot is a tall order and may take several years to achieve, but a starting point can be shelter: building a home to be the core of the homestead and doing so efficiently and inexpensively.

Development of just such a homestead was the goal of a project begun in 1982 at THE MOTHER EARTH NEWS Eco-Village, a research and demonstration center in western North Carolina. By the end of 1983, a low-cost, earth-sheltered house had been built, around which the grounds would be developed to contain gardens, a pond, and outbuildings for livestock and power-generating equipment. All these elements would be harmoniously and productively combined in a miniature ecosystem.

The 1,000-square-foot, two-bedroom passive solar home was designed to accommodate a small family comfortably and to be as inexpensive as possible to build, heat, cool, and maintain. Energy efficiency and durability were taken heavily into account in planning and construction, as was the siting of the building in relation to the rest of the project.

Because a convexly curved wall can withstand the stress of earth berming better than a flat wall can, the floor plan is based upon a 36-foot-diameter circle. The southeast section of the circumference is brought to a point so that when viewed from above, the outline looks much like a teardrop. One of the straight walls in this section faces very nearly south to catch the rays of the sun and provide heat for the greenhouse that occupies this portion of the building. Generous glazing in the greenhouse, kitchen, and south-facing clerestory provides a fair amount of solar heating, but these windows are protected from the summer sun by roof overhangs.

The structure is situated on a west-facing slope that angles downward toward a creek. On the other side of the small watercourse, a hillside rises steeply, and late on summer afternoons, deciduous and evergreen trees extensively shade the valley between the two hillsides. Consequently, the building was dug into the hillside far enough up the slope to avoid winter shading, and an attempt was made to keep the south-facing wall running as close to an east/west axis as possible.

Because the westerly orientation of the hill didn't lend itself completely to ideal solar exposure, the builders decided to extend the straight south-pointing wall beyond the house to serve as a retaining wall. This enabled them to provide deeper berming by cutting into the hillside to a point where the uphill wall would be buried to its top. The lower side of the 36-foot-diameter circle, then, is about three feet below grade. Dirt removed during the excavation was used later to increase the depth of the fill around the back of the circle to at least four feet in most places.

THE BEGINNINGS: After a backhoe had completed the major excavating, the builders dug conventional 8-inch-deep, 16-inch-wide footings around the circumference of the 36-foot-diameter circle. First they loosened the earth with a rotary tiller, and then they shoveled out the loose dirt by hand. They laid two rings of No. 4 reinforcing rod in the trench and supported these about three inches off the bottom. After that, 36-inch No. 4 starter bars were placed vertically every 32 inches around the curved section of the wall and every 16 inches along the straight portions so they would project upward into the cavities of the blocks and tie the footings to the wall when it was built. Two more bars were set where the pilasters would be located, and all the footings were filled with concrete.

A rammed-earth floor had been planned for the building, but this idea was discarded with the surfacing of a spring large enough to produce a pool of standing water within the ring of footings. Drainage was provided for the springwater, and then two courses of eight-inch block were laid on the footings. Inside this foundation, the crew dumped a 12-inch-thick layer of 3/4-inch stone and covered that with a polyethylene vapor barrier that was sealed and lapped up the sides of the block. After roughing in the plumbing, the builders poured a con-

crete slab, making it level with the top of the blocks.

Despite apprehension on the part of the masons involved in the project, laying the blocks for the walls turned out to be a fairly straightforward task. Because the curve of the wall was gentle, the larger exterior gaps between the eight-inch blocks were easily plugged with mortar. After the twelfth course was laid and the mortar had set, a form for a bond beam at the top was constructed of scrap plywood. No. 4 rebar was dropped down into the block cavities to meet the starter bars, and the other holes in the wall were plugged, reducing the amount of concrete needed to complete the walls. The upright bars were wired to two rings of steel running through the beam, and the form and unplugged cores were filled with concrete.

FRAMING AND RAFTERS: Framing began with the building of an east/west partition across the diameter of the circular section of the house. This was fairly standard 2 X 4 frame construction with the studs placed on 16-inch centers and openings left for the bathroom and bedroom doors. The job was complicated somewhat by the need for special reinforcement above the door frames and the 1-in-12 slope of the roof.

Before starting on the roof, the builders had to frame the kitchen window opening and prepare the lintel for that span. The lintel was formed from two 2 X 12's cut to match the curve of the wall.

The main rafters were flitch plate beams, which consist of plywood sandwiched between two pieces of solid lumber. These beams are less expensive than solid timbers of comparable strength and can be assembled from cut-to-size pieces right at the construction site. The ones in this low-cost earth shelter consisted of 3/4-inch plywood glued and nailed between 2 X 10's.

For the front roof, first a 2 X 10 cross rafter with a two-by ledger strip was put in place atop the west end of the divider wall so it extended over the west bedroom door. Three flitch plate jack rafters were put in place with one end of each against the cross rafter and the other resting on the outside wall. Two more cross rafters were then added to the first.

A beam constructed of five 2 X 6's and two 2 X 8's was put in place across the greenhouse opening and supported in the center by a 6 X 6 upright. The four rafters over the southeast section of the roof span the gap between this beam and the interior dividing wall. Two by ten blocking was installed between the rafters, and the roof was covered with plywood sheathing. A weatherproof covering of roll roofing capped the front half of the house.

For the rear roof, which has a 1-in-3 slope, the 22-foot-long peak rafter was the first beam set in place. This was built in two sections and supported where the pieces met by a post that would be hidden in the plumbing wall between the bathroom and the bedroom closets. Two other rafters run from the peak out to the west and east, and three others radiate outward on each side from small cross rafters that run between the front rafter and the peak rafter.

The clerestory window formed where the two roofs meet allows ample light to reach the bedrooms and bathroom, and is kept from admitting too much heat in the summer by an overhang supported by a barge rafter.

Plastic pipe and a gravel bed around the bermed portion of the outside wall provide drainage, and an asphalt-bentonite compound and plastic sheeting protect the walls themselves against ground moisture. Two layers of inch-thick polystyrene provide insulation.

Insulation for the roof consists of a total of seven inches of fiberglass batting pushed up between the rafters and stapled in place.

Double glazing was used for major expanses of window area. Four casement windows can be opened to provide ventilation, but the rest of the windows are fixed in place.

The interior walls of a dwelling such as this can, like those of a conventional house, be finished to suit the owner's taste and budget. Likewise, plumbing and electrical fixtures, kitchen and bathroom cabinets, and so on, can all be chosen according to personal preference and economics.

Ecological and financial benefits result from fitting a house into the land to create a permaculture homestead. A family can raise its own fruits and vegetables, livestock and fish. With a stream or river nearby, the homestead can even provide its own electrical power. The house, however, is the heart of such an operation.

BUYING AND RESTORING AN OLD FIXER-UPPER

Purchasing old dwellings and restoring them for resale can, for folks who are willing to invest a bit of initiative and effort, be a highly profitable enterprise or a way to own a home for much less than its final value. But buyers who don't know exactly how to choose a home to rehabilitate can easily take on a loser and end up parting unnecessarily with a lot of hard-earned money.

HOW NOT TO GET STARTED: One man, for example, found what he thought was an incredible bargain for only $23,500. The house needed repairs, but it seemed like a steal at the price. Unfortunately, as soon as work began on the dwelling, he discovered that the more things he fixed, the more he found to fix.

The wiring had been added to the house after it was built in 1910. It was all exposed and had to be brought up to code. He wound up replacing the plumbing, too, and these two jobs increased his cash outlay by $12,000. A new roof cost him $1,500, and installing a foundation after finding out that there wasn't one set him back another $4,500.

The disheartened owner next found that much of the wooden framing had been chewed to lace by an infestation of termites. Fumigation and wood replacement cost him $2,000 more.

And in addition to the surprises, there were the expected repairs to be made. The would-be home broker had anticipated putting in a new floor and insulating it, for example. That ran him $6,000, while painting, wallpapering, and kitchen remodeling consumed another $8,500.

All in all, the man poured an extra $34,500 into his $23,500 bargain, making a total investment of $58,000 in a dwelling that was finally appraised at just $45,000. If he had only known what to look for and had made a few strategic phone calls, the unfortunate buyer could have avoided the heartbreak and budget-break of getting in over his head.

HOW TO GET STARTED: However, all this can be avoided by using the following checklist as a guide to avoid pitfalls in purchasing a fixer-upper.

[1] Price the cost of repairs before making the purchase. It's best to call electricians, plumbers, carpenters, masons, and carpet layers to get rough estimates of typical jobs or the approximate price of work per square foot before you even start shopping. If a dwelling is indeed a bargain, another buyer could snatch it out from under your nose while you waste time getting estimates after looking the place over. Find out how much it costs to insulate an attic, for instance, or to replace rotted floors, or to rewire a house. With average figures in mind, you can add the cost of repairs to the price of any given house.

[2] With a specific house to consider, examine its structural condition carefully. What kind of foundation does it have? Are there shingles missing? Do water stains on the walls and ceilings indicate a leaky roof? Require that a termite inspection be made and ask the seller to pay for this and for any repairs necessitated by an infestation.

[3] Make sure that all the building's utilities are serviceable. Is the plumbing functional? Is the wiring safe? Is the furnace efficient?

[4] Find out about zoning. Should the house you're looking at be in a commercial zone, you might be able to sell it as business property, a classification that generally has greater value than comparable residential property. However, if you're looking at a lot with two houses or a duplex on it and find the zoning to be R-1 (single-family dwelling), you must realize that the site is zoned for one house, *not* two. The law may have changed since the previous owner acquired the property, but as the new owner, you could be forced to obtain a zoning variance, which is permission to use a piece of property for something not covered by its current zoning classification.

[5] Don't be put off by looks alone. Because a filthy house with unkept grounds will tend to discourage buyers who see only appearances and not potential, the price of such property is often low. A shrewd person, though, can see that by removing a few truckloads of trash and using some soap and water and elbow grease, the eyesore can become very livable. The same principle holds true for homes with superficial damage to existing paint, carpets, linoleum, wallpaper, and landscaping. Compared with the cost of structural damage, most cosmetic problems are easily and inexpensively repaired.

[6] Know the market. Before you make a purchase, have a good idea of how much people will pay to rent or buy the house. If you plan to resell, either immediately or after living there yourself for a while, subtract the purchase price and the probable repair costs from the potential market price, and the difference will represent the profit or loss. If you plan to retain ownership and rent to others, figure out your mortgage payments, estimated yearly repairs and maintenance, and any tax advantages and weigh these computations against a reasonable expected rent. Consider, too, the consequences of those times when the house could stand unoccupied.

HEDGING YOUR BET: If everything checks out favorably, it's time to make an offer. On the other hand,

few houses will be all you're looking for. When you find one that you think you'd like to buy but that doesn't measure up in every respect, consider making an offer anyway, but with contingencies that will relieve you of any obligation should the house turn out to be a nightmare. For example, you might make your offer contingent upon the building's meeting current building codes. Then if upon inspection it proves to be not up to snuff, you'll have the option of backing out of the purchase or possibly of acquiring the property for a lower price.

Adding too many contingencies to a bid, however, could leave little room for bargaining, so if your offer depends upon a number of factors, be prepared to pay nearly the full asking price.

There's a lot of work involved in fixing up a rundown dwelling either for resale or to call home, but for anyone willing to put in the time it takes to find an old house that is worth repairing, there are financial rewards and much personal satisfaction to be reaped.

(Top) This fixer-upper is in an expensive neighborhood and should resell for more than $250,000. (Lower Left) Remodeling windows, (Lower Right) putting in new tile, and (Center Right) adding a bay window are relatively inexpensive cosmetic repairs that can rapidly increase the value of a dwelling, but a house needing major renovation like (Center Left) chimney repair may be a budget-breaker. Follow the checklist to avoid pitfalls.

STACK TWO MILES OF 2 X 4'S AND MOVE IN

Holding down construction costs can do a lot for a person's opportunity to build a house, and among the methods of reducing the expense of building a home are the ones found here: providing one's own labor and using standard materials in an unconventional manner. The result was a 24-foot-square cabin with 3-1/2-inch-thick solid wooden walls, a cathedral ceiling lined with knotty pine, exposed rafters and beams, and wooden floors and walls. Inside there was a 9′ X 12′ bedroom, a full bath, a 12′ X 24′ living/dining area, and a spacious loft; outside there was an 8′ X 12′ screened porch. It took about two months to complete and cost far less than a similar structure built using conventional methods.

This house is built mostly from stacks of 2 X 4 lumber laid *broad-face down*; in fact, it took nearly two miles of them to construct the house. Now nailing down 10,000 linear feet of 2 X 4's may sound like a job for a covey of carpenters, but anyone willing to tackle such a task can, using conventional hand tools, build a similar house.

PLAN TO SAVE: If a structure is to be finished within a budget, more time must be spent planning than will be needed for the actual construction work. Before buying any materials, the builder needs to visualize every step of the process, all the way down to mentally counting the nails in the molding around the front door. Allowances must be made for plumbing, fixtures, and a metal chimney.

The first design for this house measured 16′ X 20′, but splitting up the space to obtain the rooms needed couldn't be done. Eventually, the owner considered all possible layouts before settling on the final 24′ X 24′ plan.

Paying careful attention to standard building material sizes is also important. To give an idea of what a lack of such planning can mean, imagine what could happen to a builder who thought a 2 X 4 actually did measure two inches by four inches. Since dimension lumber 2 X 4 boards are actually 1-1/2″ X 3-1/2″, the walls would come up two feet short in height, or in the case of the 24′ X 24′ bungalow featured here, 1,536 linear feet from having enough lumber to give standing room inside.

On the positive side, planning a design around standard material lengths can save both time and money. The 24-foot-square layout allowed the use of combinations of 2 X 4's ranging from eight feet to 16 feet long in two-foot increments and full sheets of 4′ X 8′ plywood. Because of the wall construction, this home required only 60 sheets of plywood for the subfloor, the loft floor, the roof, and the skirting. It was much faster and easier just to plop down a full sheet and nail it in place than it would have been to cut each piece to size with a handsaw. Furthermore, the roof pitch (when combined with the floor plan) allowed the use of 16-foot-long 4 X 6 rafter beams and combinations of full sheets of plywood.

STACKLUMBER: Why choose to construct a house of stacked 2 X 4's which many people assume is excessively expensive? Contrary to the builder's first thoughts, preliminary figures showed that a 2 X 4 house could give one built from stud walls sheathed with imitation board-and-batten plywood, and finished with inexpensive paneling, a real run for the money. The builder felt walls made with 2 X 4's would have the solidity and beauty of those constructed with logs, and yet they would be easy to build. Then, too, the beams and the pine boards used for the floors and ceiling would complement solid wooden walls, adding to the attractiveness and warmth of the home. In the end, the only nonwood materials used were 15-pound roofing felt and 28-gauge metal roofing.

BUYING AT THE BEST PRICE: Nearly all of the materials needed had to come from a lumberyard, yet the "local" yards ranged from 60 to 180 miles from the building site. Since cost was a major concern, suppliers

18

were chosen by comparing bids on a fixed list of materials. After receiving preliminary prices from a dozen different lumberyards, the three lowest were selected for detailed bidding.

The three final bidders received detailed lists describing each item as specifically as possible. At the same time, each bidder was asked to include the delivery cost and give the expiration date on the prices quoted.

When the bids came back, their totals differed only slightly, and though the closest yard to the site bid a little higher for the materials, its offer of free delivery tipped the scales. In any building project, no matter how carefully it's planned, there will be some returns, exchanges, and unforeseen purchases, and it's a lot easier to drive 120 miles than it is to travel 360 miles to do these errands.

FINAL OBSTACLES: One problem with all three of the materials bids was that they exceeded the budget. Consequently, something had to go. One sizable expense was windows and doors.

Since too little natural lighting can turn even the best space into a cell, the builder was unwilling to compromise on the window area. Consideration was given to using a lower grade lumber than planned and to using roll roofing instead of sheet metal on the roof, but both ideas were rejected as being false savings. The builder reasoned that a lower grade of lumber would contain more culls and result in more scrap and that the toll taken by the sun, hail, and snow would bring on the need to repair or replace the roofing if the rolled material was used instead of metal.

Instead, windows that had been ripped out of a doctor's house during remodeling and doors from an old telephone company office were located for a reasonable cost at a salvage yard.

Auctions also helped keep the budget intact by providing a 4-1/2′-long cast-iron bathtub for $3.00, along with a toilet, a cast-iron sink, faucets, and another old tub for a total of $5.00. (One bathtub ended up as a watering trough for horses.) The kitchen counter tiles came from another auction, where more than 100 of the 6″ X 6″ pieces cost a mere $6.50.

TOOLS: The building site had no electricity, so the only power tool available was a chain saw. The list of really necessary tools for a project like this is quite short: two well-sharpened crosscut saws, a well-balanced construction hammer, framing and T-squares, a 25-foot measuring tape, four-foot and line levels, a combination plumb bob and chalk line, a combination wrecking bar and nail puller, a keyhole saw, a brace and bits, wood chisels, a spade, a six-foot stepladder, and a 28-foot extension ladder.

FOUNDATION AND FLOOR: The somewhat unconventional foundation consists of three 24-foot-long pressure-treated 4 X 12's set on four inches of gravel in trenches deep enough to keep the tops of the wood flush with the ground. The beams were set parallel, 12 feet

apart, and a 16-inch-high wall of pressure-treated 2 X 4's and 2 X 6's was nailed along the full length of each.

The 2 X 8 joists were laid across these foundations, and 1/2″ CDX plywood was nailed on top of them with the nails four inches apart along the joists. After lapping a layer of 15-pound felt over the subfloor, the builder set 1 X 6 tongue-and-groove pine flooring at right angles to the 2 X 8's. As is often the case with long pieces of tongue-and-groove material, minor twisting of the boards required that they be forced to fit. A long 2 X 4 set alongside a reluctant floorboard and nailed to the floor at one end, combined with a six-inch piece of tongue-and-groove between it and the board to be set, makes a wonderful lever. Once the floor was in place, it was mopped with a clear sealer and preservative.

TWO MILES OF 2 X 4's: Preparing to build the walls called for laying the door frames out on the floor and carefully marking the necessary clearances. The first layer of 2 X 4's was set painstakingly on the marks, much as the sill would be in a stud-frame house. This made raising the walls just a matter of proceeding upward while keeping them plumb.

To keep the joints staggered, every other row of 2 X 4's was nailed down in an opposite direction from the one below it all the way around the perimeter. Crib construction requires only careful measurements, square cuts, attention to plumb, and a lot of nailing. Admittedly, this *is* a laborious process, but it can be sped up by laying out the materials in neat stacks according to length. That way, the longest possible pieces can be used in combination while still staggering the joints. It's also important to position the nails so that they don't hit the ones in previous tiers.

On reaching the bottoms of the window openings, a note was tacked to the portal, listing the number of tiers and the height of the opening in inches. This provided a direct reference to show how far up to carry each window opening.

As the walls began to rise above the lower edges of the windows, it became necessary to brace some of the sections until the boards once again spanned an entire side. This involved constructing an upright triangle of 2 X 4's, setting one side against the section, and then temporarily nailing the brace to the 2 X 4 stack to keep the wall plumb.

Since the interior partitions with the exception of the plumbing wall between the kitchen and bath were also built of stacked 2 X 4's, some board-end-sized openings were left in the outside tiers to help anchor the inner walls. Interlocking such right-angled stacks stiffened the whole structure substantially.

Once the walls were up far enough for the ceiling beams to go into place, the 4 X 10's were slipped through a window from the outside and then dragged onto the floor from the inside. Working alone and using 2 X 8 planks on sawhorses as a scaffold, the builder lifted first one end of each beam and then the other. This procedure was a bit tricky. Since the beams are as long as the house is wide, getting them up required turning them sideways a bit. And then one hard jerk could pull a poorly lodged beam off the narrow ledge and send it crashing onto the floor.

Filling in between the beam ends with 2 X 4 wall sections required five rows—or nearly 500 linear feet—of lumber. This quickly exhausted the supply of boards planned on for building the front porch. Fortunately, there was still some leeway left in the budget.

With the beams set and leveled, 1 X 6 tongue-and-groove pine was laid to form the ceiling for the rooms below, and plywood was added atop that to form the loft floor. This produced a solid platform from which to work on the gables and the ridge beam.

Two 2 X 4 X 16's nailed together at right angles, set against the outside of the existing wall, pushed up until the top ends reached the expected height of the roof peak, and spiked solidly in place insured that each gable continued as a straight extension of the wall below. Sixteen-foot boards extended from the peak to the walls as temporary guides to establish the pitch of the roof.

RAISE THE RIDGE BEAM:

Putting the ridge beam in its place atop the gable ends was far too heavy a task to be accomplished by lifting the 26-foot-long 4 X 10, as was done with the ceiling beams. The beam was hoisted onto the floor of the loft to lie with one end against the finished gable and the other projecting beyond the wall of the house where the gable had not yet been begun. By lifting the timber by hand and with a hydraulic jack, the builder raised the end overhanging the wall and supported it by building up the wall with 2 X 4's underneath it. When the angle of the timber became too steep to continue this, the end at the finished gable was raised and supported on wood scraps.

Eventually, something sturdier was needed to support the 4 X 10, so vertical 2 X 4 tracks were built at each end of the loft. The beam slid snugly between the boards, and each time it was jacked up about six more inches a 2 X 4 block was nailed to the tracks beneath it to support the weight. Working upward in such steps, it was finally possible to finish the second gable. Then, using a wrecking bar, the beam was jimmied until it rested firmly and squarely across the roof peak.

ROOFING: The 4 X 6 rafter shape was carefully measured, remeasured, calculated, checked, and rechecked before any cutting took place, and to be completely certain that it was right, the builder cut a pattern from a piece of scrap and after checking it, transferred the guide to each rafter board. The care proved worthwhile when that first roof-holder fit perfectly into position.

The next task, trimming the stepped 2 X 4 ends off the gables to form smooth angled edges, turned out to be quite a chore when the chain saw failed to get a firm bite on the wood and left a jagged, unsatisfactory cut. The only alternative was cutting by hand at an angle through almost 70 solid feet of wood.

The plywood sheathing for the roof was hoisted piece by piece up from the rack on the builder's pickup truck and installed from the gutters upward so that each new sheet would have a lip to hold it in place until it was nailed down. Then came 15-pound felt, which was tacked over the sheathing, and then metal roofing went on with a minimum of fuss.

HOUSEWARMING: It was two more days before the windows were in, and four more passed before the finished screened porch was ready for people to sit on in the cool of the evening and thumb their noses at the mosquitoes.

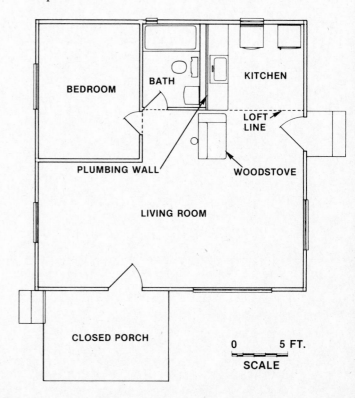

BEDROOM

BATH

KITCHEN

LOFT LINE

PLUMBING WALL

WOODSTOVE

LIVING ROOM

CLOSED PORCH

0   5 FT.
SCALE

A SOLAR DREAM CAN BE A REALITY

A high school art teacher, looking around her poorly maintained rental house and shivering from the chilly air that crept unchecked through the uninsulated walls, began taking stock of what she had to show for eight years on the job. Nancy had job satisfaction, to be sure, and she could claim a car and a small savings account among her assets. She also had huge utility bills, disappointing living quarters, and a pervasive feeling of discontent. What she *didn't* have was a sense of home. Recognizing that a change was in order, she decided to buy a house.

It took very little house hunting, though, for her to become discouraged by what was available and affordable, and she quickly abandoned the idea. Being disenchanted with conventional, fuel-thirsty structures anyway, she was wishing for an option when suddenly she remembered a little one-bedroom underground house that had been featured at an alternative energy fair. It was an idea whose time had come: She determined to build an energy-efficient, earth-sheltered home—one just big enough for herself—add a greenhouse for heat and garden space, and put an end to her housing crisis.

With her meager savings, Nancy purchased two acres of wooded land with a south-facing slope. Little did she realize that her problems had just begun. As the first person in her community to apply for a loan to build an earth-sheltered home, she was in for some special, but not exactly privileged, treatment.

FLOOR PLAN: The first step (that of designing the house) proved to be easy in comparison with the trials that

were to come. Because of her background in art, she was able—after many hours of research, discussion with experts, and work at the drawing board—to arrive at an acceptable design for her new home.

This bit of solar ingenuity was to contain 750 square feet of open living space, including one bedroom and a bath, with exposed, reinforced-concrete flooring and walls as thermal mass to absorb and hold heat. It would have a conventional shed roof (which proved to be cheaper than dirt), plus a solar greenhouse along the southern wall for capturing heat and cultivating plants.

Once the plans were completed, a builder estimated construction costs at $33,400. At that point, it was time to apply for a loan.

HARD TIMES: After waiting until interest rates dropped to 12%, Nancy took the next step. She chose the largest savings and loan institution in the area, because all the other lenders required roll-over terms which she couldn't afford on her rarely raised salary. So, in hopeful anticipation, the house plans were submitted to the savings and loan. Believing that her proposal would eventually be approved in spite of the lender's reluctance, she was shattered to be informed by the vice-president, "We don't make loans on underground houses."

The loan officer, who detected her dismay, offered to present her proposal to the loan committee. Short of building the dream house a little at a time as expenses would allow, there was little to do but to accept his offer.

To keep abreast of the situation, Nancy called the loan office daily to ask about the status of her application, and her persistence finally paid off. Two weeks after Nancy was initiated into the world of home financing, the lender agreed to the company's first loan on an earth-sheltered home. Apparently, the president had decided that the area was conducive to subsurface housing, and he wanted his lending institution to be the first to get involved in this new trend in building. Since plans for the home displayed "reasonably good construction techniques," the lenders were willing to take a chance. The long hours of research and planning had paid off after all.

PATIENCE: This breakthrough hadn't changed the fact that "conventional" was still the key word in home financing, however, and another six weeks of frustration ensued before the final approval of the loan. (The usual time for lending assessment is two weeks.) Receiving any money was contingent upon several changes that needed to be made in the floor plan, including the addition of another bedroom and central heating. (Although the original plans included a greenhouse against the south wall for heating, the three-month time limit for construction eliminated it.) Exposed-concrete floors and walls wouldn't be permitted, either.

There were compromises: Nancy was required to alter the bedroom floor plan to allow another wall to be built later, and she had to include a hallway from the bedroom along the back wall of the living area. This addition turned out well, as she later found that it provided needed privacy and also served well as a "minigallery"

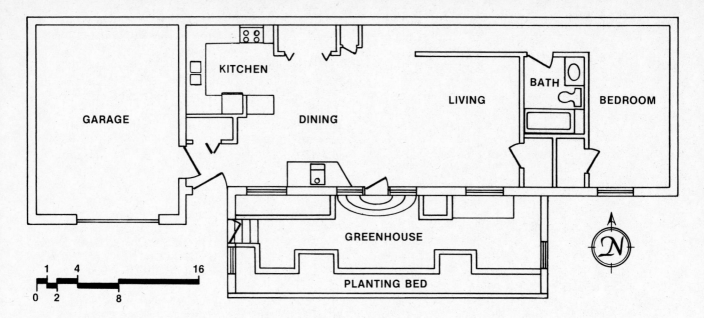

GARAGE · KITCHEN · DINING · LIVING · BATH · BEDROOM · GREENHOUSE · PLANTING BED

1 4 16
0 2 8

for her paintings.

Heating was the next issue. Although sunlight, supplemented by a woodstove, would have been sufficient, the loan officers, who were concerned with resale value, recommended the installation of three small electric heaters. As anticipated, solar gain and the woodstove keep the house sufficiently warm. The heaters have never been used.

The most difficult problem to solve in order to get the loan was how to cover the concrete walls and floors. The plan relied on using masonry for heat storage, so the usual applications, such as plasterboard, paneling, or carpet, wouldn't work; they would block the masonry surface. A man who had had some experience in covering walls in underground houses suggested a waterproofing and texturing compound called Thoroseal®. The lender agreed, and a search for a satisfactory floor covering began.

Ceramic tiles for the floors proved to be too costly. As an alternative, marble scraps were used to surface the largest areas. The shards, which were easily and inexpensively obtained from a local marble company, turned out to be a very wise choice. They were not only decorative but heat absorbent, as well! And rugs in the bedroom and living room would protect bare feet in winter.

Once all of the changes were approved by the loan office, the owner-builder was asked to submit her plans, specifications, and color sketches to an independent appraiser. It took an entire week instead of the customary three days to get a preappraisal, and the news was once again discouraging: Because the design resembled a finished basement more than a conventional house, the loan amount was limited to only $29,800 (instead of the $33,400 originally asked for). With the help of a contractor, some recalculating was done and some adjust-

ments were made in order to get by with this lower figure. Nancy agreed to reduce costs further by taking on a greater share of the labor.

TIME TO BUILD: After months of paperwork, the actual construction of the dream house began, but problems continued to develop. The builder—chosen because he'd done a good job on her parents' conventional house several years before and because he was highly respected by the loan office—was a self-acknowledged newcomer to underground construction. His initial enthusiasm for learning all he could about energy-efficient housing techniques had been deceptive. Once the loan was approved, his whole attitude changed, and he refused to consider anything that was different from the traditional construction methods he had always used in the past.

Unfortunately for Nancy, the school term started soon after construction on the house began, and she was unable to oversee all of the work. Yet despite teaching obligations, she was careful to be on hand to direct the waterproofing and insulating processes, both of which are vital to the success of an earth-sheltered house. She personally applied the two coats of tar emulsion (waterproofing) to the exterior walls—a messy, but money-saving experience.

Nancy continued to involve herself as much as possible in the various phases of construction. She arranged to be at the site to make sure that the specified perimeter insulation of extruded polystyrene was properly placed on the exterior walls, and during the backfilling, she stayed nearby to grab roots, limbs, and rocks before they could puncture the plastic around the polystyrene or destroy the insulation itself. When she had taken all the time off that her teaching job permitted, she had to trust the remainder of the hired construction to be completed without her watchful eye.

CHECK EVERY DETAIL:
She soon learned that it wouldn't be wise to take anything for granted. Getting the house built the way she wanted meant besieging the builder with nightly phone calls and countless notes left at the site. Disagreements over details became a daily routine because the builder ignored her plans and, more often than not, did things the way he was accustomed to doing them. The worst of the arguments concerned the covering of the inside concrete walls. Although drawings made it clear that the north wall (the thermal storage wall) was not be over-

layed with plasterboard, the contractor ignored the plans, feeling certain there was some mistake: "Everyone knows that concrete is always cold!"

The moral support and helping hands of family and friends made those difficult days easier. Volunteer laborers spent innumerable hours mixing mortar, painting walls, staining woodwork, installing carpeting, and putting up wall coverings. This help, lovingly given, made the house uniquely her own.

In fact, the most extraordinary features of Nancy's house were created by one of her colleagues (a vocational agriculture teacher). He not only suggested, designed, and built the eight-foot-diameter round window that's the focal point of her home, but he also obtained the marble for the floors and made the woodstove (along with the black marble platform on which it rests). What's more, he laid the interior stone for the 10′ X 34′ south wall of the living area, and he planned and constructed the steel frame for the 11′ X 31′ pit greenhouse that was added later.

Since for structural reasons the interior stone and exterior brick for the south wall needed to go up at the same time, her friend guided her in laying the brick as he worked on the stone. It was a backbreaking job that took three months of working after school and weekends, but their hard labor paid off: The total cost of Nancy's little house was $6,300 less than the final estimate on her loan commitment. She relishes every penny she saved, especially when the monthly payment comes due.

Keeping a solar dwelling warm does require an occupant's participation. When Nancy leaves for work, she must make a guess about the day's weather: If she opens the living area to the greenhouse and the day turns out to be cold and cloudy, heat is lost; if she keeps the door to the greenhouse closed and it turns out to be a sunny day, solar gain is considerably reduced.

As well as energy savings, homegrown vegetables and flowers can be enjoyed all year long. There are few things finer than the taste of fresh spinach in the winter or more cheerful than the sight of yellow zinnias in the midst of a February snowfall. These pleasures, plus the satisfaction of having overcome a life crisis by turning her dream of an energy-efficient home into a reality, have made the struggles involved seem worthwhile, if not insignificant. Nancy's overall feeling is the warm one of "Hey, I did it! I really did it!"

A SIX-SIDED OAK CABIN FOR NEARLY NOTHING

Constructing one's own home can mean a substantial saving, and if the dwelling is built of logs from the homesteader's property, the saving can be much greater. The cabin shown here was built of white oak logs, which are sturdy enough to last several lifetimes.

BEGINNINGS: The trees for the cabin were felled in the spring to take advantage of the sap flow, which makes the logs easier to peel. Some cabins are built with the bark left on the logs, but peeled trees are much less vulnerable to insect attack and season more rapidly than those with the bark left intact.

Once felled and trimmed, the logs can either be peeled on the spot or hauled to the building site before being stripped. In either case, it's best to support the logs so less bending and stooping is needed to remove the bark.

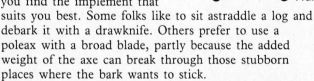

FIG. 1

Everyone seems to have a favorite peeling tool, and you'll just have to experiment until you find the implement that suits you best. Some folks like to sit astraddle a log and debark it with a drawknife. Others prefer to use a poleax with a broad blade, partly because the added weight of the axe can break through those stubborn places where the bark wants to stick.

If you intend to let your logs dry for several months, you need not debark each tree trunk entirely. Just peel a few large strips away and set the partially exposed log aside. As the wood dries, it'll pull away from the remaining bark, which can then be removed easily.

THE DESIGN: By midsummer, the cabin's design had begun to take shape, though the owners had not yet put anything on paper. Two things were certain: They wanted to build a multisided structure, something a little more aesthetic than the standard Abe Lincoln log cabin; and the dwelling would have to be constructed from the relatively small logs that a mule could maneuver without much difficulty. This meant timbers no more than 12 feet to 15 feet long and 12 inches in diameter. With these factors in mind, the hexagonal shape with 13-foot-long sides was selected.

With the design set and the trees felled and peeled,

the logs were skidded to the construction site where they were stacked in layers, with the logs in each layer perpendicular to those in the layers above and below. The timbers were left to dry until the foundation could be built and a building party arranged to raise the walls.

FOUNDATION TIME: The area where the cabin was to be built had an abundance of stone, and this was used for the foundation. Large, flat rocks cemented together formed seven piers: one at each point of the hexagon, and one in the center. Since the 13-foot-long

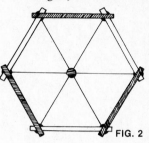

FIG. 2

logs, when notched and stacked, would overlap six inches at each end, the piers were set 12 feet apart. The bases of the columns were set 12 inches underground so they would be below frost level, and their heights were checked with a string level. The fact that the six outer columns were equidistant from each other and from the center pier made the hexagonal foundation very easy to lay out.

Next, the builders constructed twelve more columns at points halfway between each of the original seven (see Fig. 1). These were first built up to ground level and then completed after setting the sill logs, which rest directly upon the foundation. Since, in log cabin construction, the alternate sides of the building rise in half-log increments, the supporting columns must be of different heights (see Fig. 2). Besides, all logs have taper, humps, and bumps, so it's always best—whenever possible—to set the sill logs or floor joists on their main supports first, then raise the other columns to meet those sill logs.

FLOORS, WALLS, WINDOWS, AND DOORS: About 25 people of all types and descriptions showed up to help raise the cabin. Together they raised into place about two-thirds of the cabin's logs in two days.

The building team decided that the best way to join the logs in the dwelling was to cut tenons in the ends of the timbers with a bucksaw, a wedge, and a sledgehammer, and then stack the logs. The tenons were made by removing the upper and lower surfaces of the log ends,

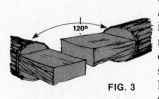

120°

FIG. 3

leaving just a rectangular tab—a *tenon*—that's half as thick as the log itself (see Fig. 3). The tenons of one row of logs would rest upon the tenons in the row of logs beneath, and so forth. This way, the weight of the logs would be what actually holds the cabin together. (With uncured oak, of course, adequate weight is no problem. For safety's sake, however, eight-inch oak pins were used to tie the sill logs together; all other logs were held together with 40-penny spikes.)

The first structural members to be set in place after the sill logs were the floor joists, which consisted of one 24-foot-long log and four 12-foot timbers, which were secured to the sill logs by means of mortise and tenon joints. The mortises were quite easily made with a one-inch chisel and provided very clean-looking joints (see Fig. 4).

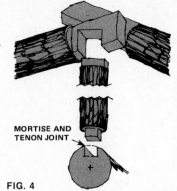

MORTISE AND TENON JOINT

FIG. 4

Next, they framed the doors and windows with 2 X 6 oak boards and began stacking the logs for the walls. The door frames were set on the sill logs before beginning the walls, and the window frames were placed on their mounts four or five layers later. Around each door or window frame, wall sections went up using logs cut to the appropriate length. As each cut-to-length timber was butted against the frame, a 40-penny spike was driven through the frame and into the log end, thus securing the bolt until small sticks could be hammered into the cracks between the logs to give more adequate support.

At the level of the twelfth log, about 7'10" above the floor joists, the loft joists went into place. These members extend from the corners of the building to a 15-foot-tall cedar pole raised earlier in the center of the dwelling (see Fig. 5). As with the main floor joists, the loft joists were tied in place by means of mortise and tenon joints. The resulting spoke and wheel arrangement makes for an exceptionally solid structure.

FIG. 5

To complete the floors the builders [1] nailed 2 X 6 oak boards on two-foot centers between the spokelike main floor joists, [2] spiked rough-hewn log sections between the loft joists, [3] overlaid both floors with one-inch milled oak, and [4] covered the oak subflooring with a layer of particleboard.

Last of all, the crew evened up the cabin's walls at the top (or sixteenth) log layer by adding half logs to the three low walls.

THE ROOF: Twelve oak saplings, each approximately four inches in diameter, come together at the apex of the building to form the roof's skeleton, giving the loft a ceiling height of 7 feet in the center and 2-1/2 feet at the walls. These rafters are bolstered with 2 X 4 oak stringers spaced two feet apart on center. The roof was finished by nailing down 5/8-inch particleboard and covering that with 30-pound rolled felt paper.

CHINKING: Once the floors and roof were finished, the time-consuming task of filling up the numerous gaps between the wall logs began.

The traditional method used involves splitting sections of log into wedge-shaped pieces between one foot and two feet long, hammering those pieces into the cracks in the wall, tacking them in place with six-penny nails, and then daubing the area with mud. The wisdom of this method is apparent when you realize that the resulting barrier has much better insulating properties than mud or cement alone.

The mud mix used consisted of two-thirds of a wheelbarrow full of hardpan clay, two shovelfuls of wood ashes, one shovelful of salt (the kind at the feed store), and sufficient water to yield a mud pie consistency. To pack the mix into the cavities, the mud was troweled off with a hand-held board.

COSTS AND ALL: Because the major part of this cabin consists of materials cut and prepared by the owner and a friendly work crew, the cash spent in the dwelling's construction was minimal. The only expenses were for cement used in the foundation, particleboard sheathing, felt roofing, recycled mill lumber, and assorted nails and spikes.

Yearly maintenance costs are virtually nonexistent, and when the roof is given a permanent covering of oak shakes, there's no reason why the logs, which provide good insulation, won't last a century or more.

A HAY HOUSE WILL MAKE A TEMPORARY HAVEN

Living in an inexpensive temporary structure while working on that dream home can often make the difference between having the permanent dwelling paid for when it is finished or facing mortgage payments that may linger for years. One couple, as the bitter Minnesota winter approached when they were just starting to build, knew it would be impossible to continue living in the screened-in hunting shack they had found on their property. Rather than use up their funds to rent an apartment in town and then have to obtain a loan to cover construction costs, they chose to spend a few hundred dollars building a hay house that would shelter them comfortably for the next two years while they completed a permanent dwelling. This allowed the major portion of their savings to be spent on materials for their new stone house.

To maximize internal space, the hay-house builders selected an open, six-sided design. The structure was framed with poles and enclosed with stacked bales of hay and was heated by their woodstove located in the center of the building, the greatest possible distance from the highly flammable walls.

FRAME AND ROOF: The homesteaders cut the poles for the framework and roof supports from spruce trees that grew plentifully on the property. But in their race against the threat of cold weather, the couple post-poned stripping the bark from the poles or coating them with preservative.

On a cleared, flat site with good drainage, the builders laid out a hexagon on a 30-foot diameter circle, and using a posthole digger, sank 2-1/2-foot-deep holes at each of the corners and midway between each of these points. Six additional holes were sunk in the center area to form another hexagon with a six-foot diameter. Poles were placed vertically in all the holes, with the posts in the center of the building slightly taller than those located around the periphery so there would be some pitch to the roof. The tops of the uprights were notched with a chain saw, and crossbeams and tie-in supports were spiked in place.

With the walls framed in, work began on the roof. The support for the composite plastic, hay, and sod covering consisted of a nearly solid umbrellalike arrangement of poles that projected far enough over the hay bale walls to protect them from rain or snow. The tops of these poles were peeled to prevent bark and rough spots from wearing holes in the plastic that made up the next layer of the roof. Then the builders broke about 45 bales of hay into pallets and spread these over the plastic, locating the hay squares as close to one another as possible. Another layer of plastic was laid over the straw insulation, and sod was cut and placed over this. Because freezing weather moved in, placement of the sod was left unfinished until the following spring, and by that time some of the second layer of plastic had deteriorated and needed to be replaced.

The center section of the roof where the stovepipe went through was the most complex part of the construction. A small mitered hexagon supported by 2 X 4's radiating in and up from the center poles comprised the frame. This was covered with boards, which, in turn, were covered with plastic. Glass-covered square holes cut in this section served as small skylights. In the interest of safety and fire prevention, no hay was used on this area of the roof.

WALLS, WINDOWS, AND THE DOOR: First, plastic was laid under the bottom row of hay bales and was folded up around them to protect them from dampness. As each bale was set in place, it was attached to those next to it with baling twine. Many of the bales were also attached to posts or to diagonal braces nailed between the uprights.

The walls went up quickly, with the bales laid in a staggered pattern like brickwork. At corners and window and door frames where only a portion of a bale was needed, the builders took a bale apart, retied as much as was needed, and saved the remaining hay for stuffing cracks later.

The couple had already obtained windows inexpensively at sales and auctions, but knew they would have to build additional frames that would be wide enough to sit on the hay bales and strong enough to support the tier of hay between the frames and the roof eave. For extra insulation they decided to pair windows for each opening. Deep frames of 1 X 6's were toenailed together at the corners, and strips made of 2 X 4's joined two matching frames to create a double-glazed unit with a dead-air space between the panes of glass. The window units were wedged in place on top of the third row of bales.

A frame was built in a similar manner to surround a door constructed of two inches of foam insulation sandwiched between wood faces.

ADDITIONAL TOUCHES: The final touches in constructing the hay house consisted of stuffing as much loose hay as possible into the spaces under the eaves and any other crevices, laying a plastic vapor barrier on the ground and covering it with rugs throughout most of the building but with linoleum in the kitchen area, and placing bricks in a bed of sand in the center section to serve as a base for the woodstove. (A fire extinguisher was installed in a handy location near the stove.)

There were also several later additions made to the house, some to gain protection from the elements and others to provide more space. Below-zero winds forced the hay-house dwellers to line both the inside and the outside of the porous hay walls with plastic. While this helped a great deal, they also found that too much heat was being lost through the building's cap, so they installed fiberglass batts against the inside surface of the roof by supporting them with wires strung from the center of the house to the ouside walls.

A doghouse of hay bales and old lumber provided shelter for the family's two Russian wolfhounds and took only about an hour to build.

With the arrival of spring, a greenhouse constructed along the south wall of the hay home provided a spot to begin seedlings early and to continue growing some warm-weather vegetables late into the fall. This was built using old railroad ties for a base, recycled lumber for the framework, and salvaged storm windows for glazing.

The following fall, the family added a 9' X 12' shop, also built of poles and hay, adjoining the house so they could move their stained glass business out of the main living area. Access to this addition was gained by replacing one window with a door, and the shop was given its own heat source, a small gas stove to be used only when someone was working there.

Living in their temporary dwelling provided enough comfort so that this enterprising couple felt they could complete their permanent home without being rushed. They could even pursue their stained glass business, enabling them to continue to pay for construction costs without taking out a mortgage. Once the stone house was completed, they could tear down their hay home without regret, recycling the materials for other uses.

DIGGING IN FOR WINTER IN A SOD IGLOO

Who would actually live full-time in an igloo made of dirt? Well, suppose that you're lucky enough to have a new homestead in the woods, but winter is just a few months away, and all that separates you from the worst the cold season has to offer are basic tools, a few hundred dollars, and your own two hands. Some kind of shelter would be in order, but suppose also that you want to create more than a mere refuge out of your limited resources: something not only warm and comfortable but also structurally graceful and in harmony with the landscape. A sod igloo could fulfill all those expectations, as a resolute Vermont homesteader proved.

Generally, these crude earth-sheltered structures aren't used as permanent homes. Most often, they're intended as quick, recyclable shelters that will serve until something more conventional can be built, or they're utilized as auxiliary retreats and hunting lodges. In this case, winter was approaching, and the aforementioned homesteader believed a sod igloo would meet his needs and be within his financial means. Soil was plentiful, and as insulation against the cold, it would be better than canvas, his only affordable option.

HOW HE DID IT: The necessary earth was stockpiled in the course of digging out the outline of the house, and the wood for the frame, roof, and walls came from nearby spruce and balsam fir trees. Many of the required slim, straight poles were culled from stands of young trees growing too close together for proper development. Because an overpopulated copse produces trees that are tall, thin, and straight, a single thicket can provide an excellent supply of building materials and the opportunity to give Mother Nature a hand by thinning out the overabundance.

The only other construction supplies needed were nails, spikes, staples, a few screws and hinges, 6-mil black plastic sheeting for the vapor barrier, glass or plastic for the windows, planking for the floor, and 2 X 6's for framing the door and windows. Salvaging some of these materials and trading for others helped costs remain low.

His tools, though basic, were well suited to the job at hand. The collection consisted of a saw, hammer, ax, hand drill, pick, shovel, drawknife, screwdriver, and staple gun. A level and square proved useful for laying the floor and hanging the windows. Peeled logs don't have many planes or right angles, so the woodsman learned to work with the wood, using its irregular curves to best advantage. He discovered that when this kind of building is constructed with sensitivity to the natural grain and form of each log, the resulting structure can be aesthetically pleasing.

Because a sod igloo is an earth-sheltered dwelling, it's very important that it be built on a well-drained site, with the depth of the excavation well above the water table. Choosing a relatively high spot in a small clearing where the ground sloped slightly to the south, the builder began to dig out a hole that would eventually measure 3-1/2′ X 15′ X 18′.

After first removing the top layer of sod in one-foot squares and setting that future insulation to one side, he got down to the single most difficult part of the task: actually excavating the site. Digging the hole, by hand and alone, required about four 20-hour weeks of backbreaking labor. Until it was completed, he couldn't get on with the more pleasant task of framing.

The first step of that job consisted of placing the pilings, beams, and braces as shown in Figs. 1 and 2. The pilings form and support the basic 9′ X 12′ rectangle that defines the house, and they had to be at least six to eight inches in diameter, since they must bear the weight of two layers of sod and as much as three feet of settled snow during the area's rough winters. For fastening the beams to the tops of the pilings and the ridgepole to the beams, square notches were cut in such a way that the log frame could withstand the compressive forces of the dirt that was applied later, and the joints were secured with ten-inch spikes.

Part of the front of the igloo was to be left uncovered to accommodate the windows, so the earthen load on the back wall would be much greater than that on the face. Without some extra bracing, the structure would eventually begin to lean away from the greater pressure and become unstable. Similarly, the side of the dwelling opposite the doorway would be subject to extra berming stress. To counter these forces on the back wall, the builder elected to install diagonal braces from the tops of the rear corner pilings to points near the bases of those in front, butting them against rocks buried below floor level. The wall opposite the door was braced in the same way, except that in this case the front prop started below the window. He ran another support from the midpoint of the ridgepole to the beam above the window for carrying the pressures from the back wall to the front without stressing the poles that would constitute the roof.

Setting the walls and roof came next. The small trees selected as raw materials were each four to five inches thick at the base. Almost 200 of them were needed, but the woods at the building site were so thick that this thinning did little more than allow a few additional rays of light to reach the clearing.

The young conifers were cut, trimmed, and scraped clean. To begin building the walls, the Vermonter leaned the poles against the frame at a slant of about 4-1/2 inches per foot of height, thereby using gravity to help hold the earth and sod against the walls and to allow the floor's dimensions to be greater than those of the ceiling. He hammered each pole deep into the soil, nailed its upper end to the top beam, and sawed off its excess length. For the sake of the inside appearance, the poles were placed as close together as possible, but an occasional gap wouldn't have done any harm, because the whole wall was sealed off by plastic sheeting later.

He set the roof poles across the beams and ridgepole, nailing and trimming them as he had done for the walls. The plastic vapor barrier was laid in place and stapled to the logs before layering the earth and sod that would provide protection against the cold.

It might have been quicker and easier to use boards or plywood for the ceiling and walls, but the small trees that he cut and peeled were free and already too thickly clustered for continued healthy growth. Another consideration for this man was the appeal of the soothing visual rhythms produced by the logs' irregular, rounded

shapes and natural wood grains, especially when seen by lamplight. Indeed, after working so intimately with earth and trees in the building of the house, he said that putting an exterior plastic covering over those gleaming shafts of wood felt like sacrilege. The vapor barrier was necessary to keep the dwelling dry and snug, but it was promptly hidden away beneath the mound of dirt and sod insulation that left the new home looking like an organic, albeit somewhat traumatized, part of the clearing.

By summer's end, the home boasted a plank floor, a door and windows, a woodstove, and a chimney. Moving day at the sod igloo came just before the first serious snow of the season fell on the Vermont landscape.

WHAT HE EXPERIENCED: During the first weeks of winter, small beads of condensation formed on the plastic sheeting between the poles, and it was thought that the shelter might become damp and cursed with mildew. But as the earth around the walls began to absorb the heat generated by the stove, the moisture disappeared. At the same time, living beneath a ceiling made from several feet of insulating soil and snow was making sense both economically and aesthetically. Inside, it was warm and cozy, and outside, the sod igloo blended into the landscape, looking like nothing so much as a large snowdrift miraculously emitting a thin trail of smoke.

No record was kept of fuel use during the winter, but generally about two hours every other day proved sufficient for finding, felling, hauling, splitting, and sawing enough wood by hand to keep the igloo comfortably warm even with subzero temperatures outside.

WHAT HE LEARNED: The first winter in the earth-sheltered dwelling proved the structure to be a pleasant and practical home regardless of outside weather conditions, but some improvements were indicated. While there was no evidence of rot attacking the underground sections of the support pilings, the owner decided it would have been prudent to treat the bases with creosote or old motor oil, or to char them as the Japanese do. He would support the beam over the windows with an additional piling (shown as "recommended" in Fig. 2) placed midway across the front wall, and although the site was well-drained and he experienced no problems with flooding or seepage (even during the height of the spring thaw), he wished he had added a floor drain to the basic construction plan.

The one serious flaw in the sod igloo was that the roof tended to leak during thaws and hard rains. The problem arose because the holes made in the vapor barrier by stapling it to the roof logs permitted water to seep through. It's also likely that two sod layers atop the ceiling are not enough, especially in a wet climate.

An improved version of the roof would call for covering the ceiling first with building paper and then with 6-mil unstapled black polyurethane sheeting, maintaining a foot of overlap all around. Above that, there would be a layer of stickless, stoneless, finely sifted earth, followed by a layer of plastic, covered by four more inches of clean dirt and topped with sod blocks. This roof would be heavier and a bit more demanding to build, but it would result in a drier home.

Overall, the sod igloo performed well despite any flaws it exhibited. Its occupant was able to stay on his homestead through the winter in good health and relative comfort despite the subzero cold and the spring thaw. The rewards tallied against the cost confirm that the sod igloo was a wise choice for someone in this particular housing quandary.

FIG. 1
SIDE VIEW

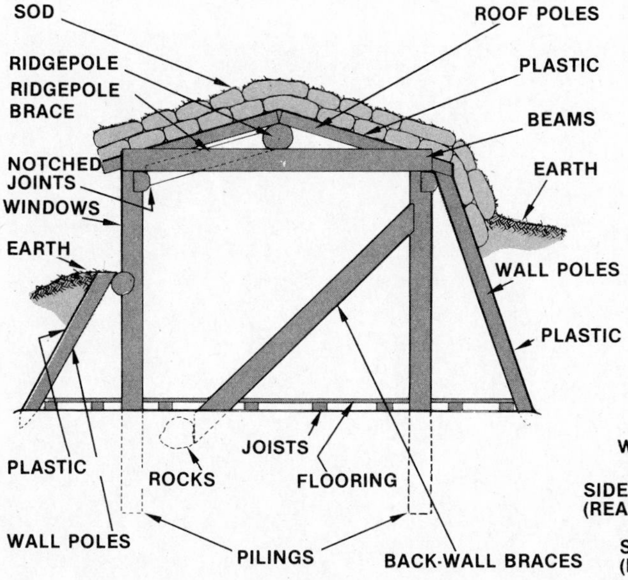

FIG. 2
FRONT VIEW

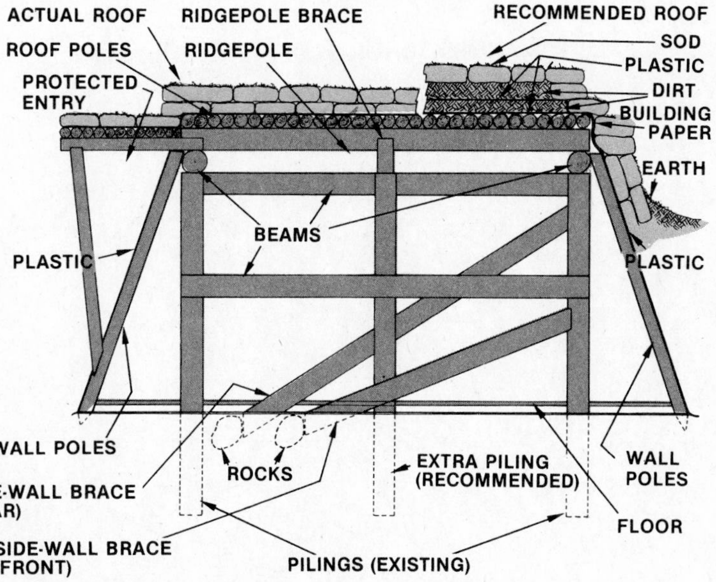

SHINGLE YOUR ROOF WITH PRINTING PLATES

Aluminum shingles are an excellent roofing material. They can last a lifetime, are fire- and rustproof, and reduce heating and cooling costs. To cover an 1,800-square-foot roof with aluminum shingles, a roofing contractor would be likely to charge a few thousand dollars, but an enterprising homeowner can reduce this outlay by an astonishing amount. By using salvaged aluminum from inexpensive, used printing plates to create shingles and by installing them without professional help, the do-it-yourselfer can roof a house for less than 5% of a contractor's fee. And such shingles are lightweight, an important consideration for the lone roofer who must carry hundreds of them up a ladder.

SHOP AROUND: The best print-shop leftovers for shingle use are .009" thick and measure 24-5/8" X 36". Telephone calls to several presses will reveal that such plates vary quite a bit in availability and in price. But many small-job printers have quantities of the used plates that they are more than willing to unload at a bargain rate. Locate the printer with the greatest number of usable plates for the lowest cost (sometimes as little as ten cents apiece).

Carefully select undamaged plates that have a sturdy, 1/8-inch doubled-over edge (created when the aluminum was locked in the press). When loading the plates into your car trunk or truck, you'll find that printer's ink blackens everything it touches, so always don gloves and old stained garments when working with this type of recycled aluminum.

CUT THEM UP: Cutting the 2' X 3' plates into fourths will produce shingles that are attractive, as well as strong enough to resist high winds. Place a single aluminum sheet—printed side up—on a work surface, measure carefully to determine the midpoint of each side, line up a yardstick across the marks, and scratch in a "cross hair." Use scissors to divide the plate into four equal sections. These rectangles become the patterns for the rest of the plates.

The sheets are not difficult to cut if stout scissors are used. While it's possible to quarter ten sheets in about 25 minutes, the job could be done much more quickly with a paper cutter. An even faster method would be to pay the print shop to cut the plates with a power knife.

A TEMPLATE AND TOOLS: Fashioning each shingle into a parallelogram works best for a number of reasons: They require only one thickness of aluminum, require few manufacturing steps, allow overlapping of each shingle on all four edges, produce slanted vertical tiles (to shed water well), are easy to mount, and make it possible to secure three of each shingle's corners with only two nails.

In order to produce the finished metal shakes, however, one must first make a template—17-1/2 inches long and 10 inches wide—from a piece of 1/8-inch paneling or something similar. Then mark two points 4-1/2 inches—horizontally—from the upper right and lower left corners. Next, scribe lines connecting these dots to, respectively, the lower right and upper left angles. Saw off the two indicated triangles to create the parallelogram form shown here.

Then, after rounding up a table knife, a 16-inch scrap of steel strap, and a 6-inch piece of 2 X 4, you can set to work.

HOW TO FOLD THEM: To fold the shingles, place one of the minisheets—shiny side down—on the work

surface. The 1/8-inch press-folded edge should be closest to you (turned under), and the sheet must protrude about one inch over the table's edge. Next, put the template on it so that the top edges line up, and the acute angles of the template are even with the sides of the printing plate. The one-inch aluminum "tongue" that sticks out toward you is then folded up and over the bottom edge of the template to form a small pocket.

At this point, use the scissors to make two small cuts just through the 1/8-inch fold at the top of the pocket, positioning them four inches from the left side of the sheet and six inches from its right edge (see photo). After making these snips, begin the next step, which is to wrap the exposed triangles of metal up and over the sides of the template. A wooden block (see second photo) is used to press each fold almost—but not quite—flat.

The last stages in shingle production are shown in the same photo. Place the piece of strap iron along the slanting fold at the right side, and bend the triangle of metal back over itself. (When the strap is removed, it will leave a small trough or pocket.) A table knife is then used to lift the 1/8-inch tab between the two bottom-fold cuts.

This may sound complicated, but after a little practice, the steps flow smoothly in a "line up, fold bottom, make cuts, fold sides, remove template, squash folds, make right-side pocket, and open 1/8-inch edge"

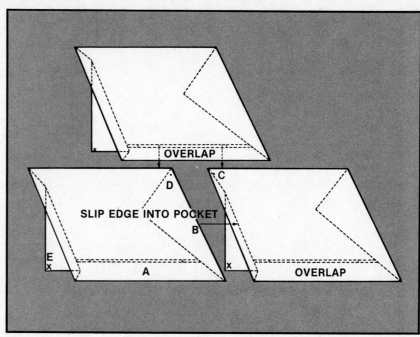

Fold a one-inch pocket over the template and snip two cuts in the 1/8-inch doubled edge. Place the strap iron along the right slanting fold, bend the metal over itself, and lift the tab between the two cuts. In laying the shingles as shown in the diagram, it's best to sit to the side and not to put too much stress on the plates.

sequence that makes production a rapid process.

At a rate of forty shingles every twenty minutes (not an improbable pace), an adult can make in the course of a week about 2,000 shingles, the amount needed for an 1,800-square-foot roof.

The following plan for mounting the finished shingles on the roof calls for sitting safely to the side, working from right to left, and placing the slippery aluminum plates—one above the other—in vertical strips.

Hook each plate's 1/8-inch lip—beneath edge A—over the top of the shingle below it and slip the right side B of the aluminum shake into the strap-iron-formed pocket of the matching shingle in the row immediately to the right. This places the upper right obtuse corner of the most recently added tile beneath the upper left acute angle of the shingle in the preceding row. These two corners, C and D, are then secured with one nail (near enough to the upper edge to be covered by the next shingle), while a second fastener is used to hold down the flap at E. In this way, all of the sides of the shingle overlap, and two roofing nails are usually sufficient to secure three corners of each of the plates. Rubber-fitted roofing nails are recommended for this job, but if these special nails aren't used, any nailheads not covered by an overlapping shingle should be given a waterproofing with black plastic sealant to prevent rain or melting snow from leaking into the house.

These homemade, interlocking shingles can not only weather 80-MPH winds and heavy snows, but they can also provide insulation effective enough to lower heating and cooling bills. Such aluminum shingles reflect the sun's glow in a particularly nice way, and the attractive diamondlike pattern of the roof belies the low cost of the covering.

AFFORDING A PASSIVE SOLAR HOME

Achieving at least partial energy independence through the use of passive solar technology can mean long-term savings for the residents of dwellings constructed or retrofitted to use the sun's energy. However, first they must be able to build that house. Under the Farmers Home Administration (FmHA) small home program, qualifying individuals who can't afford high-interest housing loans are able to borrow the money needed to build their own energy-efficient houses in rural open areas or in towns that are outside metropolitan areas and have populations of less than 20,000.

As the credit arm of the U.S. Department of Agriculture, the FmHA provides low-interest housing loans for the construction of some 110,000 homes and apartments annually. It is a decentralized agency with offices in about 2,000 counties across the country and can relate at the grassroots level to people who need to borrow at an affordable interest rate not only for building shelter but also to provide new employment, start businesses, or purchase or operate farms.

The FmHA program is hardly a giveaway plan, though, and relies almost totally on insured loans to provide up to 100% of the mortgage funds needed for building projects. Interest rates as low as 1% are available. The income range for eligible families is between $11,500 and $18,000 in the continental United States, though the range varies from one area to another depending on the local cost of living. In Alaska and Hawaii the range is somewhat higher.

Until a few years ago, Farmers Home Administration architects were concerned with structural integrity, practicality, ease of construction, and low cost, but not necessarily with energy conservation. However, after work at the state level by some progressive individuals, simple passive solar techniques began to be incorporated into the agency's basic home designs, and the plans for FmHA houses are available not only to those eligible for the program but also to anyone interested in the buildings themselves.

THE HOMES: The houses being financed under the small home program range in size from about 900 square feet to slightly over 1,000 square feet of heated area, though additions such as carports, outside storage areas, and porches can add to the overall size of any of the structures. To keep building costs down, great care has been taken to keep the plans as conventional as possible. This was done to avoid confronting contractors with demands for unfamiliar techniques that could be constructed as expensive custom work or presenting building material supplies with requirements for high-priced, unusual materials.

As a result of these measures, the homes can usually be built in the range of from $30,000 to $55,000 depending on their geographical location. These amounts should not be considered absolute parameters, and they do not include land and such adjuncts as septic systems and wells. Also, the cost of a home can be reduced substantially if it is built by the owner rather than by a contractor.

The FmHA program allows applicants a great deal of flexibility in the design, construction, and decoration of their abodes, and the agency will even provide contacts and professional consultation for any program participants who wish to become intimately involved in the creation of their dwellings.

The structures themselves depend on three standard design techniques to achieve at least partial energy independence:

First, they're oriented ten degrees east of due south to reduce insolation from the west on sultry summer afternoons while still taking full advantage of the light and heat available during the winter. Protective roof overhangs are also included in the designs to prevent the rays of the high summer sun from directly entering the homes.

Second, the insulation goes beyond the requirements of normal state and local codes to hold both artificial and natural heat in the dwelling. The walls of the homes are equipped to an equivalent of R-19, and the ceilings protected to an R-30 level. The foundation walls or slabs also have rigid Styrofoam lining. Also, all the south-facing windows are furnished with thermal curtains: frame-fitted roll-up quilts that prevent heat collected during the day from escaping out the windows at night.

Third, each house is equipped with low, broad "Trombette" walls, which are actually brick thermal storage masses placed four inches behind large, double-glazed windows or sliding glass doors on the south side of the structure. Unlike conventional Trombe walls, which because of their size are often both imposing and light-restrictive, the smaller partitions do a more-than-adequate job of storing daytime warmth and releasing it for up to six hours in the evening, while still allowing natural light to enter above the walls. They can also

function as attractive planters or shelf units. By the same token, if for any reason a resident chooses to shut out daylight, the thermal shades can be easily lowered to the level of the brick bulkheads' upper surfaces without sacrificing the heat storage capabilities of the system.

Beyond these basics, care was taken to insure that the home designs are both flexible and attractive. For example, the North Carolina plans provide for main entry from the north, south, or east to allow construction in virtually any subdivision. Material, trim, and color options are left completely to the discretion of the builder or buyer. The backup thermal system is currently zone-controlled electric baseboard heat. However, those homeowners who have adequate supplies of timber can use woodstoves, too, if they wish. Any extra summertime cooling is taken care of by a ceiling-mounted attic fan.

Calculations based on the original plans for dwellings to be located in temperate areas indicate that a full two-thirds of the structures' energy needs can be provided by the sun, and some homeowners have reported even greater savings.

OTHER PROGRAMS: Savings both in interest on building loans and on long-term expenditures for heating and cooling are also certainly possible under this program, but there are other programs operated by the FmHA that can benefit people willing to pursue the agency's several avenues of home financing. For groups whose members are willing and able to participate in building their own homes, for instance, financing and technical assistance are available through a self-help housing program. The agency also operates programs aimed at helping interested individuals develop multi-family housing.

There are several other areas in which FmHA can lend a helping hand. These include farm loan and assistance programs, community facilities development, business and industrial loan guarantees and grants, and area development aid.

If you want to know more, you can obtain some detailed information on the many individual areas of the programs mentioned here from county or state offices of the Farmers Home Administration. The offices are usually located either in the county seats or the state capitals.

FAR LEFT: The "Trombette" walls serve as both shelf area and a heat storage medium, while allowing natural light to enter. FAR UPPER RIGHT: The north side of this house has few windows in order to minimize heat loss by conduction. FAR LOWER RIGHT: South-facing windows let in the sun for both heat and light. LEFT: The "Trombette" wall behind the windows provides solar heat gain. Note the doors on either side of the windows.

BRINGING A SILO TO LIGHT AND LIFE

Two brothers, spurred by the encroaching autumn chill in the Kansas air, began discussing winter in the Midwest and how to warm a home with the least amount of heat loss. One brother, ruing the fact that one-level houses lose most of their heat through the roof, complained that someone should design a dwelling in which rooms would be stacked vertically, channeling the heat up through the living space. He was surprised to hear his sibling confide that once he had considered how to acquire just such a house. The plan relied on finding an abandoned silo, because with the basic structure already in place, the building could be remodeled at a much smaller expenditure than constructing a home from the ground up. The concept proved so exciting to the men and their families that soon they were making a concerted search for silos on the country roads in their locale.

Most of the silos they saw were built of ugly gray concrete block and wrapped with metal bands. Persistence paid off, though, and they finally found the perfect structure. Constructed of glazed and glistening red-clay tile, the silo, like a lookout, dominated the crest of a hill. On the south side of the silo there was a grain-chute opening, which the brothers believed they could adapt to accommodate a few sun-catching windows. Full of enthusiasm, the group went to explore the inside of the 14-foot-diameter cylinder and looked up to see blue sky. It was obvious that one of the first renovations necessary would be to construct a new roof.

Within two weeks, they'd located the silo's owner. Because the land wasn't being used and since one of the brothers and his wife wanted to put their own money into the renovation, the farmer offered them a free and renewable five-year lease. By that time, though, it was already early November, and winter was rapidly overtaking them.

A STEP-BY-STEP CONVERSION: Making an excavation to house a septic tank and drainage lines was the first step. In the process, the new tenants also dug a ditch from the silo to a nearby wind pump and well, and put in a waterline. Since easy access to their future home was important, they chose a spot on the silo's west side and cut out a front door opening, using a specially made concrete saw.

The couple's next project, the roof, proved to be a real challenge. In order to provide safe working conditions, a platform was built to sit on top of the structure.

It took an hour of scooting around the rim—40 feet up, in icy weather—to mark the edges so that the big scaffold wouldn't overlap the points where the rafters would later sit. Then, one by one, the wife tied the planks to a rope, and her husband hauled them up.

Once the platform was assembled, he constructed an eight-sided, tipi-shaped wooden frame and spent a number of consecutive weekends sheathing, tar-papering, and shingling seven of the roof's eight sides. The last section where they planned to build a cantilevered balcony the following spring was temporarily covered with plastic.

There was a race to pour concrete in the base of the silo before freezing weather came to stay, but first it was necessary to dig out three feet of soft earth. For someone working in a 14-foot-diameter hole, that's a lot of dirt to move by hand. Fortunately, they got the job finished just in time.

Despite freezing weather, the remodelers went on to break away the old grain chute, piece by piece, with a sledgehammer. They nailed short boards, each at an angle, on both sides of the opening to add a decorative touch. Next, they bought four long, narrow windows and built a shingled awning to be positioned above each one. The installation involved tying an awning onto a rope, climbing the bars that led up the slot, pulling up the awning and nailing it in place, climbing back down to tie on a window, hauling up the window and nailing it in place, and so on, until the arduous task was finally completed.

A WINTER OF WORK: The window wall was finished in mid-January, and the weather had turned pretty cold by then. With plywood propped over the entrance until they could afford a door, the inside of the silo provided at least some refuge from snow and slashing wind, but in order to continue working, it was necessary to purchase a woodburning stove. It was set in place on the concrete slab, and the insulated stovepipe (chosen because it had to pass through four floors), stacked 40 feet high, ran through flashing that had been incorporated into the roof for that purpose.

With a cozy fire roaring, it was easier to tackle the problem of how to contrive strong, round floors out of straight lumber designed for use in rectangular houses. The solution began with four wooden columns spaced evenly around the circumference of the solid concrete pad. Next, the carpenters built a wooden square that rested on top of the columns, and nailed stringers every 16 inches until the square was filled. To make a circle, they stood a board up along the wall between each pair of columns and set another board atop each one to span diagonally the space between supports. Sheets of plywood were cut on a curve and nailed into place, forming the sturdy circular floor.

Another quartet of columns was then placed directly above the first, and floor after floor gradually came into being. However, this fairly simple procedure was complicated by the need to leave openings for a stairway that would spiral a quarter of a circle around the inside wall for each floor, making nearly one full twist before it reached the top.

Since 48 steps rise from the first floor of the silo to the balcony, the renovators gained plenty of practice in building stairs, which they admitted "looked better and better as we got closer to the top."

By the time the staircase was complete, spring had arrived. To finish the balcony, a cantilevered, wooden platform was covered with a 4′ X 8′ sheet of plywood and secured with interior bracing. Its inside half was sheltered by a shingled A-frame section boasting two skylights. The installation of a door and a railing with a gate made it possible to escape in case of fire by climbing down an adjacent ladder, which the silo's original builders had strung up the side of the structure.

THE HOME STRETCH: With the basics out of the way, the couple began to concentrate on turning the 50-year-old cylinder into a comfortable home. A partition on the second floor served to separate the bathroom from the kitchen area, and the necessary plumbing was installed. A submersible deep-well pump hooked up to 50 feet of pipe and lowered into the casing of the well under the windmill came up with a seemingly inexhaustable supply of clear, free water.

With assistance from family members, the necessary electrical wiring was accomplished in one weekend, and suddenly they had the luxury—as they went from the first floor to the fifth—of turning on a light for the floor above and flipping off the light for the level below.

In mid-May the projected moving-in date was six weeks away. The time was spent wallpapering the kitchen/bathroom partition, installing cabinets, putting up plasterboard and texturing the ceilings, and laying carpet and linoleum.

After settling in, the family used evenings and weekends to add the necessary finishing touches. With just $6,500 and 800 work hours separating the homeowners from their starting point, the first floor had become a sunken living/dining room, from which three steps led up to the front door and to the stairs to the second-floor kitchen and bath. The third floor became the bedroom, the fourth, an art studio, and the fifth, storage space and a study. The spiral staircase rises the final four feet from that level to the balcony.

Anyone deciding to rehabilitate a silo to provide living space should be wary. It's wise to consider only older models, as some modern silos have been sealed with material that contains the dangerous chemical polychlorinated biphenyl (PCB). However, finding the right place is worth the time it takes. People who are willing to maintain a tight budget, and to endure some inconveniences during the months required for transforming such a silo into a useful living space, will be rewarded with an attractive, unusual, and energy-efficient home acquired at a reasonable price.

MOVE A HOUSE AND MOVE INTO IT

Coming up with the down payment on a house is problem enough for most people today, and high interest rates and commensurately high house payments only add to the problem of how to afford a home. However, by purchasing a house that's about to be torn down, moving it to a new location, and remodeling and making a few additions to the structure, it's entirely possible to take up residence in a new home that costs only about as much as the initial investment in an equivalent modern dwelling and that has an appraised value several times the amount spent.

THE EARLY STEPS: Finding a house to move should be done carefully, with consideration given to the soundness of the structure and the amount of work and expense of materials involved in bringing the heating, electrical, and other systems up to the standards of the new location's building codes. Some subdivisions have prohibitions against bringing in houses built elsewhere, and in some areas there are restrictions on the size, cost, or type of structure that can be placed on a lot. Distance from the old lot to the new one also must be taken into account, since most house movers charge not only for lifting the building off its original foundation, but also for the number of miles a dwelling must be moved.

There will be excavating expenses at the new lot, as well as fees for water, sewer, and electrical hookups. The building departments in some places will issue "homeowner's permits," which allow individuals to perform much of the work themselves rather than hiring professional contractors to bring the house up to standard.

When all the permit matters are settled and the perimeter of the new foundation is staked out on the new lot, excavation can begin. When the site's ready, it's time to call the mover.

MAKING THE MOVE: Relocating a house is a major undertaking, but those in the business can usually get a residential structure from one place to another in a short time. For a frame structure, holes are knocked in the foundation, long I-beams placed under the house, and the entire building raised off its base with jacks. Then, either the house and the long beams are both lifted on shorter I-beams and are pulled away from the foundation or the foundation is removed so the building and its temporary base can be towed away. Sets of wheels attached to the ends of the long I-beams allow the building to be pulled to the new location by a heavy truck tractor.

SETTING IT IN PLACE: When the movers have brought the house to the new location and have positioned it over the excavation, the four ends of the I-beams are set on pillars made by stacking heavy timbers crosswise. The wheels are detached and taken away, leaving the building on the pillars until the footings are dug and poured and the foundation or basement walls are laid to their proper level. By using jacks and removing the timbers, the structure is then lowered onto its new base and the I-beams are removed.

Electrical, water, and sewer lines can then be connected to the residence, and with backfill placed around the foundation or basement walls, the new owners are ready to undertake any renovations, improvements, and alterations they have in mind. These might include anything from such cosmetic and protective measures as caulking and painting the dwelling to structural renovations such as changing the positions of windows and doors, adding a porch or a wing, and moving partitions to alter the floor plan.

TIPS FOR HOUSE MOVERS: Anyone deliberating the purchase of an unwanted house for the purpose of moving it to a new location should consider the following advice from those experienced in the process.

First, it's best to have the building official from the new area inspect the structure to determine whether it meets the codes, needs minor repairs to do so, or requires major renovations. In an older house, for example, it's entirely possible that the wiring and plumbing will all need to be completely redone.

Second, remember that there's always more than one house on the market and that there's no need to settle for one that needs a great deal of work.

Third, since the charges for trundling the house from one location to another can vary considerably from one mover to another, obtain several bids.

Fourth, it's a good idea to make your purchase offer on a lot contingent on being able to obtain all the necessary permits for relocating a house.

Finally, a tight schedule should be avoided. Many conditions and small problems can delay the moving itself, as well as the building official's finally issuing an occupancy permit. Rainy weather can create mud, which might make it impossible for the mover to get the building off the old site or onto the new one until the ground is drier. Small electrical, plumbing, or structural problems can delay approval by inspectors until "just one more detail" is taken care of.

THE BOTTOM LINE: Even with delays of a week here and a week there, and the time taken for several renovations and alterations, it's possible to move a home and have it ready to occupy in much less time than it takes to build a comparable dwelling. And when it's done, the home is free and clear of debt.

BUYING LAND
AND HOMESTEADING

HOW ONE FAMILY ACHIEVED SELF-SUFFICIENCY

Cutting the cost of living can range from taking a few steps to reduce incidental household expenses to establishing a homestead that is close to being completely self-sufficient. The latter course was taken during the 1970's by the Dan Taylor family, which pulled up its urban roots to settle in the hills of the Arkansas Ozarks.

In 1973 Taylor, his wife Mary Lou, and their sons Mark and Brad invested ten years' of savings in 160 acres (120 are wooded hillside and 40 are bottomland) of mountain land where they hoped to supply most of their own needs for food, energy, and shelter in a manner harmonious with the environment. Because they felt that the true cost of living in the technology-based society was masked and failed to reflect the damage that was being done to the environment and atmosphere, they resolved to try to live without dependence on the conventional food supply cycle and on nonrenewable sources of energy.

The Taylors felt that the cost of food in the supermarkets would eventually rise to reflect its true cost and that this would put it beyond the means of many people. This, they felt, could very well necessitate a return to the self-sufficient way in which our forebears lived. After about four years on their farm in the hills, the Taylor family had achieved a great deal of the self-sufficiency they sought, and they were able to outline what they had done to reach that level of independence.

The homestead had a usable house on it when the Taylors bought the land, and they were therefore able to concentrate all their early efforts on food and energy production.

For 100 years before they bought it, the land was farmed to exhaustion with corn, cotton, sugar cane, and small grains, and getting anything at all from the rocky soil was a struggle. But one way or another, the family has produced almost all its own food since moving there, primarily because in the early days they were willing to eat whatever they had. They lived on little but canned black-eyed peas and green beans their first winter, and as a result those legumes still have a special place in their affections.

Foraging was very important to survival when the family first moved to the farm, and four years later it still provided a significant portion of their diet. A big bowl of crisp watercress mixed with tiny wild onions is hard to beat in the spring long before the first lettuce is ready to pick from the garden. Black walnuts and hickory nuts are real staples, and the Taylors canned 50 quarts of wild blackberries in their third year in the Ozarks. They also harvest elderberries, huckleberries, gooseberries, grapes, persimmons, and other volunteer vegetables and fruits.

Milo maize was a real lifesaver for them the first couple of years on the homestead. It grows in extremely poor soil and produces in even the hottest and driest summers. In a typical year, the family plants 5,000 feet of row with two pounds of seed and harvests 300 pounds of the grain.

They reap the milo by simply cutting the plants' heads off with a pocketknife, then beating out the grain, grinding it fine, and using it just like cornmeal. The ground grain makes a good pan bread, and when cooked in milk, an excellent hot cereal.

By plowing and replowing their garden three or four times during the first winter, working large quantities of manure and limestone into the soil over the years, and sowing a mixture of winter vetch and rye grain on the area each fall and plowing it under as green manure the following spring, the Taylors were able to build their vegetable patch into a fairly fertile piece of land.

The planning of each year's garden was probably the family's most important and the most difficult homestead activity. Homegrown fruits and vegetables made up a substantial portion of their diet, and the Taylors approached their gardening activities in a very serious and systematic way. They rotated crops for maximum utilization of soil fertility and for control of diseases and insect pests. They spread manure heavily and used a certain amount of mulch. Both standard and hybrid seeds were sown, and in many other ways these homesteaders took a middle road through all the "miracle, cure-all gardening methods" that the "experts" seem to be constantly pushing.

Their best advice to the beginning gardener is to start slowly with the old cultivation systems, such as plowing, disking, and harrowing or rototilling, that have already proven effective. Experiment with new ideas a little at a time, and beware of the agribiz industry's claims that any and all problems can be solved now and forever by the application of some magic chemical. Prepare your seedbed as well as you can, and stir the soil around your plants as they grow. Plant across the slope, and grow cover crops during the off-season to keep the ground from eroding. Learn what to expect from your soil and climate before you begin to test far-out theories and ideas, and then test such "breakthroughs" cautiously and a little at a time.

The Taylors found that Jerusalem artichokes are a true survival food. A few roots from a neighbor are all

the start you'll need, and after the first year or two, the plants should become so prolific that they'll need to be thinned for better tuber production.

The roots of this plant store themselves in peak condition in the ground right through the winter, and they can be dug and eaten at almost any time. They're good raw in salads or prepared any way that potatoes are cooked. The Taylors also used Jerusalem artichokes as supplemental feed for their hogs, chickens, and rabbits.

When the garden was in full production, the family became vegetarians. During the vegetable patch's off-season, however, they ate about 2-1/2 pounds of meat a day. For one year, this broke down to: 300 pounds of pork (two 150-pound hogs), 110 pounds of rabbit (44 fryers averaging 2-1/2 pounds), 96 pounds of Muscovy duck (24 four-pounders), 60 pounds of Bantam chickens (60 one-pound fryers), 24 pounds of Khaki-Campbell ducks (eight, weighing three pounds each), and 20

pounds of wild squirrels, rabbits, and groundhogs. Grand total: 610 pounds of meat for the four of them.

The Taylors kept two sows to raise feeder pigs for market and to produce pork for homestead use. The feeder pig business is very labor-intensive, and a lot of study was needed to learn the ropes of the game. When the market is reasonable, however, the sale of feeder pigs can substantially boost a small farm's income even when it's necessary to buy feed to bring the animals up to market weight.

Rabbits are an indispensable source of meat for the

house, and the two birds quickly became pets.

Geese are easy to keep and inexpensive to feed. In the Ozarks climate, they prefer no shelter, they eat grass, and the only grain they get is the little they snitch from the hog trough. They should be a very efficient source of meat and eggs.

A neighbor gave the family a pair of Muscovy ducks in return for help with his cattle, and the

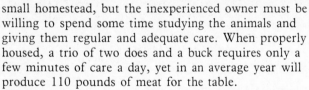

small homestead, but the inexperienced owner must be willing to spend some time studying the animals and giving them regular and adequate care. When properly housed, a trio of two does and a buck requires only a few minutes of care a day, yet in an average year will produce 110 pounds of meat for the table.

The Taylors got their start in poultry by purchasing day-old baby chicks from a hatchery. They ordered 25 Light Brahmas, 24 Araucanas, and 10 Bantams. The Brahmas and Araucanas eat a lot and lay very little most of the year, though in the late winter and early spring, they overwhelm the family with eggs.

The Bantams, however, were not a mistake. They lay reasonably well, they make excellent setters and mothers, and they forage for most of their food. The Taylors plan to butcher everything but the Bantams, add a good laying breed such as White Leghorns, and then set both Bantam and White Leghorn eggs under the Bantam mothers.

They got into the goose business on a small scale by setting two Toulouse eggs under their hens. The chickens didn't mind incubating the large eggs but refused to raise the ugly goslings, so the Taylors brooded the two youngsters, one a goose and the other a gander, in the

female sets at least twice each season. As clumsy as she appears to be, she handled the job all by herself, and in 1975, she successfully raised 25 ducklings. When butchered at about five months of age, these birds provide meat that is exceptionally tasty and tender.

The family also raises some Khaki-Campbell ducks, which, according to a USDA pamphlet, have been known to lay 365 eggs per year. Those of the Taylors's weren't nearly that productive, but they did lay well in the spring and were easy to care for. Khakis forage constantly although they do require some grain, particularly during their laying season.

The family felt their guineas were a glaring failure. The guineas certainly are excellent foragers—too good, since their favorite foraging territory was the garden. Young seedlings seem to be quite a delicacy in the guinea diet, and the birds have a particular affection for any kind of peas, beans, and squash. Guinea fowl can also spot—and peck out—the tiniest speck of pink on a green tomato.

These birds nearly destroyed a hive of bees by roaming the fields and eating a bee from each blooming flower. They also learned to stand in front of the hive and catch the pollen-laden insects as they landed.

Guineas are poor mothers, and the Taylors found that contrary to popular belief, they have little value as "watchdogs," as they screeched *all* the time. The birds are extremely wary, and after you've killed one, the only way to ever harvest the rest is with a rifle. Also, guineas like to sleep in trees, where they are easy prey for owls. All in all, the Taylors felt guineas weren't worth the effort.

The family acquired three mixed-breed cows that were bred to calve at four-month intervals. The idea was to have one of the three coming fresh and producing between three and four gallons of milk per day early in her lactation on a regular enough schedule to give a steady supply of milk the year-round. They figured that each new calf could have one gallon of the flow every day, and the other two would be for the table.

And that's just the way everything worked out . . . until one cow dropped twin heifers, leaving only a gallon of milk for daily household use.

Pennyroyal made an effective and inexpensive fly repellent for livestock. A large handful of the mint is boiled for a few minutes in water, and then the liquid is mixed with mineral oil and a couple of drops of dishwashing detergent. The mineral oil extends the effective life of the repellent by helping it stick to an animal's hair, and the detergent helps the oil and water combine into a useful emulsion when the container's shaken vigorously.

The Taylors freely admit that their goal of self-sufficiency in the purest sense was unattainable. They feel they could never, for instance, produce the iron in a plow or manufacture the implement in their backyard. For this reason, they are willing to accept what they called durable technology—a tool which uses only renewable sources of energy as its driving force, has a relatively long life, say on the order of a human lifetime, and when damaged or worn, can in almost every instance be repaired right on the farm.

The family rescued a forge from a junk pile, bought an anvil at an auction, and purchased a vise at another sale. It's hard to believe how handy it is to be able to work metal. The Taylors found annealing to be a particularly valuable skill around the homestead, and there were days when they'd fire up their forge two or three times.

They first tried farming the land with an old tractor, but it was simply impossible to operate one of the machines on their rough woodland and on the small patches of land they cultivated. Besides that, they didn't like the expense of pouring gasoline through such a piece of machinery.

Attempts at using horses proved equally frustrating. Real draft horses were few and far between and very expensive. The horses and mules that the Taylors did find they could afford were usually of the saddle type and too small to do significant amounts of work.

The family felt that horses have at least three other major drawbacks: They must be fed large quantities of grain when they're working; their harness is expensive; and many horses become excited in a confusing or tight situation and immediately make a gigantic lurch or jump. The invariable result of this action is a broken set of harness, expensive repairs, and delays.

So they turned to oxen and found that, especially when hand-fed from birth, the beasts are calm, steady, and forgiving. When confronted with an unfamiliar situation, they tend to simply stop and think things over. This is an ideal response, since it gives the teamster a chance to gather his thoughts too.

Oxen are not unduly expensive or hard to find, and they're not difficult to train. None of the family had ever seen another team of the animals work before, but they soon had their pair working together beautifully.

Also, it doesn't take a lot of money to harness a span of oxen. Following directions received by mail, the Taylors made a sliding yoke with just the crudest of tools. The only expense was a few cents for having the yoke's beam sawed out and a few dollars for nuts and bolts.

Oxen are surefooted and work well in brush and other tangles. Their simple gear is much harder to foul than the harness on a team of horses. The animals can get by reasonably well on no grain at all if they're allowed all the forage or hay they can eat.

The Taylor's span pulled a moldboard plow, disc harrow, spring tooth harrow, standard tooth harrow, row cultivator, two-row planter, mowing machine, hay rake, and hay wagon. "Bigun" and "Mawry" were also invaluable for dragging logs out of the woods and hauling firewood on a cart, and for two years they turned the sweep on a homemade irrigation rig to pump 1,000 gallons of water an hour

15 feet uphill from the Little Buffalo River to the garden.

During the summer when heat from a woodburning cookstove would make the house intolerable, many meals were prepared in a homemade solar oven. In addition, the oven saved the work and time that the family would otherwise have spent in cutting wood for summertime cooking.

Cooking is somewhat slower with the solar rig than with the cookstove, but the Taylors felt that most foods—yeast bread, pan bread, potatoes, meats, and a dozen other things—taste better when cooked slowly.

Because of the labor and expense of pressure canning 1,300 quarts of food on a wood cookstove as the Taylors did in 1975, they tried drying their food. They tried sun-drying garden produce several times, but thanks to the heavy dew every night throughout the summer in the Arkansas Ozarks, it was completely unworkable for them even when they covered the food or took it inside each evening. Electric dryers were too expensive to operate and use nonrenewable energy; the Taylors didn't care for oil-fired units because the fumes from their fuel always seemed to taint the produce.

So they built a dryer which circulates clean, controlled, smoke-free air at any temperature up to 150° Fahrenheit through anything they want to preserve. This dryer was heated by the renewable fuel the family cut from their 120 acres of woodland. It worked like a charm, and by disconnecting a single length of pipe so the smoke from the fire went up through, rather than around, the drying chamber, the rig served as a meat smoker.

The Taylors also bought two steam engines. One weighed only 100 pounds and put out five horsepower. The plan was to set it on wheels with a small boiler and pull it around from the irrigation pump, to a washing machine, to a battery charger (for some household lights, a car radio for news and weather reports, and an electric fence), to a grain thresher, to a concrete mixer, and so on.

The other powerplant served for larger jobs, such as driving a cordwood saw, thereby freeing the family from using the gasoline-eating chain saw.

The grass in the Taylor's pasture and the trees in their woods gather the sun's energy and store it for later use. The oxen then consume the grass and use the energy derived from it for draft work. The family cuts the wood and burns it in their stoves, steam engines, and food dryer. Even the nutritional value of the things they eat from the garden, orchard, woodland, and the animals they butcher originally comes from the sun.

The Taylors planted 80 Chinese chestnut seedlings and gathered their first ten pounds of chestnuts three years later. They hoped that these trees would eventually produce 100 pounds of nuts per tree. That's 8,000 pounds of food with a protein content roughly three times that of corn, or the equivalent of 24,000 pounds of corn. Pipe dream or not, they expected to feed most of the chestnuts to the livestock in place of grain. Such tree culture has been done by other people in other lands, and the family liked the idea. Once established, the crop requires no annual replanting and cultivation, and the trees protect and hold the soil better than more conventional forms of agriculture.

While the Taylor family found that their newfound lifestyle was viewed askance by some of their friends and relatives, they felt quite comfortable with their homesteading experience. They felt that while they were enjoying a heavily self-sufficient way of life, they had not retreated from the world and were still an integral part of modern society and hardly immune to economic, environmental, or social problems.

However, the family's requirements for money were lessened considerably by moving to their Arkansas mountain home, and the fruits they enjoyed there were those of their own labor.

FINDING THE FARM YOU HAVE IN MIND

Perhaps you've decided to leave the crowded city life and make the move to a place in the country. Living peacefully in a quiet hollow where you can raise your own garden and tend your own livestock might sound appealing, but it can turn into a most unpleasant experience if you impulsively flee to a section of the country or a piece of land that's wrong for you.

Finding the right country property isn't difficult; it just requires a bit of forethought and a lot of research and patience. People who leap into farm life without giving proper consideration to the part of the country where they'll be at home, or who buy their land without gathering the information, facts, and figures needed to make a calculated decision, stand a good chance of winding up back in the city, licking their wounds and feeling resigned to living elbow-to-elbow with thousands of others.

PICKING THE AREA: There are several matters to consider before even looking at farm and property listings in the real estate catalogs. Among these are the climate and topography you prefer, the distance you want to be from friends and relatives, what you can afford to pay for property, and whether you want a remote location or one with access to a large metropolitan area.

You'll need to decide whether you want four distinct seasons or year-round sunshine. Do you prefer hills and mountains to flatlands . . . the dryness of the desert or a certain amount of rainfall? Have you always yearned to live near the ocean or a lake?

If price is a factor, as it is for most people, look at population shifts to see which areas of the country have stable or declining populations. Land prices are most likely to be lower in these locations, and property is probably more readily available.

Once you've decided which type of land and climate are most suitable, contact Strout Realty and United Farm Agency, both of which maintain directories of farms, acreage, country homes, and even small businesses for sale all over the United States. You'll get a good idea of land prices, the geography, and the types of farming practiced in various parts of the country.

The next step is to find out more about the specific areas that interest you and to try to narrow the field to a single state. The public library is a good place to find information you need. Talking to people and ordering government publications can also be helpful.

LEARNING ABOUT THE STATE: Write to the state agricultural extension service for publications on soil, climate, farming, wildlife, poultry raising, beekeeping, and gardening.

Next, break the state down into counties and get the address of every county seat. Then order a map of each county and write to inquire about proposed highways, industry, and other developments. This should narrow your search to a handful of counties.

CHOOSING THE TOWN: Address letters to the chambers of commerce of small towns in the areas which interest you most. Ask about schools, churches, libraries, recreational facilities, clubs, and so forth, and when the information arrives, interpret it according to your needs and way of life.

Next, order a copy of each small town's newspaper so you can learn about food prices, real estate, cost of used farm equipment, and other matters. You can tell a lot about an area by reading editorials and want ads.

The final step is to write for copies of the local telephone directories. The yellow pages are packed with information about business opportunities, services available, restaurants, and so forth. If you need further information about people or organizations mentioned in other literature you've received, the telephone book will help you locate them.

USING THE INFORMATION: By now you will have amassed quite a pile of paper.

When writing for information, type your queries neatly and enclose a stamped, self-addressed envelope. Psychologically, a reply envelope is almost as hard to ignore as a ringing phone, and a businesslike letter indicates that you're serious about your inquiry.

When requesting maps, telephone directories, and other materials, always arrange to pay any cost involved. Keep carbon copies of all correspondence.

FINDING THE FARM: At this point, begin making lists of things to look for in your "ideal" farm. Is there an adequate water supply? Drilling a well is expensive. Is the property on a mail and school bus route? If so, roads will probably be plowed promptly in winter. Will you have to install a septic tank, a bathroom, electricity? Take nothing for granted; many old farmhouses are appallingly primitive.

Realize that you probably won't find a dream house, and keep in mind that you may well wind up renovating an older home. You can repair a building, but you can't move a piece of acreage, so pay particular attention to the land's location.

When inquiring about a particular piece of property, you may find it's already been sold. Don't give up, though; write to several of the realtors who advertise in the catalogs and ask what else is available. Some may not reply, but others will, and ultimately you'll find what you're looking for.

THE DO'S AND DON'TS OF LAND BUYING

Buying your own parcel of land instead of sinking your money into rent year after year can be an attractive prospect, but there are several considerations a person should give such a purchase, and many pitfalls that should be avoided.

Imagine you spot an ad that describes what sounds like an ideal piece of land: "Forty acres, year-round creek, partly wooded, some pasture, marketable timber, south-facing slopes, small down payment, easy terms. $26,000." It sounds like the deal of a lifetime, one you certainly don't want to pass up or miss.

However, before shelling out a large amount of cash that you may not be able to recover later, there are several matters to consider carefully.

ACCESS: It's impossible to overemphasize how important access rights are. Be certain beyond the shadow of a doubt that permanent, legal, transferable access is specified in the deed.

As an example of the problems that can arise, consider the experience of a couple who bought a lovely place and built a house on it, acting on a neighbor's assurance that he had no objections to their using his road to get to their land. Later they had a minor disagreement with the fellow, and he promptly blocked the road. The couple started walking in and out across a bordering piece of government land but were informed by the agency in charge that they'd better cease and desist or they'd be hauled into court on trespassing charges.

Becoming frightened, the people tried several other routes, each of which was eventually blocked when at least one landowner wouldn't let them through. Because the unfortunate couple couldn't afford an expensive legal battle, they were forced to abandon the place, and they lost the cash they'd invested, which amounted to all of their savings.

As you can see, it's imperative to make sure that no one can stop you from getting to your property. If it's possible to obtain access by paying for it annually, as is the case when dealing with some government agencies, make certain that the right is not revocable and will be transferable should you later decide to sell. You'll also want to find out who's responsible for the maintenance of the road.

Furthermore, don't assume that, because a piece of property is on a county or state road, access is guaranteed. If the right wasn't granted to the previous owner or if no driveway has been put in yet, you may have to get permission from the county or state. Such permits are not always automatic, and they'll generally cost some money.

WATER, SEWER, DRAINAGE, AND RELATED MATTERS: Water and soil drainage are also critical concerns. That creek running across your dream parcel may be lovely, but take the time to discover whether you have the right to use it. Your land could, for instance, be part of a city watershed, in which case it's possible that you'd be unable legally to use a single drop of the liquid. In addition, the law could require that all your livestock be kept several hundred feet from the creek or could prevent you from putting in a septic tank and drain field or an outhouse.

If a septic system is to be installed, make several percolation tests before buying. This is necessary to assure that there are some places away from your water supply where the drainage is adequate.

MINERAL RIGHTS: Many people consider mineral rights to be of minor importance, but there are examples of what can happen to a farmstead when the owner doesn't hold them. One man, for instance, bought what he thought was an ideal piece of property, built a beautiful home, and planted several hundred acres of orchards and gardens. In short, he invested a fortune in both time and money in his land. He knew he didn't own the mineral rights to the property, but the real estate agent had assured him that they weren't important.

Some 25 years later, however, after his orchards and gardens had matured and were supplying his entire income, he came home one day to find his house being bulldozed and one of his orchards already gone. Coal had been found on his land, and his deed stated plainly that the only compensation due him was the cost of the materials in his house and barns. The farmer had absolutely no legal recourse.

Just because no minerals of value have been found on a piece of property, there's no guarantee that one or more won't be discovered there sometime in the future or that a new use won't be found for a "worthless" mineral that's already known to be there.

TIMBER RIGHTS: In most cases, timber rights don't pose much of a problem. A property owner will usually receive them at least conditionally. However, be sure to find out whether there's a timber contract out on the place. If there is, extreme caution is in order. You'll want to learn when the contract expires, how many board feet and of what species the logging company is allowed to take, and how that cutting will affect the looks of the land. Also, be sure to find out what condition the loggers are required to leave the property in after the harvest.

EASEMENTS: It's also important to research easements, the rights and privileges that persons may have in another's land. First, find out what easements are available to you over other people's property. For example, if you're not on a county road, you'll want to know whether the easements all along your access road are wide enough to meet county specifications in case the local government is later willing to take over maintenance of the road. Take the case of a couple who lived on a fairly populated road that the county said it was willing to maintain if all 15 families along the route would grant a 60-foot-wide right-of-way. All but one landowner, a man whose house was almost at the beginning of the road, were eager to have that convenience, but that fellow refused to give up the 30-foot strip required.

In addition, you'll want to make certain that easements are available to you for power and telephone lines. Even if such trappings of civilization aren't important to you now, they might be later, and they almost certainly will be should you ever choose to sell your spread!

You'll also want to know what easements may apply to the land you're buying. That way, you won't plant your vegetable garden in the middle of someone else's right-of-way.

AVAILABILITY OF UTILITIES: As far as utilities are concerned, you should know that if you live at a considerable distance from a powerline, some companies have the right to refuse to put in an electric line even if you have the money and the desire to pay for the materials and installation.

CHEMICAL POLLUTION: We've probably all had our fill of horror stories associated with land contaminated by chemicals. After all, chemical poisoning can not only make your land useless but can also seriously affect your health and that of your children, your pets, and your livestock. You'll at least want to know what common sprays are regularly applied in the area, such as for roadside maintenance. Try to find out, too, what has been used on the ground in the past, what may have seeped into it, or what might come down the creek.

PERMITS AND ZONING: In most areas, permits are required to build a house, put in a septic system, and so on, so before buying, find out how the property is zoned and whether you'll be able to get the permits you want. This isn't as routine as it may sound, because there are areas with very strict codes that, for instance, allow only so many structures to be built in any given time period. If you're serious about farming, be sure the property is zoned for agricultural use. Some zoning and deed restrictions can prevent you from keeping certain types of animals or engaging in a commercial venture, including the sale of surplus vegetables.

PROTECT YOURSELF: Before purchasing property, it pays to make sure the price is in keeping with the normal land costs in the area.

Furthermore, be certain that when you do put down earnest money, you'll be allowed to make the final purchase dependent upon written contingencies. Just what

these qualifications are will be up to you, but do be sure that your earnest money agreement covers legal access, mineral rights, timber, and water, and that it requires the seller to deliver to you a deed conveying clear title. Be certain to obtain a title search, which will tell you the legal history of the property, what, if any, encumbrances are on the land, and that the seller does, in fact, own the property.

Make sure that any advance money given to the seller goes into an escrow account and will be returned if the owner can't convey a clear title. Don't leave this up to chance; insist on such an agreement, since it's entirely possible to lose property and a good bit of money if this simple step isn't taken. If there's an underlying contract or mortgage on the property, get a statement in writing that it's being paid or that you're making provision to assume it, because if this isn't specified, the holder of the mortgage has a claim on the land.

You should also invest in title insurance, and read the policy carefully in order to understand exactly what it says. Also be sure to get the transaction recorded at the public registry, which may or may not be at the county courthouse.

You will, of course, be faced with a lot of legalese when buying property. It'll be necessary, for example, to become familiar with such terms as the following: binders, mortgagor, mortgagee, graduated payment mortgage, variable rate mortgage, mortgage clause, loan origination fee, loan discount (or points), foreclosure, lien, quitclaim, and acceleration clause. An acceleration clause, for example, causes the entire debt to become due should one installment payment be late, and it's something you definitely don't want in your mortgage.

Be sure, then, to consult a legal encyclopedia or dictionary whenever you come across a term that isn't absolutely familiar to you, and to find out from a competent real estate lawyer exactly how that term is interpreted in your particular agreement.

COMMUNITY ATTITUDES: Finally, study the area where you plan to live as thoroughly as possible. The time spent on this research can be critical to your future peace of mind. A few miles can sometimes mean a lot in terms of happiness and opportunity.

It's possible that the area's only industry can close down leaving people with no money to pay for outside services. Also, people in some communities tend to be a bit hostile to newcomers. Make an effort to talk to new residents in the area where you're planning to buy and find out how they feel about living there. The answers you receive may be the deciding factors as to whether or not you purchase.

These, then, are some of the points you'll need to consider before investing your hard-earned savings in any land deal. You may decide, of course, to compromise on a few of the factors in order to make your homestead dream come true, but be sure you don't compromise so much that your dream becomes a nightmare.

SOURCES FOR LEARNING THE LAY OF THE LAND

Without a doubt, the best way of knowing that you are buying what you want when purchasing land is to examine the plot in person. However, this often involves a great deal of legwork and expense, especially for anyone looking at several pieces of property situated some distance from one another or well away from the prospective buyer's home. Maps can help cut the cost of hunting for acreage, and allow one to make a preliminary and rather thorough evaluation of a tract without ever setting foot on the land.

Soil survey, geological, and topographical maps, available from state and local government offices, contain specific facts about an area: the kind of soil, the crops the earth is likely to support, rock types and formations, and the lay of the land. Other information such as average rainfall, seasonal temperature ranges, and first and last frost dates can be obtained inexpensively or for free. With these types of data and whatever is learned from the technical maps, a person can determine whether a piece of land warrants further consideration.

MAP BASICS: Traditionally, north is at the top and south at the bottom; east is to the right and west to the left. The scale, which gives the relationship between distance on the map and actual distance, is usually found in the upper or lower margin. There is also a legend, which contains an explanation of the various symbols, numbers, colors, and shades used on the map. Any map should carry the date that it was drawn or that the most recent revision was made. This last piece of informatin is valuable, because streambeds can shift, buildings are constantly being built or torn down, and roads change. Making use of a map involves translating the symbols, lines, and colors into an image of the actual land.

TOPOGRAPHICAL MAPS: A topographical map is an accurate and detailed representation of a section of the earth's surface. These maps indicate streams, lakes, rivers, wooded areas, roads, trails, railroads, buildings, mines, and other features, but they also delineate the hills, valleys, ridges, and other natural variations of the land itself.

Water is usually indicated by blue, wooded areas by green, roads and trails by black or red solid or dotted lines, railroads by crosshatched black lines, buildings by black rectangles, and mines and other features by other symbols. The ups and downs of the earth's surface are depicted by contour lines, each of which represents a certain elevation. Depending on the map, the vertical interval between the lines is either 10 or 20 feet. Knowing the elevation interval between two lines, the distance between them, and the scale of the map, a person can get an idea how steep or gentle a slope is. If the contour lines are some distance apart, the slope is gentle; if several lines are quite close to one another, they indicate a steep slope, possibly even a cliff. For example, suppose on a certain map the difference in elevation between contour lines is 10 feet, and the scale is 1:24,000, meaning one inch on the map equals 24,000 inches, or 2,000 feet, on the earth's surface. If the distance between two lines is 1/4 inch, the land rises only 10 feet over the 500 feet between the lines. If, however, there are 20 lines grouped in that 1/4-inch map distance, the land rises 200 feet in elevation over a distance of 500 horizontal feet, a much steeper slope.

In addition to showing the natural and man-made physical aspects of an area, a topographical map contains other useful information about the land. By indicating the steepness of grades, the direction a site faces, and erosion and drainage patterns, these maps can aid in selecting building sites, appropriate and feasible places to cut access roads, and good locations for planting crops.

Topographical maps can usually be ordered from the department handling geological surveys in the state you're interested in, but it may first be necessary to order an index so you can determine precisely which sectional maps you will need.

GEOLOGICAL MAPS: Also available through state

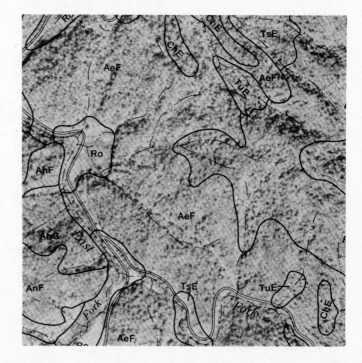

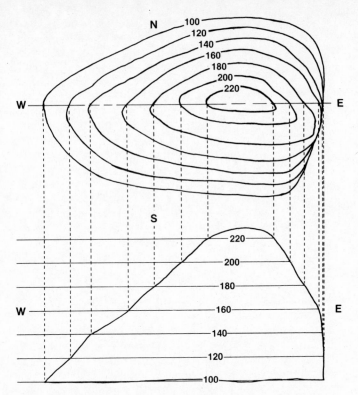

These maps are valuable during a property hunt for several reasons. Before selecting a well site, for instance, a geological map can be consulted to find the probable locations of porous rock formations—such as limestone or sandstone—that might hold water. Also indicated are what types of stone a person might expect to find that could be used as a building material. And the probable presence of mineral deposits on a piece of land should be reason enough for a prospective buyer to look into the ownership of mineral rights.

SOIL SURVEY MAPS: In addition to knowing something about the shape of the land and what lies below the surface, most people want information about the composition of the soil. This is provided by soil survey maps and accompanying literature that explains the symbols and describes the different types of soil. Similar to topographical maps in appearance, soil survey maps show the irregular outlines of each soil group, usually differentiating among them through the use of a system of color coding. By cross-referencing the map and the explanatory matter, a person can find out how the soil was formed, what its physical characteristics are, the minerals and plant nutrients it contains, and the crops that will be most suitable. Soil surveys may also contain climatic data, and they list crops that have been grown on a plot of ground in the past.

geological survey offices are specialized maps depicting the location of mineral deposits and rock formations, the planes and direction of strata, and other geological information. These maps use topographical drawings complete with contour lines as their base, but also incorporate a system of dotted lines and letter symbols to represent formations and deposits.

WORTH THE EFFORT: Though it can take some time to obtain these maps and to study them in the detail needed to really familiarize oneself with an area, doing so can eliminate an expensive scouting expedition to property that might prove unsuitable. Technical maps will tell you a great deal about the acreage you're considering before you actually see it.

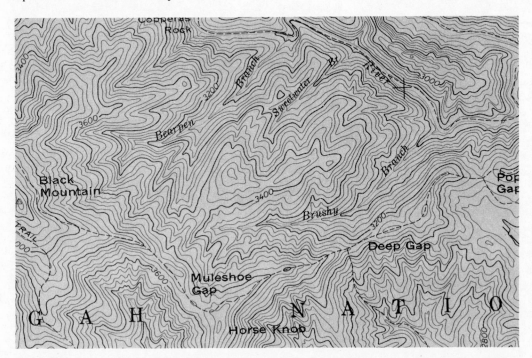

LEFT: A topographical map is the most widely available type of technical map (you can buy one from most state geological survey offices or in many office supply stores) . . . and it'll give you three-dimensional knowledge of a tract of land's natural features. ABOVE: This figure shows how topographical maps use lines on a flat plane to represent three-dimensional objects. FACING PAGE: The soil survey map—usually available, with an accompanying booklet, from the Soil Conservation Service—will tell you what kinds of soil you can expect to find on your land.

LEASE WITH AN OPTION TO BUY

Owning a home is one of the heartfelt desires of many people, but with high interest rates and the requirement for a huge down payment, this dream is increasingly just that—a dream. But there are methods of avoiding the demand for an enormous outlay of cash. One of the best ways to moderate this impact on the pocketbook is to lease the property with an option to buy.

Under a lease-to-purchase arrangement, part of the tenant's rent will go toward the purchase price of the property if that person decides to exercise the option and become the new owner of the homestead. There are several advantages to buying land or a house under a lease-to-buy plan, including the financial benefit and the ability to inspect the property more thoroughly than is usually possible before buying.

This type of arrangement gives the prospective owner the opportunity to actually live in the house under consideration before putting any money down. A renter has time to discover any quirks or problems in the plumbing, the electrical wiring, or the structure itself and can determine whether any major renovations are needed. The home can be inspected under various weather conditions and during different seasons, insuring that there will be no unpleasant surprises later on.

The option plan is attractive from a financial viewpoint, too. The usual arrangement in this type of agreement is to apply a portion of each month's rent toward the down payment, making it possible for a buyer to become a landowner without having to lay out as much cash at one time as would normally be required to purchase a home.

However, there are usually some trade-offs that must be made when leasing with the option to buy. For example, a slightly higher rent than normal might be required during the option period. This additional money will in most cases, though, be credited toward the down payment and will be lost only if the renter decides to forgo the purchase.

Depending upon the agreement, paying for minor repairs and contributing toward the upkeep of the dwelling might be necessary. Usually, however, the landlord foots the bill for all of the maintenance. Your skill as a negotiator will help determine the arrangement in your particular case.

WHERE TO LOOK: Begin searching for property in your own backyard—literally! The average landlord holds onto a house for only three years before selling it, so it stands to reason that if a tenant were to offer to buy the property for an acceptable price and terms, the rental home's proprietor might well be willing to listen to the proposal and to consider it. If the original offer doesn't spark a deal, an offer to pay a higher rent during the lease period might help capture the landlord's attention.

Should arranging a purchase with a current landlord fail, a satisfactory deal might be found in the real estate section of the local paper. It is also possible to place an ad stating the kind of arrangement you might want. If there is a particular piece of property you're interested in that is not on the market, it's possible to find out from county or city records who owns the land and make that person a proposal. Be forthright. Remember, the worst response you can get is no.

A person should be aware that many sellers will not be interested in a lease-to-buy option and that many real estate agents will not want to handle this type of transaction. However, a refusal from the first few homeowners or agents contacted is not a good reason to give up. Find out why your offers are not accepted, and perhaps it will be possible for you to make a more favorable proposal. Though locating lease-to-buy property can take some time, people who find a home they can purchase under such an arrangement usually discover that the transaction works out quite satisfactorily.

DRAWING UP THE AGREEMENT: Basically there are two parts to the typical lease with option to buy: the lease itself and the sale contract. When preparing the former, it's necessary to reach an agreement concerning the length of the lease and the amount of rent. From the buyer's point of view it's advantageous to negotiate a fairly long term. Such an arrangement could allow a person to apply several years' rent, or a portion of it, toward the down payment and substantially reduce the amount of cash needed when the purchase option is exercised. Regardless of the length of the lease, however, make sure that the agreement allows you to buy the property at any time before the term of the lease is up.

The remainder of the lease portion should contain all of the items normally covered in a standard rental agreement. You'll want to include a description of the property and the addresses of the parties involved, an explanation of how the maintenance, utility, and insurance costs will be paid, an outline of the procedure to be used to return—or not return—the security deposit, remedies to be employed should either party default on the bargain, and any other information deemed pertinent.

Because a legally binding contract will go into effect when exercising an option to buy, it's generally best to include all the essential components of a formal sale contract in the original option agreement. As an alternative, a preliminary agreement to lease with the option to purchase can contain the written understanding that more complete final documents will be drawn up prior to the date of exercising the option and that the offer to buy is contingent upon mutual approval of those documents. However, even such a shortened contract should include the purchase price and the terms of sale, any conditions of and limitations to the title, the contingencies of the sale, and the apportionment of the closing costs between the parties.

The purchase price and terms of sale detail how much the property will cost when the option to buy is exercised and where that money will come from. This information should include the amount of the down payment, the percentage of rent to be applied toward that cost, and an explanation of how the balance is to be paid. As the buyer, you're going to want the lowest possible price and the easiest terms. You might be able to convince the seller to carry the loan, so that you don't have to arrange financing through a lending institution. However the sale's financed, though, be sure to stipulate the type of loan, the amount, the payment plan, and the interest.

Clearing the title gives assurance that the parcel is free of any outstanding debts, taxes, and insurance premiums and that any limitations to the title such as land-use restrictions are clearly listed. Otherwise, you might well find yourself saddled with an unpaid bill after you've settled in. Also, be sure that the title is insured against unspecified claims.

All of the conditions that you'd like to have met prior to taking ownership of the property should be included, in writing, in the final contract. Contingencies for sale include such items as any inspections that need to be done before the sale is consummated. You might, for example, want to have the acreage surveyed and the dwelling appraised, require a termite and structural inspection, or request soil and water testing. Local or state agencies may require specific inspections before the sale can be completed.

Closing costs involve various expenses that must be settled before you secure the title. These can include the fee for recording the sale, an attorney's charges for drawing up the final contract, the costs of clearing up any contingencies, and an escrow fee paid to a go-between who protects the interests of all parties involved in the deal. Some of the payments are typically shared by the buyer and the seller, while others are usually handled by just one of the parties. In any circumstance, it's very important to make sure that the amounts of, and responsibilities for, these costs are agreed to in writing.

All of the matters concerning to the sale itself, of course, pertain to any land-buying transaction, but the details will more than likely be somewhat different and tailored more to the individual deal in a lease-to-buy arrangement. This makes it one of the least painful ways to take care of the usually large down payment that often makes home-buying almost a prohibitively expensive venture.

HOW TO SLICE YOUR MORTGAGE IN HALF

A mortgage payment is usually the largest single monthly expense a family has, and when the length of time that payment must be made and the total cost of a home by the time the debt is finally paid off are considered, the prospect of buying your own house can be foreboding.

For example, the actual cost of a house priced at $26,300 and purchased on a 30-year mortgage with an interest rate of 11.5% would be about $90,000 if the debt were paid off over the full period of the loan. However, by making extra payments against the principal, much of the interest, about $63,700 in the example given, that would be paid the lending institution over the 30 years can be eliminated.

Each monthly mortgage installment consists primarily of an interest charge and a payment applied to the principal amount of the loan, plus fees for insurance and taxes included by some lenders. As long as the balance owed is high, the interest charges will be high, accounting for all but a small amount of the monthly payment at the beginning of the loan. Therefore, by adding extra amounts of principal to each mortgage payment, a person can save thousands of dollars in interest expense.

Take the example cited here in which the payments amount to $247.50. The first 40 of the 360 payments due would be distributed as indicated on the accompanying amortization schedule. This chart shows how each payment of the loan would be broken down into principal and interest. At the end of the first year, $2,866.81 in interest and only $103.19 of the principal would be paid. In effect, with almost $3,000 paid to the lending company, the loan would be reduced by only about $100!

Starting after the first year, including five extra payments against the principal with every monthly mortgage installment for the next three years would reduce the term of the borrower's obligation from 30 to 15 years. Of course, a home costing $26,300 with an 11.5% mortgage is unlikely to be found today, but the method and its effectiveness remain unchanged, and it can save the homeowner a great deal of money wherever it can practically be used.

There are mortgages that contain prepayment penalties, which impose an extra cost upon the borrower for paying off the debt early. Also, anyone who holds an existing mortgage with an interest rate substantially below those currently being offered by lending institutions could find it more prudent to invest extra funds elsewhere at current market rates than to use the money to shorten the loan. Finally, individual savings and loan institutions have different policies concerning repayment of loans, so it's best to take these regulations into account before embarking on any early repayment plan.

HOW TO BEGIN: In order to apply the program, first obtain the amortization schedule specifically calculated for your mortgage. It will resemble the table shown here. Next, in order to identify the interest/principal breakdown on the next month's installment, calculate how many payments have already been made. When making that payment, add to the routine monthly installment the total of the payments against principal for the next five installments and pay the entire amount.

Suppose, in the example given, that 24 payments had been made before starting this plan, and when the twenty-fifth remittance was due, the principal amounts for installments 26 through 30 were combined for an additional payment of $52.75. This would make a total payment, including the regular remittance, of $300.25.

By doing this, a person would make six of the 360 payments at one time, effectively avoiding $1,184.75 in interest charges which would've been paid had the regular schedule been followed.

After one year of adhering to this procedure, 72 mortgage installments (20% of the loan's life) instead of 12 would be covered at a total extra cost of about $700, yet almost $12,000 worth of interest charges would be avoided in the process.

Not everyone can afford to add five extra principal payments each month. However, any number of additional installments will help reduce the overall interest.

$24,975 at 11.5% for 30 years				
PAYMENT	AMOUNT PAID	INTEREST	PRINCIPAL	NEW BALANCE
1	$247.50	$239.34	$ 8.16	$24,966.84
2	247.50	239.27	8.23	24,958.61
3	247.50	239.19	8.31	24,950.30
4	247.50	239.11	8.39	24,941.91
5	247.50	239.03	8.47	24,933.44
6	247.50	238.95	8.55	24,924.89
7	247.50	238.86	8.64	24,916.25
8	247.50	238.78	8.72	24,907.53
9	247.50	238.70	8.80	24,898.73
10	247.50	238.61	8.89	24,889.84
11	247.50	238.53	8.97	24,880.87
12	247.50	238.44	9.06	24,871.81
13	247.50	238.36	9.14	24,862.67
14	247.50	238.27	9.23	24,853.44
15	247.50	238.18	9.32	24,844.12
16	247.50	238.09	9.41	24,834.71
17	247.50	238.00	9.50	24,825.21
18	247.50	237.91	9.59	24,815.62
19	247.50	237.82	9.68	24,805.94
20	247.50	237.72	9.78	24,796.16
21	247.50	237.63	9.87	24,786.29
22	247.50	237.54	9.96	24,776.33
23	247.50	237.44	10.06	24,766.27
24	247.50	237.34	10.16	24,756.11
25	247.50	237.25	10.25	24,745.86
26	247.50	237.15	10.35	24,735.51
27	247.50	237.05	10.45	24,725.06
28	247.50	236.95	10.55	24,714.51
29	247.50	236.85	10.65	24,703.86
30	247.50	236.75	10.75	24,693.11
31	247.50	236.64	10.86	24,682.25
32	247.50	236.54	10.96	24,671.29
33	247.50	236.43	11.07	24,660.22
34	247.50	236.33	11.17	24,649.05
35	247.50	236.22	11.28	24,637.77
36	247.50	236.11	11.39	24,626.38
37	247.50	236.00	11.50	24,614.88
38	247.50	235.89	11.61	24,603.27
39	247.50	235.78	11.72	24,591.55
40	247.50	235.67	11.83	24,579.72

CARETAKING ON SEVENTY WILDERNESS ACRES

Matt and his wife, Mary, live on a wilderness ranch seven miles from the nearest road and neighbor. Their home is a huge log cabin that overlooks a cold, clear mountain stream. They swim and fish in deep green pools, surrounded by tall fir trees and giant granite boulders.

If you drop by at dinnertime, you may see Mary preparing fresh produce from the garden and orchard as Matt fires up the woodburning cookstove. Dinner will proceed in calm, orderly fashion: No phone will ring, and no television or radio will blare. Their thoughts and discussion will be of the day's chores and accomplishments. They'll be looking forward to the biweekly mail pickup, for they know it will contain no water bill, electric bill, or notice of rent, tax, or mortgage payment.

If what has been said isn't enough to convince you that the life they lead is a good one, you should know that they receive $100 a month for enjoying themselves in this fashion. How do they work this enviable deal? The answer is simple: They're caretakers.

OUT OF THE CITY: This wilderness life came about because Mary and Matt, like so many others, are forsaking the nerve-racking pace of city life and looking for more harmonious alternatives. Living close to the land and away from crowds was the direction in which their hopes pointed.

Still, gathering the energy to make such a transition is no easy task, and that energy must be used with forethought and economy. They admit it was difficult to decide what form their back-to-the-land movement should take. Did they want a subsistence-level farming venture like that of Scott and Helen Nearing, or perhaps a frontier experience patterned after the works of Bradford Angier? Would one of the international communities be the right choice, or did they need their own quiet Walden?

With no real experience to help them make a decision, they found themselves in a position that's all too common among people who are trying to make the move from the city to farm. They visited several established planned communities, but none seemed especially interested in the couple, and the residents, according to Matt, all appeared to have problems enough without inexperienced newcomers further complicating their lives.

They stayed with friends who were buying or had already bought land, but for one reason or another, they didn't make their big move. After checking out the possibility of renting a small farm, the couple agreed that the idea had many merits, but they couldn't abide the thought of using their savings to pay off the loan on someone else's acreage.

Just as they were growing discouraged, Matt happened to spot a newspaper advertisement for a caretaking job. Here, it seemed, was the nearly perfect situation: a chance to live in a rural setting for a trial period without the obligations of a lease or mortgage. The couple felt they could advantageously use that time to gain experience in gardening, animal husbandry, plumbing, carpentry, and other skills that they urgently needed. The caretaking deal offered the pleasant and practical prospect of being paid while they learned. It seemed to merit prompt investigation.

GETTING HIRED: Matt began by answering the ad, only to find the position filled. Undaunted, he began searching the papers for other possible openings. The positions generally fell into two categories. The first consisted of house-sitting jobs, mostly of short duration and located in the suburbs. They weren't particularly interested in these. The second, and largest, group of opportunities involved caring for summer homes, vacation cabins, and hunting clubs. Though a number of advertisers specified retired couples, some didn't mention age at all.

Finally, in the monthly newsletter of a local conservation organization, the couple spotted an offer that appealed to their imaginations and state of mind. The ad asked for a single man or couple to caretake a wilderness cabin in northern California, and it gave an address to which inquiries could be sent.

Matt wrote to the prospective employer and told the man in glowing terms how interested he and Mary were and what eager and conscientious custodians they would be. The reply stated that there were several applicants and that a choice would be made shortly. Even after learning that it would be a seven-mile hike from the road to the front door of the cabin in question, they decided to pursue this particular caretaking job. After much correspondence, the husband and wife were notified that they'd been hired and were invited to their new boss's home to discuss the details of employment. Possibly their eagerness and enthusiasm had landed them the job.

The arrangement proved better than they'd hoped for. To begin with, the length of employment was up to them. They were required to be on the property from mid-May to September—roughly, during trout season. The rest of the year was left open. They could stay all winter if they liked or could leave with the assurance that the job would still be theirs in the spring. They would receive $100 a month plus a charge account for all the hardware, tools, and supplies deemed necessary

for the upkeep of the cabin. The owner used the place for two weeks at the end of the summer; the rest of the time Matt and Mary could consider it theirs. Their single official duty was to be there in order to discourage vandalism of the house and abuse of the property. The employer suggested several projects he'd be happy to have done, but only if the caretakers were so inclined.

SETTLING IN: Since the cabin was seven miles from the road, the couple planned to hire a mule packer to carry in supplies. Unfortunately, they couldn't locate a driver with the proper permits (the property is bounded on four sides by national forest), and they were forced to trek in with the supplies on their backs. The undertaking made them doubly grateful that a sound, well-equipped cabin awaited them. It would have been impossible to backpack building materials, and the cost of transporting such a load by mule would have been prohibitive for anyone on a limited budget.

Before too long, they had hauled up most of their staples and went down for mail, beer, and diversion more than anything else. The 14-mile round-trip became a pleasant means of meditation and exercise. The couple found themselves looking forward to the hikes.

CHORES: Once the caretakers were settled at the ranch, the first job they faced was gathering wood. Their equipment consisted of an ax, a 36-inch bow saw, two wedges, a sledgehammer, and a wheelbarrow. The steep terrain severely limited any search for fuel, but fortunately, they were able to find plenty of wood lying on the ground within a short distance of the cabin.

For three reasons the couple chose to use the downed wood instead of cutting trees. First, by clearing away all the dead, dry branches that accumulate on the forest floor, they eliminated the fuel on which a forest fire burns, thereby lessening the danger in their area. Nature would eventually accomplish this cleanup in her own way, by kindling the dead material with lightning. Their second reason for preferring fallen timber was that it's already seasoned and burns better than green wood. And third, these folks liked their trees left vertical.

The cabin has both a fireplace and a cookstove, so the woodpile is divided accordingly. Into the fireplace-supply side go all the less desirable pieces: knotty, twisted logs and stumps, and damp or green fuel. Wood for cooking is stored on the other side, and for this purpose, Douglas fir is unsurpassed in their part of the western United States. Matt and Mary were lucky enough to locate several trunks of this timber left over from a small logging operation. These big slices taken off the ends of logs measured about three feet thick and four to five feet in diameter, split easily, burned hot, left little ash, and were already dry.

Working off and on for about two weeks, the couple amassed a good supply of both types of fuel. However, this stock was only for the summer months when little heat was needed. If they had stayed through the winter in the cabin, every spare moment would have been spent gathering, splitting or chopping, and storing wood.

The next venture was the garden, and they picked an open spot in the orchard which received good, steady sun and had water via an irrigation ditch. They learned later, however, that alfalfa had been grown on that very patch as hay for mules, and the crop had never been turned under to replenish the soil. Since there had been no time to compost before planting, their garden on the run-down plot of earth was a little disappointing. A compost pile was started right away, but it wasn't of any use for the first year, of course. All the same, the gardeners kept building the soil with whatever organic material they could lay their hands on, and they were later rewarded for their efforts. They did grow enough fresh vegetables for meals, and they enjoyed the cherries, apples, and pears from the small orchard. Fresh trout, wild berries, and foraged vegetables rounded out their diets.

The rest of the work consisted of mending fences, gates, barns, and plumbing and whatever maintenance jobs seemed necessary. Neither of the caretakers hesitated to take a break whenever they wanted to go fishing or swimming—or just to sit and think.

Mary and Matt say that they learned, for the first time, the joy of labor. Like so many others, they had always equated tasks with drudgery, but in this job they discovered the self-discipline needed to be one's own boss and soon became proud of their achievements. Work was no longer toil. Of all the lessons the experience taught them, they believe that self-mastery has been the most rewarding, because it's a tool that makes all other things possible.

CARETAKING HANG-UPS: And what about the job itself? Part of their only official task was to discourage camping on the property. Matt was given no real rules to enforce but was told simply to use his own discretion regarding the use of the land. He was willing at first to overlook the presence of passing hikers because he felt that the majority would have enough courtesy to treat the campsites with respect. Unfortunately, this was not true, and after finding equipment stolen or abused, sites left a mess, and litter strewn all along the trail, he closed the area to camping.

That was a sticky situation to handle, but one which everyone who owns or takes care of private property encounters sooner or later. It's unfortunate that for some people the attitude is "the land belongs to all of us, so I can do anything I want, but you're living here, so you clean it up." There may not be a fair solution to this problem, other than a caretaker's decision to prohibit all camping or trespassing. If you don't believe that there *is* such a thing as private property (in other words, if you can't accept that an individual has a right to buy and control land and thereby keep others off it—if you feel that the earth belongs equally and unconditionally to everyone . . .), you may not enjoy being a caretaker. You will be policing an area that belongs to someone else, and though you may have much latitude in your decisions, you will be obliged to carry out the owner's instructions concerning intruders. Find out exactly what your official position entails so that you'll have no misunderstandings with your employer, friends, and passersby. If you can't ethically consent to the conditions of the job, don't accept it.

However, should you take the position, be ready to stand by your employer's requests even if your firmness makes you out to be a villain in the eyes of someone else. Responsible caretakers will agree that this is the best policy. As a custodian, you're a middleman and may be called to task both by your boss and by people who want to use the property. Be as honest as possible in your dealings, and ill feelings can be minimized.

A NEW SEASON: For Mary and Matt, time left over from caretaking and household duties was filled with swimming, reading, and relaxing. At the end of their first wilderness summer, they were brown, healthy, serene, and $400 richer. The freedom to leave after the vacation period was over was one of the greatest assets of their job. They were able to travel, work, plan, and play with the assurance that they'd be back at the cabin the next spring.

That was the first year. The second time around, the couple managed to engage a driver and pack mules to haul equipment and supplies to the cabin, and their employer offered to foot the bill this time.

As soon as the caretakers resettled themselves, they put in their garden, and because of the composting done the year before, it began to flourish. They anticipated a long, hot summer with a bumper crop of tomatoes and other fresh foods. Mary became increasingly skillful with the cookstove, and the variety and quality of food that came out of its oven constantly delighted the diners.

THE REWARDS OF CARETAKING: Mary and Matt consider their experience as caretakers to be one of the most rewarding adventures of their lives and believe that many others would find such a situation equally exciting and educational.

Locating the right job is a mixed matter of stubbornness and serendipity. If you're industrious, you should be able to find enough openings to let you be choosy. Because of the low pay and occasional isolation, such jobs are not in great demand, and the market is definitely in the employee's favor.

These tips from longtime caretakers may help: Pick a region that interests you and check the help wanted sections of the local newspapers. Spend some time talking to the neighborhood realtors and postmasters. Read the bulletin boards in supermarkets, coin laundries, and churches, and then leave a card with your name, address, and phone number, stating that you would like a caretaking position. With conscientious footwork and a little faith, you may find a way of life as satisfying as that of the wilderness caretakers profiled here.

A FREE FARM FROM A MIXED BAG PURCHASE

A husband and wife in Morenci, Michigan, are proudly homesteading 36.5 acres of land which they, quite cleverly, acquired for free. The property contains a spring-fed creek, 10 acres of bottomland, 15 acres of woods, and more than 10 acres of pastures and sandy hills. The farmstead abounds with hawks, owls, deer, muskrats, and other wildlife.

HOW THEY DID IT: The couple's pleasant landholder status didn't occur overnight, but neither did it take so long to become a reality that they grew discouraged. The secret to winding up with a 36.5-acre farm for free depends on buying it first, as part of a larger parcel. After saving their money for several years, the would-be homesteaders purchased 120 acres with $20,000 down and a land contract for the remaining $34,000, payable at $1,000 a year on the principal and 5% interest on the balance. The amount of their down payment was negotiable. They could have bought the original 120 acres with a much smaller investment.

The important part of their secret is the fact that the couple wanted only 36.5 of the 120 acres. They didn't want the 83.5 acres of "good" cropland that all the local farmers wanted; they prized the "worthless" bottomland, buildings, and woods that would make an ideal homestead.

This, of course, gave them a tremendous advantage in their land dealing. Most people looked at the whole 120 acres and tried to balance the cost of "improving" the rough 36.5 acres against the profit that could be made farming the other 83.5 acres of field crops. Other potential purchasers would mentally calculate how long they'd have to farm the whole 120 acres to make enough money to be able to buy yet another piece of property and expand their holdings even further.

The homesteaders, on the other hand, had no intention of "improving" that rough 36.5-acre tract at all, because they liked it just the way it was and figured that 36.5 acres was a big enough "place in the country" for them. They had no desire to parlay it into "bigger and more efficient" landholdings of any kind.

So by "cash-renting" those 83.5 acres of fields to a local farmer, they made enough money to cover the land contract payments and real estate taxes for the entire 120 acres. This arrangement lasted for four years, during which the farm earned all the land and tax payments that were due, without the owners having to lift a finger.

When they checked out the local market, it was discovered that those 83.5 acres would sell for $800 an acre. (That's a total of $66,800 for 36.5 fewer acres than they had paid $54,000 for, just four years earlier!)

And so the couple sold their "good" land, but not through a real estate agent. They knew the property was worth $800 an acre, so they simply offered it for that amount to a neighboring farmer, who accepted.

It cost about $1,000 to have the 83.5 acres surveyed and a legal description drawn up. Another $100 went to a local lawyer for handling the contract. The owners accepted $6,000 as a down payment from their neighbor and allowed him one full year in which to come with the rest of the sale price. (Their lawyer drew up a land contract which stated that no interest would be charged on the principal if it were paid within 90 days. After that, 10% interest retroactive to the signing of the contract would be due, and the entire amount would be due one year from the contract's closing.)

While they could have made more money by taking out a 30-year contract with the buyer at a higher interest rate than the 5% they were paying on the existing contract, they chose not to do that. Thirty years of making payments and receiving payments seemed complicated, so they elected to "take the money and run." After all, the real purpose of the transaction was to acquire a place in the country, and that was being accomplished.

THE BOTTOM LINE: As it turned out, the buyer took nearly a year to arrange his financing, and that year cost him $6,080 in interest. It also cost the sellers the loss of one year's rent on the 83.5 acres and one year's interest on their own debt (a total of $4,500).

The settlement, then, looked like this: The homesteaders received a final lump-sum payment of $66,343.35 from the buyer. From this, they had to pay $50.00 for title insurance, $25.00 for document preparation, $4.00 for recording fees, $73.70 for state tax stamps, $597.40 for real estate taxes, and $30,500.00 to close out the balance on the original land contract. This left them with $35,093.25! Even when the capital gains tax that they paid was subtracted, they still got back more than their original investment, plus 36.5 acres with buildings free and clear. Their homestead, in short, was free!

HOW YOU CAN DO THE SAME: If you'd like to work the same economic miracle for yourself, just remember the facts of life in today's real estate market: Two kinds of property—the minifarm of a few acres and the big farm made up almost entirely of tillable fields— are in great demand, and both types of property are overpriced.

There are, however, countless small farms and family holdings of 60, 80, and 120 or more acres scattered throughout the United States and Canada. A great many of these places are mixed bag properties: various amounts of cleared and tillable land combined with some rough acres and a few old farm buildings. Big farmers who look at such acreage are usually put off by the rough land and old farm buildings (which they don't want to fool with). Back-to-the-landers generally don't consider these properties at all, because they are looking for only 20 or 40 acres, instead of 80 or 100 or more.

And right there is where you come in. Save up a nest egg, and then use it to buy a larger piece of mixed bag property than you need. Next, cash-rent the good fields to someone while local land prices rise. Eventually, survey and sell the tillable farm acreage for more than you paid for the entire original parcel. This move will leave you—free and clear—with a picturesque little homestead and some money in your pocket.

Play the mixed bag game skillfully the way this husband-and-wife team did, and you shouldn't have any trouble duplicating their success. Just don't get greedy. Don't make a fetish of buying at the absolute bottom dollar and then lying awake nights scheming to sell at the maximum top dollar. Instead, buy at a fair price, wait for the market to go up, split your property, and sell at a fair price.

HOMESTEADING IN MICHIGAN'S UPPER PENINSULA

A young couple named Francie and Jeff decided to flee their city situation, and they laid elaborate and detailed plans. They were going to combine savings with some friends, buy land together, and leave Grand Rapids in the fall. Their urban partners backed out at the last minute, however, and Francie and Jeff hadn't enough money of their own to swing a farm purchase. Just as the thought of spending another dreary winter in their apartment seemed more than they could bear and just when their spirits were at an all-time low, they met a sympathetic young farmer at an outdoor market. "As far as I can see," he said, "the only way to get to the country is to go there." His observation was the impetus they needed.

ESCAPE: Francie and Jeff loaded everything they

owned into the back of their old pickup truck, put their two-year-old son, Aaron, and their faithful Alaskan malamutes between them on the seat, and with a road atlas propped on the dash, headed north to Michigan's Upper Peninsula.

They hoped to settle in the U.P. because they had camped there many times and had become enamored of its unspoiled countryside. Furthermore, land in the rugged region was still inexpensive. For example, real estate listings for that area in 1982 included a three-bedroom home on 39 acres with drilled well and a barn for $9,250, a 120-acre spread at $160 an acre, and some property as low as $100 an acre. Of course, prime farmland or plots with lake frontage commanded higher prices, but compared with most parts of the United States, land there was a real bargain.

TRAVELS AND TROUBLES: The family was only about a half day's travel beyond Grand Rapids when it started to snow, which was enough to slow them down a bit but not enough to dampen their adventurous spirits. Without mishap, they reached Houghton/Hancock,

twin cities with a combined population of about 14,000 on the Keweenaw Peninsula, where their migration came to a halt. Providentially, a little farm located just a quarter-mile from the Lake Superior shore was available for rent at only $140 a month. They snapped it up and had barely unloaded the truck when the snow began to fall in earnest, piling up more than a foot overnight!

Although the adventurers were grateful to have a roof over their heads, their adjustment to the new environment wasn't all that easy. They had arrived in the north country just in time for the first real snows of winter without the slightest idea of how they would make a living, and Christmastime was upon them. Much of the holiday season was spent gathering wet wood, which was all they could find, to stoke the woodstove. Family outings during this time consisted of driving the 15 miles into town through a blizzard to call their folks from a pay phone on Christmas morning and feeble attempts to explore the terrain despite regularly harsh winter conditions.

Gradually, though, things began to improve. Neighbors dropped by with loads of dry wood and gifts of food, a local co-op extended membership to the newcomers, and both Francie and Jeff managed to find work that at least paid well enough to keep them from overdosing on lentil soup and boiled dinners.

Best of all, they discovered that they weren't alone. The family met many kindred souls who had been drawn to the U.P. by an honest appreciation of nature and who like themselves, were willing to take any kind of job in order to stay. Some were survival role models for Francie and Jeff.

GETTING BY AND GETTING BETTER: Determining ways to make a living can be an exercise in creativity: One couple, Dennis and Janet, worked as substitute teachers. To supplement their meager salaries, Dennis sold drawings and photographs at local markets, while Janet peddled her craft items. Jay, another new acquaintance, had a degree in forestry, but he was washing dishes to make ends meet while he got started in his own firewood business. A neighboring family, Jerry and Christiane and their four youngsters, had started a log-home operation.

Then there's Bill, who had worked part time at the Keweenaw Co-op for several years. He spent his winters as a tax accountant in California to help subsidize his summers in "Superior country." Bob and Becky, on the other hand, put in a couple of months each winter planting trees "down south" in lower Michigan, but they returned to Bob's grandmother's blueberry farm for the rest of the year to help out with the crop.

Although Francie and Jeff didn't find what they consider ideal employment right away, one thing is certain: Their lifestyle in the north country was far more healthful than their city existence was. Jeff's stress-related stomach condition disappeared, and the fresh air put color in their cheeks. Both husband and wife accepted

having to change their career goals somewhat in order to live in an environment that contributes so positively to their physical, mental, and emotional well-being.

Despite their adaptability and cheerful outlook, the two did a lot of soul-searching that first cold winter, especially during the many snowbound weeks that passed without their seeing another person. But spring finally came, and at last they could see what the surrounding territory actually looked like without a blanket of snow to mask it.

And what a spectacular sight it is! There are hills (of up to 2,000 feet) and trees everywhere, and there is eye-filling Lake Superior. The world's largest inland sea is an amazing expanse of fresh water that measures some 31,800 square miles and has depths as great as 1,333 feet! The lake and its winds can cause unpredictable storms and harsh weather, but Superior also can be dazzling to onlookers, counting among its attributes exquisite sunrises across the water's surface and a generous scattering of agates along the shore.

SOME FACTS AND FIGURES: The Upper Peninsula of Michigan has a land area of well over 16,000 square miles, around 90 percent of which is forested, and 1,700 miles of shoreline. It offers 17 state parks and two national forests, and boasts 4,000 inland lakes and some 12,000 miles of streams. No mention of the wilderness area would be complete without a word about fishing: In good weather, anglers come from all over just to try out the trout-filled waterways, and the deep, dry snow during the cold months is perfect for winter sports.

HOME IS WHERE THE HEART IS: There are, of course, a few thorns in any paradise. Because of lengthy and severe winters, large undeveloped areas, and a declining job market, population on the Keweenaw Peninsula has decreased in the last few decades. Homesteading in this rugged part of the country is clearly not for everyone. The main challenge is that of earning enough money to live on. The best opportunities for employment are in the fields of forestry and tourism. (Many of the once prominent copper mines have shut down as a result of the depressed economy, adding to the already unfortunate employment problem.) Jeff and Francie may yet have to shift their base of operations long enough to acquire the skills and training that will make them more marketable as workers in such an isolated area. Francie, for instance, would like to become a midwife and practice on the Keweenaw Peninsula. Though the couple may have to move south for a time to accomplish such a goal, they know where their home and hearts really are. The sight of their son, Aaron, bolting out the back door and grinning from ear to ear at the prospect of unlimited space in which to frolic, proves to them that they did the right thing by leaving the inner city to make their way in the north country. Even severe winters and financial problems can't dissuade them from their plans for the future.

SOLVING SUBURBAN HOMESTEAD PROBLEMS

While there are several demonstration projects across the United States and Canada designed to show that a metropolitan-based homestead is feasible, most of these have gardens created by professional horticulturists, solar facilities designed by engineers and built by professionals, and labor provided by hordes of volunteers. But can a suburban family with moderate homesteading knowledge and skills realistically expect to achieve the self-reliance these demonstration projects promise, especially while one or two members maintain full-time jobs and also look after children? The answer is, "Yes, definitely." However, there are pitfalls that should be taken into account before anyone actually embarks on such an ambitious project as suburban homesteading.

PHILOSPHY AND VALUES: Setting up a homestead in the suburbs or the city takes a great deal of work. Even though saving money in the long run is a valid reason to attempt such a venture, people also need a philosphical justification to fall back on during those inevitable occasions when things don't work out as smoothly as they'd hoped. Essentially, a person has to believe that the individual can make a difference in the state of the world today. After all, saving energy and re-using resources won't always bring immediate and direct cash savings, but both will contribute to a global resource saving, which is just as important.

Many other value questions will have to be addressed and resolved in developing the homestead operation: Will gardening be done organically or with chemical fertilizers and pesticides? Should building be done with power tools or by hand?

CASH OUTLAY: Before starting a homesteading venture, read as much as possible about all the money that can be saved with a 600-square-foot vegetable garden, a solar water heater, or other money savers, no matter how small. Most publications don't stress how much money you have to spend before you begin to save, but capital investment in a sophisticated suburban homestead can be significant. There are certain constraints inherent in suburbia that will tend to increase the demand for capital investment over what it might be in a rural area. Space, for one thing, is limited to probably about a quarter of an acre. There are often minimum square-footage requirements in some suburbs, as

well as neighborhood expectations of aesthetic standards. And because in many suburban households both the husband and wife have full-time jobs outside the home, equipment that can be used efficiently is a necessity in order to save time. All of these factors will add to the cost of outfitting a homestead.

One way to help reduce these capital investment costs is cooperative ownership. If handled sensibly, this can save a great deal of money. For example, a shredder purchased in partnership with a neighbor, or the ownership of an old pickup truck shared with another friend, can reduce the individual cost considerably. Of course, it's possible to get burned in arrangements of this kind, so one must always be cautious when entering into co-ownership agreements.

TIME: No one ever seems to have enough time, and this is especially true when one becomes involved in suburban homesteading. Managing gardens, greenhouses, chickens, and woodstoves takes time—a lot of it—and that soon exerts a painful pressure.

A small vegetable garden might demand only two to four hours of care a week during the growing season, but as the garden gets larger, and canning and freezing the edibles begins, the time factor may increase to as much as eight hours per week. Add to that the labors of tending livestock and managing energy devices, and you'll soon find yourself working 20 hours a week on things you never had to do before you got into suburban homesteading.

Of course, a lot of pressure can be eased if all members of a family pitch in and help with the work load. There are also ways of saving time that will come with experience. It's likely that a task which at first took two hours a week to complete might take only 20 minutes a week when experience is gained in handling it.

The lesson to learn, then, is not to take on anything new unless there's time to continue the activity. If it takes five years to get a homestead all together, then let it take the five years. Taking on, all at once, more than can be maintained can lead to frustration and possibly to giving up on the whole idea.

FAMILY SUPPORT: This issue is a critical one. True, one member of a family can manage suburban homesteading all alone, but it's difficult at best. If you are an ardent conservationist and the rest of the family wastes energy, water, and food, your frustration level will most assuredly rise. If your brood won't eat the bounties from your organic garden, then those beautiful vegetables are almost a waste of time and energy. If you don't mind turning down the thermostat to 63°F while wearing more clothing and using the woodstove to compensate, but everyone else gripes constantly about the chill, then family tensions will undoubtedly build.

Adopting a surburban homesteading lifestyle will affect the lives of the whole family in significant ways. Negotiations and compromises can often provide workable solutions, but cooperation and support of the entire group—even without actual labor from everyone—is essential. Without this, the homesteading attempt can be a negative, potentially destructive family experience.

SKILLS AND KNOWLEDGE: Discouragement comes quickly to those who don't respect the amount of education that will be required to pursue such activities as managing a large garden, processing a year's supply of food, tending chickens and fish, and operating a solar greenhouse. These are practically as complex as those involved in running a small farm, and most of us would not even consider jumping into the job of managing a fully stocked 150-acre farm. So it's usually best that folks interested in suburban homesteading think of it as a long-term project. The necessary knowledge and skills must be developed gradually for the project to be successful.

were originated for reasons of health and safety: for example, the standards set for woodstove installation and operation. Others, such as the laws prohibiting or restricting the raising of farm animals, may have wound up technical information on one particular subject.

The next best sources are friends, acquaintances, and the county extension agent. Friends who have been gardening a long time will be extremely helpful, but keep in mind that they may pass along bad as well as good information. Since county agents work mostly with commercial farmers, they will usually emphasize chemical agriculture, but they can help with certain problems.

Finally, look into adult education courses. Short seminars on small engine repair, basic horticulture, welding, woodworking, plumbing, and electrical work are extremely helpful and provide lots of hands-on experience.

NEIGHBORS, ZONES, AND LAWS: Everyone has seen newspaper stories depicting a group of neighbors up in arms because somebody in their area angered them. Well, suburban homesteading is occasionally the cause of such friction.

Most towns have zoning ordinances restricting what you can do with or on your property. Many of them were originated for reasons of health and safety: for example, the standards set for woodstove installation and operation. Others, such as the laws prohibiting or restricting the raising of farm animals, may have wound up on the books because someone complained about a problem. The secret to suburban homesteading is to avoid creating new problems, and therefore more restrictions, by keeping your neighbors happy. And two ways to keep neighbors on your good side are to inform them of your plans, activities, and sincere intentions, and to share your bounty.

THE OUTLOOK: In many cases, there are few limits on how a suburban homestead can develop. A large organic garden, berry patches, and fruit trees might grace the landscape and can be supported by a composting system that will provide much of the nourishment the plants need. Solar greenhouses and cold frames can enable a family to grow fresh food year-round, and a root cellar used in conjunction with a canning and freezing program can store the surplus harvest. A woodstove supplementing an attached solar greenhouse can drastically reduce fuel bills during the heating season. Even raising bees, chickens, and fish is not out of the realm of possibility.

With planning, and time to develop a working system, it's possible for a family to produce about 80% of its food supply and at least 50% of its energy needs on as little as a quarter-acre suburban lot.

AVOID URBAN PIONEERING CONFLICTS

The attempt to produce more and purchase less is often associated with rural life, but an increasing number of people are realizing that urban areas also offer prime opportunities for resourceful living. Pioneering in the city, however, isn't always the simple life, as one urban homesteader discovered.

When Marian first saw her house, the building in Grand Rapids, Michigan, had been condemned and vacant for four years. Most of the windows were broken, and a mountain of rubble lay on the floors. The roof sagged and, consequently, leaked. The building had no basement stairs, insulation, or heat source. Its plumbing and wiring systems needed a major overhaul. Still, the 104-year-old structure was built of sturdy brick, and it stood on a tree-lined residential street close to the heart of the city. There was a large, unkempt backyard and a vacant lot next door. To anyone else it may have appeared desolate, but to Marian it looked like the right place for new beginnings.

She purchased the property for $350 in back taxes, and later bought the vacant lot for $1.00.

Marian moved into her new home and began the arduous task of repairing and renovating. A friend helped her remove truckloads of debris from the house. The two then became super scroungers. They obtained replacement sheets of glass for all the broken windows in the house from trash dumpsters behind the local glassworks, hunted for various other discarded materials to use in repairing and outfitting the house, and gathered stovewood from power right-of-ways, construction scrap piles, and dead trees to use in the newly acquired woodburning stove.

Slowly but steadily they renovated. Marian learned to cut glass to fit the graceful arched shapes of the windows in the house. Insulation was added, and cellar steps were built. Because the home's plumbing was such a wreck, Marian didn't try to fix it, but simply connected up to the city water system with a hose in the basement that ran up to the kitchen sink.

She and her friend cleaned up the backyard, set fruit and nut trees out in the vacant lot, and converted an old wooden structure next to the house into a rabbit hutch. A solar greenhouse was attached to the residence, and a gray-water drainage system was laid out from the sinks and bathtubs into the greenhouse soil beds.

Basic amenities were handled on a basic level. There was no electricity, so candle and lantern light sufficed. The woodburning stove was used for cooking and heating. Marian and her friend built their own composting toilet, which consisted of a 55-gallon oil drum fitted into the floor, with a vent pipe and a privy-type seat with a cover mounted on top. Fresh sawdust was sprinkled into the drum after each use to absorb the liquid and help neutralized the acids. The residue was placed in large, heavy plastic drums that were sealed and stored for six months in the heated solar greenhouse to "digest."

PUBLICITY: During her first winter in the house, Marian was approached for an interview by a reporter from *The Grand Rapids Press* who had heard of her experimental urban homestead. Afraid of censure by city inspectors, Marian demurred. The reporter persevered, and eventually Marian decided that perhaps it would help the cause of conservation and environmentalism if other people learned what she was doing and why. The result of the interview was a sensitive four-page article that appeared in the Sunday supplement magazine. The writer managed to convey, along with the facts, the essence of Marian's character and her strong commitment to live a life that is less wasteful and more in touch with the earth. Unfortunately there was also a faint suggestion that the project, though courageous and ingenious, was unrealistic.

The city of Grand Rapids certainly thought so. Within two weeks, Marian's fears were realized. Housing inspectors descended upon the house, checked the facilities, and cited her for violation of several city ordinances: [1] no electrical service, [2] no hot and cold running water to the kitchen and bath, [3] no proper connection from the kitchen sink and bathtub to the city sewage system, and [4] no flush toilet in the bathroom. The chief inspector said that the city had received a complaint about the house from a neighborhood organization whose president claimed the people wanted impartial treatment in the enforcement of city codes. (If they had to hook up to city systems, so did she.) The house was again condemned, and the owner was required to appear in court.

IMPASSE: At the hearing before the Housing Board of Appeals, she was accused not only of violating several city ordinances, but also of refusing to vacate her condemned house. She entered a plea of not guilty. A pretrial hearing was set, then postponed. A full trial was scheduled . . . postponed . . . rescheduled . . . and postponed again, and so it went.

The most controversial issue in the case has been the system of waste control. The city's position has been that Marian—without checking requirements and obtaining permits—installed a substandard toilet facility that is maintained in a manner that doesn't meet the housing code. According to regulations, city-approved alternative toilets are allowed, but the waste material they produce

must be packaged and deposited in a landfill designated by the Health Department.

For her part, Marian claimed that she telephoned city hall before she started and was told there didn't seem to be any problem with what she proposed to do. She said that she did a great deal of careful research on the matter of composting and using waste material safely, and believed she complied with healthful procedures.

The city disagreed. At the time of inspection, the waste material was kept in sealed drums for approximately two to three months before being put into the ground. A six-month period was recommended; yet an employee at the city's waste treatment plant stated that the city makes sludge available for free to anyone who wants it for fields, gardens, or landfills—sludge that has been processed in sealed tanks at 94°F for only one and a half months! Urban pioneers find themselves doubly frustrated when a metropolis fails to live up to its own standards!

Despite such incongruities, Grand Rapids does not readily fit the role of short-sighted villain in this drama. At one time, years ago, the Michigan municipality had an anaerobic digester system that produced both commercially salable fertilizer and gas that was used to power municipal engines, including those that ran the treatment plant. The arrival of electroplating industries in the area, however, changed all that, because the industries' waste products killed the anaerobic bacteria in the city's digesters.

Not only that, Grand Rapids does run an urban homesteading program of its own and actually supported an experiment by the National Sanitation Foundation that tested and approved the Clivus Multrum composting toilet. Purchasing a Clivus Multrum, however, is an expensive proposition that may be beyond the means of many homesteaders.

To be fair, the city did try to reach one compromise with Marian by arranging for "emergency" funds to pay for hooking up the house into the city sewer system—even if she chose not to use the system—thus helping her "obey" the housing code. Marian, though, turned the funds down. She felt that if the city could find extra money, there were other good people in the area who needed it much more than she did. Her attitude seemed unreasonable to city officials, but it was clear that her argument against spending thousands of dollars on a plumbing system that wouldn't be used did have some merit.

BREAKING NEW GROUND: So, how are such issues resolved? Ideally the two parties eventually work out a reasonable compromise, one which allows city homesteaders to pursue a self-reliant lifestyle yet takes into consideration the health and expectations of others. Perhaps Marian's laudable intention to live simply and in harmony with the environment and the attempts of Grand Rapids to deal fairly with a difficult problem can make similar situations easier for the next urban pioneers.

IT'S POSSIBLE TO LIVE WITHOUT THE POWER LINE

A husband and wife who purchased 31 acres in the Ozarks immediately started working toward a way of living which, in their thoughts, was fraught with both fact and fantasy. Scott and Nancy bought their land with the full knowledge that they would never be able to hook up to a power company's grid. A national wilderness area borders the property on three sides, and the nearest accessible electricity was more than a mile away from the fourth side of the property. There were numerous vertical rock ledges and a year-round stream between their home and that lone pole, and they didn't wish to destroy the beauty of the glades and brook with a big, cleared power line right-of-way.

UNNECESSARY CONVENIENCES: A year and a half after their land purchase, the couple moved into an octagonal, square-beamed home that they had built with hand tools. Just before that happy event, they held a garage sale, during which they parted with their television, iron, hair dryer, toaster, blender, and

various other gadgets they have long since forgotten and have never missed since that day.

To those who wonder how the couple can get along without such "conveniences," they say, "It's not complicated at all!" They have replaced electricity with kerosene, propane gas, wood, a car battery, and the heating and cooling properties of the thermal mass in their house.

Mantle-type kerosene lanterns provide illumination for evening reading and work. Five of these—two in the living room and three in the kitchen—give off plenty of white light, which is easy on the eyes and necessary for doing close work. Throughout the rest of the house, standard kerosene wick lamps produce a soothing yellow glow. Their lighting system probably isn't any less expensive than electrical lamps would be, but it does create a mellower atmosphere and isn't subject to brownouts, blackouts, and the pricing whims of the power company.

During the day the home's many windows and two skylights provide plenty of light; in designing the house, the builders were careful to base the placement of the openings on the daily and seasonal positions of the sun. The kitchen, which is the center of most household activity stays bright and cheerful all day long as a result of its southwestern exposure. There is no problem with excessive summer heat buildup, because the dwelling is nestled in the trees, and their leaves filter the sun during the intensely hot months.

CENTRAL HEATING: The family heats with wood, using a fireplace with an insert built into it. Most such arrangements are fitted with electrical fans to move the warm air, but the owners wisely built the fireplace in the center of the house and installed vents on four sides of the massive rock chamber. This system directs heat into the living room, bedroom, bathroom, and kitchen. Each of the rooms has a floor vent near its outside wall to return cool air to the fireplace, and convection keeps the indoor air circulating.

The fireplace's mass acts as an indirect heating and cooling system. In cold weather the 400 cubic feet of rock heats up after about the first 36 hours of continuous fire. The stone mass then remains warm to the touch all winter and contributes to the occupants' comfort, even when the fireplace is not in use. Likewise, in the summer the rock stays much cooler than the air and helps keep the inside temperature agreeable even in the dog days.

One of the home's skylights is also used for cooling

purposes. In the summer, the rooftop window is opened every morning, and the fresher outside air pours into the lower half of the opening as the warmer air is pushed out through the top half. Cool air is also drawn

in through the doors and lower windows. Such thermal conditioning doesn't cost any money or make any noise.

KITCHEN NEEDS: For about eight months of the year, all the cooking is done on a woodstove. However, when the weather is too warm for comfortably firing up the range, propane is used to operate a small two-burner stove. The same gas is used to run the water heater and a Swedish-made ammonia absorption refrigerator, an extremely efficient unit that operates on a 600-Btu pilot light.

The cold and hot water tanks are in a closet in the loft area. Water is lifted up to the elevated tanks with a gas pump. (All of the drinking water is boiled.) The house has complete plumbing, operated by gravity flow, and the water pressure is excellent!

The house was wired for DC current in the hope of someday producing a useful quantity of electricity with wind or water. A car battery powers two car lights, which are mounted under a shelf above the kitchen sink, and the same unit runs an FM car radio which is tucked away on a bookshelf. The battery gets boosted about once a week with a charger.

The fact that this couple gave up most of their powered appliances doesn't mean that they lack for kitchen tools. A hand beater, chopper, food mill, and ricer take care of most food preparation and preservation chores. An 1890-model meat grinder, which can be used to mince many edibles other than meat, and a grain grinder also provide assistance. Such devices may not be as fast as their electrical counterparts, but they do get the job done.

These homesteaders are proud of an alternative garbage disposal system that is definitely more efficient than conventional models: Twenty Araucana and Aus-

tralorp laying hens do a splendid job of gratefully gobbling up kitchen scraps and give a bounty of eggs in return.

OTHER ALTERNATIVES: During the winter months, sewing with an old and treasured treadle machine is a productive pastime. The only time Nancy irons is when she sews, and she uses a flatiron (the type which usually serves only as a doorstop these days) that's heated atop the stove. It isn't a joy to use, but it works well.

Neither Scott nor Nancy miss the convenience of a hair dryer. They spend a few minutes combing their hair in front of the fire or in the sunshine and have found that they enjoy such silent, meditative times—in contrast to performing the same task, usually in a frantic rush, with hot, dry air and a noisy motor roaring in one's ears.

The truth is that a nonelectrical house is a wonderfully quiet house. There's no refrigerator or furnace clicking on and off, and peaceful evenings are enhanced with books and musicmaking, instead of being dominated by a blaring television.

Scott and Nancy readily admit that they went to extra trouble for independence from the power company, but they have found a deep satisfaction in living this way. It is especially rewarding when someone complains about the power being off for hours during a storm, and this couple can nonchalantly respond, "Oh? We didn't miss it a bit!"

MAKE YOUR MOVE IN AN OLD SCHOOL BUS

· There are any number of popular songs that make movin' on down the highway sound like a fulfilling, even exhilarating, experience, but when a change of job or lifestyle makes relocation necessary, most folks find the task a good bit less than pleasant. In fact, moving can be not only a tremendous hassle but also a very expensive one.

That second concern loomed pretty large several years ago for a family of four that had to leave Minneapolis for the western part of Montana, a distance of about 1,200 miles. They couldn't afford to hire a professional moving company, and even the fee wanted by the local truck agency was a bit beyond their budget. In short, they knew they had to come up with a lower-cost way to make the move.

Happily enough, after a few hours of deliberation, they hit upon what turned out to be the perfect answer: buying a used bus! After all, they reasoned, with its seats removed, a bus would have a lot of cargo space, it would be equipped with an engine designed to haul hefty loads, and they could probably sell the vehicle at the journey's end or at the very least put it to use as a portable outbuilding.

The idea proved to be a practical one, too. The couple has changed homes twice since that jaunt to Montana and used a bus on each occasion.

FINDING THE BEST DEAL: Of course, the first thing you, as a would-be bus owner, will have to do is shop around for a vehicle that satisfies your needs and won't empty your pocketbook. The couple's initial buy was a 48-seater that they purchased secondhand from a transit company. School systems and churches can also be counted on to sell old buses from time to time.

Use care and be patient when making your choice. Remember that the ideal machine will not only haul all your belongings a long way, but also provide you with a profit upon resale. It's best to buy from either a reputable transit company or a good school district, because such organizations generally make every effort to keep their buses in working order and will often have up-to-date maintenance and safety inspection records for each one. Mileage data and information on individual vehicle oddities will often be scribbled in the margins of the forms as well. Ask to see the sheets and check them carefully, and you should be able to eliminate a lot of potential buys on the basis of their service records alone.

Once you've narrowed the list to buses that seem to be worth looking at, it's time to go on out to the lot and examine the vehicles. When you do, don't let such cosmetic problems as slashed seats, scratched paint, and graffiti worry you. Those eyesores may well be among the reasons why the bus is for sale in the first place, but they have no effect on the potential of the vehicle as a moving van.

However, while minor scars can be ignored, you will want to be sure that the doors swing wide open for ease of loading and unloading and that the lights, horn, mirrors, fans, heaters, and other accessories are in good working order.

Crawl under the vehicle and check the security of the tailpipe. While you're down there, also look for leaks. Wipe off any wet spots, and after a test drive, go below again to make sure there's no new fluid on those places. Be certain to inspect the underside for any signs of severe rusting.

If you're still happy with the bus after your initial inspection, the next step is to take it out on the road. Should you be unable to start the engine at first, it's all right to let the person who is showing you the vehicle crank it into action. It may have been standing unused for quite a while and thus be difficult to start. Once it's been started, though, turn the motor off and fire it up yourself. Remember, you're the person who'll have to get that loaded monster down the highway.

If you doubt your own ability to determine the health of a motor, you'd do well to enlist the services of a friend with more mechanical know-how. A bus does represent a substantial investment, and you'll want to cover every possible angle in order to make an informed choice.

When you're satisfied with the sound of the engine at idle, take the bus for a spin. Don't be alarmed if the test vehicle seems cumbersome compared with your car; you'll get used to handling a bigger rig in time. Start off slowly, though, and allow yourself plenty of driving space to maneuver.

Once you've found a bus that's to your liking, it's time to begin dickering. You may be able to get minor repairs and removal of the seats included in the bargain. But even if these can't be arranged, you can probably find an affordable deal. The couple's first bus cost them roughly the price of renting a truck big enough to move their household, and when they got to Montana, they sold it to a country music band for $1,200.

RENOVATION: After you've purchased your vehicle, you may want to paint it. Indeed, if you've got yourself a potential moving van colored school-bus yellow, you must do so, because a federal regulation requires that at least half of the original hue be covered. One alternative is simply giving the vehicle a couple of coats of primer in order to prepare it for whatever color its next owner might prefer.

If the seller didn't do the job for you, you'll need to remove the seats to open up the cargo area. The best tools for this task are a cold chisel, a hammer, and a strong arm. Begin by forcing the heads off the bolts that hold the legs of the seats to the floor. Just place the chisel blade at the base of the bolt head and then apply the hammer with enthusiasm until the ornery little fastener is decapitated.

Most of the seats will probably be secured to the side of the bus as well as to the floor. The wall bolts can be difficult to get at with hammer and chisel, so you may want to spray them with penetrating oil and take a wrench to them. If they turn out to be too stubborn even for that approach, you'll have to enlist the service of a torch and cut the heads off. When you do, though, be sure that you have a full bucket of water and a pile of wet rags nearby to cool down the floor and the sides of the bus as you work. Don't use the torch on the bolts near the gas tank.

With the passenger seats out, go on to remove the stop sign and any special warning lights from the front and rear of the vehicle. These modifications are required by law, and they're jobs that can be easily performed with a screwdriver.

It might be worth your while to try to sell the seats, sign, and lights, or you may be able to barter them for help on moving day. They're just excess baggage to you, and you might as well turn them into gas money if you can.

MAKING IT LEGAL: You're almost home free at this point, but before you can load up and get on down the road, you'll need to weigh the empty bus in order to obtain either a license or a permit. Every state has different rules about such things, and this may be more complex if you're moving from one state to another. You'll just have to call your local license bureau and the nearest highway patrol office and then take the least expensive option available. Try for a permit. A license can be expensive, whereas when the couple moved to Montana, they needed only a 21-day permit, which set them back a mere $4.00.

LOAD UP: Before the time comes to pack, you'll want to scrub out the interior of the bus thoroughly. Then buy a couple of 4′ X 8′ sheets of hardboard and cut them lengthwise to cover the windows inside the bus. These panels will protect your investment's glass from attacks by rocking chair arms and the like.

It's best to load through the rear doors and to begin by putting your mattresses and box springs behind the driver's seat. There they'll serve to protect the operator from anything that might come rolling forward in the event of a sudden stop or skid. Be sure, as you pack, to consider weight distribution, and make efficient use of space by fitting such unwieldy objects as bicycles around the wheel wells.

Admittedly, the tasks involved in converting a people-hauler into a moving van and then in trying to remarket that converted vehicle at a profit will seem pretty imposing to some folks. But anyone who's dollars down or simply thrifty ought to give the idea some consideration. Can you think of any other way to get your family moved and make a profit in the process?

PAYING RENT WITH WORK, NOT CASH

Richard, a married graduate student with two small children, paid rent for three years on a tiny apartment near Purdue University where he was earning his master's degree in horticulture. He and his wife really wanted to homestead, and although they read books on the subject, made lists, and planned, the dream always seemed to stay well ahead of the small amount of cash they could save from Richard's salary as a graduate assistant. Rent and bills pretty well used most of their income. Still, when he finished at Purdue and planned to move on to Penn State to work for his doctorate, he and his wife decided to hunt for a small place in the country. The search revealed only exorbitant prices and imposing interest rates.

While they were disappointed, they weren't surprised or despondent. Their extracurricular reading on homesteading had taught them that successful homesteaders are characterized by a willingness to look at things in new ways and that clever ideas are often worth more than cash.

Ideas were plentiful. They placed a classified ad in the county newspaper in the area where they'd been househunting: "WANTED TO RENT. NEED SEPTEMBER. Country home 15 miles State College. Two, three bedrooms, garden, yard. Christian student/family. Rental preferred, purchase possible. Experienced handyman, will trade rent for repairs."

They mailed the ad, waited, and prayed. The first response offered a rental for cash plus labor, but even then, the amount was more than their budget could afford. A second reply said they sounded like "nice people," but the woman's house didn't need any work and was far too expensive for them to lease. The idea was to pay as much of their rent as they possibly could with labor, not cash.

Offer number three was the charm, though. A man wrote to say he and his wife had just purchased a farm as an investment. The former owner had begun to do some remodeling but hadn't completed the job. The owners wanted the remodeling completed and felt that the house should be lived in and the property maintained.

The couple visited the place and fell in love with it. The homestead was better than any they had ever dreamed of owning. There were grapevines, apple trees, a huge yard, garden space, two creeks, a barn, and a pasture. The two-story farmhouse featured five bed-

rooms and had a woodburner, and there was even a timber lot from which to harvest their fuel supply.

The big drawback was the daily 60-mile round-trip to school. The family decided that the trade-off was well worthwhile, however, and worked up a rental agreement with the landlords: At least half of the rent each month would be paid with labor. They initially gave the owners one month's payment in cash. After that, any work they did would be deducted at an agreed-upon hourly rate from the following month's rent.

Naturally, it would have been in their best interest to work all the rent off, but Richard's studies didn't allow him that much time to spend on the remodeling jobs. Each month's payment included 34 hours of labor, which kept him busy for about three Saturdays every month. The landlords provided all the necessary building supplies, and when the tenants needed to buy additional materials, they deducted the costs from the cash portion of the next month's rent. Such a setup works very well as long as accurate records of time and materials are maintained.

Projects in lieu of rent money included ripping out an old porch and using the wood to make compost bins, painting and electrical work, and clearing away fallen limbs and chopping the wood for fuel. A nearby farmer volunteered to plow their quarter-acre garden space "just to be a good neighbor," and for the same reason, the couple gave him a considerable portion of their winter squash at the end of the season.

Shortly after Richard moved his family to the farm, a friend of the landlords began to board her horse with them. In return for their keeping an eye on the animal and feeding it, the owner supplied the family with fresh goat's milk.

When Richard learned that another of the owners' friends needed a place to pasture his small herd of cattle, he jumped at the chance to practice livestock tending without having the financial responsibility. Not only did the man bring five beef steers, but he also brought a cow and calf, 24 bantam chickens, and eight cats!

As a result of becoming farmsteaders, both husband and wife learned to milk cows, give vaccinations, and doctor sick animals. They can claim what is called "a farmer's eye," which enables them to spot and head off certain livestock problems. A resident Holstein is the source of the family's milk, butter, and cottage cheese. Richard delivers three gallons of milk to the landlord each week, and the price of it is deducted from the rent. The bantam hens that are boarded on the farm provide enough fresh eggs for the family of four. These homesteaders have engineered a rather impressive series of swaps, to say the least.

Besides getting a farmer's education for free, they are enjoying homestead life without either the mortgage or the cash outlay that many people believe is inevitable. Determination, fresh ideas, and initiative truly are enviable assets.

GARDENING

THE LAZYBONES' LOW-LABOR GARDEN PLOT

Raising its own vegetables can certainly help a family reduce its grocery costs, but planting and maintaining a garden capable of providing food for several people often calls for a heavy investment in time and labor. This demand can be held to a minimum—and bountiful harvests can still be reaped—by using several labor-reducing techniques, including rotating the planting areas, mulching and tilling on a sensible schedule, choosing hardy and disease-resistant varieties, companion planting, and encouraging natural controls for insects, disease, and weeds.

FOR STARTERS: Plan to have as large a garden as possible. The maximum size of a plot will be determined by the amount of land available, the tools on hand, and the quantities of manure that can be obtained for fertilizer. A large garden allows room for nice wide paths between double-width rows—a layout that provides built-in soil relief and easy crop rotation. Vegetables use lots of soil nutrients, and they grow especially vigorously in earth that has lain idle for a while. The paths between the crops should rest under mulch one year and can be put into production the next.

A good-sized garden will also provide habitat for a variety of insects, making it less likely that any one particular bug will become a problem. A diverse population of these small creatures in the garden will limit the chances of an infestation because the separate insect types will control each other. A productive and healthy garden is not insect-free but is a balanced system in which the gardener works with, rather than against, the other creatures of the earth.

With plenty of space, more food than is needed will probably be grown, and there'll most likely be enough to feed you and your insect population, which means that you won't have to worry about their snacking.

SOIL NUTRITION: In order to produce a lot of food, the ground must receive a lot of food—so feed the garden! In addition to the mulch and crop residues that should be worked into the earth, spread about an inch of chicken manure or four inches of cow manure on the soil every year and turn it under.

To get that plant food underground, the whole garden will need to be tilled—or turned by some other method —at least twice in the spring and once in the fall. This may sound like a fair bit of heavy labor, but it's a fast way to kill weeds and to get organic matter into the soil. Also, by turning the soil this way, time-consuming composting won't even be necessary: Simply spread vegetable wastes along with other mulch, and leave this until tilling time.

It's a good idea to grow a cover crop during the garden's fallow seasons. Buckwheat and annual rye both make good covers, because neither will develop a persistent root system or set seed before the first spring tilling. Such plants protect the soil from erosion and supply valuable green manure.

When planning a "minimum intervention" garden, it's important to concentrate on soil building. Plants grow faster and stronger, become more insect-resistant, and are better able to take care of themselves when they grow in healthy, humusy, fertile soil.

CHOOSE AND PLAN WISELY: Taking into account which crops best suit the climate, choose disease-resistant varieties whenever possible. Most seed catalogs note which cultivars have a certain amount of built-in insect and disease resistance. With good soil and strong seed, the battle will be half won.

During each winter, draw up a garden chart for the following spring, and in this plan make certain that the crops are rotated from year to year. Even if a garden is quite small, the annual movement of crops is very important, because many insect eggs remain in the soil over the winter. Shifting the vegetables' positions at least keeps the varmints from multiplying on their preferred host plants year after year.

MIXED VEGETABLES: Companion planting, another technique for warding off insect pests, should be kept in mind when drawing up a garden plan. The scents of some plants mask the insect-attracting odors of a neighboring cultivar; other plants actually repel insects. Rather than planting related vegetables such as cabbage, cauliflower, kale, and broccoli together, separate them with patches of onions, tomatoes, potatoes, and beets, which are unattractive to the bugs that consider the plants of the genus *Brassica* a delicacy.

Marigolds are particularly beneficial throughout the garden—both as general soil conditioners and because of their strong insect-repelling odor. Nasturtiums, basil, parsley, summer savory, and sweet marjoram act in the same manner.

PLANTING TIME: Sowing the garden as late in the season as possible increases the number of times all the weed sprouts can be tilled under before the seeds are in the ground. This will reduce the amount of painstaking hoeing around each young vegetable plant later in the year. While it might take only about two hours to till an entire half-acre, it can take about two days to hoe around the plants in a plot that size.

Plan to turn the soil once as soon as it becomes workable in the spring. Then wait about two weeks for a good flush of weeds to appear and till the plot again. If it's possible to wait a few more weeks before planting the seeds, till the soil a third time. The delay will pay off in the long run, and save hours of hand weeding and hoeing. The repeated tillings will also destroy most of the cutworms that have wintered over in the soil.

A relatively late planting could make it difficult to grow such cool weather crops as lettuce unless plenty of mulch is applied. A good organic ground covering will keep the soil cool and moist, build fertility and humus as it's turned under from year to year, and shade out most of the weeds that survive the spring tilling.

Cool-weather crops and root vegetables should be mulched to within a few inches of the seeds as soon as they're planted. Squash, corn, tomatoes, beans, and other hot-weather crops should not be mulched until the soil has warmed up considerably. It's also a good idea to mulch the garden's paths even more thickly than the rows. Heap the organic matter on the paths to a good foot deep.

Even after these many preparations—which will insure that your vegetables have all the growing advantages you can give them—there's still going to be the problem of dealing with the weeds and bugs that remain. Also, the newer a garden is to organic culture, the more uninvited plants and insects you should expect.

However, much of the remaining control work can be done by "helpers." To keep the problems in hand, just call on toads, birds, and if possible, chickens. It won't take much to attract such assistants to the garden, and by harvesttime your efforts will have been paid back many times over. A single toad, for instance, will eat up to ten pounds of insects during one season, and snails, slugs, and cutworms are among this amphibian's favorite treats.

It's pretty easy to get a few toads to take up residence in the garden: Simply sink a small water-filled tub in the ground, and near its rim place a few upside-down flowerpot caves with tunnel entrances beneath them. A sticky-tongued midnight pest patrol will move right in.

Wild birds, on the other hand, can help control insects during the day. They'll eat just about any bug that moves. To attract them, provide nesting sites and water. A stream is best, but a small birdbath will do if it's kept really clean. Birdhouses can be put up when there's not much natural shelter nearby. The backyard songsters will also need high places to perch near the vegetable patch. Garden fenceposts make great lookout towers for insect-hunting birds, and a few tall poles set among the rows will provide similar vantage points.

Chickens are birds of a different feather. They're great weeders and cultivators and will eat grubs, ants, and worms. However, they can be too thorough at scratching and cultivating if they're not controlled. If let into the garden early in the season, hens may well wipe out all the newly sprouted seedlings.

When the crops are well along, chickens can be a real asset. Their dirt scratching will control weeds; they're efficient and methodical insect hunters; they'll eat your household food scraps; and they'll provide wholesome fresh eggs in return for the privilege of sharing your garden. The biddies will even supply fertilizer while they work. Chickens require minimal housing and care, and the hens, at least, are quiet creatures that are not inclined to roam.

Even city dwellers may be able to keep some chickens around if local ordinances permit. If a small flock is allowed, city ordinances usually specify that premises must be maintained in clean and sanitary condition. A call to the local health department can determine whether raising these birds is permissible.

SAVINGS: Even with these gardening methods, raising a successful vegetable crop will require hours outdoors spent spading the beds, tilling the soil, and sowing the seed. But cooperating with nature will produce a more abundant yield and still save a great deal of time so you can pursue those other pleasant summertime activities.

FINDING GARDEN SPACE IN THE CITY

Urban gardening is as old as city living itself, and now, more than ever, it's an essential practice for city dwellers who want to retain a link with nature and to save money by growing some of their food.

By the year 2000, more than half of the planet's population could be concentrated in metropolitan centers. Much of the developing world is wisely turning to urban agriculture, aquaculture, and small-scale energy production as a way to recover the value of the cities' vast discards and to cope with burgeoning populations. Americans, especially—despite our "use it up, throw it away, and buy a new one" cultural conditioning—are looking anew at urban detritus (organic wastes, recyclable building materials, and unused space) and discovering refreshing ways to utilize it productively.

What city gardeners lack in the way of ready-to-use soil, panoramic landscapes, and unobstructed sunlight, they make up for in resourcefulness, persistence, humor, and the satisfaction of making the concrete desert bloom. The fact that plump cabbages and dazzling dahlias can be successfully nurtured amidst traffic and towering buildings is enough to make any city gardener believe that with a few basic horticultural techniques and a little specialized know-how, great things are indeed possible.

SITE SELECTION: All gardens—no matter where they are—need sun, water, and fertile soil. The differences between a rural and an urban vegetable patch are, in fact, largely superficial. A "back forty" could be just a row of old dresser drawers filled with soil, and the first spadeful of city dirt could unearth only rusty nails, broken glass, and other archaeological evidence of your metropolitan forebears. Perhaps the backyard measures only 7' X 7' with trash cans on half of it and laundry flapping overhead. So what? City growers must seek new definitions of the word "garden." Look around. Does your building have south-, east-, or west-facing walls? A flat roof? Sunny windowsills? An exposed porch? Does a neighbor have such spaces that he or she might share in exchange for fresh produce? Is there a vacant lot nearby—or an unused corner of a local park—that united efforts could turn into a community garden?

Finding a site that gives you everything you want may be impossible, but you can begin with what you have. You'll be amazed at what you can do with a less than perfect location. Besides, being an uptown gardener means envisioning your garden as you wish it to be, making the necessary compromises, and coming as close as possible to the original dream.

SUNLIGHT: At least some solar exposure is essential for growing food. In examining a potential garden (yard, porch, windowsill, whatever), keep in mind that the sun shines from the south, that it is highest and casts fewest shadows in the summer, and that most herbs, flowers, and fruiting crops—such as squash, cucumbers, and tomatoes—do best with a minimum of eight hours of daily direct sunlight throughout the growing season. Anything tall (such as a tree) on the south side of a garden will cast a shadow all day long, and anything on the east or west will do so in the morning and afternoon respectively.

Be ruthless in making an evaluation. You can adjust your garden's design to the path of the sun, but the sun and the buildings that may block its rays aren't equally flexible. Wishful thinking will *not* convince tomatoes to grow without adequate sunlight. While vegetables such as lettuce, chard, and spinach can grow in partial shade, a garden must get some sun.

ADEQUATE WATER: Generally, city gardeners are close to a source of piped water. Those who aren't—like many farmers—must rely on rainwater, which can be collected in barrels or steel drums located beneath downspouts. Rainwater can also be conserved in the soil by mulching heavily (don't use an impervious material such as matted leaves, however). Another possibility is to use plastic jugs to bring water from some other site to the garden patch.

With access to an outside faucet, you can save labor and money by using a drip irrigation system, either a commercial sort (such as a perforated "trickle hose") or something along the lines of a system invented in Boston, which uses plastic jugs with pinholes burned into their handles and bottoms. The containers are set, bottom down, among the plants—at two-foot intervals— and filled with water and liquid fertilizer or manure tea once a week or so.

Unfortunately for urban gardens, city water has usually been treated with "purifying" chemicals that kill virtually all bacteria, including the kinds that break down organic material into plant nutrients. Letting such water stand before using it gives volatile chemicals a chance to evaporate. Take care to empty the containers often, however, because mosquitoes breed in stagnant water.

Once you begin gardening, you'll probably notice a gradual change in your perspective on weather. On rainy days, when nongardeners stomp around under their umbrellas and mutter to each other about how awful and wet it is, you'll find yourself feeling grateful for the raindrops trickling down to your plants' thirsty roots.

SOIL CONSIDERATIONS: Before doing anything about the soil (or lack thereof), you should consider the possibility of lead contamination. Lead—a toxic heavy metal that even in small quantities can cause serious and irreparable damage, especially to young children—has dangerously contaminated soils throughout residential areas of the United States. It's particularly concentrated in older neighborhoods where lead-based paint has been routinely scraped off the exteriors of houses prior to the application of a new coat and then simply left on the ground.

The Environmental Protection Agency office, the extension service in your area, or a local laboratory may be able to test your soil for toxic minerals. In any case, keep in mind a few basic facts: Any wooden house built before the 1950's (when lead was banned in exterior house paints) is likely to have some lead-contaminated soil around it—out to about ten feet from the edges of the structure—with the greatest concentration nearest the building. The older the home, the higher the level of lead is likely to be. And remember, too, that the poison will be primarily in the top three inches of soil, because lead tends not to leach deeply into the earth.

Therefore, if the only available space for planting vegetables is close to an older house—and especially if you have children under the age of six—*remove the top three inches of soil* from around the building and treat the material as a hazardous waste. Keep in mind that lead contamination can also occur near heavy traffic—

particularly within 100 feet of a street—and in rubble containing the paint from walls (exterior or interior) of demolished buildings. Heartbreaking as it is (especially if your soil is otherwise ideal), heavily tainted earth should be thrown out or used only for growing ornamentals. If necessary, you can purchase topsoil in bulk from a supplier (look in the yellow pages) and have it trucked in.

SOIL IMPROVEMENT AND THE MUD-PIE FACTOR: Assuming that you've found poor to average soil among the buried treasures in your backyard, your next step is to improve its quality. This you will do by adding "soil amendments." The amending process varies from individual to individual and is largely dependent on how that person went about making mud pies as a child and on the predilections and prejudices that developed in the process.

If, say, you're neither squeamish nor broke—and never much cared for mud-pie making—chances are you'll go to a garden store and buy fancy bagged amendments labeled "composted cow manure" and "bone meal," for example. If you're squeamish but somewhat less well-off, you can compost leaves and organic kitchen wastes such as vegetable trimmings, coffee grounds, and eggshells (avoid meat and fish, though, because they attract rodents). If, regardless of your income, you're *not* squeamish and *loved* concocting exotic mud pies in your youth, you may develop an outright fervor for composting and building up soil.

Enthusiastic urban composters and soil amenders have been known to ferret out such obscure sources of organic wastes as vats of spoiled bean sprouts, masses of hair clippings from barber shops, and leather dust from shoe factories. Those individuals view their urban surroundings as a veritable treasure trove of organic riches. Truly passionate urban composters can be observed shuttling back and forth between their gardens and the local police stables or the municipal zoo on weekends, and they can also be seen tirelessly toting bulging plastic bags of leaves and grass clippings from suburban lawns, pine needles from the woods, and dripping seaweed from the beach. These people don't take *trips* out of the city . . . they make *forays*.

There are many methods for making and using compost, and you'll find an explanation of most of them in any good gardening book. If you don't have room for the usual compost piles, however, try this technique: First, dig a knee-deep hole the size of a standard door. Then fill it halfway with well-mixed compostables and put the soil back in the cavity on top of the material. If you have any finished compost or a bagged soil amendment, combine it with several inches of dried grass clippings, hay, straw, or shredded leaves. To plant seeds or seedlings, just make a hole or furrow in the mulch.

GARDEN DESIGN: Whether you like tidy, weedless

rows of vegetables or a somewhat more overgrown and cluttered look, you'll need to do some planning in order to make the most of available space and solar exposure.

First, measure your chosen location and draw a map of it to scale. Note the locations of trees, fences, or adjacent buildings, and be sure to take into account the areas of the plot that do and do not receive direct sun.

Now, think about the kinds of things you'd like in your garden: Do you want benches to sit on . . . paths to stroll . . . a toolshed . . . compost bins . . . a cold frame? Whatever you decide, make and cut out scale drawings of the items, so that you can arrange them as you wish on your map and get a bird's-eye view of the various design possibilities.

For growing vegetables, intensive raised-bed gardening will give the biggest yields in the smallest space. A series of 3' X 6' plots positioned in the sunniest part of the garden makes a good arrangement. Use less-exposed areas for seating or sheds and for shade-tolerant plants. Try to position tall botanicals (corn, sunflowers, pole beans, dwarf fruit trees) on the north side of the garden where they won't shade other plants. If you can't find a suitable place for a particular crop, look for a reasonable substitute that you can grow. For example, your plot may not have enough exposed space to support fruit trees, which must have lots of sun, but you can almost certainly find enough room somewhere for a few raspberry or blueberry bushes.

Do take advantage of *vertical* growing space: sunny walls, fences, and even lampposts will support climbing vines such as beans, peas, or morning glories. A tree or post makes a fine place to hang baskets of strawberry plants, and you can espalier fruit trees against a trellised wall or fence.

Because city gardens may be the exception instead of the rule in your neighborhood, residents and other passersby will naturally want to see (and maybe even taste) its bounty. You can avoid unnecessary self-torment by resisting inbred territorial urges from the start and viewing your garden more communally: as a gift of sorts to the neighborhood. Be generous within reason, unless your conscientious work is being undone by the inconsiderate or destructive behavior of others, of course. Plant cherry tomatoes, grapes, or raspberries along the sidewalk edge of your garden and encourage people to sample the fruit in season. Or sow morning glories, which are strikingly beautiful (and bountiful), to twine along an exterior fence for everyone to enjoy. Help your neighbors up and down the street start their own gardens and flowerbeds, too. Gardening can be contagious, and it's to your benefit for everyone to catch it!

Generally, vandalism and theft are not much of a problem. In fact, they're almost nonexistent in gardens (whether in front of private homes or in public housing developments) that have become a source of pride within the community. In town-bound agriculture, neighborliness plays a very important role!

THE BUCKET GARDEN WEIGHT PROBLEM

An apartment gardener, living many stories above the ground, can raise enough food on the edge of a 30-foot balcony to equal the produce from a 6' X 20' country garden. The setup costs little more than the price of the seeds, doesn't drip or damage the decking, and can be tended in the little time left at the end of a long workday. Hard to believe maybe, but it's been proven.

High-rise horticulture became a consuming interest for a soil management major at U.C. Berkeley who wanted to grow her family's vegetables at home. She set out to develop a high-yield method of urban gardening for rooftops and balconies that would be drip-free, safe for decking, lightweight, able to survive several days without watering, simple to care for, inexpensive, and attractive (a tall order!). As a result of her efforts, which had the support of U.C.B.'s Plant and Soil Biology Department, a method evolved that works beautifully and should be successful for other city gardeners .

CONTAINER GARDENING: The obvious alternative to hauling numerous loads of dirt and lumber up to an apartment, perhaps many stories high, is to grow crops in containers. This option presents two notable problems: drainage and weight.

It's important to avoid using any kind of drainage system at the base of balcony plant boxes because of the mess and the possible rotting of the deck floor, to say nothing of complaints from neighbors below! Also, hot-weather wilt is a major drawback to gardening in drained containers. At temperatures above 95°F, large plants in these vessels, though thoroughly watered in the morning, can be severely dehydrated by midafternoon. Vessels with no drainage, on the other hand, can hold water in reserve that will carry the plant over a two- or three-day period, which allows the owner to leave for a weekend and find the garden still thriving upon his or her return.

For containers without drain holes, a special planting medium is needed: something spongelike to hold water so that it doesn't pool in the bottom of the planter, drowning the roots. This problem occurs routinely in drainless containers filled with dirt as the only medium. Even good soil is heavy, and in pots or planters it usually settles and hardens into a bricklike mass which discourages vertical growth. The perfect nutrient system

—soft, lightweight, and inexpensive—is a mass of leaves. And as these naturally occurring premixed packages of trace minerals and plant residue decay, they support a variety of microorganisms essential to plant growth and health. The gardener needs only to add water, fertilizer, and seed—nature does the rest! Besides that, leaves are easy to get (free for the raking) from parks and lots all over the city. In many neighborhoods, they're bagged and sitting by the roadside, waiting to be carted away.

LEAVES AT WORK: To set up a bucket garden that will be roughly equal to a 6′ X 20′ plot, you'll need a large load of fallen leaves, four gallons of potting soil mix, about 20 nonmetallic, light-colored, drainless containers (plastic paint cans, polystyrene foam coolers, trash cans, baby baths, or wooden boxes, buckets, or tubs), a water source, and a variety of seeds. Try one package each of tomatoes, carrots, squash, radishes, lettuce, Kentucky pole beans, a cole such as cauliflower or broccoli, and two packages of snow peas. Climate and season may dictate starting seeds indoors and later transplanting the seedlings to outdoor planters. Egg cartons or shallow, plastic-lined cardboard boxes can serve nicely as seed flats. If indoor space and light are inadequate for such flats, consider purchasing bedding plants for some or all of the crops.

Select a sheltered space that receives at least three hours of direct sun each day. Then fill the assorted containers with well-packed leaves, water them (using 1/4 gallon of water per gallon of container volume), and repack with leaves as needed. Add a regular commercial fertilizer, fish emulsion, or packaged cow manure in amounts appropriate to the size of the container.

Cover the surface of the packed leaf layer in each container with three inches of potting soil or humus. Plant most of the buckets with a variety of vegetables and flowers, and make two other buckets "quick crop" containers for fast-growing vegetables such as lettuce, radishes, and peas. Keep soil surfaces slightly damp until the young plants grow to be about five inches tall.

TENDING THE BOUNTIFUL BUCKETFULS: To help determine moisture requirements as plants become established, insert a pointed wooden stick in each container and leave it there. When the stake is dark and wetly glistening from one to four inches above the soil, moisture conditions are perfect. If drippiness occurs along the stick as far as five inches above the soil's surface, excess water is present and must be poured out. Dried-out, whitish patches on the stake indicate a need for water. (A rule of thumb: Full-grown plants require about a gallon of water per container every other day.)

Because a bucket garden has a limited amount of soil from which to draw nutrients, fertilize vegetables and flowers as heavily as possible. If green leaves wilt or shrivel, the plant food is too concentrated. If older leaves turn pale or yellow and if growth slows down, more nitrogen is needed.

High-rise horticulturists seldom have serious garden infestation problems. Nematodes and cutworms are precluded because of the use of dried leaves and sterile potting mixtures, and any insects that do appear are usually predatory and pollinating types attracted by the fragrant flowers, dense cover, and colorful variety.

When bucket plants grow to four or five inches tall, thin a single container's contents to three of the healthiest bean plants (or whatever), three of the best peas, and two of the most vigorous tomatoes. When tomatoes reach ten inches in height, thin them to one per container. Most plants can be allowed to grow naturally; only those which intrude on a deck's or balcony's walking space need staking.

As quick-growing crops reach maturity and are harvested, replant the container. By successive planting, you can harvest fresh produce throughout the growing season and achieve high yields. From a five-gallon plastic paint bucket, you might expect, for example, several bowls of leaf lettuce, 2 heads of lettuce, 35 snow peas, 20 pole beans, 4 radishes, 25 tomatoes, and 2 carrots!

THE SAFETY FACTOR: Balcony bucket gardens have proved to be labor-saving, productive, recreational, and attractive, but some gardeners will wonder if the produce might be contaminated. Because the leaves may have been gathered and the vegetables grown in an auto-filled city, lead content is a legitimate concern. Vegetables grown in leaves from a busy parking lot were sent to researchers at U.C. Berkeley for testing. The verdict: No more lead was present in these plants than is normal for any garden vegetables.

So, enjoy the success to be had with the foliage method for superb plant production in buckets or other containers. As the handsome leaves and flowering vines of beans and squash trail gracefully along railings, and lovely white pea blossoms alternate with the bright green of ruffled lettuce and the red and orange of decorative tomatoes, you can reap a bounty not only of food but of beauty.

BIODYNAMIC/ FRENCH INTENSIVE GARDENING

Maximizing the crop yield for a given amount of space has long been a necessity in many countries in the world and is a desirable goal for many North Americans who must plant their gardens in limited areas or in places where poor soil makes cultivating large plots economically prohibitive. Biodynamic/French intensive gardening is a method that combines the economic use of space characteristic of the gardening practices found in turn-of-the-century France with the biodynamic theories developed by Rudolf Steiner in the early 1900's in Austria.

The techniques were demonstrated in 1966 in California by Alan Chadwick, an English horticulturist, and were later subjected to careful testing and modification by John Jeavons of Ecology Action of Mid-Peninsula in Stanford, California, in an effort to produce the optimum yield from the smallest possible space. Yields on a per-acre basis of between four and six times the national average have been obtained, and in rare cases, gardens have recorded yields of 31 times the national average for a given space. The system uses no fuel-requiring tools, no toxic pesticides, and no highly processed chemical fertilizers. It improves the soil with each crop grown and requires only a hundredth as much energy and an eighth as much water as does commercial agriculture.

HOW IT IS DONE: All facets of the biodynamic/ French intensive method help the gardener to produce as many healthy plants as possible on a given piece of land. The raised beds that are characteristic of such gardens serve several purposes. Since the growing areas are wider than are "normal" garden rows (approximately five feet, which still allows the gardener to reach plants in the middle without stepping on and compacting the soil in the bed), less space is needed for walkways. The rectangular beds are raised four to ten inches above the original ground level, and their edges are angled at a 45° slope, which provides more surface area than if the same piece of ground were left flat.

Most important of all, though, the beds are double-dug to a depth of two feet. Because of the resulting deep cushion of well-worked soil, plants have less trouble sending their tiny root hairs down to gather in the water and the nutrition supplied by compost, ashes, bonemeal, and other such organic plant foods that are necessary to healthy, insect-resistant, nutritious, delicious vegetables.

The arrangement of the plants in the bed is also a bit unusual. The seeds or flat-started seedlings are placed in such a way that the foliage of each mature plant will just barely touch that of all its neighbors, creating a living mulch, which keeps weeds down, helps moderate the swings of soil temperature, and improves the bed's ability to retain water. Close-quarters planting is another reason for the gardening technique's incredible yields.

It's difficult to give a rule of thumb for plant placement in a biodynamic/French intensive bed. The spacings recommended on seed packets will often work out well, since the plants grown this way tend to spread farther than their conventionally raised cousins.

Of course, a technique that can enable an average homeowner to raise an abundant crop in a small backyard involves more than merely digging beds deeply and planting vegetables close together. Further preparation of the soil includes [1] the use of a specially prepared compost that has aged for at least three months and consists by weight of one-third dry vegetation, one-third wet vegetation or kitchen scraps including bones (but not meat), and one-third earth, [2] an organic fertilization program specifically designed to meet the needs of each crop, and [3] daily light waterings with special hose nozzles and cans that simulate the fall of rain.

COMPANION PLANTING: The way in which the growing space is used is at least as important to successful biodynamic/French intensive gardening as the prepa-

PREPARING A DOUBLE-DUG BED:
[1] Dig a foot-deep "spit." [2] Loosen the earth, a second foot down, with a garden fork. [3] The soil beneath the bed's borders is forked loose, too. [4] A second trench is dug, and its soil is piled into the first ditch. [5] The subsoil in the new spit is loosened. [6] Pile the soil removed from the first trench into the final ditch. [7] The whole plot can now be tilled. [8] The bed is covered with compost and fertilizer, then shaped and smoothed.

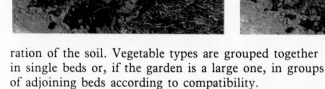

ration of the soil. Vegetable types are grouped together in single beds or, if the garden is a large one, in groups of adjoining beds according to compatibility.

Intensive gardeners believe that different plants grown in proximity affect each other in a number of ways. For example, the vegetables must be placed with a regard for simple physical compatibility: A slow-growing variety shouldn't be planted where it will soon be overshadowed by a rapidly maturing plant.

But companion planting goes far beyond such commonsense dictums. Certain vegetables, flowers, and herbs are actually mutually beneficial when grown together, helping eliminate each other's insect pests, and even influencing the quality of each other's produce. For instance, when planted near beans, potatoes can be very helpful in controlling the Mexican bean beetle, and Bibb lettuce will taste better if it's grown in companionship with spinach.

In order to make the most efficient use of both garden space and growing season, gardeners using this method also practice succession planting, a kind of companion planting in time, or a short-term, small-scale form of crop rotation. This practice allows the grower's plot to yield the greatest possible amount of produce.

A significant aspect of succession planting as practiced by biodynamic/French intensive gardeners is the alternation of plants that are heavy feeders (such as corn, cucurbits, and tomatoes), which take large quantities of nutrients from the soil, with varieties that are heavy givers (such as peas and beans). The heavy givers then return to the soil some of the nutrients that have been removed by previous plantings.

Planning for any garden should start long before the first warm days of spring beckon one outdoors. With proper planning, there's no reason why a biodynamic/French intensive bed only five feet wide and twenty feet long cannot yield a full year's supply of vegetables for one person.

MAGIC IN THE CABBAGE PATCH

Discovering one of those time-honored "tricks of the trade" can magically increase your gardening satisfaction. "You can grow more than one head of cabbage per plant, you know," an old-timer may remark sagely, and he would be right. Anyone can do it, and the technique should be especially helpful where the growing season is too short for producing both spring and fall crops.

LEAVE A LITTLE TO GROW ON: The procedure is easy. When you harvest the main cabbage head, leave just enough bottom leaves to constitute a viable plant (see the photograph). If you cut *below* the lowest leaves, the stubble will wither quickly and die. The idea is for it to live long enough to be the sprouting surface for a second crop. Now, make believe that what's left is a whole new plant. Treat it like one by cultivating it, watering it, and even working some rich manure into the first inch of soil around the base (being careful not to injure the roots).

Soon small sprouts will form around the rim of the main head's stub. Continue to treat the plant with care, and in time these little offshoots will grow to the size of a fist. There may be as many as six of the secondary cabbages, and together they'll provide almost as much food value as the big main head did . . . but with a delightful difference. The cores of these little cabbages will be pale green—almost white—leafy, and tender. The outer leaves will be darker green, but still tender and tasty. They're all, in fact, simply delicious!

The small size and fine quality of the minicoles make them especially suitable for Chinese stir-frying, delicate steaming, or adding to soups and stews. (If you harvest them in the late fall when the first chill winds are blowing, the savory leaves are particularly appropriate for soup.)

Broccoli, too, responds well to this treatment, and will yield second, third, and even more succeeding crops from the same plant, though the later pickings will not be as large as the first head.

This bit of cabbage magic isn't difficult to perform, and it can increase your *Brassica* yield dramatically. That should make it a very worthy addition to your bag of garden tricks.

THE LITTLE GARDEN THAT COULD

Just because the available gardening space a family has is limited to a small fenced-in plot behind an apartment, there is no reason to forgo having at least some freshly grown produce for the table. A lack of tillable ground did not deter a Tucson, Arizona, couple whose backyard consisted of a 15' X 29' area, about a quarter of which was paved with concrete and more of which was lost to a path leading to the electric meter.

In addition to having only limited space, their yard was flanked by a tall wooden privacy fence on three sides and the apartment building on the fourth. Each day the enclosure received only a few hours of the scorching desert sun, which seemed more likely to burn the plants than nourish them.

The native flora in the tiny patio's parched soil consisted of a few especially stubborn weeds, which the couple pulled up and stuffed into the open spaces under the fence to form a crude retaining wall. They hoped this dike would help keep desperately needed water in the garden space. Once that was done, the path to the meter was outlined with discarded bricks, and the rest of the earth inside the fence was dug to a depth or eight or ten inches.

The soil was rich, but it packed down quickly. In order to keep the sunbaked earth loose, the couple mixed in ten cubic feet of peat moss. Where the patio sloped up to the far-back corner, they built terraces with small clay walls to help hold the precious, life-giving water.

FROM PLAN TO PLANTS: With everything ready for planting and with space alloted for various plants, six hybrid tomato seedlings were set out in the area between the path and the house, which received direct sunlight from 10:00 AM till noon. A few mint sprigs and some purple and blue violets went in as a border.

The very back corner of the patio was sunny from noon until 3:00 PM, so that became the cornfield, with hills 15 inches apart in three rows. Four mounds of yellow squash, two rows of beets, and a patch of lettuce and parsley rounded out the vegetable section. Near the end of the yard, they established plantings of pansies and marigolds in a small plot surrounded by water-saving dikes. White clover provided ground cover over the remaining barren spots and served to replenish the nitrogen in the soil at the same time.

WASTE NOT, WANT NOT: The yard didn't have room for a compost pile, but as the plants grew, they received a mulch of clippings from the apartment lawns, with vegetable and fruit peels, coffee grounds, tea leaves, and other kitchen scraps added. This waste soon crumbled in the desert sun and was mixed into the dirt, preventing odor and pest problems in the process.

Pouring dishwater and wash water into the garden helped reduce the amount of irrigation necessary, and though the soil still needed to be soaked thoroughly three times a week, the series of little dikes and canals reduced the runoff and captured every possible drop of precious moisture during the rare Tucson rain showers.

Surprisingly, insects didn't prove to be a problem at all. Occasional aphids were washed off the plants with soapy dishwater, inchworms were squashed, and tomato worms snipped in two with shears. The bug control program was simplified, thanks to a large number of praying mantises and lizards who took up residence on the patio.

SWEET REWARDS: Although the small garden didn't provide all the vegetables the couple needed, they were more than happy with the results. They harvested over 75 juicy, red fruits from the tomato plants, and the parsley and mint were so profuse that some was dried for winter use. The corn yielded a couple of sweet ears per plant, after which the stalks were pulled up and zinnias planted in the reopened space. The lettuce lasted until late June, when the blistering Arizona summer heat finally killed it. The squash produced abundantly throughout the hot weather, and the couple was still eating beets well into the winter.

In addition to the fresh vegetables, the patio garden also provided many lovely flowers. The violets bloomed early in the spring, the pansies from March to late June, and the marigolds and zinnias from early June until late fall. By the time the pansies had finished flowering, sunflower, millet, kafir, corn, and other seeds that birds had scattered from the bird feeder were already up and growing. As these matured, the couple was able to enjoy the antics of various finches as they fed from the tops of swaying stalks.

When the plants died or finished bearing, they were pulled up and returned to the soil. Organic matter from the kitchen, plus a little dried manure, was added throughout the winter, and the following spring, more peat moss was dug into the soil.

When the garden was begun, not a single earthworm could be found in the dry, hard ground, but just 12 months later, every shovelful of soil was rich with the squirming, helpful little creatures, and thanks to these natural composters, the second year's garden was even more lush and productive than the first had been.

GROWING PLANTS WITHOUT SOIL

The growing of plants without soil is known as hydroponics, a food production system in which vegetables can be raised in a nutrient solution. In view of the world's diminishing natural resources and increasing human population, hydroponics appears well worth studying. And for the urban dweller or small-scale gardener with little space and time to maintain a conventional vegetable patch, this essentially soilless method may be the key to raising a wider variety of plants and harvesting greater yields.

Hydroponics isn't a new concept, but because of its particular advantages, growers are continually experimenting with improved hydroponic techniques. Most of the current systems, resulting from research in plant chemistry, use an inert medium (such as perlite, vermiculite, gravel, sand, pumice, peat, or even sawdust) to which a nutrient formula is added. The solution must provide *all* of the vital elements that would normally be provided by a well-prepared soil bed.

EXAGGERATED CLAIMS: When hydroponics first came to the attention of the media, overzealous proponents of the idea—including writers and the distributors of commercially manufactured equipment—claimed that such water-culture gardens could produce yields 15 times greater than those of "normal" plots, bring plants to maturity 30% faster, use only 10% of the water and fertilizer required by crops grown in soil, and allow a considerable saving of space without a comparable loss in produce. Because the claims were greatly exaggerated, and many hydroponic greenhouses subsequently failed, home gardeners became justifiably skeptical.

Despite exaggerated or poor press, however, hydroponics can offer several advantages to the home horticulturist: complete fertilization control, utilization of small areas, a yield approximately one and a half times greater than that of soil-grown plants, and the elimination of guesswork regarding moisture requirements. Most important, hydroponics makes it possible to grow plants anywhere light and warmth are adequate, such as on rooftops, windowsills, or parking lots. Even basements can become impressively productive garden spots if supplemental lighting is provided.

HOMEBUILT BEAUTIES: There are quite a few hydroponic outfits on the market, but many people don't want—or can't afford—to buy systems and would much rather build a setup with their own hands. For these intrepid souls, there's a wide variety of simple do-it-yourself hydroponic designs to choose from. The development of lightweight plastics has made it possible to avoid the high construction cost associated with earlier concrete-bed systems, and newly available small pumps, time clocks, and solenoid valves allow today's units to be almost completely automated.

No matter what type of system you design or buy, though, it *must* do three things: [1] provide support for your plants, [2] allow for the proper distribution of nutrients, and [3] give adequate aeration to the roots. Generally speaking, hydroponic units fall into one of two broad categories: those in which the nutrient solution is stored, or "standing", below the growing medium, and those in which the solution flows—either constantly or at regular intervals—*through* the medium.

Of the standing solution types, the wick systems are probably best for small-area, low-work setups. In this design, the nutrient solution stands in a container directly beneath the growing medium and is drawn up through wicks made of cotton, glass wool, or the like. (This method is similar in operation to the common clay pot and gravel-filled saucer arrangement.) A simple unit could consist of little more than a trough or pan of nutrient covered by a lid or shelf with several holes in it. The wicks are presoaked and run from the solution up through the lid holes. Then the wicks' ends are frayed open, and a seedling in its starter cube is set on top of each one. Every two weeks or so, the nutrient formula will need to be changed, but otherwise the system is virtually maintenance-free. This design is most suitable for small containers such as pots, hanging baskets, window boxes, or pans not exceeding 6″ X 2′ X 2′ in size. Unfortunately, this method doesn't supply the nutrient fast enough to satisfy large plants or those with lush foliage.

The tank method is another example of a standing solution hydroponic design. In such a unit the plants are supported by an inert medium which rests on top of plastic or nylon mesh. Their roots grow through the

mesh and extend down into a container of solution below. The submerged roots are provided with oxygen by an aquarium pump that bubbles air into the nutrient.

The basic "slosh" method, the simplest of the flow systems, is very easy to set up but quite demanding to maintain. In this design, the plants are set in an inert growing medium, and the nutrient solution is placed in a bucket that's attached to the garden container by a tube. When the bucket is lifted, the solution floods into the growing medium. When the bucket is lowered, the solution drains back out. Of course, unless you use a growing medium that retains moisture adequately, someone will have to lift and lower that bucket at least twice every day. Many gardeners would find this method a bit confining.

THE NFT VARIATIONS: Particularly appealing is a variation of the slosh method that's automated and involves the use of float valves, a recirculating pump, and a continuous flow of feed formula. The Nutrient Flow Technique, called NFT, evolved from the work of Dr. Allen J. Cooper of the Glasshouse Crops Research Institute in Littlehampton, England. Dr. P.A. Schippers further developed the technique.

In the NFT system the nutrient solution flows from a container through a growing bed that's placed on a 3% to 4% slope and filled with a coarse grade of perlite. The solution runs into a receiving basin at the far end of the growing bed. A float switch in the nutrient container operates a recirculating pump located in the receiving basin. When the life-sustaining mixture falls below a certain level in the first tank, the float switch is activated and turns on the recirculating pump, and the solution is sent back into the first container. A second float valve, connected to an outside water source, is placed in the receiving basin and acts to compensate for loss of water through transpiration and evaporation. (The outside water source can be either another tank, which must be filled periodically, or a domestic waterline, which would further automate the system.)

The NFT system can accommodate several physical layouts, but the basic trough design is both inexpensive and versatile. The required troughs can be constructed

WICK METHOD

STARTER CUBE

SHELF

AIR

SUPPORT

NUTRIENT SOLUTION

WICK

TANK METHOD

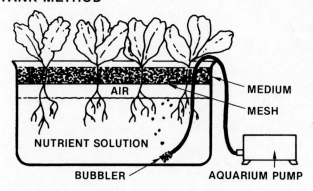

AIR

MEDIUM

MESH

NUTRIENT SOLUTION

BUBBLER

AQUARIUM PUMP

out of 1 X 6 pine or plywood and then lined with black polyethylene. A screen (or screen-protected drainage tube) is placed at one end, and the container is filled with perlite. The nutrient tank must be placed higher than the bed to allow gravity flow. Moreover, it's important that all elements in this design—nutrient container, receiving basin, *and* refill tubes—be both enclosed and opaque. Any light striking the rich solution will stimulate the growth of algae, which could eventually clog the system. The basic trough design can easily be enlarged into what's called a "flat bed." In such a system, a 4' X 8' sheet of plywood is fitted with 6" sides to make a large garden-growing area.

PVC pipes have also proved very useful in the construction of hydroponic systems. Large (8" or so in diameter) pipes, with a 2-1/2" to 3" channel cut in them, can be employed as single troughs, or 3" pipes can be channeled and suspended from an A-frame in what is called a "cascade" design.

Still another design utilizes PVC pipes suspended not horizontaly, but vertically, with 2" holes drilled at strategic points along their lengths. Young plants are inserted in the holes, and the pipes are then filled with perlite. The nutrient-bearing liquid simply flows down through each pipe to its receiving basin and is recirculated.

The vertical design proves particularly useful in areas where space is at a premium, and it works well with such relatively small crops as herbs and strawberries. Large plants, such as tomatoes and cucumbers, are suited to the basic trough design, while the flat bed lends itself to leafy crops like spinach, chard, celery, and lettuce.

FEEDING FACTS AND FANCIES: There are a number of effective plant food mixes on the market, but it's also possible to go the whole route and mix your own. If you're just starting a hydroponic garden, it's probably a good idea to use a prepared mix, but eventually you may well find it less expensive—and more satisfying—to make you own.

Be aware, though, that hydroponics is more of a science than an art. It involves substituting controlled, artificial systems for those natural systems found in a regular soil garden. The more one attempts to supply substitutes for such natural elements as soil fertility, light, temperature, humidity, pollination, and pest control, the more complicated and prone to instability the artificial system becomes.

The major problem facing the small-scale hydroponics gardener probably is monitoring and correcting the pH and fertility levels in the nutrient solution. Imbalances can easily occur, and too often these go undetected until the plants exhibit visible signs of distress. However, an inexpensive, simple test kit can reveal any imbalances in pH, N (nitrogen), P (phosphorus), K (potassium), or the minor elements. When used on a weekly basis, the test will help you insure that an adequate fertility level is being maintained.

ORGANIC OR INORGANIC: The question of whether organic or inorganic nutrients are best for a hydroponic system is principally a matter of cost, preparation time, availability, and personal conviction. The so-called chemical (inorganic) nutrients do fit more easily into an automated, strictly controlled system. Because they contain additional and variable elements, organic fertilizers such as fish emulsion, seaweed extracts, and manure tea generally need to be more carefully monitored and more frequently adjusted. On the other hand, the very presence of the additional trace elements can be seen as an advantage, since *soil* routinely provides many such nutrients which, though minute in quantity, contribute to the well-being of the plants. Chemical fertilizers warrant a few philosophical and economical considerations as well. After all, such intensively processed fertilizers are made from nonrenewable resources and consequently are becoming more and more expensive.

CONTINUING RESEARCH: Small-scale hydroponic gardening is evolving, and more experimentation and study will reveal its full potential. But even now, venturesome people who have limited space, time, and energy to devote to gardening can benefit from this efficient, low-maintenance crop-raising method that provides a thrill and challenge to the little bit of scientist that exists in us all.

BASIC SLOSH METHOD

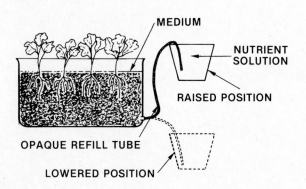

MEDIUM

NUTRIENT SOLUTION

RAISED POSITION

OPAQUE REFILL TUBE

LOWERED POSITION

NFT

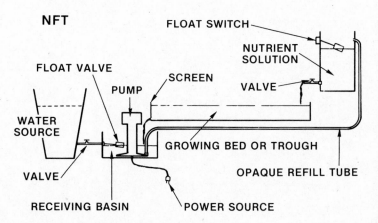

FLOAT SWITCH

NUTRIENT SOLUTION

FLOAT VALVE

SCREEN

PUMP

VALVE

WATER SOURCE

VALVE

GROWING BED OR TROUGH

OPAQUE REFILL TUBE

RECEIVING BASIN

POWER SOURCE

CONSTRUCT A LAMP GARDEN FOR SEEDLINGS

Living in an apartment is a necessity for some people and a convenience to others, but whatever their reasons for residing in the space-stingy dwellings, the residents often find there is no space for growing anything but a few houseplants. For these folks, one way of starting seedlings and even raising a few fresh vegetables might be the use of a lamp garden.

Such an indoor growing stand need not be fancy, and the design and size can easily be altered to match the builder's skills. The dimensions can also be adjusted to take full advantage of any materials on hand and those that can be inexpensively or easily obtained.

The major concerns in building a lamp garden are that the structure is long enough to contain whatever light fixture is used and that the fixture can be moved up or down to accommodate the height of the plants be-

ing grown. When seeds are sown, the bulbs should be suspended three or four inches above the soil-filled flats. They should be raised to maintain that distance above the foliage as the plants grow.

After making a rough sketch of the envisioned structure, the next step is rounding up the required materials. While a real grow-light bulb works better than a standard fluorescent fixture, the latter will do the job, and a secondhand one such as the 48-inch, twin-element unit shown can often be found and purchased inexpensively. Other materials needed include an eight-foot 2 X 4, five feet each of 1 X 6 and 1 X 10, two 1/4" X 5" roundhead bolts with wing nuts, a pair of cup hooks, and a handful of nails.

Though the dimensions might differ from those shown, the configuration shown in the illustration outlines how the different parts fit together into a sturdy unit. One major refinement might be drilling additional holes in the uprights, which would allow the lamp to be further adjusted.

To use the unit, simply fit the lamp with bulbs and plant the shallow trays with seeds. Water the flats regularly and move the lamp up as the plants grow. When seedlings have reached the proper size and the weather permits, the young plants can be moved to permanent homes in an outdoor garden plot. If the lamp garden is being used to grow wintertime produce such as tomatoes, keep moving the lamp until the plants reach their finished height and bear fruit.

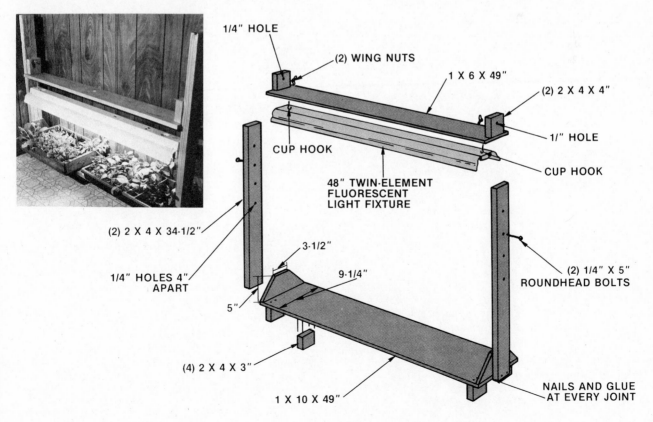

81

TAMING WILD APPLES AND BERRIES

With rural land being rapidly urbanized, it's increasingly difficult to forage many once-common wild delicacies. However, grafting a few scions from an old roadside apple tree to commercial rootstocks can insure that wild apples will still be available even if their present field is bulldozed for a new shopping mall. And brambles transplanted to the backyard can eliminate long expeditions to a favorite berry patch.

ADAPTABLE AND HARDY: Most wild fruits and berries will thrive in home gardens, since such varieties are typically very hardy. In fact, in northern sections of the country where winter temperatures often reach well below zero, many domestic species can't survive, while transplanted native berries and fruits, born to withstand the rigorous weather, are strong and productive.

However, anyone planning to collect wild edibles to plant in their garden should be careful to select only healthy stock; wild plants sometimes harbor diseases that can attack and devastate tender, virus-free, commercial breeds.

Because there is a possibility that leaf curl, orange rust, verticillium wilt, or other diseases might spread from wild brambles to fancy hybrid raspberries and blackberries planted nearby, the wild cousins should be planted as far from the domestic bushes as possible. For the same reason, locate the transplants well away from tomatoes, peppers, eggplants, potatoes, apple trees, or maple trees, and don't plant wild stock where the tame species have grown within the previous two years.

There are three seasonal stages in domesticating wild fruits and berries. First, as the fruit ripens on the plants in their original habitat, mark the healthiest, most productive plants or trees with a stake or some bright ribbon tied to a cane or branch. Then, later in the fall, work organic matter into the soil of the beds that will receive the native plants and correct its pH balance if necessary. The following spring, go forth with a shovel and burlap sacks, dig up the prizes, and as soon as possible, replant them in the new location.

SUCCULENT STRAWBERRIES: The large, commercially grown hybrid strawberries developed from native North American wildings have never matched the delectable, aromatic flavor of most of their undomesticated ancestors. The perennial wild strawberry (genus *Fragaria*) is among the most delicious of all fruits, but sample the berries a season before tranplanting because some wood strawberries (*Fragaria vesca*) are practically tasteless.

Wild strawberries are so vigorous and transplant so well that it's difficult to make a mistake with them. Simply fill the new bed with well-tilled, slightly sandy, compost-enriched loam and make sure the pH range is between 5.8 and 6.5. But because the plants can't tolerate standing water, good air circulation and water drainage are more important than either pH levels or soil composition.

In early spring before the plants have flowered, dig up the previously selected, shallow-rooted strawberry crowns with a trowel, keeping plenty of soil around the roots to lessen the shock of transplanting. Leaving 12 inches between plants, set them out in rows three feet apart, being careful not to cover the crowns with earth. During the first season after transplanting, pick off any flowers that appear, and in the late summer, snip off any runners that sprout. These prunings assure heavier fruit production in subsequent years.

In order to meet their early ripening schedule, the plants almost always put out blossoms before the last of spring's treacherous weather is over. Therefore, in the North they must be planted on a slope that's above frost pockets if they're to give the highest possible yields. Even so, should the temperature take a plunge, you should cover the plants to protect their tender blossoms.

By late August, we have several rows of flourishing dark-green plants, which promise a good yield during the coming summer. After the first few fall frosts, mulch the plants with straw or dry calamus or cattail leaves. When spring comes the covering is removed and spread between the rows.

VERSATILE ELDERBERRIES: One of the most useful woodland plants is the elderberry; the flowers and fruits can be used to make superb wine, jelly, fritters, pies, muffins, pancakes, chutney, and a deliciously refreshing nonalcoholic drink. In the Northeast, several kinds of elderberries grow wild, but the common elderberry (*Sambucus canadensis*) is the most familiar.

Transplant these bushes in the spring by digging up plants of a manageable size and packing the roots in moist mulch before taking them home. If a bush is tall and rangy, prune it back by half and then plant it an inch deeper than it grew in the woods.

Common elderberries enjoy damp habitats and tend to spread vigorously if not cut back. The best place to plant one is in a moist area near a compost heap, for they're reported to help speed the formation of compost and produce a fine humus around their roots.

The easy-to-care-for wildings are prey to very few insects and diseases, but over 43 species of birds place elderberries high on their list of delicacies, so be prepared to use protective nets as the fruit ripens.

ZESTY WILD APPLES:
Wild apples might be either neglected old cultivars found in abandoned orchards, or seedling crabapples descended from domestic trees. Since apple seeds don't propagate true to type, the majority of wild trees revert to the characteristics of their ancient crab-stock ancestors and produce small, tart fruits that make excellent pies, jellies, sauce, and superior cider.

Young trees growing in the wild can be dug up and transplanted to develop into mature specimens, or they can be used as rootstock after a year of adjustment to their new locale. Whichever purpose the seedlings are used for, the transplanting must be done while the trees are dormant.

Before uprooting a wild fruit tree, prepare a roomy hole to receive the seedling and replace any hardpan or poor earth with rich topsoil. As soon as the tree's dug up, wrap its roots in burlap or plastic and rush the sapling to the prepared planting site.

Once there, snip off any shovel-frayed roots, spread the rest out on the bottom layer of rich, well-worked soil, and position the tree about an inch deeper than it grew in the wild. Build up the earth around the roots, pat it firm, and tamp down the final layer of dirt to make a two-inch-deep water-holding depression all around the tree. After that, give each new transplant a bucket of water, which should soak the earth and help collapse any hidden air pockets.

Top-pruning is also important, both to balance root loss and to conserve the tree's vigor during its period of adjustment. Slice off any crossed, dead, and obviously weak or badly angled branches flush with the trunk, prune the remaining limbs, and cut the top halfway back. Finally, paint the pruning wounds with a special tree sealer or nonleaded paint. If the weather is dry, water the trees every few days. Don't add any fertilizer during the first season: Strong substances could injure trimmed and weak roots.

If the wild seedling is to be used as rootstock, wait at least a year before making the graft so the tree can recover from transplantation shock. Because they're suited to your climate, established wild apple seedlings can provide especially hardy rootstock for your grafting experiments. All apples are related through the genus *Malus*, so all are compatible for grafting. Be sure, though, that the trees from which you choose scions can also tolerate the region's weather. It's useless, for example, to expect a warmth-loving Granny Smith scion to survive a cold Vermont winter simply because it's been grafted onto a northern New England tree's rootstock.

BLACK AND RED BRAMBLEFRUIT:
Both wild blackberries and raspberries should be transplanted in the spring while the bushes are still dormant. While they are both members of the genus *Rubus*, these two fruit-bearing cousins seldom grow together in the wild and should not be planted near one another because raspberries can be an unaffected carrier of anthracnose, a disease that can destroy blackberries.

A few of the approximately 122 species of blackberry sport small prickly spikes along the canes, but the most common wild species protect themselves with stout, fierce thorns that can tear the skin and draw blood. With the plants set in orderly rows, harvesting the fruit is much less hazardous than picking the berries in a clump of wild bushes. The thorns on raspberries are less threatening.

Pruning is needed for the canes of both these plants when they are moved, but raspberries should get a less radical cutting than blackberries. Cut raspberry canes back to just above the first bud on each cane, but not more than six inches above ground level. Blackberry canes should be cut back to the roots. Yearly pruning of old, unproductive growth will keep your brambles healthy and your yields high.

The bushes should be set about 30 inches apart in well-prepared soil. To minimize the chance of any fungal diseases spreading in the patch, leave six to ten feet between the rows. Try to pick a spot that is similar to the one where the bushes were growing in the wild. Raspberries will need frequent waterings in dry weather, and a hay or grass-clipping mulch will help retain the moisture in the soil and keep weeds in check.

A FINAL NOTE:
To-be-transplanted wild fruits and berries should be dug *only* from your own acreage or from the property of a landowner who has granted you permission. Furthermore, certain wild plants may be in danger of extinction in your area: Consult your state chapter of the American Federation of Garden Clubs for information on local endangered species. Always be careful not to disturb surrounding habitat while gathering your transplants, and leave enough trees or bushes *in the wild* to make sure that the grove or patch you have "borrowed" from will survive.

The adventurous may wish to experiment by transplanting other untamed fruits. Wild cherries, serviceberries, blueberries, and others can be moved from their happenstance homes to a cultivated plot.

USING SAFE HOMEGROWN PEST REPELLENTS

Growing vegetables to supplement the home food supply can certainly help keep the cost of living down, but much of the economy of this move toward living on less can easily be lost if four-legged and eight-legged produce-plundering creatures get to the crops first. Homegrown pest repellents and pesticides can inexpensively and easily reduce the loss to insects and animals, deterring the bandits from taking their toll on the valued crops.

While taking preventive measures at the beginning of the gardening season is undoubtedly the best course of action, there are also remedies that can be taken after the cherished plants are up and beginning to bear.

PROTECT CUCUMBERS, SQUASH, CORN, AND TOMATOES: Maturing cucumbers and squash can be protected by using an always-handy kitchen discard—onion skins. Simply strew a big handful of these leftovers loosely across the top of each hill, and let the legendary pungency of the *Allium* drive away the most stubborn of cucumber beetles. Further guard the mature plants by spraying a mix of equal parts of wood ashes and hydrated lime in water on the upper and lower surfaces of the spreading foliage. For advance protection, you might border *next* year's hilled areas with orange nasturtiums (*Tropaeolum majus).*

One of the high points of summer, the first menu that includes field-fresh roasting ears of corn dripping with butter, can quickly turn into one of the low points if raccoons, squirrels, or earworms get to the dinner first. To prevent such a catastrophe, consider trying a few of the following plans of attack.

Surround this native American crop with soybeans, which will tempt any furry, four-footed invaders to fill their bellies with beans before they reach the succulent maize. It's best to choose a soybean variety that matures at the same time as the corn. In addition, the color and pungent aroma of nasturtiums (which also repel aphids and Mexican bean beetles), marigolds, and mustard rebuff numerous gnawing pests. Roasting ears can be further protected by putting a pinch of cayenne pepper on the silks.

Some folks also place crumpled newspapers between the rows, scatter sections of garden hose cut in one- to three-foot lengths to resemble snakes, hang pieces of a broken mirror about, string Christmas tree lights all through the rows, and even play tape recordings of shotgun blasts to discourage produce pirates.

Sowing dill (*Anethum graveolens*) and borage (*Borago officinalis*) around the tomato patch in the early spring will help repel hornworms as the fruit matures and ripens. These two flavorful herbs are also useful in their own right for adding zest to both cooked and fresh foods.

MARIGOLDS AND MOLE PLANTS: While both French and African marigolds (*Tagetes erecta*) help rid soil of nematodes, the Mexican marigold (*Tagetes minuta*) apparently exudes a substance from its roots that's actually toxic to certain invasive weeds. Try sowing the potent flowers as a cover crop in the autumn, and when the next year's planting time rolls around, the plants can be turned under for one of the finest, most soil-cleansing green manure crops available. Mexican marigolds also repel rabbits and destroy innumerable soil-born pests. Be extravagant with the flowers; scatter them throughout the orchard, surround roses with them, and use some of the foliage to brew up a tea to spray localized areas.

If the garden plot comes under attack by moles, try planting a few mole plants (*Euphorbia lathyris*) around the edges of your garden next time around. The exotic-looking biennials with their thick, milky sap have long been known as mole deterrents, and they'll reseed themselves for the second year, providing seedlings to place in other mole-ridden spots.

Two other plants that can be sown to help eliminate moles are the castor bean (*Ricinus communis*), which also fends off flies and mosquitoes, and the common dandelion (*Taraxacum officinale*). Castor bean seeds are poisonous, so take caution when growing this plant.

SLUGS, BEETLES, AND MOTHS: Slugs, which are among the most damaging aboveground pests, can be discouraged with a preparation made from silicon-rich horsetails (*Equisetum arvense*). Once dried, the plants produce a powder which slugs find highly unpleasant. A second method of deterring slugs involves placing discarded cabbage leaves, grapefruit rinds, or even old boards throughout the garden in the evening. When day breaks, check underneath, remove the occupants, and either add them to your ducks' breakfast menu or squash them.

If Japanese beetles appear to be your primary enemy, try plantings of castor beans, white-flowering geraniums, zinnias, and garlic throughout the garden.

For more general purpose garden protection, consider the roadside herb, yarrow (*Achillea millefolium*). It not only repels a number of pests, but is commonly believed to enhance the growth and flavor of plants growing nearby. Furthermore, yarrow's friendly qualities can be utilized throughout the year by brewing the foliage into a liquid fertilizer and watering periodically with the "tea."

When cole family vegetables face an invasion of cabbage moths and their larvae, which can mutilate plants in just a few days, rely upon an item from the kitchen. Simply pour soured milk over the young cabbages and other crops. It will keep the moths aloft and the worms away.

INDOOR REPELLENTS: Tender greenhouse tenants need protection too, so always allow a few shoo-fly plants (*Nicandra physalodes*) several places of honor in the solarium. The attractive, fast-growing annuals are toxic to all pests that chew them and rebuff the white flies that often plague enclosed gardens.

Homegrown repellents can also keep the kitchen and food storage areas free of unwanted guests. For example, a couple of bay leaves (*Laurus nobilis*) in the bottom of grain containers will keep them bug-free, and tiny cloth bags of ground black pepper will prevent weevils from infesting dried beans. If silverfish are setting up housekeeping in cupboards, just place fragrant leaves of costmary (*Chrysanthemum balsamita*) in each section of the cabinets to make the squatters move on.

MODERATION IN ALL THINGS: Resourceful gardeners have found innumerable common plants that have pest-chasing abilities. Sprays, for instance, can be made from many different species and used for a variety of purposes. The alkaloid exudates from nearly every type of tomato foliage will deter aphids; stinging nettle (*Urtica dioica*) spray encourages healthier plants; a turnip or anise mist will rid crops of spider mites and aphids; basil spray discourages flies; and onion, garlic, horseradish, mint, and chamomile-flower sprays all have bug-chasing qualities.

In putting organic pesticides and repellents to use, bear in mind that a few insects will not pose a threat to the vegetable crop. In small numbers the invaders simply provide food for such natural predators as swallows, each of which may consume 2,000 insects a day. Every concerned gardener should respect the natural balance and use even the suggested repellents only when pest populations threaten to become excessive.

PLANT NO-PAMPER PERENNIAL PRODUCE

Thanks to today's escalating food costs and shortages, as well as a growing concern over the chemical additives often found in supermarket produce, gardening is booming as never before. Perhaps you've joined the "home-grown is better" movement yourself.

But are you still growing only annual vegetables—carrots, corn, radishes, beans, and so forth—that must be planted and laboriously tended every year? If so, it's time to move on to some perennial plants such as asparagus, rhubarb, dandelions, bamboo, Jerusalem artichokes, Egyptian onions, and other edible lilies (onions, for example, belong to the lily family).

ASPARAGUS:
To many people, asparagus is the "choicest of the choice" of all the spring vegetables. In addition to the plant's palate-pleasing qualities, another attribute is that an established bed of asparagus will just keep on  filling your plate with its early spring spears for 20 years or more.

This perennial thrives best when grown in areas where the winters are cold enough to freeze the ground to a depth of at least five inches. In general, this covers much of the continent north of upper Georgia.

Plant asparagus in sandy soil that receives six to eight hours of direct daily sunlight during the summer and that is located away from trees and shrubs.

Many asparagus growers prefer to plant roots rather than seeds in order to avoid waiting an extra year for their first harvest. Prepare the bed the fall before planting, if possible, by digging trenches at least 15 inches deep and about 10 inches wide. Tamp a three-to-four-inch layer of well-rotted manure into the bottom of each trench and cover this with four to six inches of rich garden loam that has been mixed with sand, compost, bonemeal, and some lime. (Asparagus prefers a slightly acid soil with a pH between 6.4 and 6.8.)

The following spring, after giving the soil a good soaking, place one-year-old asparagus plants or crowns in the trenches. Space them 18 inches apart with their roots widely spread and their crowns or buds pointed up. Firmly and carefully pack two inches of sandy soil around the plants without smothering their roots, and continue to water for two weeks.

This will leave an indentation in the soil along the length of each trench, but since the plants tend to rise as the season advances, cultivate the earth in and around the ditch frequently to remove all weeds and gradually fill it in until the trench's surface is leveled off with the surrounding ground.

The chief enemies of asparagus are beetles and rust. Both can be avoided to some degree by cultivating only strains of the plant that are resistant to such problems.

As time goes on, you'll sometimes notice that seed stalks appear on your asparagus plants during either early or late summer. This is generally because poor varieties have been planted, the temperature is too high, or the bed lacks fertility, water, or both. Remove the seed stalks by cutting them off at an angle with a sharp instrument as close to the base of each plant as possible.

If you really want your asparagus patch to bear bountifully year after year, take the time to bed it down each winter. Some gardeners advise cutting off all the plants' summer growth before spreading three inches of mulch over the bed. Others—most notably Ruth Stout—say, "Just leave the stalks where they are. Like everything else, they'll die when their time comes, so let them rest in peace. Besides, they add a certain amount of organic matter to the mulch you spread around the asparagus patch."

You can also take your choice when spring rolls around: Some gardeners prefer to pull the mulch back from their asparagus plants so the sun can warm the earth around them faster and encourage their early growth. Others—especially those who've seen late frosts ruin their early produce—simply leave the mulch where it is and let each year's new growth of asparagus find its way up through the covering.

Try (if you can resist the temptation) to avoid harvesting any of your succulent asparagus spears until the plants are three years old (if you originally put out one-year-old sets, you can start to cut the second spring after they went into the ground). Don't make more than three cuttings the first season, but after that you should enjoy an extremely liberal six- to ten-week-long harvest (the cooler the season, the longer the plants will bear) each and every spring for 20 or more years.

Gather asparagus spears when they're four to eight inches tall, just before the scales on their tips begin to open. Always harvest in the morning and, to avoid damaging other nearby sprouts, either cut each spear individually or snap the shoot by bending it across your index finger with your thumb.

Asparagus is delicious, it's easy to raise, and—after the

mild amount of labor that it takes to establish a bed—it'll put pounds of fresh, green food on your table every spring for years to come.

RHUBARB: Rhubarb—like asparagus—prefers a rich, slightly sandy soil with a pH of 5.5 to 6.5. However, it prefers colder winters than asparagus and, as a result, grows well from the upper southern states all the way north to Alaska. Check nursery catalogs to find which varieties will do best in your area.

Although rhubarb can be propagated from seed, it's a longer and slower process than most gardeners want to tackle. For that reason, new beds of the plant are usually started from root cuttings. (A rhubarb crown is dug up and divided into several pieces, each of which contains one or two good "eyes" or buds.) Plant the cuttings in the spring just as soon as the ground can be worked, usually four to six weeks before your area's last frost date.

Rhubarb sets are generally planted three feet apart in rows spaced four feet from each other. Dig a hole about two feet in diameter and two feet deep for each cutting and place a half bushel of manure in the bottom. Then fill the pit to ground level with a mixture of compost and topsoil. Plant the crown three or four inches deep in the center of the prepared soil and cover it with earth. The top of the root, where the buds are, should lie about two inches underground.

Five to ten good roots will supply enough "fruit" (this is the only vegetable that is truly used as a fruit) for a year-round supply of stewed rhubarb, pies, and preserves for ten years . . . *if* the patch of plants is well

fertilized each fall with a plentiful cover of compost, straw, and manure. Pull the mulch back or not, as you see fit, in the spring, and water the rhubarb regularly during dry weather. It's important, too, to remove flower stalks as they develop during the growing season.

Rhubarb occasionally suffers from "foot rot," which causes its stalks to rot off at the base and fall over. The best cure for that infrequent ailment is to move the patch, but it can usually be prevented by choosing a well-drained location. Once in a while, rhubarb is attacked by the rhubarb curculio, but the beetle can be picked off the plants quite easily. This insect also likes wild dock, and gardeners who clear that plant away from their rhubarb beds are seldom bothered by the beetle.

Wait until the second year to begin harvesting stalks that are ten inches long or more (not including the leaf) and an inch thick at the base. Cutting the rhubarb with a knife can cause root injury and disease, so just twist as you pull them from the ground, and they'll come up easily. Rhubarb is usually one of the very first plants that you can eat in the spring, and its stalks are tender enough to be edible for four to six weeks. CAUTION: *Only the stems of the plants*—NOT ITS LEAVES OR ITS ROOTS—*should be eaten.* A good rhubarb bed will bear for ten years or more, but most gardeners like to divide and replant their patches every five years or so.

DANDELIONS: Why would anyone want to cultivate dandelions when wild ones grow so profusely? One reason is that far too many of the lawns and fields where wild dandelions grow have been chemically treated, and another is that cultivated dandelions—just like cultivated asparagus and cultivated rhubarb —can be tastier, more tender, and otherwise more palatable than their volunteer cousins. In addition, they will grow almost anyplace. Most of the larger seed companies now sell packets of dandelion seeds, so leaf through a few catalogs and try the varieties that especially appeal to you.

Dandelions prefer a soil pH of 6.0 to 8.0. Work manure, rock phosphate, and other natural fertilizers into the earth and then plant your seeds in rows 18 inches apart. Thin the sprouts so that they stand a foot from each other as they develop and, at least in more frigid sections of the country, cover them during the winter with three or four inches of mulch. An annual mulching is about all the care that these hardy plants will ever need.

Dandelion leaves (greens), crowns, and roots may all

be eaten in a variety of ways, especially in the spring and fall. Surprisingly enough, dandelion greens from cultivated plants (unlike their wild relatives) are generally also tender and flavorful right through the summer, and the roots of the cultivated varieties can even be dug up and eaten in the winter. Consult any good wild foods cookbook for recipes.

BAMBOO: Although it's a mainstay of Chinese, Philippine, and other Asiatic schools of cooking, bamboo as a vegetable is hardly known on this continent. More's the pity. Bamboo—or "cane" as it's sometimes called in our southern states—does very well in almost any section of the country where there's rich, well-drained soil and plenty of water. If there's any complaint about cane, in fact, it's that the plant sometimes does *too* well: Once given a start, it's been known to take over whole gardens. The ideal site for a stand of bamboo is in rich loam adjacent to a brook that's partially shaded by a canopy of large trees.

About 70 species of cane can be raised on this continent and almost any issue of most gardening magazines will contain ads run by growers who have the plants for sale. Bamboo is best propagated in the spring by dividing starts from its thick, tangled network of roots. Shoots are also "layered" from the stems. Either method of propagation is better than attempting to start cane from seeds.

When allowed to grow to heights of 25 feet or more, the stalks of the bamboo plant have myriad uses: fishing

poles, rafts, furniture, pole vaulting poles, rug rollers, and so forth. If picked while still young and tender in the spring and summer, however, the shoots of the plant are delicious sautéed in butter, added to salads, and prepared in many other ways. Any good Chinese cookbook will have more serving suggestions than you'll be able to try in a year.

JERUSALEM ARTICHOKES: Despite their misleading name, Jerusalem artichokes are really a member of the sunflower family and are native to North America. They seem to do best across the middle and north-

ern United States, but their range extends far into Canada and south to all but the driest and most southern states.

Sunchokes, as they're sometimes called, will grow in almost any kind of soil though it's easier to dig their tubers from looser and sandier earth. Once established, they must be harvested regularly to keep them from getting out of hand.

Most of the larger nurseries sell the plant's tubers. Generally it's best to order the smooth, white "French" strain, instead of the smaller, red, native variety. And don't go overboard! You'll probably get all you need by putting only three or four of the roots into the ground. Plant them three to four feet apart and four to six inches deep in a sunny, well-watered spot any time between mid-October and mid-December.

Jerusalem artichokes are harvested by digging up their tubers after the first frost. Additional tubers may then be dug right through the winter and well into the early spring. Dig them only as you need them, because they store better in the ground than in a root cellar, and don't worry about harvesting all you need, as you only have to leave a few tubers in the ground to ensure an

even bigger crop the following year.

Jerusalem artichokes contain no starch (which makes them a prescribed food for diabetics) and are loaded with vitamins and minerals. Enjoy them pickled, oven-fried, boiled and mashed, in soups and stews, even cooked and crushed and added to cakes and breads. One way or another, this prolific plant seems to have only one mission in life: to feed you year after year.

EGYPTIAN ONION: Another perennial that too few gardeners know about is the Egyptian onion, also known as the tree or multiplier onion.

Like all onions, this variety prefers a continuous supply of moisture and does well when generous amounts of rotted manure, compost, and bone meal are worked into the soil until the whole onion bed is of a fine tilth.

The bulbs, which look like tiny acorns, are planted in the fall 12 inches apart in rows spaced 30 inches from each other. Some of these mother bulbs can then be left in the soil, where they'll grow larger year after year and produce a crop of new little bulbs on top of three-foot stalks.

In late summer, after these baby bulbs have set and have started showing signs of drying, they can be harvested and dried thoroughly in the sun, then stored in a cool room in a mesh bag.

Southern gardeners are advised to remove the stalks from each mother bulb before winter sets in. Vegetable growers up north, on the other hand, find that the frozen stalks, plucked during the winter, thawed quickly, and used as scallions, taste as sweet as baby spring onions.

Once started, this unusual onion just keeps on producing for your enjoyment. Just lift the parent bulbs every three or four years, separate them, and replant the divisions.

DAY LILIES: Although they're cultivated in nearly every section of North America, day lilies are grown almost entirely for the beauty of their blossoms, and very seldom for their four edible parts: spring shoots, flower buds, blooms, and tubers. All are so delicious, however, that it's little wonder the residents of many other countries of the world—especially China and Japan—look upon the day lily as an important food crop.

This hardy member of the lily family can be grown from seed and once started, is perfectly capable of spreading underground until it forms dense clumps along roadsides and across whole abandoned fields. It is, in short, an extremely carefree perennial to raise.

When plucked in the spring and simmered in a little water and butter, the fresh shoots and outer leaves of the plant taste much like asparagus. Later, as buds develop, they can be gathered, dipped in a batter, and sautéed. During June and July, the flowers themselves (which, as the plant's name implies, each bloom for a single day) can be prepared the same way. The buds and blossoms can also be dried and added as flavoring to fall and winter soups and stews.

Any time of the year when the ground isn't frozen, the crisp, nutty flavored little tubers of the day lily can be dug, cleaned, and eaten raw, either alone or in a salad. Or if you prefer, boil the miniature "potatoes" in salted water till they're tender and serve with butter.

THERE'S MORE: There are many other perennial plants—horseradish, ground cherry, garlic, sea kale, comfrey, and chicory, for example—that can be added to the garden. While each has its strong points and defenders, all are easier to cultivate and all give a bigger return for the time, money, and energy invested than do the annual plants that most gardeners specialize in.

ASSEMBLE A CUT-RATE COLD FRAME

When the spring weather's too chilly to sow seeds in the garden, get a head start on the season with a cold frame. By getting your seedlings started well before the growing season begins, you'll enjoy the good taste, nutriments, and savings of homegrown vegetables just that much earlier in the year. A solar nursery need not be expensive and can be constructed in very little time with readily available materials.

The ideal cold frame admits sunlight to the plants within, supplying them with the heat and light they need to prosper and allowing them to be hardened off before being exposed to the outside world. At the same time, it provides the seedlings with adequate protection from bitter winds and chilling cold.

This particular model requires little more than one-inch-thick polystyrene insulation board, some scrap lath and molding, a 36-inch length of 3/4-inch dowel, assorted hardware, foil tape, and a section of fiberglass-reinforced plastic glazing measuring just over 2' X 4'. Old storm windows, the glass from them, or even heavy-duty clear plastic can be used as a suitable, and much less expensive, substitute for the ordinary glazing.

To build the cold frame, just cut the various pieces to the sizes called for in the drawing, then form the ten holes that hold the night cover's support dowels and the dowel spine. These openings should be about 19 inches apart and 10 inches above the walls' lower edge. They can be made most easily by gently heating a short length of 1/2" copper pipe (using a torch and a pair of pliers) and letting this hot tool serve as a "drill" to cut the perforations. It's important not to apply too much heat to the pipe, though, or the holes will be too large and the dowels won't fit snugly. Do not breathe the fumes given off during this process, since they contain noxious gases.

Assemble the frame by first joining all four corners, inside and outside, with aluminum tape. Then press the 3/4" X 24" dowel through the two center holes to make the spine that connects the front and back walls, and push the remaining pegs into the rest of the openings in such a way that they protrude past the inner surface to form shelves at strategic points around the frame. Keep the spine in place by fastening body washers, scavenged milk jug lids, plexiglass disks, or some other material to its exposed ends with No. 6 X 3/4" flathead wood screws. Complete the frame by attaching the two handles to the night cover, again employing disks as stops.

The light-admitting lid is merely a framework constructed from 1 X 2's, which holds the glazing in place beneath lath strips tacked to its upper surface. To make it, first miter the ends of each of its side and end rails with 45° cuts. Then cut a 3/8"-wide by 1"-deep rabbet into the lower inside edge of each board, and fashion a 1/4" X 1" dado—centered—in the upper surfaces of the two longest rails.

Fasten the casing together with three No. 3 X 1/2" oval-head wood screws at each corner, then tack the 1/4" X 7/8" X 25-1/4" cross brace to the dadoed rails. Finish the job by laying the glazing over the framework and driving brads or finishing nails through the lath strip molding skirt to secure it.

Because polystyrene is apt to deteriorate after long exposure to direct sunlight, it's best to protect it—and the wooden parts of the cold frame—with acrylic latex exterior house paint, which won't adversely affect the insulation board.

To put your budget cold frame to use, just sink it about half a foot into the earth or set it on top of some turned-up soil, making sure its sloped lid is facing in a

southerly direction. If you choose not to bury the frame, secure it against gusty winds by driving a pair of stakes into the ground and fastening them to the ends of the spine with screws.

In order to provide for necessary ventilation, you can either remove the lid completely on sunny days or just prop it open by placing some 2 X 4 scraps at the corners when the weather is overcast. Hold the propped lid in place with a restraining cord tied over it and behind the spine stops. The night cover should be installed in the evening and left in place until the sun rises the next day. On especially cold nights, or if you should want to use your cold frame as a hothouse, you can always put a few strips of electric heat tape (the kind used to keep pipes from freezing) several inches beneath the soil or just set up a light bulb within the container.

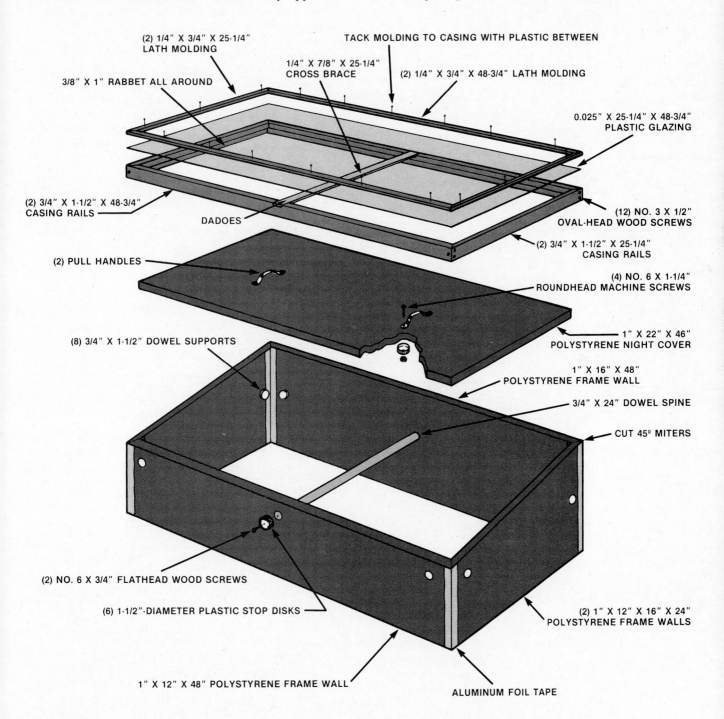

GREENHOUSE GARDENING IN YOUR BACKYARD

Homegrown vegetables can be a definite asset to a household's budget, and the savings can be even greater if a family has the capability of raising its own edibles all year rather than just during the normal gardening season. For this, a greenhouse is a necessity but not necessarily an expensive one.

The 8′ X 10′ structure shown here has proved an excellent habitat for plants, takes about two days to assemble, and costs less than a quarter as much as small prefabricated conservatories.

This homebuilt model consists primarily of a framework covered with fiberglass-reinforced plastic. Vents in the structure's roof peaks allow air to move through the greenhouse and let excess heat escape, and the door at one end can provide extra ventilation when needed.

The 1/2-inch electrical metallic tubing used for the sides of the arch is shaped with an arc roller. The 12 support tubes should be cut 104 inches long and bent so there is a straight-line distance of 97 inches between the innermost points of the ends of each tube.

It's a good idea to double-check all measurements of each component before it is cut, especially the wooden members used to frame the ends of the building. Also, pieces can be custom fitted to one another by marking one piece from the one that adjoins it.

Plastic used to cover the framework can often be obtained from a local surplus or salvage house, and further savings can be had by keeping an eye out for used lumber and conduit.

In all but the coldest regions of the United States, this backyard greenhouse can be used for growing vegetables throughout the year, and in the really cold sections of the country this conservatory will be used to extend the growing season considerably.

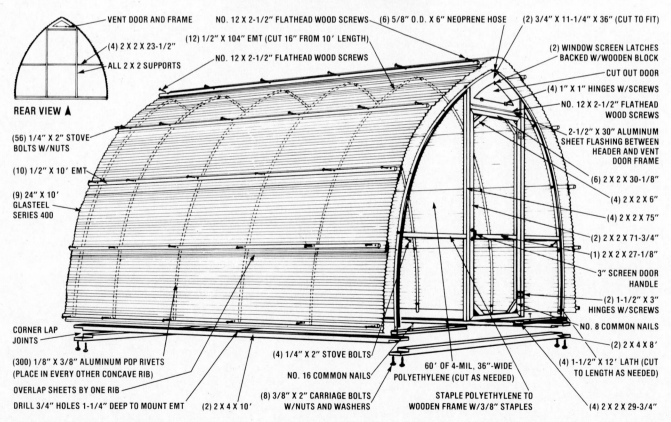

VENT DOOR AND FRAME

(4) 2 X 2 X 23-1/2″

ALL 2 X 2 SUPPORTS

REAR VIEW ▲

(56) 1/4″ X 2″ STOVE BOLTS W/NUTS

(10) 1/2″ X 10′ EMT

(9) 24″ X 10′ GLASTEEL SERIES 400

CORNER LAP JOINTS

(300) 1/8″ X 3/8″ ALUMINUM POP RIVETS (PLACE IN EVERY OTHER CONCAVE RIB)

OVERLAP SHEETS BY ONE RIB

DRILL 3/4″ HOLES 1-1/4″ DEEP TO MOUNT EMT

NO. 12 X 2-1/2″ FLATHEAD WOOD SCREWS

(12) 1/2″ X 104″ EMT (CUT 16″ FROM 10′ LENGTH)

NO. 12 X 2-1/2″ FLATHEAD WOOD SCREWS

(6) 5/8″ O.D. X 6″ NEOPRENE HOSE

(2) 3/4″ X 11-1/4″ X 36″ (CUT TO FIT)

(2) WINDOW SCREEN LATCHES BACKED W/WOODEN BLOCK

CUT OUT DOOR

(4) 1″ X 1″ HINGES W/SCREWS

NO. 12 X 2-1/2″ FLATHEAD WOOD SCREWS

2-1/2″ X 30″ ALUMINUM SHEET FLASHING BETWEEN HEADER AND VENT DOOR FRAME

(6) 2 X 2 X 30-1/8″

(4) 2 X 2 X 6″

(4) 2 X 2 X 75″

(2) 2 X 2 X 71-3/4″

(1) 2 X 2 X 27-1/8″

3″ SCREEN DOOR HANDLE

(2) 1-1/2″ X 3″ HINGES W/SCREWS

NO. 8 COMMON NAILS

(2) 2 X 4 X 8′

(4) 1-1/2″ X 12′ LATH (CUT TO LENGTH AS NEEDED)

(4) 2 X 2 X 29-3/4″

(4) 1/4″ X 2″ STOVE BOLTS

NO. 16 COMMON NAILS

(8) 3/8″ X 2″ CARRIAGE BOLTS W/NUTS AND WASHERS

(2) 2 X 4 X 10′

60′ OF 4-MIL, 36″-WIDE POLYETHYLENE (CUT AS NEEDED)

STAPLE POLYETHYLENE TO WOODEN FRAME W/3/8″ STAPLES

CANNING AND PRESERVING

A YEAR-TO-YEAR FOOD PLAN THAT WORKS

Dirt farmers espouse a particular brand of conservation economics. Long-range plans are fundamental to a rural way of thinking and living, and back-to-the-landers who lack the vision and determination necessary to put such plans into practice soon return to their cities and towns, where paychecks come once a week, or on some other regular basis, instead of with the yearly harvest. On the other hand, folks who make long-range plans work can count on getting safely through most disasters —created or natural.

The inflation fighting and conservation techniques described here will deal specifically with the family food supply, but the philosphy behind these methods can be applied to our personal management of all the earth's resources available to us.

YEAR-TO-YEAR SHOPPING: Time and money-saving techniques should first be applied to shopping: Before considering bulk purchases, read the local newspaper (a first-rate tool for fighting inflation) to compare the prices at the area's supermarkets, keeping a special eye out for seasonal and house-brand sales. When the cost of a particular item is right, buy as large a quantity of the bargain goods as money and storage space will allow.

If inflation continues (as it surely will), stocking your cabinets with adequate supplies of staple necessities can be a great form of one-upmanship against ever-rising prices.

Before soaring food costs can again attack everyone's budget, as happened in 1973-74, for example, purchase supplies (varying from one to three years' worth, as determined by each item's perishability) of salad oil, shortening, syrups, honey, coffee, tea, milk powder, dried beans and lentils, and sugar for cooking and canning. Another strategy is to stockpile canned food that you can't satisfactorily process at home: evaporated milk, tuna, salmon, pineapple, whole and cream-style corn, and pork and beans.

In addition to food, you might want to accumulate—at sale prices—a number of household staples. Toilet and facial tissues, detergents, cleansers, bleaches, and paper towels can be purchased by the case, and soaps, shampoos, and other personal hygiene articles by the dozen. This means that on some necessities, inflated prices can be avoided for as much as three years. (Remember, at its peak, the 1973-74 inflation rate was 17% annually! Money spent at that time on these basic items wouldn't have earned nearly as much interest in a savings account as it would have on someone's pantry shelves!)

The ideal plan is to keep at least a year's supply of regularly used provisions on hand, since the savings realized on products bought on sale justifies such a practice.

It certainly takes no longer to buy a case than it does to purchase one item, so you also save a tremendous amount of time by buying in quantity. If you live a good distance from the closest town, large-scale purchasing can eliminate many miles of travel and thus conserve gallons of gasoline. Those special (expensive and impulsive) runs for a few groceries become unnecessary when you have your own stockpile at home.

BEATING PRICE INCREASES: While the hoarding of items that are in short supply is neither ethical nor advisable, it is only smart to listen to the news and pay attention to trends. If the government makes a price-raising deal with sugar cane growers, increase your stores of sweetener before the supermarkets increase the price. If disastrous weather destroys a major portion of the cacao bean crop in South America, replenish your supply of chocolate items. Should you run short of a particular product between sales or when prices are abnormally high, buy just one or two of the needed items; then wait to restock your shelves until increased supplies or sales lower the cost again. There will always be a rise and fall in various prices. Being aware of such cycles and taking advantage of them can keep you in control of your yearly budget.

Some may consider this method of saving money to be too complicated or self-serving, but there is hardly a simpler or more commonsense way to level out the wild swings (that seem to be mostly upward) in the marketplace. Volume buying encourages a shopper to purchase more carefully than would be necessary on a week-to-week or day-to-day plan, and certainly a long-range food plan doesn't use up any more of the earth's resources than does ordinary grocery shopping. In fact, when transportation is taken into account, the toll exacted from these resources will be less.

COLD STORAGE FOR STAPLES: Most large-scale purchases can be stored on pantry, basement, or root cellar shelves. Any sale purchases that require low storage temperatures can be kept in a freezer. A spare refrigerator can be used to hold large quantities of such foods as crackers, flour, instant milk, margarine, cornmeal, and cracked wheat. (Airtight jars would serve to keep weevils out of such items, but the food would become stale faster if stored on a pantry shelf, nullifying any saving.)

During the coldest months of winter, a garage makes a marvelous walk-in cold-storage facility in which to keep cases of apples, grapefruit, and oranges or sacks of locally grown potatoes, yams, onions, and carrots.

NO MONEY FOR PLANNING AHEAD: Perhaps many of you on stringent budgets or small incomes are thinking: "Hey! You don't know what it's like out here! How can we buy a year's supply of anything when we don't have money even for next week's groceries?"

When money is a problem, simply start small, but start. Instead of buying a case on sale, buy two or three cans, boxes, or packages. When there's extra money (and there will be at some point), you can buy a sale-priced case. Gradually, a little cash should become available to buy a case of some other sale item, and so on. You'll soon be well on your way to working within a full-scale year-to-year plan. Be patient. It's worth the time and effort.

TIME/MONEY-SAVING GARDENING: It's evident that the list of supermarket commodities mentioned so far is rather limited. A garden, even a small one, and fruit trees can supply much of the balance of a family's food needs. An important part of your food supply planning should involve the home production of some fresh foods.

However, since growing food can demand an almost unlimited amount of time, plan very carefully to get the most from your gardening efforts. By planting late, perhaps two weeks to even a month later than other gardeners in your area, it's possible to avoid competition from early weed species and much violent spring weather (including hailstones, sandstorms, and deluges), permitting the plants to grow with less stress.

Buying bedding plants isn't a must. Cabbage, tomatoes, and peppers can be seed-sown in the same space they'll occupy during the entire growing season. You can also start seeds indoors and then transplant the seedlings. Thus, the gardener saves money and time and knows exactly what variety will appear, which often is not the case with purchased seedlings. Because the late-planted vegetables encounter less damaging weather, they're generally healthier and produce longer and more prolifically.

Besides an annual cultivated garden, another source of fresh food would be perennial vegetables set out in protected, slightly shadowed spots around the edges of the lawn, or grown in containers on patios, decks, or balconies. A very limited amount of hand weeding will take care of beds of garlic, chives, onion, poke, asparagus, spearmint, and rhubarb, while New Zealand spinach, leaf lettuce, dill weed, and wild lamb's-quarters will spring up voluntarily from unharvested seed in sheltered areas. Peaches, apricots, plums, cherries, apples, and a grapevine can be grown in most areas.

AN INVESTMENT OF TIME: Any bounty harvested from the garden and orchard that isn't eaten fresh can be preserved for later use. The fruits may be juiced, canned for salads and desserts, or made into preserves and jellies, delicious pancake syrups, and fillings for fruit pies (to be frozen and baked later). Any vitamin-rich fresh fruits that are still around late in the season may be either dried or turned into delicious fruit leathers.

Tomatoes, which may be canned whole or as juice, will provide a base for meat-rich sauces. Homemade soup combinations such as tomato, zucchini, and onion—or tomato, okra, and onion—are wonderful ways to stock pantry shelves, too. Various relishes and sauces can be created by using tomatoes, ripe or green, as a base. Caliente sauce, a Tex-Mex distillation of liquid fire made with tomatoes, onions, and jalapeño peppers, is one example, and there many variations on basic ketchups, barbecue sauces, and tomato sauces. Dried tomato slices can later be pulverized for instant additions to soups and casseroles.

If the value of home-processed food is measured in money only, there might be no way to justify the lavish amount of time one could spend on it. But there is another measurement: the quality of the finished products.

The excellence of stored homegrown food may be assured in a number of ways. For one thing, chemicals needn't be routinely applied to your soil or to the plants that produce your fruits and vegetables. Crops should be harvested at peak perfection and immediately processed to preserve as much of their natural nutrition as possible. Furthermore, the preservation processes will be according to your demanding requirements for sanitation, and unless you choose to, no artificial preservatives will be included. Balance that knowledge along with the cash and time invested, and you will probably consider your hours well-spent.

ECONOMICAL CONSUMPTION: The ultimate test of a year-to-year food plan is using the goods in an economical manner. It's always possible, of course, to "throw more out the back door than can be brought in the front," unless you continue to plan carefully after you buy.

When you serve a roast, for instance, remember the proverbial hog butcher who uses everything but the squeal. Leftover meat and drippings can provide a head start in creating a delicious, nutritious, stomach-filling casserole, and the leftover casserole can serve as a basis for a tasty, full-bodied soup. Even after that you can store the remaining soup in the freezer; then on a busy day, thaw it and serve it up with hot corn bread. No one will notice that you've used, reused, and used again the original roast. As for the leftovers of the leftovers, use your imagination before adding them to the diets of your miscellaneous animals.

Only your vision and determination need limit your conservative use of food, which is one of the earth's scarcest resources.

From a personal perspective, commonsense planning means money in your pocket, food on the table, and abundance in the pantry—a reassuring buffer against whatever hard times may come.

PUTTING UP YOUR SUMMER'S HARVEST

If your garden is well into its prime, it probably seems like quite a spell since that first shovelful of soil was disturbed to form the beginning of a backyard plot. Now that some of the homegrown delectables are ready to be harvested, the produce may be ripening faster than you can consume it. After all your working and waiting, it would be a shame to let any of that bounty go to waste, especially when it's possible to cache some of that food for next winter by preserving it.

Getting an overly abundant supply of produce stowed away for off-season feasting can seem like a formidable task to a first-timer. As with any project, the beginning step is to get an overview of what's involved. Knowledge is a great antidote for feelings of apprehension.

SOME LIKE IT HOT AND SOME LIKE IT COLD: The first decision that a prospective food putter-upper faces is what method of preserving to use. The process or processes that you choose, whether freezing, canning, drying, or root cellaring, will depend on the amount of time, space, and money you have available and on what types and quantities of foods you plan to preserve. Many homemakers weigh the pros and cons of each method and conclude that a combination of canning and freezing will best meet their particular needs.

Canning, for example, is a relatively inexpensive way to garner the backyard bounty, as long as you "put by" enough food to justify the initial outlay for processing equipment: canning jars and lids, a pressure canner, and various specialized utensils. With this versatile method, you can preserve pickles, relishes, jams, jellies, and soups, as well as fruits and vegetables. But canning does take time.

Freezing, on the other hand, requires little in the way of time and holds the garden-fresh flavor better than most of the other food-processing methods. However, the cost of purchasing a freezer makes a definite dent in the budget and may be prohibitive for folks just getting started in a self-sufficient lifestyle.

Dehydration, a technique that's been around for a long time, is still a prime method of preserving foods, especially in areas of the world where other means aren't feasible. Drying doesn't require the initial investment needed for canning or freezing. (If you decide to dehydrate on a large scale, however, you may well want to purchase or build a solar or electric food dryer.) Dried foods can be stored in a smaller space than frozen, canned, or fresh produce, and if kept dry, the foods will remain edible for years. The drying process does, of course, change the texture of the food, so it's advisable to experiment some before dehydrating large quantities of food.

Root cellaring—storing food in a cold, moist atmosphere for several months after harvest—was once a popular method of food preservation, being easy and inexpensive. Today, most homes have cozy, dry basements instead of cool, damp cellars, and root cellaring has become less common. However, if you do have access to a root cellar or to the labor and materials required to build one, this can be an excellent way to squirrel away root crops, cabbages, apples, and other "winter-tough" orchard and garden gleanings. The foods that can be stored in this manner will be "preserved" without being processed at all!

CANNING: The whole canning process can appear slightly overwhelming to a novice preserver, and if enough stories of food poisoning have made the rounds, canning may even seem a questionable practice altogether. Actually, it is a simple and safe method of handling surplus harvest, but following instructions is a must.

HOW IT WORKS: Canning interrupts the natural decomposition process of perishables by heating, and thereby sterilizing, them and at the same time sealing the food's containers to protect the edibles from outside contamination during storage. This heating and sealing technique destroys potentially harmful microorganisms such as bacteria, molds, and yeasts, and it denatures the enzymes in plant tissues which could otherwise cause toxic substances to form in the canned goods.

As you might expect, different foods promote the growth of different types of microorganisms that cause spoilage; therefore, processing times and temperatures must vary accordingly. In general, though, all canned foods are divided into two groups: low-acid and high-acid types. High-acid foods (all fruits, including tomatoes, are in this category) either naturally contain plenty of acid or have been acidified by the addition of vinegar, as in the case of relishes, pickles, and sauerkraut.

Low-acid comestibles are just what their name implies: foodstuffs with little or no acidity. Vegetables, meats, poultry, seafood, and soups are grouped in this category.

WHAT IT MEANS TO YOU: This distinction is of concern to the canner-to-be because the natural "sourness" of a food determines how it's to be processed. In tomatoes and other fruits, the high-acid content protects against harmful bacteria, while molds, yeasts, and enzyme toxins can be easily destroyed by heating jars of these foods in a briskly boiling water bath. Low-acid foods such as snap beans, on the other hand, allow the growth of heat-resistant bacteria (notably *Clostridium botulinum*, which causes botulism). These eatables, therefore, must be specially treated by being heated to 240°F in a pressure canner in order to destroy any bacteria. (It's also a good practice to boil all low-acid home-canned produce for 20 minutes before eating, just to be on the safe side.) Consult a canning manual to find the appropriate method and the prescribed amount of processing time for each food you harvest. Properly adhering to these guidelines is the key to successful canning.

THE EQUIPMENT YOU'LL NEED: Once you've determined what sort of canning process you'll be using,

your next step will be to gather all the proper preserving accoutrements. If you plan to put up only an occasional batch of pickles and relishes or to make just a few pints of Aunt Sally's conserves, common kitchen utensils will be adequate to meet most of your needs. For instance, a big pot (20- to 21-quart capacity) with a tight-fitting lid will serve nicely as a boiling-water-bath container. All you'll have to do is find or fashion a canning rack to keep the jars from touching each other as they are processed.

If, on the other hand, you have visions of packing the pantry clear to the ceiling, you'll require some specialized canning equipment. A pressure canner is a must for putting up all those low-acid carrots, beets, and beans basking out back in the sun. However, if you can't afford to part with the $30 to $80 required to purchase a canner (and if you plan to process only pint jars), a pressure cooker will suffice if it has an accurate gauge and will hold ten pounds of pressure. Because pressure *cookers* heat and cool more quickly than the larger canners do, you should add 20 minutes to the recommend-

ed processing times if you use this "make-do" method.

Regardless of how much or how little squirreling away of summertime victuals you plan to attempt, you'll need to buy canning jars and lids. Most people who can are partial to the newer two-piece, self-sealing lid that has a nonreusable rubber-rimmed top and reusable outer band, but the older-style lids (such as the "Lightning" glass tops with rubber rings and the zinc caps with porcelain liners) work perfectly well, too.

The jars themselves should be the standard half-pint or quart canning jars. Be certain to buy an ample supply early in the season, so you won't be left containerless just when the produce is at its prime. Mayonnaise-type jars are not tempered to withstand the heat and pressure involved in low-acid canning, so never use anything but the regular canning jars in a pressure canner.

Employing "ordinary" mayonnaise containers in a boiling water bath is a common practice in some canners' kitchens, but it is cautioned against by the experts of the trade. There is always a risk of cracked jars with the ensuing loss of both produce and time.

You'll find that a jar lifter or holder especially made for grasping containers of boiling foods will prove itself well worth the small purchase cost. A canning funnel that helps guide hot vegetables and fruits into the jars is equally helpful.

The remainder of the necessary equipage—tongs, saucepans, knives, chopping boards, spoons, a timer, hot mitts, and dish towels or a cooling rack—may already be right on your kitchen shelf.

READYING YOURSELF AND READYING THE KITCHEN: Once you've bought up a supply of jars and lids, located a pressure canner, and rounded up the rest of the necessary canning gear, you'll no doubt be eager to begin packing food away. Before rushing outside to gather armloads of your garden's offerings, however, take the time to make sure you really are properly prepared.

For one thing, you should be sure you know precisely how you'll preserve the harvest. For example, you must determine whether the folks who'll be enjoying your canned tomatoes would like them better whole, in juice, or as a sauce, or whether you might want to can them in a combination of ways.

In addition, you need to decide whether to use the hot- or cold-pack canning technique with the particular kind of produce you're about to put up. (In general, hot packing—precooking the food and adding the heated product to the jars—is used when the victuals need to be softened to fill their containers solidly. Cold packing—putting raw food into the jars—is used for low-density eatables, such as tomatoes, to allow the food to better retain its shape.)

Next, you're ready to read through the recipe and assemble all of the ingredients. Frantically rushing from store to store in search of spices while vats of cucumbers are waiting at home, awash in pickling brine, is not a recommended procedure, so be sure that you have everything that you'll need! Amass all the canning equipment and examine the jars for hairline cracks or nicks. Then wash and rinse the unblemished jars and leave them immersed in hot water. Put the jars lids in a saucepan, so you'll be ready to sterilize them in a boiling-water rinse.

Perhaps most important, allow yourself plenty of time to complete the entire canning process. Rushing the operation will only increase the chances that you'll make mistakes, and you can't afford mishaps in canning. The wise worker will schedule a hassle-free time for the canning operation and put off cleaning the barn or basement until another day.

Once you've determined that everything inside is set to your satisfaction, you can head out to gather the harvest. It's best to get the goods from the garden to the jar in about two hours in order to retain the maximum nutrients in the final product. Reap only enough for one canning run. Trays of cut, but not yet processed, food will all too soon become fermenting masses that are unfit to can or eat. You should pluck only ripe, unblemished food, since the quality that comes out of the jar will be no better than what originally went into it. One piece of overripe produce can spoil an entire batch.

MAKING A RUN: Although an in-depth canning guide will include more details on the step-by-step process, here is the basic information. Pack the food into the jars, wipe the rims of the containers clean, and screw on the sterilized lids. Then carefully load the jars into the water-filled canner. (A pressure canner is required for low-acid foods, and the instructions for using the particular canner should be read carefully before processing is begun.) Fasten the processor's lid and heat for the recommended time.

Once the jars have been processed in the prescribed manner, let everything cool down until you can safely remove the lid of the canner and then the jars. Then place the canned foods where they can finish cooling slowly. Before long, you'll be treated to an unusual sound that is one of the delights of canning, because as each lid seals tight, it will bend inward with a clearly audible PING or POP! After the jars have "rested" undisturbed for a day, you can store your sealed, cooled, and ready produce in a dark closet, and look forward to some good eating this winter!

Keep in mind one last bit of canning advice: Have

fun. The return to a self-sufficient food supply can be a budget booster and an enjoyable experience. Canning won't seem like drudgery if you allow enough time for the job and do no more work than you can comfortably handle. Another idea is to make canning a group effort. (It takes longer than you may think to cut up all the ingredients for soups, pickles, and relishes!)

PUTTING IT ON ICE: If free time is the limiting factor in your food storage program, you might be wise to freeze the rewards of your summer's labor. Frozen produce retains its nutrients, its texture, and that fresh-from-the-farm flavor quite well, and this form of processing involves little in the way of equipment and time. On the other hand, the freezer itself consumes energy, offers a limited storage space, and is a hefty capital investment.

EQUIPMENT FOR FREEZING: The main "utensil" required for freezing is, of course, the freezer itself. You'll have to decide what size and shape (chest, upright, or a combination freezer-refrigerator) will be best for your situation. Providing six to ten cubic feet of freezing space per person is generally a pretty good guideline to follow if you intend to freeze a major portion of the food that your group needs. (If you're not yet ready to purchase your own appliance, you might want to rent a freezer locker in a nearby cold storage warehouse for the first year to help determine how much food-stashing space you'll actually need.)

Whatever cooling plan you decide on, don't consider the small freezer section of your refrigerator to be adequate for long-term storage unless that unit has a separate door, an independent temperature control, and a good bit of room.

THE WRAPPING FOR THE PACKAGE: After storage space has been determined, the next consideration is what type of packaging to use. The freezer container has three purposes: It keeps the victuals from drying out (an occurrence known as freezer burn), it preserves their flavor, texture, and color, and it helps them to retain their valuable nutrients. Therefore, you'll want packaging materials which are moisture-vapor-resistant. Waxed cardboard freezer boxes with inner plastic freezer bags and ties are easily stacked in the freezer and help to conserve limited storage space. However, you'll find that other appropriate containers, such as plastic boxes and glass freezer jars, will also work well.

FROM SOIL TO STORAGE: Preparing your garden's produce for freezing is quick and easy after you assemble your equipment and gather up the edibles. As with canning, it's best to preserve the food within two hours after picking, if possible. Therefore, you should pluck small quantities of your best homegrown harvest. Then simply trim the vegetables as if for table use, blanch them, and package in freezer containers.

FREEZING FRUIT: You'll need to make one preliminary decision when freezing fruit: whether to "dry pack'' or "wet pack" the edibles before you put them in bags. When you wet pack, you add sugar or a sugar syrup to the fruit, but when you dry pack, you simply freeze the fruit in its natural, firm, fresh state. (If you choose to use syrup, be sure to allow some space for the liquid to expand, and be certain that the container is sealed tightly to prevent leakage.)

If you plan to freeze apples, apricots, pears, peaches, or any other fruit that discolors in storage, another factor to consider is whether or not to add ascorbic acid

(vitamin C) to prevent the food from darkening. You could also use plain lemon juice to achieve the same effect, but ascorbic acid won't change the taste of the fruit as much as the lemon juice will.

CHILLING THE VEGETABLES: The method for freezing vegetables is slightly different from that for fruit. Such low-acid foods require blanching to arrest those enzymes in the plant tissues which can cause the foods to become tough and lose their flavor. (This pre-heating is necessary for all vegetables except sweet green peppers.) To illustrate this technique, let's consider the snap bean.

On the day that you decide to freeze some "snaps," you go out to the garden and pluck the young, tender beans. After washing the green beans in several rinses of cold water, remove the "strings" and tips and either snap or cut into bite-size pieces or slice them length-wise (French style). Next, put the prepared vegetables in a wire basket, lower them into a pan of boiling water

(or place them in a steamer), and blanch the beans for the time specified in your freezing guide. (Don't over-cook the legumes, or you'll end up with a bag of "mush" when the food is thawed.)

Immediately after the blanching process, dunk the heated beans in ice-cold water and then rinse them until they're cool to the touch. They can be promptly packaged and placed in the freezer.

GIVING IT A NAME: Once you've gathered, processed, and packaged the harvest, you'll want to label each food container. A felt-tipped pen filled with waterproof ink works well for recording the name of the food and the date it was preserved.

It's also a good idea to write down the food type—and the amount frozen—on a chart, so that you'll have a running list of your iced inventory. By taping the list to the freezer door, you can conveniently cross off each parcel that is removed from storage. Also, a rough map of where a given food is located in the freezer will help you keep your own "cool" later on, as you try to locate something like that last pouch of pod peas!

KEEPING IT IN THE DEEP FREEZE: When you have your summer reapings packaged and labeled, place them in the freezer at 20° below 0°F for the first 24 hours. The food can then be stored at a constant 0°F.

This preserving method works by allowing the extreme cold to retard the growth of microorganisms and slow down the enzyme activity in the food. Because freezing does not sterilize the produce, you'll have to make sure that the edibles stay sufficiently cold and that they are used within a reasonable period (not more than a year). There will be a gradual but inevitable loss of quality as the food ages.

THE RESULT: Putting up your own food is essentially a matter of involvement. There are few things more satisfying than walking into a pantry that houses a rainbow of brightly colored jars put there by you, or peeking into a well-stocked freezer.

And remember, it's not just nostalgia for the "olden days" that's sending more and more folks back into the kitchen to make their own pickles, relishes, jellies, and canned or frozen goods. By turning back to gardening and preserving, it's possible to control the quality of your food and to pare down that ever-rising grocery bill.

A TROUBLESHOOTING GUIDE

Once the garden's in and harvesttime approaches, you may be thinking about putting up some of those delicious homegrown fruits and vegetables for year-round enjoyment and lower winter food bills.

Canning food can be as easy as it is rewarding. There are, however, some difficulties that occasionally plague even the most experienced canner. This chart will tell you just what might have caused your past batches of preserved goodies to turn out not quite as you expected, and how to avoid similar problems this summer.

CONDITION (product usable unless spoilage is indicated)	CAUSE	PREVENTION
Foods darken in top of jar.	Liquid did not cover food product.	Cover food product with liquid before capping jar. (See "Loss of liquid" reference.)
	Food is not processed long enough to destroy enzymes.	Process each food by recommended method and for recommended length of time.
	Manner of packing and processing did not produce a high vacuum.	Pack and process as recommended.
	Air was sealed in the jars either because headspace was too large or air bubbles were not removed.	Use recommended headspace. Remove air bubbles by running nonmetallic kitchen utensil between food and jar.
Fruits darken after they have been removed from jar.	Fruits have not been processed long enough to destroy enzymes.	Process each fruit by recommended method and for recommended length of time. Time is counted when water reaches a full boil in the canner.
Corn is brown.	Corn was too mature for canning.	Use freshly picked corn which has plump, shiny kernels filled with milk.
	Liquid did not cover corn.	Cover corn with liquid before capping jar. (See "Loss of liquid" reference.)
	Jars were processed at too high a temperature.	Keep pressure in canner at recommended pounds . . . gauge may be faulty and should be checked.
	Variety of corn used.	Use different variety next time.
Pink, red, blue, or purple color in canned apples, pears, peaches, and quinces.	A natural chemical change which occurs in cooking the fruit.	None.
Green vegetables lose their bright green color.	Heat breaks down chlorophyll, the green coloring matter in plants.	None.
Some foods become black, brown, or gray.	Natural chemical substances (tannins, sulfur compounds, and acids) in food react with minerals in water or with metal utensils used in preparing food.	Use soft water. Avoid using copper, iron, chipped enameled ware, or utensils from which tinplate has worn.
Green vegetables turn brown.	Vegetables were overcooked.	Time precooking and processing exactly.
	Vegetables were too mature for canning.	Asparagus tips should be tight and the entire green portion tender. Pods of green beans should be crisp and meaty and the beans tiny. Peas, lima beans, and all other beans and peas which are shelled should be green.
Crystals in grape products.	Tartaric acid, which is naturally found in grapes.	Carefully ladle juice into clean hot jars; cap and reprocess original length of time.
Yellow crystals on canned green vegetables.	Glucoside, natural and harmless substance, in vegetables.	None.

FOR THE HOME CANNER

Spoiled food should never be eaten. The most obvious signs of dangerous spoilage include gas bubbles and spurting liquid . . . mushy, slimy, or moldy food . . . cloudy liquid or liquid with sediment in it . . . leaking jars . . . bulging lids . . . and odd odors and colors.

For safety's sake, be sure to boil all of your canned low-acid foods at least 15 minutes before you taste them. If the liquid foams or if the food has an unnatural odor when it's heated in this manner, the dish is very likely to be spoiled and should definitely be discarded.

CONDITION (product usable unless spoilage is indicated)	CAUSE	PREVENTION
White crystals on canned spinach.	Calcium and oxalic acid in spinach combine to form harmless calcium oxalate.	None.
White sediment in bottom of jars of vegetables. (May denote spoilage.)	Starch from the food.	None.
	Minerals in water.	Use soft water.
	Bacterial spoilage . . . liquid is usually murky, food soft. (Do not use.)	Process each food by recommended method and for recommended length of time.
Fruit floats in jar.	Fruit is lighter than the syrup.	Use firm, ripe fruit. Heat fruit before packing it. Use a light to medium syrup. Pack fruit as closely as possible without crushing it.
Cloudy liquids. (May denote spoilage.)	Spoilage. (Do not use.)	Process each food by recommended method and for recommended length of time.
	Minerals in water.	Use soft water.
	Starch in vegetable.	None.
	Fillers in table salt.	None, except using a pure refined salt.
Loss of liquid during processing. (Food may darken, but will not spoil. Do not open jars to replace liquid.)	Food not heated before packing.	Heat food before packing.
	Food packed too tightly.	Pack food more loosely.
	Air bubbles not removed before capping jar.	Remove air bubbles by running nonmetallic kitchen utensil between food and jar.
	Pressure canner not operated correctly.	Pressure should not be allowed to fluctuate during processing time. Allow pressure to drop to zero naturally . . . wait 2 minutes before opening lid.
	Jars not covered with water in boiling water bath canner.	Jars should be covered (at least one inch) by water in canner during the processing period.
	Starchy foods absorbed liquid.	None.
Jar seals, then comes open. Spoilage evident. (Do not use.)	Food spoilage from underprocessing.	Process each food by recommended method and for recommended length of time.
	Disintegration of particles of food left on the sealing surface.	Wipe sealing surface and threads of jar with clean, damp cloth before capping.
	Hairline crack in jar.	Check jars . . . discard ones unsuitable for canning.
Jar of food fails to seal. (Correct cause and reprocess the full time or use the food immediately.)	Many factors could be involved, such as failure to follow instructions for using jar and cap, or a bit of food forced up between the jar and lid during processing.	Carefully follow methods and instructions for using jars and caps and for foods to be canned.
Hollow pickles.	Cucumbers were stale when pickling was begun.	Pickling process should be started within 24 hours of picking cucumbers.

CANNING MEAT THE RIGHT WAY

(Much of the following material was excerpted and adapted with permission from the Ball Blue Book: The Guide to Home Canning and Freezing, *published by Ball Corporation, Muncie, Indiana.)*

There are any number of good reasons to can meat. For one thing, doing so can save a lot of future cooking (for those times when you need to prepare a meal in a hurry), and it's also a practical solution to the "overstuffed freezer" problem. Many people, though, hesitate to can meats, because they think it might be dangerous. However, that simply isn't so. Canning meat is as safe as processing any other low-acid food in the same manner. You just have to follow the correct procedures.

Bacterial growth is hindered by the acid in food, and meat is very low in acid. Worse, certain harmful bacteria thrive where natural acidity is low, and these cannot readily be destroyed at the boiling point of 212°F. To can meat, therefore, you must superheat it to 240°F, which means it must always be processed by pressure canning.

Be aware, too, that the flavor and texture of any canned meat will depend upon the breed, the feed, and the manner in which the animal was handled at the time—and immediately after—it was killed. If you want to process your own livestock, contact your local county agricultural agent for complete information on slaughtering, chilling, and aging it.

CLEAN AND READY: The first step in meat canning is to assemble the needed equipment and utensils and to wash them thoroughly. Clean the petcock and safety valve of the canner by drawing a string through the openings, and if you have a dial gauge, be sure it's accurate. If it's not, the processing won't be correct, and some bacteria, including botulinum, may not be killed. (Again, your county extension agent or the manufacturer of the canner will know where to have dial gauges checked.)

Look over your jars for nicks and cracks, and wash the containers and their closures in hot, soapy water. Rinse them well and keep them in hot water until they're ready for use. Don't use wire brushes, steel wool, or washing soda for cleaning these receptacles, as they're likely to damage the glass. In handling the jars, take care that they don't crack or break because of sudden changes of temperature. Never put a hot jar on a cold surface or in a draft, and never pour boiling liquid into a cool container.

"One trip" jars, such as ones in which you buy commercially made mayonnaise, peanut butter, or instant coffee, should not be used for canning purposes.

MEATY FACTS: Cut slabs of meat about an inch thick, slicing across the grain; then cut with the grain until you have pieces of an appropriate size for the jars you're using.

Be sure to trim away gristle, bruised spots, and fat. Too much fat is likely to give the meat a strong flavor and may also damage the compound used for sealing the jars. Furthermore, you should not let meat stand in water, with the exception of strong-flavored game, which should be soaked in salt water before it is canned.

Prepare and pack the meat according to the recipes here, and process it for the time prescribed. Keep in mind, though, that because air is thinner at higher altitudes, it affects both pressure and boiling point. The times given in the recipes here are for foods to be processed at altitudes under 2,000 feet. For higher elevations, half a pound of pressure is required for each additional 1,000 feet above sea level. So, if you live at a high elevation and your pressure canner has a weighted gauge rather than a dial one, use 15 pounds of pressure instead of 10. Do not raw-pack meats for pressure processing at altitudes above 6,000 feet.

Only enough food for one canner load should be prepared at a time. Special care should be taken in filling the jars. Headspace, the area in the jar between the inside of the lid and the top of the food or liquid, should be carefully measured to achieve proper venting and sealing. If too little headspace is allowed, the food may expand and bubble when air is being forced out from the lid during processing, leaving a deposit on the rim of the jar or lid that will prevent the container from sealing correctly. If there is too much headspace, the food at the top is likely to discolor, and the jar may not seal properly because insufficient processing time won't drive all the air out of the container.

After the food has been packed in the jar, any air bubbles present should be removed by running a clean wooden spoon or plastic paddle between the food and the jar. Knives and other metal devices may nick the bottoms of the jars, leading to breakage.

The tops of the jars, screw threads, and top surfaces of rubber rings (if they're used) should be wiped with a clean, damp cloth, as particles of spilled food could prevent a tight seal. When placing closures on your containers, follow the manufacturer's directions carefully, since the method varies with the type of jar used.

To minimize the possibility of contamination by microorganisms, process the meat immediately after the containers are closed. Put two or three inches of hot water in the canner (or whatever amount is recommended by the manufacturer), set it on your heat source, and place the jars inside in a manner that allows steam to flow freely around each vessel. Fasten the canner's cover securely, making sure that steam escapes only through the petcock. Allow steam to vent steadily (according to the manufacturer's directions, or for ten minutes) to drive all the air out. Otherwise, you'll have air pressure as well as steam pressure inside, and you'll get a faulty gauge reading. When that's done, close the petcock, or—if the gauge is weighted—put the weight in place. Follow the manufacturer's instructions to determine when ten pounds of pressure has been reached, and start counting processing time at this point. (Refer to those instructions before opening the canner, too.)

CANNED ROAST: Begin by cutting your favorite meat into chunks, and then bake or roast them until they're well browned (but not done through) . . . or brown them in a small amount of fat. After adding salt to suit your taste, pack the hot meat into your preheated jars and cover the meat with hot gravy or broth, leaving an inch of headspace. Adjust the caps, and process the jars at ten pounds of pressure for an hour and 15 minutes for pints, an hour and 30 minutes for quarts.

HOT-PACKED STEAKS OR CHOPS: Cut the beef, veal, lamb, mutton, pork, chevon, or venison into one-inch slices, removing any large bones as you do so. Quickly brown the meat in a small amount of fat and salt it to please yourself. Pack the freshly cooked slices into hot jars, cover the meat with steaming gravy (leaving an inch of headspace), and adjust the jar caps. Process pints for an hour and 15 minutes, and quarts for 15 minutes longer . . . both at ten pounds of pressure.

COLD- OR RAW-PACKED STEAKS OR CHOPS: Slice any of the meats mentioned above into one-inch thicknesses, removing all large bones. Pack the meat into hot jars, leaving an inch of headspace. Add 1/2 teaspoon of salt per pint (a whole teaspoon for a quart), adjust the caps, and process pint jars for an hour and 15 minutes at ten pounds of pressure. Quarts need another 15 minutes at the same pressure.

WILD RABBIT AND SQUIRREL: Soak the meat for an hour in brine made by dissolving one tablespoon of salt per quart of water to be used. Rinse the meat, and then—omitting the salt—use any of the following recipes for canning poultry. (In most states, the storage of game is regulated by law. Conservation officials can supply information on this subject.)

BONED BIRD: For canning, one- and two-year-old fowls are better than younger ones. Cut up the picked and cleaned bird, rinse and dry it, and chill it for six to ten hours. Don't salt the poultry.

Steam or boil the fowl until it's about two-thirds done. Next, remove the skin and bones. Pack the meat into hot jars, leaving an inch of headspace, and add 1/2 teaspoon of salt to a pint (or one teaspoon to each quart). Skim off the fat, then reheat the broth to boiling and pour it over the meat, maintaining the inch of headspace. Finally, adjust the caps. Processing should take an hour and 15 minutes for pints, and 15 minutes longer for quarts, both at ten pounds of pressure.

HOT-PACKED BIRD ON THE BONE: After preparing and chilling the fowl as directed for boned bird, boil, steam, or bake it until it's two-thirds done. Pack the pieces into hot jars and add 1/2 teaspoon of salt per pint (or one teaspoon for each quart). Cover the meat with boiling broth, leaving an inch of headspace, and adjust the caps. At ten pounds of pressure, processing should take an hour and 15 minutes for pints, and 15 minutes longer for quarts.

FINISHING UP: After processing, your product should be allowed a ten-minute cooling period before the jars are removed from the pressure canner. If they're lifted too soon, a cool draft could cause the glass to break.

If food has boiled out of the tops of the containers during heating, don't try to readjust the lids, since this would probably break the seals. Instead, wipe the residue away when the jars are thoroughly cool. If, for any reason, a jar has obviously failed to seal, repack it, put on a new lid or rubber, and reprocess the container for the full length of time called for in the recipe.

When you remove jars from the canner, place them a few inches apart (to facilitate cooling) on cloths or wire racks, keeping them away from drafts to avoid breakage. Thoroughly cooled jars should be checked to see if a proper seal has been obtained, following the manufacturer's directions as to the types of tests to use.

Generally, the seal of closures using rubber rings can be tested by tipping the jar. If any leakage occurs, or if bubbles start at the lid and rise through the contents, the jar isn't sealed correctly.

Modern, two-piece vacuum lids with metal screw bands are easily checked for a proper seal. A slight pinging noise may be heard as the jar cools, and this indicates that a vacuum has formed, sealing the meat. The center of the lid is pulled down by the vacuum, creating a slightly concave surface. If you're not sure that the surface is concave, push down in the center. If it doesn't push down, the container is sealed. If it does, the jar isn't sealed, and its contents have to be eaten or reprocessed promptly. If the lid is not concave, but it pushes down and holds, the seal is questionable. In this case, remove the screw band and lift the jar by the edges of the lid. Care should be taken in doing this, because the jar may spill or break. When you've determined that a tight seal exists, remove the screw bands (if you haven't already done so). Bands left in place may become corroded, making the jars difficult to open.

Your containers of canned meat should be allowed to cool for 12 to 24 hours before being stored in a cool, dark, dry place. Remember that light hastens oxidation and destroys certain vitamins, and that dampness can cause the metal lids and closures to corrode or rust, endangering the seal. It's a good idea to label each jar, including the date on which the food was canned.

IMPORTANT: Canned meat and other low-acid foods should always be cooked at a boiling temperature for 15 to 20 minutes before they're tasted or eaten.

GROWING, RAISING, AND FREEZING SOYBEANS

You don't have to raise goats, chickens, cows, or any other livestock to grow your own protein. This essential nutrient can be grown in your garden in the form of green soybeans for eating and freezing.

However, before you go out and plant your own plot of protein, you should be aware that there are two types of soybeans grown in this country: a field variety that's used for livestock fodder, oil, and industrial products; and vegetable soybeans, which are bred for flavor and table use.

THE CHOICES GROW: Years ago the few catalogs that included soybean seed usually labeled the legumes as "novelty" vegetables. Recently, though, many cooks have discovered (as the Chinese did over 2,000 years ago) the value of these nutritious beans as people-food, and most seed companies offer a number of varieties listed under "vegetable" or "edible" soybeans.

When you're ready to select the type of soybean you want to plant, keep in mind that the crop will require an average of three months of warm weather to mature. Therefore, if you live in a cold climate, you should seek out an early-ripening breed. The seed catalogs usually give pretty accurate tips on which soybean varieties grow best in given areas of the country.

Face the fact that frosts sometimes occur sooner than expected, and plant two or three soy varieties "just in case." The precaution may not always be a necessary one, as all your crops may ripen before winter sets in. On the other hand, by growing a number of different types, you'll be sure that your beans don't all mature at the same time, which allows you to put them up in smaller batches.

PLANT THEM PROPERLY: Plan to purchase one pound of seed for every 150 feet of garden row, and at the same time, buy nitrogen-fixing bacteria (also called a "seed inoculant") to help them along. Some inoculants will specify that they should be used for soybeans, while other mixtures are designed to aid the growth of any one of several kinds of legumes. The proper bacteria, when present in the soil, will help the beans absorb nitrogen from the air and store it in their root nodules. This process not only aids plant growth and bean production, but it also improves the soil's fertility.

In order to get an early start on your crop, sow the seed as soon after the last expected frost as possible. (Soybeans are somewhat hardier than snap beans and can be planted a week earlier.)

Although the nutrient-packed vegetables will grow in any ordinary nonacid soil, the plot should be thoroughly cultivated. If the ground is already well-nourished, don't fertilize it further, because too many nutrients can actually retard the growth of soybeans. If, however, the area hasn't been enriched in the past, the addition of organic matter such as well-rotted manure or compost will improve the yield.

Just before planting time, dampen the bean seeds with water and mix in the nitrogen-fixing bacteria. Then place the seeds 1-1/2 inches deep in rows two feet apart. Later thin the seedlings, which will grow very much like bush snap beans, to four inches apart.

RABBITS AND WEEDS: Few crop failures are due to the choice of variety, but there are other reasons that a soy crop may not thrive.

This otherwise remarkably pest-free vegetation does have some mortal foes: rabbits! The ravenous little beasts will eat an emerging crop before you even realize what is happening. Erecting a temporary fence around the bean patch before the plants sprout usually discourages raiding rabbits.

Weeds pose another threat to newly sprouted seedlings, choking out a crop that is left untended during this vulnerable stage. Be sure, therefore, to keep the young soybeans weed-free, at least until they're big

Nitrogen is stored in the root nodules of the plant, and the crop is harvested in late summer when the pods are plump and green. After being plucked from the plants, the pods are washed, blanched, and chilled. The beans squeezed from the pods are placed in containers and popped in the freezer.

enough to stand on their own and shade out the competition. From then on, they'll grow quite nicely with very little attention from you.

PUTTING THEM UP: If you plan to use the soybeans green and freeze them, they'll be ready to harvest when the pods become plump in late summer. Don't put off the picking and processing task, though, because the pods and plants turn from bright green to yellow in only a few days. Once that change occurs, your beans will be too mature to freeze.

One of the easiest ways to harvest soybeans is simply to pull the plants up or to cut them off with pruning shears at ground level, depending on how easy it is to get the roots out of your soil. Then you can pick a comfortable spot to do the pod plucking.

When you have a big pan full, wash the pods and blanch them to aid in the removal of the beans. If you don't have a blanching kettle, just fill any large pot with enough hot water to cover the legumes. Bring the liquid to a rolling boil, put in the beans, allow the kettle to return to a full boil, and then blanch the pods for five minutes.

Meanwhile, fill the sink or another large pot with very cold water, and when the boiling time is up, immerse the steaming vegetables in the cold bath. Add more water, if necessary, to cool them completely. Let the pods remain in the chilly soak for another five minutes.

Removing the beans from their hulls is easy: All you

have to do is squeeze the seeds out over a bowl or pan. If youngsters help, they'll probably soon discover that when the pods are squished just right, the beans will shoot a great distance. (A bit of fun at first may help them to accomplish the rest of the job very quickly and efficiently.)

Next, transfer the shelled beans to freezer containers, leaving an inch or so of head room. Then seal, label, and freeze them. Transfer the empty hulls to your compost heap.

Although green soybeans contain only about one-third as much protein as the dried variety, they're still higher in this essential nutrient than any other vegetable, and their succulent, nutlike flavor makes them the most palatable, nutritious, low-starch garden produce available. Besides containing vitamin C, which dried soybeans do not have, the green soybeans are also richer in vitamin A.

The tasty legumes are ideal for use as a meat extender. It's possible to use less meat by adding soybeans to recipes for soups, stews, and sauces, and the same technique can be employed when preparing hamburgers, meat loaf, and almost any casserole that calls for ground meat. The remarkable vegetable has a distinctive taste and can also be used as a side dish all by itself.

It's good to know that livestock animals, game, and supermarket meat counters aren't the only repositories of protein-rich foods. You can stock up on inexpensive, quality protein from your garden by raising and freezing soybeans.

WHAT TO DO WHEN YOUR FREEZER FAILS

Freezing is one of the best methods available to preserve edibles, particularly if food quality and convenience in preparation for storage are of primary importance. Unfortunately, however, the process does force you to rely upon a fallible electrical appliance. You can almost bank on the fact that sometime, somehow—probably through no fault of your own—that freezer is going to stop cooling, usually giving you little or no notice.

Spring storms, for example, sometimes knock out electrical power to entire neighborhoods for days at a time. The appliance itself may develop a problem, or a household pet could accidentally unplug it. But no matter how the malfunction occurs, there are a number of reliable ways to prevent food spoilage until the problem is solved.

RULES TO REMEMBER: The first thing NOT to do when your freezer fails is open the door to check on the food! Little, if any, thawing will take place during the first 12 hours, provided the temperature within had been set at or near 0°F. An unopened, *fully loaded* freezer can actually keep food safe for up to two days without electricity, while a partially loaded chest will be effective for up to one day. The moral is *keep your freezer full*, even if you have to use plastic gallon jugs filled with water to take up the empty spaces. Other rules of thumb: The colder the food at the time of the mishap, the longer and better it will keep, and the larger the freezer capacity, the longer the food will stay frozen. Also, properly packaged freezer food will thaw more slowly than will carelessly wrapped goods.

So if you're reasonably certain your electrical power will resume within 24 hours—or if you've replugged the freezer and scolded the puppy (in this case, you may have to open the appliance to determine how long ago Fido tripped over that cord)—it's probably best to leave your frozen edibles alone. But should it appear that the device will be out of service for longer than a day, it's wise to try to move your goods to a friend's freezer—or to a rental cold-storage locker—for the duration of the power loss, because even a large, fully loaded freezer just might not be able to recover and refreeze the huge quantities of food it contains before spoilage starts to set in. If you do move your frozen edibles to another location, remember to insulate them well for the journey by wrapping the items in several thicknesses of newspapers and blankets.

If you don't have any convenient way to move your food, try purchasing some dry ice instead. Twenty-five pounds will maintain a ten-cubic-foot freezer for two to three days. To determine the amount of ice necessary to keep your freezer cold, just multiply the cubic-foot capacity of your appliance by 2.5.

You can locate sources of dry ice by consulting the yellow pages of your phone directory. Outlets may be listed under ice cream manufacturers and refrigeration suppliers, or you might try firms that sell compressed gas. Local dairies, fish markets, or electric utility companies may also be of assistance in locating a source.

Remember always to wear heavy gloves or use tongs when handling dry ice to minimize the risk of being "burned" by the substance. Also, be certain the area around your freezer has adequate ventilation during the loading process, because the thawing ice gives off tremendous amounts of carbon dioxide. Place the blocks of dry ice (*always* on a heavy piece of cardboard) directly over the food, since cold air moves downward, and then close the door. If your freezer is only partially full, move all the food containers and packages close together.

MELTDOWN: Let's suppose the worst has happened. You unsuspectingly open the freezer door one day and discover that all the packages inside are well on their way to being completely defrosted. What do you do? First, check the foods to see if any still contain ice crystals. Those that do are safe to eat, and many of them can be refrozen. *Cold* foods, even if no ice crystals are present, can also be considered safe but must be cooked before being returned to the freezer. It's important to remember that refrozen foods, or frozen cooked foods, need to be used as quickly as possible to guarantee maximum nutritional quality. A mushy texture can result if the foods are kept too long.

Never refreeze thawed vegetables (they may contain botulism spores, which would have ample time to grow and reproduce during the time it takes to refreeze), casserole dishes that contain meat, fish, or poultry, or melted ice cream. Naturally, you should always use good judgment and toss out *any* food that looks or smells even a little suspicious.

Breads, rolls, unfrosted cakes, and highly acidic fruits can usually be used after thawing, even if they have remained at room temperature for quite some time. Though flavor and texture may suffer, the safety risk isn't great. Items made with fruits, such as pies or juice concentrates, and other sweets such as ice cream or sherbet, are questionable, however.

Finally, carefully read the accompanying chart and use it to help you determine how to handle specific categories of edibles. Remember, if there's any doubt, throw it out. No food, no matter how much time you spent growing and preserving it, is worth the risk of poisoning yourself or someone else. While it's disheartening to discard the products of your labor, sometimes it's the only safe practice.

IS IT SAFE TO REFREEZE?	Partially thawed, but still firm to the touch	Still cold (less than 40°F) with some ice crystals still present	Completely thawed and warmed to room temperature for less than 3 hours	Completely thawed and warmed to room temperature for a prolonged or unknown time
Breads, rolls, unfrosted cakes	Yes	Yes	Yes ... but they'll dry out some	Yes ... but they'll dry out some
Fruits	Yes	Yes	Yes ... but some flavor and texture will be lost	Yes ... if fruits are highly acidic (discard others)
Fruit pies	Yes	Yes	Yes ... but best to use at once	Questionable ... safer to discard
Fruit juice concentrates	Yes	Yes	Yes ... but reconstituted juice will probably separate and have poor flavor	No ... discard (fermentation may cause cans to explode)
Garden vegetables	Yes	Questionable ... some loss in quality if refrozen	No ... serve immediately, or cook and refreeze	No ... discard
Prepared vegetables, packaged dinners, etc.	Yes	Questionable ... consult package directions	No ... discard	No ... discard
Meat (beef and pork)	Yes	Yes	No ... cook thoroughly, then serve or refreeze	No ... cook unless there's "off" color or odor (in which case, destroy)
Variety meats (liver, kidney, heart, etc.)	Yes	No ... but safe to refrigerate	No ... cook and serve immediately	No ... discard
Poultry	Yes	Yes	No ... unless fully cooked before refreezing	No ... cook and serve unless there's "off" color or odor (in which case, destroy)
Fish	Yes	Questionable ... better to cook and serve	No ... but usable unless color or odor is "suspicious"	No ... discard
Shellfish, seafood	Yes	No ... but safe to refrigerate	No ... cook and serve if appearance and odor are "normal"	No ... discard
Soups	Yes	Yes ... unless they contain meat, fish, or poultry	No ... discard	No ... discard
Ice Cream, sherbet	Yes	No ... but safe to eat immediately	No ... discard	No ... discard
Casseroles, stews, and other precooked meals	Yes	Yes ... unless they contain meat, fish, or poultry	No ... but safe to eat if thoroughly heated	No ... discard

DRY YOUR FRUITS AND VEGETABLES AT HOME

Dehydration as a method of food preservation has been around a long time. Primitive man dried victuals by the heat of the sun or with the aid of fire and then ground the stores into a long-lasting powder. Now, thousands of years later, dehydration is still one of the most widely used methods of food preservation in the world, and there are good reasons:

[1] Drying retains the vitamin, mineral, protein, and fiber content of foods more successfully than can preservation techniques that expose the viands to great changes in temperature.

[2] Dehydrated foodstuffs often are actually more flavorful than the original, undried food. Frozen and canned edibles, on the other hand, are usually less tasty than their fresh or dried equivalents.

[3] It costs little or nothing to dry foods, whereas both freezing and canning require a potentially large initial investment in equipment.

[4] Dried goods can be stored in a smaller space than either frozen, canned, or fresh foods. (For instance, 20 pounds of tomatoes, when canned, will fill 11 one-quart jars. When dried, the same quantity of tomatoes weighs a little more than a pound and occupies a single No. 10 can.)

[5] Dried foods that are kept dry remain edible almost indefinitely.

By buying fruits and vegetables in bulk at low, in-season prices, you can enjoy your favorites year-round, in season or out, for just a fraction of what you'd pay by buying them throughout the year whenever the mood strikes.

HOW TO GET STARTED: If you want to dehydrate foods quickly and if you don't mind warming up the kitchen, you can dry your fruits and vegetables in the oven. This method, however, has the disadvantage of usually causing a greater change in the color, flavor, and vitamin content of foods than does open-air drying.

A better, though more time-consuming, way to dehydrate foods is to use a cabinet-type food dryer or to rely on the sun alone to do the job. Sun-drying requires little in the way of equipment: just a couple of tables that can be set up outside, some cookie sheets, aluminum foil, or butcher paper on which to dry the edibles, and a protective netting to keep insects off the food.

There's nothing complicated about preparing victuals for drying. The key things to remember are: [1] The food should be clean and ripe. (Don't expect green or overripe fruit to taste anything but green or overripe after it's been dried.) [2] Juicy items should be cut up before they're dehydrated. [3] The individual pieces of food must be arranged on the tray or table in such a way that air can circulate freely around them. If you crowd the pieces together, mold can quickly ruin the entire batch.

HERBS DRY WELL: Edible herbs have to be among everyone's favorite dryable foodstuffs. There's something invigorating about going out on a spring morning after the dew has dried to harvest nettles, comfrey, mint, and lemon balm. After bringing them inside, wash them lightly and blot the pickings on a towel before putting them out to dry. You rarely need a food dehydrator to dry herbs: All you have to do is tie the plants in bundles and hang them in a dry place (such as the attic) for a few days. When the herbs are crackling-dry, they can be crushed and put into jars or freezer bags and stored in a dark place. The seasonings can then be used in teas, or ground fine and added to soups, stews, or other dishes.

FRUITS ARE NATURALS FOR DRYING: Virtually any kind of fresh fruit can be dehydrated satisfactorily. Pineapples and bananas, which can be bought year-round, are particularly good when dried, especially if they've been purchased in a very ripe condition and cut into thick chunks before being processed. These fruits—in their desiccated state—have a sweetness and a delightful chewiness that are hard to beat.

Few things are more fun to dry than the seasonal fruits: cherries (sour and sweet), peaches, apricots, apples, pears, and plums. It's a very satisfying feeling to have a year's supply of these delicacies in storage and to know that you didn't have to spend hours scalding, packing, and canning the fruit to get that supply.

Stone fruits—apricots, peaches, and plums, for example—need only be sliced in half and pitted prior to drying; no peeling is necessary. (Hint: The dehydrating goes a little faster if you turn each fruit half inside out by pressing on the skin side with your thumb.)

To dry pears, quarter the fruits and place them on the rack, skin side down. The same goes for apples, which you can also slice into rings, if you prefer. Coring is optional. Apples will turn brown (due to oxidation) when dried, but the color change doesn't affect the flavor.

To make your own raisins, simply pull seedless grapes from bunches and spread them out on the drying tray or table.

All of the above fruits should be "hard dried"; that is, they should contain no moist spots when done. Bacteria and mold can grow only where there's water. Hard-dried fruits can be softened by soaking them in water or juice before they're eaten, or they can be left lying out in the kitchen for a while to be softened naturally by al-

lowing them to absorb some moisture from the air.

One of the most satisfying things you can do with your fresh fruit (or with softened dry fruit) is to make fruit leathers. These snacks sell for nearly a dollar a roll at the grocery store, but you can produce them for pennies at home. To make your own leather, [1] cut one or more kinds of fruit into chunks, [2] throw the pieces into the blender, [3] blend until smooth, and [4] pour the puree out onto plastic wrap or wax paper to dry. (Note: As the sheet of pulp dries, it'll begin to curl up, so tape the corners of the "carrier sheet" down or put pennies on each corner to hold the plastic or wax paper flat.)

If the fruit is extra-juicy (as is the case, for instance, with most berries), you may want to add apple chunks, which are high in pectin, to the puree while it's still in the blender. This will stiffen up the leather. (Or you can use one tablespoon of ground flaxseed for each cup of blended fruit.) For added fun, try stirring small seeds or chopped nuts into the fruit blend before you dehydrate it.

When your leather is finally dry, peel the plastic or wax paper off its back, roll the sheet of pulp into a "scroll," and rewrap the scroll in the plastic wrap or wax paper to keep for future use.

YOU CAN ALSO DRY VEGETABLES: In addition to fruits, many kinds of vegetables—including beans, peas, peppers, beets, carrots, turnips, potatoes, yams, onions, squash, and cereal grains—can be dehydrated. Corn can be dried on the cob (after which the kernels come off easily). Even the corn's silk can be powdered and added to soups for seasoning. Dried onion and leek tops, likewise, make fine condiments for use in soups and salads. Zucchini and cucumber slices can be dehydrated to make delightfully good-tasting chips suitable for dipping.

Many vegetable parts that aren't normally used—stems, tops, roots (in some cases), and blossoms—can be dried and later added to soups, stews, sauces, and broths, or the parts can be ground into powder and blended with cheese to make delicious spreads.

DRIED FOODS WILL KEEP FOR YEARS: Regardless of what you decide to dehydrate, remember that dried foods keep safely only as long as they remain dry. This means you should always store your dried goods in airtight containers (plastic bags or glass jars are best), away from bright light. If you follow this precaution, your dehydrated foods should remain dry and edible for many years.

GIVE DRYING A TRY: Drying foods at home can be a source of much joy and satisfaction, and it's a time-tested way to [1] cut your yearly food bill, [2] free up valuable cupboard and freezer space, and [3] enjoy a greater variety of more flavorful foods. This simple preservation method can be a boon to your health and your finances.

ECONOMICAL STORAGE IN A ROOT CELLAR

A man-made cave dug into a hill and sealed shut with thick double doors: That's a root cellar, and it's a refrigerator in spring and summer and a freeze-proof pantry in fall and winter.

Not long ago, just about every family living in the world's colder climes had one of these harvest keepers. Nestled in the earth, away from the heat of the kitchen, a root cellar maintained a temperature just above freezing, and throughout the winter it provided a practical storage bin for root crops, apples, meats, cabbages, and other goods.

Of course, the heyday of the home root cellar ended a good while ago. When folks gained access to refrigerators and supermarkets, underground food storage seemed rather unnecessary and in most areas was abandoned.

With the revival of interest in practical, inexpensive ways of putting up food, more and more people are rediscovering the wisdom of constructing a place to store unprocessed, homegrown edibles. Even though building a cellar requires a fair investment in labor and materials, the finished shelter usually requires no operating energy and demands no maintenance beyond periodic cleaning.

A do-it-yourselfer in Three Lakes, Wisconsin, built the root cellar shown in the accompanying photo. The 8' X 8' X 20' cavern was excavated with a backhoe.

The bottom of the cellar was lined with sand for drainage purposes. In building the walls, though, the builder laid a concrete base that had an upwardly protruding inner lip. The L-shaped foundation would both support the weight of the cedar log walls and brace the base of those rounds against the tons of sideways "cave-in" pressure inherent in an earth-banked structure.

Every cedar log was peeled and then cut square (on each of two opposing sides) in order to make sure that the vertically stacked timbers would all fit snugly in place. The ceiling cedars were notched where they rested atop the wall logs so that—like the concrete base lip—the horizontal beams could help brace the sides.

Double doors, which were separated by an air space to keep out the cold, sealed off the front of the root cellar. An acetylene torch was used to cut the rustic-looking hinges and hasp shown in the photo. The storage house is also wired for electricity. When especially cold nights bring temperatures as low as 40° below zero, the cellar's incandescent light warms up the inside temperature a few degrees, insuring that the cached food doesn't freeze.

With the assistance of this "emergency" heater, the finished root cellar stays a few degrees above the ice-up point throughout the entire Wisconsin winter, and it maintains an even temperature during warm March thaws, when mourning cloak butterflies migrate over gray snow, or through sudden, stark May blizzards. Around midsummer the earth-sheltered space warms up to about 55°, but winter-stored crops are gone by then, and there are fresh vegetables in the garden.

A root cellar will eventually pay for itself by allowing its owner to store up food that is either homegrown or practically free for the picking at harvesttime. Here is just one example of economical food hoarding: If you gather five or ten bushels of unblemished apples late in the growing season (when they'd otherwise only fall and rot on the ground), the inexpensive edibles will keep for months in the cellar and provide you with a winter's worth of fresh fruit for eating, cooking, and making juice.

A root cellar is also a good place for storing your game, smoked meats, and cheeses. Such shelters offer complete protection from mice, raccoons, and other pests. The wife of the builder of this cellar uses it to store the huge potted ivies which decorate her patio in the warmer months but cannot live through Wisconsin winters. The crop holders are useful in summer, too, for storing wine, live fish bait, and other items that profit from a cool, protected environment.

All in all, it's plain to see that people who want the independence of being able to eat their own fresh, home-stored food should learn the deep, dark secret of building a root cellar.

CROSS SECTION OF THE ROOT CELLAR

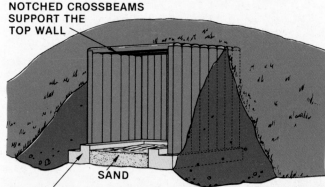

NOTCHED CROSSBEAMS SUPPORT THE TOP WALL

SAND

CONCRETE STRIPS SUPPORT THE WALLS AT THEIR BASES

FORAGING

PICKING WHEN THE TIME IS RIGHT

You can take to the countryside in late April or early May, even as far north as Idaho, and expect to find wild greens in abundance. Imagine foraging copious quantities of miner's lettuce, watercress, yellow monkey flower, spearmint, dogtooth violet, wild hyacinth, plantain, salsify, burdock, and other delicious free fare. Some of the tastiest, most nutritious vegetables and herbs in the entire plant world are yours for the taking when you know where to find them and when to harvest them.

WATERLEAF: AN UNCOMMONLY GOOD FIND: One of the more abundant springtime "volunteer vegetables" is waterleaf (*Hydrophyllum capitatum*), a delicate, leafy herb that grows in moist, rich, shaded soils throughout the West at elevations ranging from sea level to 9,000 feet. (Two related species — *H. canadense* and *H. virginianum*—thrive in the northeastern United States, where the plants are sometimes called "John's cabbage.")

The nice thing about waterleaf is that the roots, stems, blossoms (when young), and leaves are all edible. The stems, in particular, are especially delightful, either in salads or pickled. Even after the plant's purplish flowers, each of which resembles a cat's paw, have appeared and the leaves are old, there's usually no bitter taste.

Try steaming enough of this plant's leaves and stems to make two cups of cooked greens. Then for ten minutes simmer together one tablespoon each of vegetable oil and honey, the juice of half a lemon, two tablespoons of cider vinegar, two unpeeled, chopped or sliced green apples, and one teaspoon of mace or allspice. Combine the steamed greens with the hot, seasoned, cooked apples and serve the resulting "Sweet and Sour Waterleaf" as a delightful meal for two.

NETTLES FOR NUTRITION: Offhand, you wouldn't think that the common stinging nettle with its thousands of bothersome needle-sharp hairs would be a good potherb, but it is.

When less than a foot tall, the stinging nettle (*Urtica dioica*) is a delicious and nutritious spinach substitute. Its heart-shaped leaves are packed with protein, iron, vitamin A, and ascorbic acid.

Few plants, wild or otherwise, are as versatile as the weedlike nettle. Europeans have valued the spiny herb as a source of textile fibers for centuries. When dried to destroy the many stinging hairs, nettles make an excellent livestock feed, and when the cows and chickens are done with it, the plant returns to the ground as a nutrient-rich organic fertilizer. The dried greens also can be used to make tea.

You'll want to harvest nettles as you would prickly pears—that is, armed with heavy gloves, a pair of scissors, and a paper bag in which to carry the plant's tender tops. Once the foliage has been dried or boiled, it is safe to handle and to eat.

Nettle roots are edible, too, although they tend to be a bit fibrous. Chop and cook the roots, strain them to remove their fibers, and then for an unusually savory soup, combine them with onions and milk, heat, and season to taste.

Nettles have a mild taste, and you may wish to combine them with more flavorful wild edibles such as older dandelions, dock, or plantains. Some cooks like to add onion tops and bulbs, Indian celery, sweet and hot peppers, and watercress to fresh nettles, cook everything in a small amount of water, and purée the mixture in a blender to create a creamy soup.

If you get a chance, try making some nettle rennet, too: Just dissolve two cups of salt in three cups of strong nettle tea. A teaspoon of the resulting liquid, when added to a pint of lukewarm milk, will set it just as well as store-bought rennet does.

The next time you see a nettle plant in your backyard, don't curse it . . . cook it! You'll be delighted with the results.

MINER'S LETTUCE: Miner's lettuce (*Montia perfoliata*) was a favorite of the vegetable-starved forty-niners. It's one of the most plentiful wild edibles in the western United States and is easily recognized. It's also one of the few native American plants that have been introduced into Europe, where it's known as winter purslane.

Miner's lettuce grows in moist, rich soils in forests, along streams, and at the bases of cliffs. You'll recognize the plant by its distinctive saucer-shaped leaves, which have the appearance of having been stabbed through the center by their supporting stem. At its tip, the stem bears one or more small, five-petaled flowers which are usually white, but occasionally pinkish.

The succulent, vitamin C–rich leaves and stems of miner's lettuce are delicious on sandwiches, and some say they are far superior to store-bought lettuce. Combined with watercress or other cresses, wild onions, and Indian celery, they make a delicious wilted salad, too. The greens are also good cooked, as are the plant's roots. When puréed they form the basis for a unique creamed soup.

WONDERFUL WATERCRESS: Connoisseurs who savor the peppery taste of watercress (*Nasturtium officinale*) say they'd gladly trade any domestic variety of lettuce for this spicy member of the mustard family.

Watercress is naturally tolerant of cold weather, which means that the herb may be harvested year-round in many parts of the United States. (Watercress sometimes is found in protected streams in midwinter.) Thus, you should have no trouble locating successive crops of young plants. Even the older, flowering specimens, which can be quite peppery, are worth eating, seed pods and all.

Identifying watercress is no problem, especially if you're at all familiar with the high-priced version sold in supermarkets. Look for a prostrate, floating plant with masses of glossy, rounded leaves and numerous threadlike roots in slow-moving rivers and streams, or moist, seepy places. Pick the leaves, complete with small stems, but leave the roots in place to generate more of the tangy greens.

When you do find a colony of wild watercress, make sure that the water in which the plants are growing isn't polluted. If you're uncertain whether or not the water is tainted, you can sterilize the cress by first soaking it for half an hour in halazone-treated water, then rinsing the leaves twice in clean water. (Halazone is available in most drugstores and sporting goods outlets. Follow the label directions.)

Many folks think of watercress as strictly a salad vegetable, especially when wilted in hot oil with sorrels, dock, miner's lettuce, purslane, dandelions, and other greens, but the plant is also delicious when served in other ways: on sandwiches, for instance, or boiled, or in soups.

A number of other cresses—winter, spring, alpine, mountain, and upland, to name a few—can be found in fields, on hillsides, and along roads and riverbanks throughout much of the United States. These species grow in more arid habitats and aren't as succulent as watercress.

WILD LETTUCE: Many natural foods experts speak glowingly of the dozen or so species of wild lettuce, all of which—like domesticated lettuce varieties—fall under the genus *Lactuca*. Try some of these greens yourself, and you'll know why.

The two most common species of wild lettuce are *L. canadensis* (also called horseweed or tall lettuce) and *L. scariola* (variously known as prickly lettuce, compass plant, and wild opium). Both of these relatives of the sunflower can grow to a height of seven feet, both contain milky sap, and both are widely cursed as weeds.

Unlike cultivated lettuces, wild lettuce (regardless of species) becomes tough and bitter within a fairly short time, and the weedlike herbs should be harvested well before they reach maturity. Pick as much of the young plant as you can find; the leaves can be frozen for future use.

When harvested early, wild lettuce tastes like a zippier version of regular lettuce, and it's good in salads. The leaves, which have a slightly acrid taste, cook well in combination with milder potherbs, such as nettles, lamb's-quarters, and young dock.

SOW THISTLE: Another lettucelike wild edible that belongs to the sunflower family is the sow thistle (*Sonchus asper*). You'll find this prickly plant growing almost anyplace where wild lettuce thrives—along roadsides and streams, in meadows and vacant lots, and in similar weedy habitats.

BRACKEN FERNS: In contrast to many other types of ferns that thrive only in damp, shaded areas and aren't very palatable, the bracken fern (*Pteridium aquilinum*) grows in open habitats and is edible when young and tender.

Throughout the spring months, these coarse, hairy, black-rooted ferns send up shoots that are commonly called fiddleheads because of their resemblance to the tuning end of a violin. The nascent leaf structures are considered a delicacy in New Zealand, parts of Europe, and Japan, but they remain largely unappreciated in the United States, except by certain Indian tribes.

Bracken ferns have gained a reputation in some circles as being poisonous, and livestock have, in fact, been known to suffer ill effects after eating large quantities of the plant. Only the old plants are toxic, however; the tender fronds (fiddleheads) of young, six- to eight-inch-tall plants are completely harmless.

While raw fiddleheads are quite good in salads, you may prefer to cook them; when raw, the tips tend to be chewy. A popular way of preparing the fronds is to dip them in an egg batter and bread crumbs and fry them lightly. Fiddleheads also make a savory addition to casseroles, especially if the dish in question contains hyacinth bulbs, dogtooth violets, and other wild, foraged vegetables and herbs.

You'll also find that fiddleheads complement the flavor of cheese extremely well, and that the juice extracted from them can be used to thicken soups.

HARVESTTIME: With winter barely past, you can pick waterleaf, stinging nettle, miner's lettuce, watercress, horseweed, wild opium, sow thistle, and bracken ferns. Later there will be such palatable wild edibles as curly dock, lamb's-quarters, sheep sorrel, wood sorrel, purslane, green amaranth, burdock, fireweed, mustard, and plantain. So what are you waiting for? Grab your gloves, pick up the shears, and head for the hills. Wild greens are ready to be harvested.

NUTRITIONAL VALUE OF FORAGED EDIBLES

Because of the skyrocketing prices and questionable nutritional value of many commercially available foods, a multitude of Americans not only employ organic gardening as an alternative source of wholesome edibles, but they also supplement their homegrown diets with free-for-the-finding wild foods.

Although most foragers have assumed all along that the gratuitous fare—free of additives and genetically unchanged—is naturally wholesome, the increased public interest in wild food plants has created a demand for some hard facts on how nutritious these edibles are.

While many wild plants contain substantial amounts of nutrients and do not contain the additives usually found in supermarket fare, the untamed edibles can absorb toxic chemicals from the soil, the air, and water. Anyone foraging for food, then, should be careful where they pick. Plants along the roadside, for instance, can absorb pollutants from vehicle exhaust, and there is no telling what chemicals might exist in plants growing over a landfill or downstream from an industrial facility. Agricultural sprays can also land on and taint wild edibles.

JUST HOW GOOD THEY ARE: Having taught courses in foraging for some years, Robert Shosteck had been challenged many times with the query, "How do you know this plant is nutritious?" In most cases, he could only quote the author of a book on wild foods as his source. As often as not, this writer referred to the work of an earlier writer who may well have based his statements on folklore.

This lack of solid data led Shosteck to work up a systematic collection of all available scientific research on the subject and then to compare each particular wild edible with the Recommended Daily Allowance (RDA) established by the National Academy of Sciences' Food and Nutrition Board. The RDA represents the absolute minimum requirement for nutrients needed by normal, healthy people.

A typical male adult, for example, needs 5,000 I.U. (International Units) of vitamin A per day, and he can get much more than that in only half a cup of cooked dandelion greens! Or take that bane-of-the-farmers, amaranth: Just 10 ounces of the leaves or tips of this prolific plant can provide an adult's daily calcium needs plus almost all the iron requirement of men and half that of women, while only 3.5 ounces of the greens will meet the daily needs for vitamin A, thiamine, and ascorbic acid.

You see, then, that you can assure yourself of a well-balanced diet by combining produce from your garden with wild edibles in season. Beyond that you can freeze, dry, can, or pickle many of your surplus foraged foods for use later in the year.

TABLE TALK: The blank spaces in the accompanying chart—"The Nutritional Composition of Wild Food Plants"—indicate that an edible has not yet been analyzed for those particular food elements. Some variation from the figures given can be expected with differences in climate, soil conditions, and time of harvest. Similarly, where "spp." is noted beside the genus, it's an indication that more than one species in the genus is edible, so some differences can be expected among species. Usually, however, such variations are small and don't affect the food's overall nutritional quality. Included in the table also are a number of fruits, berries, and field crops which are actually cultivated varieties that can often be found in the wild.

CAUTION: The listing of a plant in this article doesn't necessarily mean that it's edible under all circumstances. People should inform themselves fully by consulting a good field guide as to any wild food's safety before consuming it, since frequently a plant may be poisonous at one stage in its development and edible at another, or—as with domestic rhubarb and potatoes—one part of the plant may be edible, while other sections are poisonous.

In order to get some overview of the various nutrients covered in the list, a highlighted sampling of plants and nutritional categories is in order. First are the foods that provide the most calories. Most folks have no trouble consuming enough starches, sugars, and fats for their energy needs (on the contrary, such elements are in oversupply in the average North American's diet), but among the wild edibles, only nuts, seeds, tubers, and a few fruits provide such "energy to burn" in significant amounts. Most wild foods have less than a gram of fat per 100 grams, and they're often low in carbohydrates as well, usually containing only several grams. This means that you can fill up on many wildings without putting on weight.

Most people also get enough protein in their diets from meat, poultry, fish, and dairy products. However, if you're a vegetarian or want to supply part of your minimum daily need (50 grams of protein) from vegetable sources, the following plants will provide five or more grams of protein for each 100 grams (about 3-1/4 ounces) consumed:

Soybean	35.1
Sunflower seed	24.0
Butternut	23.7

Black walnut	20.5
Beechnut	19.4
Wild rice	14.1
Hickory nut	13.2
Filbert	12.6
Garlic	6.2
Alfalfa	6.0
Nettle	5.5
Pawpaw	5.2
Mugwort	5.2

NATURE'S NUTRIENTS: Wild foods can also play an important role in satisfying your body's daily vitamin and mineral requirements. For example, the average person needs a minimum of 800 to 1,200 milligrams (mg) of calcium, the body's most abundant mineral, every day. Here's how a few wild plants stack up in comparison with milk (the most commonly mentioned, and a highly touted, calcium source) in milligrams per 100 grams of food:

Lamb's-quarters	309
Mexican tea	304
Rape	252
Mallow	249
Galinsoga	245
Soybean (dry)	226
Dayflower	210
Filbert	209
Shepherd's purse	208
Mint	194
Dandelion	187
Watercress	151
Knotweed	150
Water primrose	144
Milk	118

Iron is usually obtained from meats, shellfish, and whole grains. Adult males need 10 mg of this mineral daily; females, 18 mg.; and children, 15 mg. Here's a sampling of wild foods and the amounts of iron they offer per 100 grams as compared to beef liver, one of the best supermarket sources:

Primrose-willow	12.7
Mallow	12.7
Soybean	8.5
Water primrose	8.0
Sunflower seed	7.1
Galinsoga	7.1
Butternut	6.8
Black walnut	6.0
Amaranth	5.6
Curled dock	5.6
Alfalfa	5.4
Mexican tea	5.2
Sheep sorrel	5.0

Shepherd's purse	4.8
Fame flower	4.8
Beef liver	8.8

Liver and kidney are among the best "conventional" sources of vitamin A, while deep yellow and dark green vegetables supply carotene, which the body can convert into this important nutrient. Adult males need 5,000 I.U. of vitamin A daily, while females require 4,000 units. The following wild edible plants contain more than either of those I.U. requirements in a 100-gram serving:

Dandelion	14,000
Dock	12,900
Lamb's-quarters	11,600
Peppergrass	9,300
Pokeweed	8,700
Violet leaves	8,200
Storksbill	7,000
Nettle	6,500
Mustard greens	5,800

Three of the B vitamins—thiamine, riboflavin, and niacin—are usually obtained from meat, milk, whole grains, and especially from the organ meats. But since adults require a daily minimum of only 1.25 mg of thiamine, a "standard" serving of many wild foods can help to fill the need for this nutrient. The following plants contain from 0.25 mg to 2.0 mg per 100 grams, and the amount they have is compared to that which beef liver contains:

Sunflower	2.00
Arrowhead	1.60
Pecan	1.00
Pokeweed	0.80
Soybean	0.66
Filbert	0.46
Wild rice	0.45
Lamb's-quarters	0.44
Galinsoga	0.27
Burdock	0.25
Dandelion	0.25
Shepherd's purse	0.25
Beef liver	8.80

BETTER HEALTH FOR FREE: In the past, some people were justifiably skeptical of unsupported allegations regarding the nutritional content of many well-publicized wild foods. However, now that the scientific evidence for more than 80 plants is in (and included in the accompanying chart) there's no reason not to forage a large proportion of your meals. You can eat better, stay healthier (just getting outdoors to find the plants is a good start), and watch your food budget shrink instead of constantly growing!

THE NUTRITIONAL COMPOSITION OF WILD FOOD PLANTS (per 100 grams)

Name	Calories	Protein (grams)	Fat (grams)	Calcium (mg.)	Phosphorus (mg.)	Iron (mg.)	Sodium (mg.)	Potassium (mg.)	Vitamin A (I.U.)	Thiamine (mg.)	Riboflavin (mg.)	Niacin (mg.)	Vitamin C (mg.)
Alfalfa, or Lucerne (*Medicago sativa*)	52	6.0	0.4	12	51	5.4	—	—	3,410	0.13	0.14	0.5	162
Amaranth, or Pigweed (*Amaranthus spp.*)	42	3.7	0.8	313	74	5.6	—	411	1,600	0.05	0.24	1.2	65
Arrowhead, or Duck Potatoes (*Sagittaria spp.*)	107	5.0	0.3	13	165	2.6	—	729	—	1.60	0.40	1.4	5
Asparagus (*Asparagus officinalis*)	20	2.2	0.2	21	50	0.6	1	183	900	0.16	0.18	1.4	26
Bamboo (*Bambusa spp.*)	27	2.6	0.3	13	59	0.5	—	533	20	0.15	0.07	0.6	4
Beechnut, American (*Fagus grandifolia*)	568	19.4	50.0	—	—	—	—	—	—	—	—	—	—
Beggarticks (*Bidens bipinnata*)	33	2.8	0.6	111	39	2.3	—	—	—	—	—	—	—
Blackberry (*Rubus spp.*)	58	1.2	0.9	32	19	0.9	1	170	200	0.03	0.04	0.4	21
Blueberry (*Vaccinium spp.*)	62	0.7	0.5	15	13	1.0	1	81	100	0.03	0.06	0.5	14
Burdock, Great (*Arctium lappa*)	89	2.5	0.1	50	58	1.2	30	180	—	0.25	0.08	0.03	2
Butternut (*Juglans cinerea*)	629	23.7	61.2	—	—	6.8	—	—	—	—	—	—	—
Cherry, Sour Red (*Prunus cerasus*)	58	1.2	0.3	22	19	0.4	2	191	1,000	0.05	0.06	0.4	10
Cherry, Sweet (*Prunus avium*)	48	0.9	0.2	15	13	0.3	1	130	60	0.02	0.02	0.2	3
Chestnut (*Castanea spp.*)	194	2.9	1.5	27	88	1.7	6	454	—	0.22	0.22	0.6	—
Chicory (*Cichorium intybus*)	20	1.8	0.3	86	40	0.9	—	420	4,000	0.06	0.10	0.5	22
Chives (*Allium schoenoprasum*)	27	2.7	0.6	83	41	0.8	—	—	—	0.10	0.06	0.5	32
Chufa, or Yellow Nut Grass (*Cyperus esculentus*)	311	4.4	17.2	59	155	2.4	—	—	—	0.90	—	—	—
Crabapple (*Pyrus spp.*)	68	0.4	0.3	6	13	0.3	1	110	40	0.03	0.02	0.1	8
Cranberry, Large (*Vaccinium macrocarpon*)	46	0.4	0.7	14	10	0.5	2	82	40	0.03	0.02	0.1	11
Currant, Garden Red (*Ribes sativum*)	50	1.4	0.2	32	23	1.0	2	257	120	0.04	0.05	0.1	41
Dandelion (*Taraxacum officinale*)	45	2.7	0.7	187	66	3.1	76	397	14,000	0.19	0.26	—	35
Dayflower (*Commelina spp.*)	43	2.3	0.4	210	52	—	—	—	—	—	—	—	—
Day Lily (*Hemerocallis fulva*)	42	2.0	0.4	87	176	1.2	24	170	3,000	0.16	0.21	0.8	88
Dock (*Rumex spp.*)	28	2.1	0.3	66	41	1.6	5	338	12,900	0.09	0.22	0.5	119
Dock, Curled (*Rumex crispus*)	21	1.5	0.3	74	56	5.6	—	—	1,385	0.06	0.08	0.4	30
Duckweed (*Lemna spp.*)	18	2.1	0.3	142	4	—	—	—	560	0.06	0.13	0.6	5
Elderberry, Common (*Sambucus canadensis*)	72	2.6	0.5	38	28	1.6	—	300	600	0.07	0.06	0.5	36
Fame Flower (*Talinum spp.*)	23	1.9	0.4	90	21	4.8	10	392	1,790	0.09	0.19	0.6	58
Fennel (*Foeniculum vulgare*)	31	2.9	0.5	114	54	2.9	—	338	1,566	0.12	0.15	0.7	34
Filbert, or Hazelnut (*Corylus americana*)	634	12.6	62.4	209	337	3.4	2	704	—	0.46	—	0.9	—
Galinsoga, or Quick Weed (*Galinsoga parviflora*)	42	3.2	0.5	245	45	7.1	—	—	1,120	0.11	0.27	2.1	30
Garlic (*Allium spp.*)	137	6.2	0.2	29	202	1.5	19	529	trace	0.25	0.08	0.5	15
Grape, Concord (*Vitis spp.*)	69	1.3	1.0	16	12	0.4	3	158	100	0.05	0.03	0.3	4
Ground-Cherry, or Husk-Tomato (*Physalis spp.*)	40	1.6	0.5	10	34	0.9	—	—	25	0.90	0.04	2.4	6
Hickory (nuts) (*Carya spp.*)	673	13.2	68.7	trace	360	2.4	—	—	—	—	—	—	—
Honewort, or wild Chervil (*Cryptotaenia spp.*)	18	2.0	0.1	81	45	1.8	7	490	488	0.15	0.20	0.5	60
Horsetail, Common (*Equisetum arvense*)	20	1.0	0.2	58	93	4.4	—	—	180	—	0.07	5.6	50
Jerusalem Artichoke (*Helianthus tuberosus*)	77	2.3	0.1	14	78	3.4	—	—	20	0.20	0.06	1.3	4
Knotweed (*Polygonum spp.*)	64	3.6	0.3	150	46	—	—	—	—	—	—	—	—
Kudzu (roots) (*Pueraria lobata*)	113	2.1	0.1	15	18	0.6	—	—	—	—	—	—	—
Lamb's-Quarters, or Pigweed (*Chenopodium album*)	43	4.2	0.8	309	72	1.2	—	—	11,600	0.16	0.44	1.2	80

Name	Calories	Protein (grams)	Fat (grams)	Calcium (mg.)	Phosphorus (mg.)	Iron (mg.)	Sodium (mg.)	Potassium (mg.)	Vitamin A (I.U.)	Thiamine (mg.)	Riboflavin (mg.)	Niacin (mg.)	Vitamin C (mg.)
Leek, or Ramp (bulbs) (*Allium* spp.)	52	2.2	0.3	52	50	1.1	5	347	40	0.11	0.06	0.5	17
Mallow (*Malva* spp.)	37	4.4	0.6	249	69	12.7	—	—	2,190	0.13	0.20	1.0	35
Mallow, High (*Malva sylvestris*)	28	3.6	1.4	90	42	3.7	—	—	1,989	0.17	0.29	0.5	24
Maple (sugar) (*Acer saccharum*)	348	—	—	143	11	1.4	14	242	—	—	—	—	—
Mexican Tea (*Chenopodium ambrosioides*)	42	3.8	0.7	304	52	5.2	—	—	1,210	0.06	0.28	0.6	11
Milkweed (*Asclepias syriaca*)	—	0.8	0.5	—	—	—	—	—	—	—	—	—	—
Mint (*Mentha* spp.)	32	3.0	0.7	194	48	3.8	2	179	1,296	0.13	0.16	0.7	64
Mugwort, Common (*Artemisia vulgaris*)	35	5.2	0.8	82	40	1.5	—	—	1,284	0.15	0.16	3.0	72
Mulberry, White (*Morus alba*)	53	1.7	0.4	30	32	3.7	37	152	—	0.03	0.06	0.7	5
Mustard (greens) (*Brassica* spp.)	23	2.2	0.4	138	32	1.8	18	220	5,800	0.80	0.14	0.6	48
Nettle, Stinging (*Urtica dioica*)	65	5.5	0.7	—	—	—	—	—	6,500	—	—	—	76
Oak (acorns) (*Quercus* spp.)	48	0.2	0.1	12	314	0.2	—	—	6	0.02	0.40	0.5	0
Pawpaw (*Asimina triloba*)	85	5.2	0.9	—	—	—	—	—	—	—	—	—	—
Pecan (*Carya illinoensis*)	610	11.0	84.0	86	341	0.8	—	712	150	1.00	0.15	1.1	2
Peppergrass (*Lepidium* spp.)	32	2.6	0.7	81	76	1.3	14	606	9,300	0.08	0.26	1.0	69
Persimmon (*Diospyros virginiana*)	127	0.8	0.4	27	26	2.5	1	310	—	—	—	—	66
Pokeweed (spring greens) (*Phytolacca americana*)	23	2.6	0.4	53	44	1.7	—	—	8,700	0.80	0.33	1.2	136
Prickly Pear (*Opuntia humifusa*)	42	0.5	0.1	20	28	0.3	2	166	60	0.10	0.30	0.4	22
Primrose-Willow (*Jussiaea* spp.)	41	3.3	0.4	57	300	12.7	—	—	3,555	0.00	0.01	2.8	3
Purslane (*Portulaca oleracea*)	21	1.7	0.4	103	39	3.5	—	—	2,500	0.03	0.10	0.5	25
Rape, or Field Mustard (*Brassica rapa*)	32	3.6	0.6	252	62	3.0	—	—	1,355	0.12	0.29	1.1	118
Raspberry, Black (*Rubus occidentalis*)	57	1.2	0.5	22	22	0.9	1	168	130	0.03	0.09	0.9	25
Raspberry, Red (*Rubus idaeus*)	73	1.5	1.4	30	22	0.9	1	199	—	0.03	0.09	0.9	18
Rice, Wild (*Zizania aquatica*)	353	14.1	0.7	19	339	4.2	7	220	—	0.45	0.63	6.2	0
Sheep Sorrel (*Rumex acetosella*)	77	1.9	—	55	82	5.0	—	—	—	—	—	—	—
Shepherd's Purse (*Capsella bursa-pastoris*)	33	4.2	0.5	208	86	4.8	—	394	1,554	0.25	0.17	0.4	36
Silverberry (*Eleagnus* spp.)	51	1.3	0.9	7	20	0.4	—	—	12	0.03	0.05	0.4	10
Sow Thistle, Common (*Sonchus oleraceus*)	20	2.4	0.3	93	35	3.1	—	—	2,185	0.70	0.12	0.4	5
Soybean (*Glycine max*)	400	35.1	17.7	226	546	8.5	—	1,504	6	0.66	0.22	2.2	0
Storksbill, or Alfilaria (*Erodium cicutarium*)	—	2.5	—	—	—	—	—	—	7,000	—	—	—	—
Strawberry, Wild (*Fragaria* spp.)	37	0.7	0.5	21	21	1.0	1	164	60	0.03	0.07	0.6	59
Sunflower (seed) (*Helianthus annuus*)	560	24.0	47.3	120	837	7.1	30	920	50	2.00	0.23	5.4	—
Vegetable Oyster, or Salsify (*Tragopogon porrifolius*)	89	1.4	0.2	48	50	1.4	—	—	—	0.04	0.04	0.3	10
Violet (leaves) (*Viola* spp.)	—	—	—	—	—	—	—	—	8,200	—	—	—	210
Walnut, Black (*Juglans nigra*)	628	20.5	59.3	trace	570	6.0	3	460	300	0.22	0.11	0.7	—
Watercress (*Nasturtium officinale*)	19	2.2	0.3	151	54	1.7	52	282	4,900	0.08	0.16	0.9	79
Water Hyacinth (*Eichhornia crassipes*)	30	0.5	0.1	—	—	—	—	—	—	—	—	—	—
Water Primrose (*Jussiaea repens*)	43	2.5	1.0	144	65	8.0	—	—	1,725	0.04	0.12	0.8	87
Water Shield (*Brassenia schreberi*)	10	0.7	0.2	9	23	2.0	—	—	6	0.03	0.03	0.3	0
Wood Sorrel (*Oxalis* spp.)	—	0.9	—	—	—	—	—	—	2,800	—	—	—	—
Yucca (flowers) (*Yucca aloifolia*)	33	3.1	0.2	47	73	0.5	—	—	10	0.14	0.09	0.6	—

PICKING WILD FOODS FROM YOUR GARDEN

Native Americans and pioneers alike picked wild plants from the forests to supplement their diets. And since the renewed interest in natural foods in the early 1960's, an increasing number of people have trekked the woods, seeking everything from Jerusalem artichokes to wild wintergreen. But it's not at all necessary to hike hither and yon to reap a bountiful harvest of volunteer vegetables. The fact is, you need not look any farther than your own yard or garden to find plenty of free-for-the-plucking plants.

It's entirely possible that the wheelbarrow load of "weeds" hoed and pulled from the yard and garden will be full of excellent soup and salad greens rather than just throwaways fit only for the compost pile. It's no accident that many wild plants also bear the name of a common domestic vegetable preceded simply by the word "wild." For instance, the leafy plant known commonly as lamb's-quarters is also called wild spinach.

Chances are, your backyard, lawn, or garden is well stocked with free edibles such as these few common good-to-eat weeds.

LAMB'S-QUARTERS (*Chenopodium album*): Lamb's-quarters—also known as pigweed, goosefoot, and wild spinach—is a relative of spinach and one of the most widely distributed plants on earth. In years gone by, Europeans and native Americans cultivated this leafy annual for its abundant yield of seeds, which contain an average of 16% protein compared to wheat's 14%.

As a green, however, it is delicious and surprisingly nutritious. The uncooked plants are richer in iron, protein, and vitamin B_2 than both raw cabbage and raw spinach.

Mature plants stand from two- to seven-feet tall and can be identified by their jagged-edged, diamond-shaped leaves, the undersides of which are powdered with coarse, whitish particles accounting for the Latin name *album*, or "white." The short leafstalks may be either plain green or reddish-streaked. Both the stems and leaves of young plants are a mealy white.

While only the tender growing tips of mature *Chenopodium album* are mild enough to eat, every part from the ground up is tasty when taken from plants less than a foot tall.

Some folks like to use this green in salads, but it's also excellent cooked as a substitute for spinach and is especially good when creamed. It is also quite tasty when wilted in hot dressing, as follows: Fry one small,

diced onion in 1/2 cup of salad oil. Making sure the oil in the frying pan isn't hot enough to splash, add 1/4 cup of vinegar, 1/4 teaspoon salt, and pepper if desired. Throw in four cups of lamb's-quarters, stir-fry until limp, and serve.

GREEN AMARANTH (*Amaranthus retroflexus*): A milder-tasting relative of lamb's-quarters that can be prepared in the same manner is green amaranth, also known as redroot, wild beet, and (coincidentally) pigweed.

You'll recognize green amaranth by three main fea-

amaranth an odd taste and can cause digestive upsets.

Brief cooking will drive saponin out of the plant's leaves and create a vitamin-rich vegetable side dish that's sure to please. Because the plain, cooked greens have a very delicate flavor, you may wish to serve them with a stronger-tasting vegetable such as curled dock or with cheese sauce.

Boiled, wilted, fried, creamed, or steamed, green amaranth is an uncommonly delicious find.

PURSLANE (*Portulaca oleracea*): If you want a weed you can safely eat raw, try purslane.

A native of southern Asia, purslane is at present widely cultivated throughout Europe and the Orient for use as a salad green and potherb. In America, however, relatively few gardeners have discovered how flavorful and nourishing this small, ground-hugging plant can be.

Although purslane rarely grows taller than two inches, it can, and will, quickly spread its fleshy, reddish-purple stems and paddle-shaped leaves over a large portion of a garden. All aboveground parts of this semisucculent are edible and are rich in iron and calcium. Harvest only the tender, growing tips, though, if you want to keep your purslane productive all summer long.

The leaves or tips add a welcome and slightly acidic flavor to salads. In addition, the foliage is delectable, either boiled, or fried in butter with salt or pepper.

Purslane's texture is somewhat gooey or mucilaginous. If you find this disagreeable, try dipping the plant in a beaten egg, rolling it in a mixture of bread crumbs and flour, and then frying the vegetable until it's brown. The glutinous quality of the leaves is rendered unnoticeable by the procedure. This gooey property makes purslane an excellent substitute for okra in soups, sauces, and almost any recipe calling for a thickener.

CURLED DOCK (*Rumex crispus*): The docks are some of the hardiest, most widespread, most persistent weeds found anywhere. These plants are found practically anywhere you'd expect a weed to grow: alongside streams, roads, and driveways, and in pastures, vacant lots, and gardens.

Of the 15 Rumex species called docks, all are edible. None, however, is as well-known or delicious as curled dock (also called narrow-leaved dock and yellow dock). The plant's name refers to the fact that its slender, lance-shaped leaves, most of which sprout directly from the ground, have wavy edges. Often, these leaves reach two or more feet in length, while the weed's spindly flower stalks grow to four or five feet in height before they bear small, green blossoms.

Curled dock's glossy foliage is unusually flavorful—frequently, and especially if the leaves are more than a foot long, to the point of tasting bitter. There are two ways of dealing with this unpalatable pungency.

The first is to boil the plant through two waters. In other words, place the leaves in cold water in a pan, bring to a boil, and drain the hot water off. Then add more liquid to the container and cook the foliage until

tures: a stout, hairy stem; rough-to-the-touch, pointed oval leaves borne on stalks almost as long as the leaves themselves; and a crimson-colored root. The height of the plant varies, though the mature plant usually grows no more than three feet tall.

While some people suggest ways of preparing raw amaranth leaves, others recommend eating the leaves only after they've been cooked, because of the fact that the foliage contains a substance called saponin. Used commercially as a foaming and emulsifying agent and detergent, saponin imparts to the raw leaves of green

it's tender. By doing this you are pouring some vitamins down the drain, but the steaming-hot greens that remain in the pan are among the best-tasting of all wild, foraged vegetables.

A second effective way to rid dock leaves of their astringency is to cream them. To do this, simply mix a tablespoon of flour with a tablespoon of melted butter in a pan, add two cups of chopped dock leaves and 1/2 cup of milk to the butter and flour paste, and cook, stirring constantly, until the sauce thickens. The result: a gourmet's delight without the bite.

SHEEP SORREL (*Rumex acetosella*): A close relative of curled dock and a frequent inhabitant of neglected gardens is sheep sorrel, also known as sourgrass.

Although the light-green, arrowhead-shaped leaves of sourgrass are a bit acid tasting and shouldn't be eaten in excess, this shouldn't keep you from using small amounts of the foliage to add zest to your salads, soups, and other dishes. Place a few leaves of *acetosella* (literally, "small vinegar plant") in a salad and you can use dressing without vinegar.

The crisp tartness of sheep sorrel makes it a perfect accompaniment to fish. Verify this for yourself by including some chopped sourgrass leaves in your favorite seafood sauce, or the next time you bake a whole, stuffed fish, add a small quantity of sorrel to the stuffing mix.

Sheep sorrel may also be substituted for rhubarb in pie recipes. Just cook the sorrel leaves, combine them with the remaining ingredients, and pour the resulting mixture into a pie shell. Then top with a layer of crust, pop the whole thing into the oven, and bake according to the recipe's directions.

Another sheep sorrel dish, puree, goes back many years. The dateless instructions say to boil three pounds of the leaves until tender, drain them, and press the cooked foliage through a sieve or spin the leaves, with a

little water if needed, in a blender until they're smooth. Then pour the pureed greens into a saucepan containing two tablespoons of butter, and simmer while stirring for ten minutes. Finally, add more butter or milk or cream as desired, and salt and pepper to taste.

WOOD SORREL (*Oxalis acetosella* and other species): This fragile plant, held by some to be a descendant of the original shamrock, grows in shady areas alongside houses and fences. It can be recognized by its familiar triple heart-shaped leaves. Most of the dozen species of *Oxalis* known as wood sorrel bear yellow flowers, though some have white blossoms and others have violet or pink blooms. Regardless of the species, the pointed seedpods of wood sorrel are always good for a refreshing, lemony nibble on a summer day.

Wood sorrel is similar in taste to sheep sorrel; thus, one plant can replace the other in many recipes. However, because the wood sorrel's stem can be stiff and hard to chew even after cooking, you'd be well advised to harvest only the leaves from *Oxalis* species.

You'll find that raw wood sorrel leaves add a delightful flavor to sandwiches, and that the shamrocklike foliage makes a decorative and tasty garnish.

FOOD IS WHERE YOU FIND IT: You can use any of the plants described here alone or mixed as soup greens or the base for a puree. Also, it's no chore to store the wild edibles for year-round use. All you have to do is blanch the greens by placing them in a small amount of boiling water for two minutes, cool the foliage quickly in prechilled water, pack the victuals in airtight containers, and put them in the freezer.

Give the lamb's-quarters or redroot or purslane or curled dock or either of the sorrels described here a try. Add an extra measure of nutrition to your meals and watch your grocery bill go down at the same time. It makes good sense to stop thinking of garden weeds as ornery pests and to begin accepting them for what in many cases they actually are: natural, free foods.

BRITCHES FOR THE BERRY PICKER

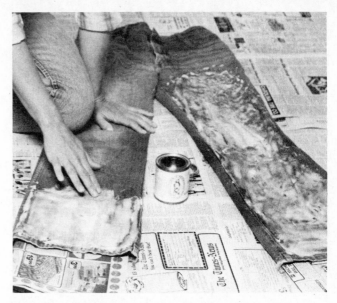

In late summer and early autumn, giant succulent blackberries tantalizingly suspended from thorny canes can lure the most sedate person into a battle with bristly thickets. At the end of such a skirmish, the berry picker usually crawls out of the prickly patch glaring wildly, clutching a hard-earned bucketful of berries, and bemoaning thorn-scarred legs.

Some try to thwart the thorns by donning three pairs of trousers to protect their vulnerable shins, but the weight of so many leggings proves to be almost as unbearable as the prickly thorns. Furthermore, those layers of clothing become particularly uncomfortable in the early morning dew, and few things can take the joy out of woods-roaming more thoroughly than slogging around in three pairs of soggy drawers.

One fortunate berry picker discovered, quite by accident, the solution that now allows her to tramp unscratched through the thickest of blackberry patches. It all started when a pair of her well-worn blue jeans developed a severe tear during an encounter with a barbed wire fence. Rather than sew up the laceration, she temporarily glued a patch over it with some fabric cement. To her amazement, the repair stayed on as if it had been woven into the fabric, and even repeated trips through the washing machine and clothes dryer failed to dislodge the stubborn mend. With some curiosity, she examined the patch and saw that the adhesive had completely penetrated the fabric, making the material both waterproof and extremely tough.

"Aha," she reasoned, "if I coat the front of my jeans with the rubbery substance, I'll have a durable and inexpensive pair of berry-picking pants!" So she applied some more fabric cement to a pair of old dungerees and found to her delight that the covering stood up against the sharpest thorns and even helped keep her dry while she walked through rain-soaked thickets.

Since that first experiment, she has refined the technique that transforms ordinary denims into brush-buster britches. The only items required are an old pair of pants (jeans work best, but any trousers made of a heavy material will do), some newspaper, and a six-ounce bottle of fabric cement. There are several satisfactory brands of the adhesive on the market, and they are sold at most hardware stores, canvas and awning supply shops, and shoe repair services.

To construct your own pair of brush-busters, assemble the materials and spread newspaper over your work surface. (The floor or a wide table will suffice for this operation.) The next step is extremely important: Place several thick folds of newspaper inside the pant legs to prevent the cement from bonding the layers of cloth together. In using any of these exceptionally aggressive bonders, be careful not to spill the fabric cement on the floor or to apply it to any garment you may later wish to restore to its original condition, since the substances simply can't be removed.

After you've readied the jeans, place them zipper side up on your work surface and squirt about one-quarter of a bottle of fabric cement on the front of each leg. You can paint the milky substance onto the cloth with a brush, but the originator of this idea says it's better to spread it with your fingers. The fabric must be evenly coated from the top of the thigh to the hem. After ten minutes or so, the rubbery compound will dry and become transparent.

Coating the seat and the back cuff areas as well as the front is a good idea. This provides adequate "rear guard" protection while still permitting the pants to breathe through the untreated material at the back of the legs.

You'll notice that the coated cloth has a slightly tacky feel to it at first, but this will disappear as the britches are worn. The berry picker who invented these armored jeans has washed them at all temperatures and dried them without harm in an electric clothes dryer, but she recommends that the pants be laundered in warm water and hung out to dry on a clothesline for longer wear. (Fabric treated this way should never be dry cleaned, because the solution used in that process softens the cement.)

Before bearding the elusive blackberry in its thorny lair again, why not earmark an old pair of denims for your own briar-beater britches? For a small investment, you'll have an edge on the wild bounties of summer.

THE BERRIES OF SUMMER

Wild berries! Nothing's as likely to set a mouth to watering and a body to thinking about pies and jams and jellies and other such excruciatingly delicious treats. And there's no better time than midsummer for gathering nature's fruits from fields and forests, roadsides and city streets, meadows and open slopes. The berries you see here are only a small sampling of the myriad types and varieties that can be found in virtually any corner of North America, and you shouldn't have much trouble locating at least one tasty species within a few miles of your own backdoor. When you do, try your best to get as many of the bite-size morsels past your mouth and into a collecting bucket as you can (a formidable test of willpower, to be sure), and remember to return later to the same spot if you see any flowers of fruit yet to come. By carefully observing where and when each variety in your region ripens, you may well be able to go berrying from late spring until the first few weeks of fall!

BLACKBERRIES: Blackberries are the forager's delight and the eternal bane of botanists, who thus far have only been able to pin down the number of individual species to "somewhere between 50 and 390." True blackberries are borne on thorny upright canes (as opposed to trailing vines) and can be found throughout most of the continent, including even Arctic regions, along roadsides and hedgerows and in abandoned meadows. Rich in vitamins A and C, the fruit—which is preceded by large white flowers in early spring—can usually be harvested from late June to early August and beyond. Pick the berries when they're really sweet (one or two days after they've turned black).

CRANBERRIES: The American cranberry (*Vaccinium macrocarpon*) thrives in peaty bogs and similarly semimarshy areas from Nova Scotia to North Carolina and westward to Minnesota. The coast of Massachusetts and other relatively cool regions near large bodies of water are particularly prime territory for this small shrub, which is easily identified by its thick oval-shaped evergreen leaves and nodding pink or red flowers that blossom between June and August. The tart berries (best when cooked with honey, for sauces and jelly) turn ripe-red during September and October and

cling to their branches throughout winter. They're especially good when picked soon after autumn's first frost.

STRAWBERRIES: Although roughly half a dozen species of wild strawberries (genus: *Fragaria*) grow in this part of the world (ranging from the Arctic Circle to Florida and west to California), the fruit is found in greatest abundance in the Northeast and eastern Canada. The plants sport three coarsely toothed leaves, produce small five-petaled white flowers in the spring, and bear fruit (which is most often red, but sometimes white) between May and July. Look for this sought-after forager's prize in open woods and clearings, on exposed slopes, and along roadsides, streambeds, and railroads. Harvest them soon after sunrise, when they're still glistening with the early morning dew.

HUCKLEBERRIES: If you pop an especially dark "blueberry" in your mouth and promptly bite down on ten stone-hard seeds, you can be sure that what you really have is a huckleberry. This fruit's unfortunate preponderance of pits, however, is but a small obstacle—overcome by straining the pulp through a sieve—to folks who've come to savor its unique and somewhat spicy flavor. Most species of huckleberry (genus: *Gaylussacia*) are small shrubs that favor acid soil, grow from a foot to three feet tall, and range throughout most of the eastern, southern, and northwestern states. Look for the almost-black-skinned fruit from June to September in oak woods, bogs, sandy or rocky areas, and clearings.

GOOSEBERRIES: Gooseberries are relatively common in moist woods throughout Canada and across the northern border states of this country, sometimes occurring as far south as Colorado in the West and New Jersey in the East. Mountainous regions from Massachusetts to North Carolina may also be the home of this tart round fruit. There are several species of gooseberries (genus: *Ribes*), each of which ripens to a different shade of reddish purple. The berries are usually picked when green, though, and flavored with honey or some other sweetener in pies, jellies, and sauces. The shrublike plant stands from two to four feet tall, displays greenish or purplish flowers in May and June, and produces a bounty for the resourceful forager during July and August.

DEWBERRIES: For practical purposes, most foragers simply distinguish dewberries from blackberries (both of which belong to the genus *Rubus*) as "the ones that grow on trailing vines rather than on canes." The consensus is that dewberries are the choicest of blackberrylike fruits. They're bigger, fatter, juicier, and tastier. Look for the telltale white flowers of this ground-hugging plant in the spring, and be prepared to harvest its bounty beginning in mid-June, or about two weeks earlier than the "ordinary" blackberries in your area are ready for picking. The dewberry favors dry soil, and it ranges from the eastern United States as far west as Oklahoma.

CURRANTS: All species of wild currants, which ripen during July and August, belong to the genus *Ribes* and grow on small shrubs that sport maple leaf-shaped foliage and favor cold, wet woods. Most varieties of the fruit are smooth, but a few are covered with short "bristles," and nearly all exude a slightly disagreeable odor resembling that of skunk cabbage. Red currants range throughout southern Canada, along the Rockies to Colorado and the Alleghenies to North Carolina, and in parts of New Jersey, Indiana, and Minnesota. Black currants—which are relatively rare—can sometimes be found in moist forests from Nova Scotia to Virginia and west to Kentucky, Iowa, and Nebraska.

BLUEBERRIES: Blueberries (genus: *Vaccinium*) are one of the world's most widespread fruits. They occur from the tropics to northern Alaska. The two most abundant species in the United States are the low-bush blueberry, which rarely exceeds a foot in height, and ranges from New England west to Minnesota, and the high-bush variety, which can reach a height of up to six feet, and grows throughout the Atlantic coastal plain from Maine to Georgia and west to Lake Michigan. Both ripen between July and September, and thrive in areas of acid soil, particularly burned-over fields and old pastures. Less common types can be found from the mountains of the West Coast to the swamps of New Jersey.

RASPBERRIES: The wild red raspberry (*Rubus strigosus*) is found in dry or rocky areas from Newfoundland to British Columbia, south in the Alleghenies to North Carolina, and in the rockies to New Mexico. The tangy, widely favored fruit is borne on canes that grow from two to five feet tall and are covered with many weak, bristly spines. Look for

the promising three- or five-petaled white flowers between May and July, and make a mental note to bring a bucket back with you several weeks later (mid-July to September) when the canes will be laden with plump, ripe-for-the-picking berries. You'll have to add commercial pectin to the fruit if you intend to put it up as jam or jelly.

MULBERRIES: If you never ended a day as a child gloriously stuffed full of—and stained head to toe with—red mulberries (*Morus rubra*), you might consider trying it now. Nobody ever has or ever will "go 'round the mulberry bush" because the plant is actually a tree, and can be found in fields and along roadsides (and even city streets) throughout the eastern United States to as far west as the Great Plains. The fruit ripens during July, when the elongated berries turn deep purple and can easily be shaken from their branches into a blanket spread over the ground below. You can dehydrate mulberries for winter storage by stringing them up and drying them as you would the green beans called "leather breeches."

ELDERBERRIES: The sweet or common elder (*Sambucus canadensis*) is a four- to twelve-foot-high shrub that grows along roadsides and in open fields and woods throughout the eastern half of the United States and Canada. In July, the plant produces abundant clusters of tiny white flowers—themselves a delicious treat when fried in batter like fritters—that fill the air with a heady perfume and by early August give way to equally numerous bunches of berries. When green, the fruit can be pickled and used to flavor sauces as a substitute for capers. Most foragers, however, wait until September when the berries have ripened to a sweet deep purple and virtually beg to be picked by the handful.

BLACK RASPBERRIES: The wild black raspberry (*Rubus occidentalis,* sometimes known as "thimbleberry") is more widespread than its red-colored cousin and is a bit more hazardous too. The canes' strong sharp thorns have left many a berry picker scratched from the ankles up. You're most likely to find this outrageously tasty species along roadsides and fencerows and in neglected fields from Quebec to Ontario and south to Georgia and Missouri. The plant seems to have a special liking for old tree trunks and rocky places, so keep

an eye out for such spots when you're searching. Black raspberries ripen during July and early August. Harvest them when they're plump and heavy with juice.

HARVEST FROM HICKORY TREES

A favorite autumn activity for many families is sitting around the fire and cracking hickory nuts, but even such a pleasurable pursuit can become pretty darn frustrating when the nuts continually shatter into tiny fragments trapped in the mazelike compartments of their shells. According to popular conceptions, one of the worst offenders in the hard-to-husk category is the hickory nut, a member, as is the pecan, of the genus *Carya*.

Hickory nut meats are rarely found on grocery store shelves, simply because the kernels are difficult to extract in large pieces. However, you can easily gather a bushel of hickory nuts in one afternoon and shell them yourself to reap a wealth of large, beautiful nutmeat "halves." Every fruit, nut, or seed has a hidden "zipper" or "door," and all a person has to do is find the combination that opens it.

THE MYSTERY IS SOLVED: A lot of folks think that hickory nuts—which are native to most areas of eastern North America—are well-nigh impossible to crack neatly, but if you strike one of the nuts in just the right spot, the shell will fracture along clean lines almost every time, because of the interior architecture (or framework) of the shell itself. A membranous partition called the septum divides the kernel in such a way that when a nut is struck near its stem end, where the thickest part of that membrane attaches to the outer hull, the shock waves travel along the septum and through the shell, causing the rugged casing to fall apart in six separate pieces.

FORAGING IN AUTUMN: Hickory nuts usually begin to drop from the trees in early autumn, as soon as they're loosened by rain or frost. If you want to forage a good supply, be sure to head for the nearest grove as soon as the nuts start falling, because this wild food is a favorite of squirrels. The plume-tailed scavengers are skillful hickory hunters, and if you're not quick, they'll beat you to the scene and may plunder the entire local crop before you have time to collect any nuts at all.

Take a bucket or sack with you on foraging trips (or just wear an apron with big pockets) and use a small stick to scratch around in the leaves under each tree. Most of the nuts you pick up will still be encased in their rough, dark hulls, which have to be removed before you can start cracking them. Some gatherers stamp on their crop to dehusk the "fruits," while others pick the sections of the outer coverings off carefully, one at a time. Whichever way you remove the hulls, though, don't throw away those hand-staining pods, as they can be used as mulch for your garden.

Once you've toted your harvest home, you'll need to sort through the pile and remove any "rotten apples." Discard nuts with discolored shells, grub holes, or a dry and wrinkled appearance. The husked nuts should then be washed and dried before they're opened: Thoroughly rinse off all mud and debris and spread your hoard in the sun for a few days. It helps during this period to stir the nuts around every once in a while, so they'll dry out evenly.

THE "MEAT" OF THE MATTER: Once it's completely dehydrated, the crop will be ready to be cracked open. First, assemble the few tools you'll need: a hammer, a nutpick, a brick, and a pan. Don't try to use a lever-type nutcracker for this operation, because it will crush the meats into fragments.

Place the brick on a hard, level surface and set the pan next to it. Then grasp a nut between the thumb and forefinger of your left hand, with the stem end pointing toward the right. Balance the nut on top of the brick (narrow edge downward) and aim your hammer at a spot about one-third of the way down from the stem end of the nut.

Whack that spot with a short, sharp blow, and the nut will pop right open. The shells may not split perfectly every time. The single most important factor will be the striking force of the hammer blow, which you'll have to learn through experience to control.

As you open each nut, drop the meat-containing sections into the collection pan at the side of

the brick. When you've cracked a good supply of hickories, you can use a pick to remove those delicious kernels. You can toss the shell fragments into the bird feeder. Feathered visitors love to peck at any tiny morsels you may have missed.

EAT 'EM UP: Once you've accumulated a large panful of nutmeats, sit back and relax. When you want to put the tasty crop to use, you can enjoy the oil-rich nuggets raw, toasted, or added to cake and cookie recipes.

It's easy to roast the chewy pieces, either on the stove or in the oven. For range-top toasting, use a dry, unoiled pan or cookie sheet set over medium heat. Spread the nutmeats evenly across the pan and stir them often, until they turn light brown. Then quickly move the seeds to a cool surface.

For oven roasting, simply warm the nuts in a shallow pan at 200°F until they're a golden color. You can make a wholesome nut butter from your roasted hickories by grinding the meats in a blender, along with enough safflower oil to produce the desired texture. Then salt to taste.

You can enjoy the wild flavor of hickory nuts in lots of dishes, once you've mastered the art of removing the meats. As you now know, it doesn't have to be as hard to crack hickories as their "bad" reputation suggests.

Hickory nuts can also be used as delicious substitutes for expensive pecans or walnuts in bread and dessert recipes by simply using the same amount of the wild nuts as you would customarily use of the other varieties. You might, for instance, want to try Old-Fashioned Hickory Molasses Pie.

The several varieties of hickory can be found from the Texas plains and the Florida swamps to New England and the Great Lakes. The bark of this member of the walnut family ranges from smooth to rough and shaggy, and the fruits can range in size from 3/4-inch to 2-1/2-inches in diameter. The name "hickory" comes from *pawcohiccora*, an American Indian word for an oily food derived from the nuts.

OLD-FASHIONED HICKORY MOLASSES PIE
  To make the family-pleasing dessert, fold together the following ingredients: 1-1/2 cups of unsulfured molasses, 4 beaten eggs, 2 tablespoons of whole wheat flour, 1/4 teaspoon of sea salt, 1/2 teaspoon of nutmeg, and 1 tablespoon of butter. When the ingredients are well blended, stir in 1 cup of finely chopped hickory nuts and pour the mixture into a 9- or 10-inch unbaked whole wheat piecrust. Then cook the pie in a moderate (350°F) oven for 35-45 minutes.

125

WILD YEAST FOR THE BAKING

The leader of a survival camping expedition in the rugged terrain of the Pacific Northwest routinely distributed to each member of the party a ration of whole wheat flour sweetened with a lump or two of raw sugar. This basic food served as a supplement to gathered wild fare. In the evening, the flour would be mixed with water, and the resulting paste shaped into a kind of tortilla and cooked in the hot coals of the fire. Such "ash cakes" tasted good the next day, and by the third day were still edible. However, by the eighth day in the woods, everyone hungered for fresh-baked, leavened bread. Little did they know that the means of satisfying their craving was growing all around them.

On one of the daily foraging hikes, a biochemist in the group picked a handful of ripe Oregon grape berries and explained to curious onlookers that the white powder covering the fruit was actually an atmospheric fungus commonly known as yeast.

Wild yeast spores grow nearly everywhere, and if they happen to land where there's moisture, sugar, and warmth, the delicate plants will begin to grow and multiply. The airborne microflora are especially attracted to the sweet skins of berries and grapes.

The same yeast that ferments the sugars in the juices of grapes and other fruits will serve as a leavening agent when mixed with dough. Legends about the prospectors in California and Alaska indicate that they guarded their sourdough bread starter more closely than they would a poke of gold. The perpetually fermenting yeast culture was the wellspring of every meal, and it meant the difference between feasting on fresh bread and choking down a weevil-infested, rock-hard biscuit.

The prospectors' sourdough starter was made by combining equal amounts of flour and water and allowing the mixture to sour in an earthenware pot for three to five days. Yeast would be found and added, and the dough would become a bubbling mass with a pleasant, slightly alcoholic aroma.

From then on, the culture was kept growing by constant use and subsequent replenishment of the flour and water. A prospector would protect the brewing mass from the below-freezing northern temperatures by wrapping the sourdough crock in his bindle or by placing the pot in a pouch that could be tucked under his long johns, where body heat would keep the yeast alive. (The legends go on to say that if the winter winds howled too fiercely, some gold seekers would hole up in their cabins and slurp down the nectarous liquid—or "hooch"—that formed on the surface of the well-fermented starter. The potent brew would send the miner on a bender that sometimes went on until the weather cleared!)

It's no wonder that the sour starter soon lent its peculiar homebrew aroma to a prospector's cabin and clothing. Eventually the starter and the bread it produced became so well-known that the gold miners themselves took on the name of "sourdoughs."

It would hardly occur to most of us to forage for yeast in view of the ready availability and low price of the packaged commercial product and in light of the time-consuming nature of sourdough baking. However, being in the middle of the forest with plenty of time on her hands, the leader of this expedition set her sights on making a batch of wild yeast sourdough. Her attempt was succesful, so the next time that you're away from civilization and have a yen for real sourdough bread, you may want to try her method.

A BACKWOODS BAKERY: It's easy to spot the powdered blue berries of the Oregon grape (*Berberis aquifolium*), a fall-ripening, hollylike evergreen shrub that grows profusely in the mountain ranges of the Pacific coastal area, and in no time at all, you can collect dozens of miniature fruits. Both juniper berries and the bark of the aspen are other good sources of wild yeast, which appears in the form of a powdery white coating. When harvesting aspen bark, be especially careful not to harm the tree.

To prepare the "sponge," simply put a handful or two of the berries or the bark in a scalded quart jar or crock, add two cups of whole wheat flour, and stir in two cups of lukewarm water. Next, loosely screw the lid onto the container to allow the gas from the fermenting process to escape and—at the same time—to protect the yeast culture from contamination. Then, after placing the starter jar on fire-warmed rocks, merely wait for the prolific yeast to multiply.

After just two days, tiny bubbles will appear in the mixture, and you'll know that the yeast is working. (A single whiff of the fragrant concoction will leave no doubt as to whether the procedure is successful; it will smell like a miniature brewery!) Always remove the berries or bark promptly once the yeast is brewing, because an undesirable flavor may be imparted to the dough, or the starter may spoil if the berries are allowed to ferment in the mixture. They are no longer needed as a source of yeast, because the culture can now perpetuate itself.

Now, armed with a vigorous starter, you can set to work to produce some loaves of real sourdough bread. Before mixing the batter, check again to make sure no berries or bark remain in the sponge. In a large bowl, combine one cup of the starter with six cups of whole wheat flour, and add just enough water to make the mixture easy to handle. The next step is to knead the dough thoroughly, adding about four more cups of flour

in the process until the mix becomes stiff and no longer sticks to the sides of the bowl. Shape the dough into two loaves and set them by the fire to rise, which may take three hours (or a little longer) on the warm rocks.

You can put that time to good use, however, by building a stone oven. A primitive cooker can be fashioned by setting a large flat rock directly in the coals of the fire, then forming three sides with inch-thick stone slabs and covering the top of the enclosure with a fifth large chunk of rock. Place the two loaves on the floor of the crude oven and close the "door" with a final stone. During baking, the heat can be regulated by simply piling up or scraping away the coals around the sides of the oven. The sourdough should cook to perfection in about an hour.

You'll find that the flavor of these golden loaves of wild yeast bread is more robust and a bit more sour than that of baked goods made with packaged leavening, and it's a far better taste than you'll find in the airy loaves found on supermarket shelves.

Once you have treated your taste buds to the hearty flavor of genuine sourdough bread, you'll never want to be without a crock of starter again. So go ahead. Gather a crop of yeast-bearing bark or berries and brew your own sourdough sponge in the kitchen or in camp.

TIPS FOR FISHING THROUGH THE ICE

Just because a cap of ice covers your favorite fishing hole, there is no reason to forgo enhancing your diet with fresh fish. Many people stretch their warm-weather food budgets by fishing, and this practice needn't end in the cold months. However, before venturing out onto the frozen surface of a wintry lake or pond, make certain the ice is thick enough so there won't be any danger of breaking through for a life-threatening dunk.

Most experts consider six inches of solid ice that's neither slushy nor brittle to be the absolute minimum thickness to safely support an adult, and with a shelter and other equipment, the thickness should be greater.

WEATHER BEATERS: Your time on the ice will be more pleasant and productive if you take a few steps to protect yourself from the weather. Warm clothing is essential when ice fishing. Many winter anglers wear snowmobile suits, and others dress in several layers of lighter clothing.

A knockdown frame covered with canvas makes a good windbreak that will help keep the chill off the angler. The frame for one of these can be made of scrap lumber, bolts, and wing nuts. Bolt holes should be pre-drilled, so an angler wearing mittens can assemble and

NORTHERN PIKE
(Esox lucius)

Range: Throughout most North American ice fishing waters.

Size: From an average of about two feet in length to a maximum of about four feet.

Bait: Wobbling spoons (the Dardevle brand is a good choice) or perch or suckers of under ten inches in length.

RAINBOW TROUT
(Salmo gairdneri)

Range: Throughout North American ice fishing waters.

Size: From an average of about a pound to a maximum of 40 pounds.

Bait: Worms, grubs, minnows, artificial flies, spoons, or salmon egg baits.

disassemble it on the ice. A sled or stool will keep your backside off the cold, solid surface of the lake and will also allow you to sit comfortably and to stay low behind the windbreak. Many people like to have a little added warmth, and a bucket filled about one-quarter full of sand makes an excellent portable wood or charcoal stove. Charcoal lighting fluid or paper and some reliable kindling will help get a fire going.

SPOTTING THE FISH: After drilling or chipping a hole in the ice, you can peer down into the water below to make certain there are actually fish where you're fishing. To enable you to see into the depths, cover yourself and the hole with a dark cloth to cut out the daylight.

LOCAL LORE: It usually stands to reason that a concentration of anglers indicates the presence of hungry fish. The novice at ice fishing can often follow the crowds to a spot where a big catch can be taken. Cour-

tesy demands, however, that a newcomer to the scene not crowd the folks already there, so without an invitation, don't drill your hole closer than about 20 yards from another angler. You'll also find that people who fish regularly in one area are usually willing to share information about worthwhile locations, what baits to use, the best times of day, and even the nearest or best tackle shops around.

TACKLE TIPS: Though just about any fishing rod can be used for angling through the ice, a pole between two and three feet long will allow you to sit nearly over your hole and respond immediately to even the slightest nibble. For small trout and panfish, the rod should be fitted with two- to four-pound-test line to which is tied a small hook anywhere in size from No. 6 to No. 14. When going after pike or lake trout, use 10- to 15-pound-test monofilament line and, depending on the size of your bait, a No. 4 or larger hook.

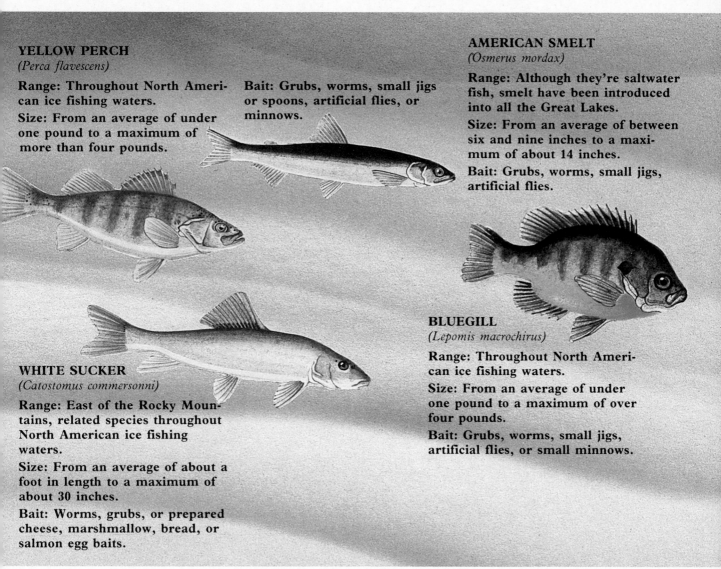

YELLOW PERCH
(Perca flavescens)

Range: Throughout North American ice fishing waters.

Size: From an average of under one pound to a maximum of more than four pounds.

Bait: Grubs, worms, small jigs or spoons, artificial flies, or minnows.

AMERICAN SMELT
(Osmerus mordax)

Range: Although they're saltwater fish, smelt have been introduced into all the Great Lakes.

Size: From an average of between six and nine inches to a maximum of about 14 inches.

Bait: Grubs, worms, small jigs, artificial flies.

WHITE SUCKER
(Catostomus commersonni)

Range: East of the Rocky Mountains, related species throughout North American ice fishing waters.

Size: From an average of about a foot in length to a maximum of about 30 inches.

Bait: Worms, grubs, or prepared cheese, marshmallow, bread, or salmon egg baits.

BLUEGILL
(Lepomis macrochirus)

Range: Throughout North American ice fishing waters.

Size: From an average of under one pound to a maximum of over four pounds.

Bait: Grubs, worms, small jigs, artificial flies, or small minnows.

A FEAST FROM ALONG THE SHORE

Clam chowder so rich you can savor the taste of the steam and mussels so delicate they defy description don't have to mean an enormous bill at an exclusive seafood restaurant. These and other delicious foods are free for the taking to almost anyone within foraging range of an ocean, and it doesn't take days to fill a kettle.

Expensive equipment is unnecessary to pursue and harvest a bounty of shellfish. A good field guide, the desire to spend the day surrounded by the sounds and smells of the beach, and a willingness to brave water, mud, sand, and rocks are about all a person needs to get started.

BOUNTIFUL BIVALVES: Bivalves, mollusks with two hinged shells, make up the bulk of most people's seashore scavengings simply because they're readily available and awfully fine eating. Even a novice forager can harvest plenty of these creatures without difficulty on the first trip out.

Before getting down to specifics, however, a few words of caution are in order. Most mollusks feed by siphoning in water and straining out and absorbing the small bits of food that they happen to suck in with the liquid. This, unfortunately, means that if the water is

contaminated, these creatures can become tiny store-houses of poison. Always make sure of the water's purity by contacting the local health department before collecting and eating bivalves from any beach, tidal flat, or other coastline location.

Calling the area's state fish and game department office to determine seasons, size and bag limits, and licensing requirements is also a good idea. Most local sporting goods stores can sell you a permit if one is needed, and they can usually supply you with a yearly tide table. The latter will help you plan your expeditions around the prime foraging times, which in most areas are from two hours before until two hours after low tide.

Finally, never eat any shellfish that isn't unquestionably fresh. A general rule is to discard each and every bivalve that doesn't resist your efforts to open its shell, or that doesn't close itself more tightly when touched.

MUSSELS: The quickest way to make the collecting sack bulge is with a passel of tasty mussels.

Members of the genera *Mytilus* and *Modiolus* (varieties of mussels) can be found along just about any portion of the North American coastline, east or west. Westerners should limit their gathering to a season running from November through April, since during the rest of the year, the bivalves found in their area may ingest microscopic dinoflagellates which can cause illness in humans. The old rule to harvest shellfish only during months that contain an "r" should do quite nicely for folks on the East Coast.

Once the season begins, a sharpened tire iron or heavy-bladed knife and a gunnysack are the only tools needed to go musseling.

Finding a bed of delicious mollusks to dig into should present no problem. Locate a rocky area near the low tide line, and if mussels are present, you'll be hard pressed not to walk on them. In large colonies where the shellfish are packed together like mosaic tiles, it's obviously an easy matter to pry off enough for a filling, delicious meal.

While foraging for mussels, have a look around the rocks for a clump of the long-stemmed, white-shelled goose barnacles, which are closely related to crabs, though they look like a cross between a mushroom and a gander. These bizarre creatures of the genus *Mitella* on the West Coast and *Lepas* on the East Coast have a

flavor like lobster and are easy to collect. Scrape the black stems off their rocky perches and try for a compromise between getting the maximum amount of stalk with the minimum of grit and sand.

The mussels can be steamed right on the beach in a large kettle, and the barnacles can be popped into the water right along with the mollusks. Their white-shelled tops can be discarded after steaming, the stems cut open, and finger-sized pieces of meat pried out. Furthermore, since their taste is similar to that of the clawed crustaceans, goose barnacles can be substituted in any recipe that calls for crab or lobster.

Those patches of gravel surrounding the masses of stone that harbored the barnacles should be foraged too, as they're often the homes of small clams and of several types of mollusks called cockles.

Along the Atlantic coastline "cockle" usually refers to members of the genus *Cardium*. On the Pacific shore, however, the term is applied to mollusks of at least four different genera. Confusion is seldom a problem, though, because in local usage "cockle" most often seems to translate as "good eating clam." See what the area's residents gather, double-check with your field guide, then have a go at foraging on your own.

You'll be thankful, as many a sore-backed digger has been, that cockles have no breathing siphons at all. Because of this, they must limit their below-ground travel to within an inch or two of the sand's surface. A clam rake, a hoe, or a shovel should be the only tool needed to gather the tasty little rascals. However, because of the rocky nature of the sand in which cockles are generally found, even a small amount of digging will be anything but easy. And after leaving the seaside, remember that a freshwater rinse will greatly extend the life of your foraging equipment.

THE WEST COAST'S LARGE, ECONOMY-SIZED CLAMS: The Pacific Ocean is a huge body of water, and some of the clams that inhabit its North American coastline are nothing less than giants. The most common of these monsters is the horse clam (*Schizothaerus nuttalli*), found in mud and sand flats from Alaska to San Diego.

It isn't necessary to wait for a particularly low tide to snare a few of these whoppers, which run up to four pounds each. The only real job after sighting the spouts from their squirt holes between the low and high water marks is digging them out. Even when they're spraying water three feet into the air, these clams may well be buried a yard deep in the sand. Dig the giants out anyway; when properly cleaned and prepared, they're more than worth the effort.

The flavor of horse clams and other bivalves found in muddy sand can be improved by storing the shellfish alive in a cage sunk beneath the surface of the ocean or in a large, shaded tub of seawater for about 48 hours. If you add cornmeal to the water in the tub the critters will replace any silt in their bodies with the grain. This simple treatment will make most bivalves taste better, even species that the local diggers may think are inedible.

No discussion of clams, at least in California, would be complete without a mention of the pismo. This, the Golden State's most famous mollusk, is a tourist attraction in its own right and is found in open, sandy areas from Half Moon Bay near San Francisco all the way to southern Mexico. The pismo clam (genus *Tivela*) supports an entire digging industry, complete with chauffeured boat rides to prime beaches and shoreside equipment rentals. Unfortunately, despite rigid size and bag limits, the pismo's population is threatened in popular clamming areas. It should be looked upon as a special treat rather than a regular source of wild food.

Clams can be steamed right on the seashore, the same way mussels and barnacles are prepared, and with any of these shellfish it's easy to collect a great many more than can be eaten in just a post-foraging feast.

TAKING SOME WITH YOU: Since uncooked shellfish spoil rapidly if left uncooked, it's best to go ahead and steam the entire day's harvest on the spot and carry any cooked but uneaten meat home to the freezer for use in chowders, soups, and other seafood recipes.

Steaming is the simplest and easiest way to cook shellfish and requires only a kettle equipped with a tight-fitting lid, some water, and a driftwood fire. White wine can be substituted for the water to make a flavorful treat.

Heat just enough liquid to cover the bottom of the pot and not boil away before the morsels are done. Add the shellfish and cover the kettle. Clams and mussels will be done after about 20 minutes of steaming; they are ready when the shells open wide. Barnacles take about the same amount of time.

Served with butter, French bread, and wine, all three of these seashore delicacies produce an excellent meal.

OUT IN THE WATER: Not all the coastal treats are found on exposed areas of rock or beach when the tide is out. Fish, crabs, and shellfish other than the mollusks, clams, and barnacles mentioned earlier must be pursued in waters along the coast.

When it comes to pulling in a passel of fish for the frying pan, the lowly cane pole (about 14 feet of bamboo) and accessories—some string, a bobber, a sinker, and a few small hooks—are all you really need.

The two most consistently productive types of shoreline saltwater fishing seem to be angling in tidal pools and off wharfs. Since many (but by no means all) of the fish you're likely to tie into in such areas are relatively small, the fastest way to fill your stringer or catch bucket is by using a tiny hook—in the No. 6, No. 8, or even No. 10 size range—on the end of your line.

Other anglers may look askance at your minuscule grapplers, but you'll have the last laugh. Bait up with rock snails, mollusks, and little sea worms foraged near your fishing site and then proceed to haul in as many big ones as the people using larger hooks are catching, plus a healthy assortment of the small, tender, tasty fish that the other folks can't catch at all.

Smelt (*Osmerus mordax*), for instance, average only about six inches in length, but you can catch them by the bucketful when you find a school. It's hard to name any fish, regardless of size, that has a more delicate and delicious flavor when fried in browned butter.

These feisty little fish are abundant in most coastal waters of the United States. They look like miniature barracuda and have an appetite which matches their vicious appearance. They'll grab most anything you drop in front of them.

Another fish that can keep your bobber dancing if you live along the eastern seaboard between North Carolina and Labrador is the pollack (*Pollachius virens*). This member of the cod family often grows to more than two feet long and isn't at all shy about latching onto a foraged bait. Locals frequently look down on this plentiful fish because of its many tiny bones, but a fillet taken from this cod's meaty back above the rib cage is both bone-free and wonderfully tasty.

Tie half a dozen of these fillets in a piece of cheesecloth, lay the package in the bottom of a sizable kettle, and add two quarts of water, one tablespoon of salt, and the juice of one lemon. Bring the water to a quick boil and simmer for five minutes. Remove and unwrap the pollack and serve the fillets hot with a dill or anise sauce. This fish doesn't taste "fishy" and is also excellent fried, baked, or broiled, especially when seasoned first for an hour in a marinade made of one large finely diced or ground onion, two tablespoons of salt, two tablespoons of vinegar, and one teaspoon of mace. Rinse the fillets in cold water after their soak and then fry, bake, or broil them.

There are, of course, literally hundreds of other species of saltwater fish that you can harvest along the shoreline with a pole and line. Despite the fact that some are a little offbeat, most are delicious when cooked slowly until their meat just flakes. Don't, for instance, overlook shark, which has a taste and texture much like cod and is frequently sold in the market as grayfish. Another not to throw back is the ray. Cut off the wings of a common skate (*Raja erinacea*) close to the body, slice them into strips parallel to their "airfoil," peel off the skin, pop out the cartilage in the middle, and cube the remaining meat. Dip it in a mixture of beaten eggs and either bread or cornmeal crumbs, and deep-fry it; you'll think you're eating scallops.

CRABS: The heads of the fish you catch have their use too: as crab bait. Few crabs can resist a fresh fish head, chicken neck, or chunk of salt pork. Tie the bait to a line, add a sinker, and toss the rig into the muddy water along shorelines, estuaries, and tidal streams where crabs are known to lurk. When you think a crab's latched onto the bait, just pull the line in very slowly and easily and slip a dip net under the crabs which will cling to the bait all the way to the surface.

That's the way individuals, couples, and whole families go after the luscious blue crab (*Callinectes sapidus*) up and down the East Coast, and they sometimes come home with baskets full of the tasty crustaceans.

The same approach works just as well on the West Coast with the Dungeness crab (*Cancer magister*) and its Pacific seaboard relatives, even though most folks in that part of the country seem to prefer to catch their crabs in store-bought ring nets and crab traps.

Unless they live in polluted water, all true crabs are edible, and as long as you obey the pertinent game laws, you can enjoy any of the critters that are big enough to take a nutpick to. Just drop the crustaceans alive into boiling water (it's the quickest and most humane way to kill them), leave them until their shells are bright red, and then pick out and eat their meat, hot or cold, with melted butter or a light white sauce.

SOME SELECTED MOLLUSKS: It's unfortunate that the delicious abalone (*Haliotis refescens*, *H. fulgens*, *H. cracherodii*, and *H. kamtschatkama*) has become known as the king of seafoods. Thanks to that publicity and the resulting demand for the mouthwatering steaks cut from these univalves (one-shelled animals), legal-sized "ab" are now quite scarce throughout much of their range along the Pacific coast.

That's all the reason you need to forget abalone entirely as a foraged seafood and concentrate your efforts on a number of the shellfish's far less renowned, but equally delectable, relatives.

The West Coast intertidal zone from northern California to southern Mexico is the home of the often ignored owl limpet (*Lottia gigantea*). These huge gastropods, whose shells look like squat tipis and are often more than three inches across, are abundant in many areas and can be gathered at low tide simply by popping them off their rocky perches with a sharpened putty knife.

As with all univalves, only the owl limpet's fleshy foot, which yields a steak about two inches across, is eaten. Tenderize the cut of meat by pounding it and storing it in the refrigerator overnight before it's cooked. Then dip the steaks, of which you'll need several for every eager eater, in an egg-and-bread-crumb or cornmeal batter and fry them to a golden brown. The flavor will wake up even the most jaded taste buds.

Other West Coast limpets and *Acmaea testudinalis*, an East Coast variety, are generally considered to be too small to bother with. As the late Euell Gibbons pointed out in his writings about foraged foods, however, that idea is nonsense. They might not be big enough to eat as steaks, but the meat of almost any limpet is worth going after for chowders and soups.

To prepare one of those chowders, put a quart or more of limpets into a covered kettle with one cup of water and steam the shellfish for ten minutes. Remove the limpets, saving the broth, and as soon as the gastropods are cool enough to handle, remove their meat and discard the shells and viscera. The meat is then ground in a food chopper with a medium blade, returned to the broth, and placed over a low heat.

Next, dice one large onion and four slices of bacon and fry them together until the onion is translucent. Add two cups of diced potatoes, cover everything with water, and boil the mixture until the potatoes are soft. Then stir in the limpet meat and broth, and immediately add one quart of milk and one-quarter teaspoon of finely ground black pepper. Allow the mixture to simmer while you blend one tablespoon of flour into one-fourth cup of milk and slowly stir this mixture into the chowder. Continue stirring the soup as it simmers for approximately ten minutes, and serve it with crackers on the side.

Another East Coast family of related mollusks, the chitons, or sea cradles, are also quite tasty, though they are only about two inches long, and few people ever give them the chance to reach the dinner plate. It's a different story, however, on the West Coast. All the way from Alaska down to Baja California, a forager can find the giant sea cradle (*Amicula stelleri*), which reaches a length of 13 inches.

The brick-red giant sea cradles can be found at low tide along rugged beaches. The vegetarian animals often hide under overhanging ledges and are sometimes difficult to see, but it's not unusual to stumble onto dozens of them clustered together along the low water mark of rough northern California beaches in the spring.

Chiton meat has a tendency to develop a strong fishy smell within two hours of the time the animal's caught. However, when they're cleaned immediately, the steaks packed in ice, and the meat cooked as quickly as possible, sea cradles are so delicious that you may want to get right up from the table and begin picking your way through slippery coastal rocks in search of more.

If you want to collect your seafood without any competition, watch for various members of the whelk family. These marine gastropods look so much like snails that few folks ever give a thought to eating them.

The best whelk pickings are found on the East Coast from Newfoundland to Florida and around the Gulf Coast all the way to the tip of Texas. Look for the three- to four-inch-long waved whelk (*Buccinum undatum*) along the upper East Coast south to the Carolinas;

the 12-inch-long knobbed whelk (*Busycon carica*) and six-inch-or-longer channeled whelk (*B. canaliculatum*) just off the sandy shores from southern New England to Florida; the six- to nine-inch lefthanded whelk, sometimes called the lightning whelk (*B. contrarium*), south from Cape Hatteras; and the three- to five-inch-long pear conch (*B. spiratum*) from Hatteras, south around the tip of Florida, and westward to Texas.

If you're a scuba diver, you can probably find all the whelks you'll ever want, anytime you want, by checking the ocean's bottom 12 to 18 feet down, off any sandy beach that sports a few washed-up whelk shells. They can also be found by walking the shore after a heavy storm and picking up those fresh, live specimens that have washed onto land, often by the bushel. Since these mollusks are meat eaters, you may be able to make a deal with commercial operators, who frequently find whelks stealing bait from their crab and lobster traps and would welcome the chance to dispose of them.

Whelks can be broken open with a hammer and the fleshy foot, the edible part, cut out. This meat can then be pounded or rolled, seasoned, and fried to a light brown. The foot can also be ground or diced.

Whelks can be pickled by boiling a pailful of them in heavily salted water until they can be slipped from their shells with a pin or a nutpick. Discard the viscera above each mollusk's foot and pull or slice off the operculum, the horny plate that closes the shell. Then place one packet of crab boil and three bayberry leaves in the bottom of a quart jar and pack the container loosely with alternating layers of cleaned whelks and finely sliced onions. Finally, fill the jar with boiling vinegar, seal it, and allow the meat to soak for at least a few days.

Once you've discovered how good whelks can be, you may also want to go after moon shells, which look like miniature whelks. Look for the Lewis moon shell (*Lunatia lewisi*), a grayish-brown five-incher, on sandy bottoms from British Columbia to Mexico; the one- to

three-inch-long Recluz's moon shell (*Polinices reclusianus*) from California to Mexico; the northern moon (*Lunatia heros*) from Newfoundland to the Carolinas; and the shark eye (*Polinices duplicatus*) from Cape Cod to Texas.

All the moon shells are good to eat. They're generally found in the same kinds of places that you'll find whelks, and you should look for their rounded burrows in the sand as you walk along a beach at low tide. Their feet are both savory and tender when prepared properly. Just slice them into half-inch-thick steaks, pound the meat, separate the slabs with wax paper, and store the pieces in the refrigerator for 24 hours. Dip the steaks in egg, roll them in bread crumbs, and fry the meat to a light brown.

ONLY THE BEGINNING: There is much more to be taken along the edge of the sea, of course. There are oysters, scallops, seaweed, sea eggs, beach plums, bayberry leaves, grunions, blennies, lancelets—the list of saltwater seafood available to the discerning forager goes on and on.

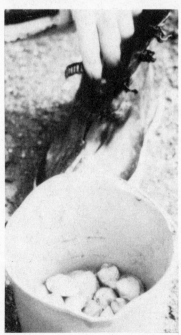

LIVESTOCK

THE BEST BACKYARD LIVESTOCK COMPARED

Raising small livestock—from babes to butchering—is no more difficult than cultivating a garden, and many types can be reared even in areas as limited as a large backyard or an urban lot. However, choosing the animals that will best suit your needs is crucial to small-space meat production.

Although economy is obviously important, other factors are bound to influence your choices as well. The accompanying chart lists some basic aspects of livestock raising—such as housing needs, feeding requirements,

labor involved, and expected harvest—that must be considered in selecting your stock. Some of the individual advantages and disadvantages of the five most popular types of livestock should help you make the final decision as to what you'd like to raise.

REGARDING REGULATIONS: First of all, before building any pens, hutches, coops, or sties, be sure to check local restrictions and laws regarding the types and number of animals that may be kept. In many well-populated areas such regulations are very specific, limit-

BACKYARD LIVESTOCK COMPARISON CHART

	LAYING HENS	BROILERS	DUAL-PURPOSE CHICKENS
HOUSING AND FENCING	2–3 sq. ft./bird 1–1½ sq. ft./bird if pasture available 8″ roost/bird 1 nest/4 birds chicken wire for pasture	2–3 sq. ft./bird 1–1½ sq. ft./bird if pasture available 4–5 sq. ft./bird if kept 10 wk. chicken wire for pasture	2–3 sq. ft./bird 1–1½ sq. ft./bird if pasture available 10″ roost/bird 1 nest/4 birds chicken wire for pasture
MISCELLANEOUS NEEDS	hanging feeders starter feed trough waterers brooders (incubator)	hanging feeders starter feed trough waterers brooders (incubator)	hanging feeders starter feed trough waterers brooders (incubator)
FEED	per 100 chicks: 40 lb. starter ration for first 2 wk. 250–300 lb. starter for 2–6 wk. change to growing ration at 6 wk., to layer ration at 18–20 wk. 100 adults: 24–30 lb./day (1 adult: 85–90 lb./yr.) 2–5 lb. oyster shell/yr. 1 lb. grit/yr. 300–500 pullets: 1 acre pasture	per 100 chicks: 500–600 lb. starter ration for first 6 wk. change to finishing ration at 6 wk. 300–500 pullets: 1 acre pasture	per 100 chicks: 40 lb. starter ration for first 2 wk. 250–350 lb. starter 2–6 wk. change to growing ration at 6 wk., to layer ration at 18–20 wk. 100 adults: 25–35 lb./day (1 adult: 85–90 lb./yr.) 2–5 lb. oyster shell/yr. 1 lb. grit/yr. 300–500 pullets: 1 acre pasture
WATER	per 100 birds: 6–8 gal./day	per 100 birds: 6–8 gal./day	per 100 birds: 6–8 gal./day
YOUNG PER YEAR	none unless incubated low production for hybrids	none unless incubated low production for hybrids	none unless incubated low production for hybrids
RATIO MALE/FEMALE	for eggs: no male needed to incubate: 1/20	NA	for eggs: no male needed to incubate: 1/10-15
LIFE SPAN	1 yr. egg production (decreases each following yr.)	5–15 wk. (see HARVEST)	butcher meat hens at 20–22 wk. butcher layers at end of first egg season
LABOR	feed, water, collect eggs: 1–2 times/day butcher: 15-min. process	feed, water: 1–2 times/day butcher: 15-min. process	feed, water, collect eggs: 1–2 times/day butcher: 15-min. process
HARVEST	first egg harvest: 20–22 wk. 250–290 eggs/yr./hen (drastic drop after first yr.) butcher 1-yr. hens	butcher "Cornish game hen" at 5 wk. butcher broiler at 8 wk. butcher roaster at 11–15 wk. 1 lb. meat/2.5 lb. feed	first egg harvest: 20–22 wk. 200–270 eggs/yr./hen 4–6-lb. adults for meat

NA = not applicable

ing the number of animals per household and requiring that shelters be placed a specified distance from adjacent property lines. You can save yourself a great deal of annoyance and extra work by checking the rules before you build or buy.

Even if there are no detailed livestock laws where you live, you should strive to keep noise, odors, and flies from becoming nuisances to your neighbors. Indeed, if you live in an area where backyards tend to be small, you'll have to make your prospective project's effects on others a prime consideration.

WHERE ARE THE COWS: As you read on, you'll notice that this analysis is limited to rabbits, chickens, sheep, goats, and pigs and has left out the most popular mainstay of the American barnyard: the cow. The reason for that omission is that although a beef or dairy cow could probably be kept in a very large backyard,

cattle pose many more problems than do other domestic animals for the livestock raiser with a limited amount of space.

For one thing, a cow's contribution to the manure pile can be pretty sizable. Bovine animals also require very sturdy fencing, and butchering one of them demands a great deal of help and effort. Also, the 500 to 600 pounds of beef harvested will stuff a freezer so full that you'll have no room left for other food. Finally, cows need considerable grazing room—at least an acre of lush pasture, which is more land than many homesteaders can spare.

Varieties of fowl other than chickens have also been omitted. Actually, many kinds of poultry—such as geese, guinea fowl, ducks, quail, and pheasant—can easily be raised in backyards. There are too many species of winged livestock to cover in this analysis, however, so

RABBITS	SHEEP	GOATS	PIGS
all-wire hutches, 24" X 30" X 36"	15-20 sq. ft. shed/adult plus pasture 10-15 sq. ft. shade/adult 39"-high, 12"-grid woven wire or 2-strand electric	15 sq. ft. shelter/goat plus pasture or pen 54"-high sturdy wire or 3-strand electric or 52" X 16' stock panel	8-10 sq. ft./shelter/pig plus outside area 36"-high welded wire with sturdy bottom or 2-strand electric or 32" X 16' hog panels
nest boxes crocks for food and water	manger and feed bunk creep feeder for lambs (shearing equipment)	feed bunk and hay manger milk stand and equipment	feeders waterers mud wallow
120 lb. pellets/10-lb. adult 24-30 lb. additional pellets/pregnancy 65-100 lb. pellets/litter mineral and salt spools	3½-4 lb. hay/day/sheep, 5-6 lb. during pregnancy and lactation (700-850 lb. hay/year with 6 mo. pasture) Grain: 15-20 lb./year/adult	3 lb. hay/day/goat (540 lb./yr. w/6 mo. pasture) ½ lb. grain/lb. milk produced (500-1,000 lb. grain/yr.)	400-600 lb. balanced ration from weaning to 230-lb. pig (or 1,400 lb. garbage)
1 gal./day/rabbit	2-3 gal./day/sheep	2-5 gal./day/goat	1-3 gal./day/pig
4-6 litters of 8/yr./doe (optimal, 32-48 total)	1.5/ewe	1-3/yr./doe	NA
1/10	1/30-35	1/20-30	NA
4-5 yr.	5-6 yr.	5-6 yr.	one summer
feed, water: 1-2 times/day butcher: 5-min. process	feed, water: 1-2 times/day shear each spring butcher: 30-min. process	feed, water: 1-2 times/day milking: 2 times/day milk handling butcher: 30-min. process	feed, water: 1-2 times/day butcher: 30-60-min. process
first harvest: 10-12 mo. 2 lb. meat/4-lb. bunny hides	first harvest: 1-yr. ewe should produce first litter + 8 lb. wool 50-65 lb. meat/100-lb. lamb 8 lb. wool/year/animal	first milk harvest: 1 yr. milk: 1 gal./day (305-day lactation period) meat hides	4-6 mo. after purchase of 30-lb. piglet 135 lb. meat/200-300-lb. pig hides

the focus is upon the most commonly raised backyard birds.

CHICKENS: The most popular barnyard birds can be highly efficient meat or egg producers. A broiler, for instance, proves its weight-gaining efficiency by yielding nearly a pound of meat for every two pounds of feed. Moreover, a good egg-laying hen will supply about a dozen eggs for every five pounds of feed. And certain dual-purpose breeds will give a fair supply of both products.

Chickens aren't fussy eaters and are good foragers. They'll eat everything from meat scraps and bugs to weeds and kitchen leftovers. However, their voracity can easily prove devastating to a garden, so guard your crops against disaster by fencing in either the vegetables or the birds.

These fowl are well suited to a small-space operation. Stout fences aren't required (the appropriately named chicken wire is usually the least expensive and easiest enclosure material to use). The birds will, however, learn to fly over five- or six-foot barriers, so you must either fence over the top of your pen or clip the chickens' wings to keep them earthbound. In addition, predators may well try to raid your flock, so be sure your coop's fencing and flooring are at least strong enough to deter rats, owls, coons, opossums, and canine prowlers.

Be forewarned that chicken coops in an urban neighborhood tend to cause more human commotion than does the appearance of a few rabbit hutches. Neighbors are often concerned—and perhaps rightfully so—that the birds will get loose and dig up their prize petunias, that the flock will create odor and fly problems, or that you'll decide to keep a rooster, forcing them to put up with a living alarm clock. Although these difficulties can be prevented by proper management, you might be wise to sound out the folks next door and prepare them for their new neighbors. (The promise of an occasional gift of fresh eggs might be one good way to make the introduction.)

RABBITS: Quiet, clean, and prolific, rabbits are the most nearly ideal animal to raise in a small space. If they're kept in all-wire hutches and the manure is cleaned out regularly from under their cages, they are odor-free and won't attract flies. Rabbits also give an excellent return for the amount of feed and labor invested. The litters from one ten-pound doe, kept in a 30" by 36" hutch, can yield up to 80 pounds of meat a year. In addition, the pelts, although generally not strong enough for clothing, can be used or sold for trim on coats.

In spite of all the good things to be said about rabbit raising, the species does have one serious disadvantage. The gentle creatures are prone to attack by predators, so unless you build your hutches or fences strong enough to keep prowlers out or enclose your rabbits in a shed or garage, your stock will be easy prey.

SHEEP: Calm, quiet, almost odor-free, and easy to keep penned, sheep are a good addition to nearly any meat-producing homestead, especially rural households with an acre or so of unused pasture. Sheep are excellent grazers. In season they can be raised entirely on good grassland without supplemental grain. When pastured exclusively, they're probably the most economical animal to raise on your backyard farm. You can harvest about 100 pounds of meat and 8 pounds of wool from each adult ewe, and an acre of lush pasture will support four or five ewes and their lambs. (Some European breeds, by the way, are raised for milk in addition to meat and wool.)

Sheep don't require much regular caretaking, either. They do need to be shorn every year, however, and this can be a problem for the backyard homesteader. Shearing must be done correctly if it's to produce a quality fleece for spinning, and few small-flock owners have the time to learn the skill or the money to buy the expensive equipment. Since it may be difficult to find a professional shearer who's willing to work on just a few animals, you should contact—in winter, well before the shearing season begins—someone who shears larger flocks in your area and arrange to have your sheep included in that person's rounds.

Labor requirements for your backyard flock can also be high at lambing time. Ewes will need to be watched (and assisted, if necessary) to be certain they care for their lambs properly, and you'll have to guard the timid creatures constantly against predators.

Overall, though sheep require less daily maintenance than do either rabbits or chickens, raising them demands more livestock husbandry skills than managing those smaller species. The pasture, for instance, must be managed to prevent overgrazing, and your flock will require a good veterinary care program.

GOATS: Perhaps the most intelligent, and certainly the most companionable, of backyard livestock animals, goats are highly efficient milk producers and good friends to have around the homestead.

A good doe will yield a gallon of milk each day from a feeding of three to four pounds of grain and a few pounds of hay (the latter helps keep her rumen—part of the animal's digestive system—healthy). Goat's milk tastes similar to cow's milk, yet many people who can't drink cow's milk can tolerate the smaller creature's givings. Then, too, although the popular breeds in this country are not usually raised for meat production, caprine meat (called chevon) is delicious, and tanned hides from the animals can be used for rugs, and vests, jackets, and other garments.

For all these reasons, many new homesteaders think a goat is the first animal they should have for their farm, especially after they've had a chance to play with one. But before you run out to purchase your own goat, it's best to be aware of the disadvantages of keeping the beasts. First, a dairy goat must be milked twice a day, seven days a week, through her entire ten-month lactation period. This is a caretaking requirement many homesteaders might find too confining. Second, although goats don't require much space, they are difficult to keep penned, and third, in addition to their fence-attacking tendencies, some of the little fellows are pretty good noisemakers. Neither the second nor the third quality will endear you or your goats to the neighbors.

Bucks are another matter entirely. During fall breeding season, the male of the species will spew his odor far and wide, letting people for blocks around know there is a billy goat in the area. This isn't an ordinary country smell. It's foul, rank, and to some folks even nauseating. So if you're thinking of getting into the goat-breeding business, plan to live far removed from other humans. As an alternative, you might talk some farmer friend into keeping your buck for you.

If you intend to get the highest and most economical milk production from your goat, or any dairy animal for that matter, you must have a good understanding of its nutritional needs during lactation and dry periods, and provide good veterinary care. You should know, too, that the tiny fat droplets in goat's milk, unlike those of cow's milk, are mixed throughout the liquid. Thus the butterfat doesn't rise naturally to the top (it can be separated mechanically), which means that making butter or cheese is a bit difficult.

Probably the hardest aspect of goat raising, though, is culling a favorite doe—no matter how poor her milk production is—because the creatures are so lovable to have around. But if you're not willing to get rid of your caprine companions, it won't be long before one cute doe, at two or three kids per year, multiplies into a sizable herd that must be milked twice a day for ten months of the year and fed all year-round.

PIGS: Among the best waste-to-meat converters, pigs will turn kitchen scraps, garden greens, grains, roots, surplus eggs, or offal from other butchered livestock into hams, pork chops, bacon, and fresh side meat. In other words, a swine can be the finest garbage disposal available. Alternatively, when fed a well-balanced store-bought diet, a good hog will gain a pound for every 2-1/2 to 3-1/2 pounds of feed.

Pigs don't require much room. You can raise one or two from weanling to market weight in a pen 16 feet square. For backyard meat production, pigs should be purchased as weanlings in the spring and raised through the summer to their market weight of about 220 pounds each. Using this method, you'll avoid the considerable husbandry problems associated with handling newborns, piglets, and those 400- to 500-pound boars and sows. All you'll have to do until butchering time is feed and water your stock twice a day and clean out the manure as often as needed.

Most pigs are not jumpers, but they will try the best of fences at ground level, so your enclosures must be absolutely "swine tight" at the bottom. Commercial hog panels, each of which consists of 16 feet of 32"-high welded wire, are just about the ideal fencing for a backyard pigpen.

Along with the tendency of pigs to root their way out of captivity, pig raising has other drawbacks, such as the work involved in butchering a 200-pound hog. There's even the problem of trying to find room for 100 pounds of meat in your freezer. The biggest disadvantage to these otherwise excellent meat producers, however, is the public's general reaction to the aroma. Be sure to consider your neighbors before you set up a pig sty behind your house.

TAKE YOUR PICK: While these are some of the objective pluses and minuses of each of the five best minifarm animals, don't forget that one of your chief considerations should be your personal preference. The homesteader who really enjoys a particular species of livestock will give them more care and attention. The animals, in turn, will be more comfortable and therefore more productive. So if, for example, you like the soft clucks of a flock of chickens but find the thought of raising pigs distasteful, don't let cold economics alone determine your choice.

There's one final consideration. It's possible that the hardest part of livestock raising for you would be butchering the animals you've nurtured since birth. If this is an insurmountable problem, you would do better to limit your operation to milk-producing goats (you can sell their offspring) or egg-laying chickens.

ACQUIRING FREE STOCK FOR YOUR FARM

By the time novice homesteaders have invested in property, their financial reserves may be pretty well exhausted. There you are, proudly looking over a nice piece of farmland, with perhaps a comfortable little house and maybe a barn and some outbuildings. You visualize a brood of clucking chickens providing eggs, a rooster noisily greeting the dawn, some ducks and geese swimming in the pond, a few goats giving you milk, and a family of rabbits living in the hutch. And what farm could be without a couple of romping dogs and a tabby with cuddly kittens!

However, buying this assortment may be way beyond

your means at this point. What can you do? You'd probably be amazed at the number of people who have animals they no longer want or can no longer care for. You can reach these people by running an inexpensive ad for several weeks in your local newpaper. The ad could say, for example, "WANTED: Ducks, chickens, rabbits, and any other farm animals you no longer need." If your experience is anything like that of others who have tried this, the response will be overwhelming.

Before pursuing this course, though, there are a few factors you should consider carefully. First, analyze your needs and space restrictions, and be prepared to turn down offers of animals that you have no desire to care for. If your plans include raising stock for meat production, you'll need a tactful, as well as honest, answer when someone asks for reassurance that "you're not going to butcher them, are you?" More than a few people get misty at the thought of their "babies" winding up on someone's dinner table.

Second, know how to take care of the animals you do choose to accept. Since it's not likely that anyone will offer a cow, horse, or pig, it's best to concentrate on how to raise smaller livestock. Learn all that you possibly can from the people who answer your ad.

Check to see if your existing farm structures are adequate and suitable for your planned livestock acquisitions. The animals will need shelter (in most climates) and protection from predators. If providing this will require a good deal of new construction or fencing, you may find you can't actually afford "free" animals. Also, be sure to have the facilities ready before bringing the orphans home. Your homesteading experience could really be soured, for example, if newly acquired goats eat a neighbor's prize tulips before the fence is put up.

Finally, make sure you're able to feed the livestock you intend to keep. You'll want them to be healthy and productive, and for this, good, nutritionally balanced food is essential.

By following these few suggestions, your vision of a thriving, well-populated homestead can soon be realized. There'll be meat and poultry in the freezer, goat's milk in the refrigerator, and enough eggs left over to sell. It's a good life!

PRODUCE A FISH CROP IN CAGES

Raising fish on a small scale in cages is an economical way for an individual or family to put literally hundreds of pounds of fish on the table or in the freezer. Even a first-time grower should be able to reap a seasonal harvest of about four pounds for each cubic foot of cage space, and under demonstration conditions, yields of over 15 pounds per cubic foot have been recorded.

HOW CAGE CULTURE WORKS: To understand just how fantastic that rate of production is, imagine a water-filled 3′ X 3′ X 3′ hole in your backyard. Then visualize 100 pounds of fish swimming around in it. That's the beginner's yield.

Actually trying to produce fish in a small hole would create serious problems long before that 100-pound harvest could be achieved, primarily because the creatures' wastes, along with any uneaten feed, would soon drastically pollute the water. If such contamination didn't kill the fish outright, it would certainly retard their growth.

Of course, a person could use some costly combination of circulation, aeration, and filtration devices, but cage culture solves the problem of pollution in a small space, because there is a constant exchange of water between the screen-walled cage and the larger body of water it floats in. After all, even landlocked, supposedly stagnant ponds have some natural circulation as a result of wind and convection currents, but the major source of water movement in a cage is often a natural pump—the swimming and breathing of the fish themselves. The stock's containers are, in addition, normally floated in the upper layer of a body of water that's at least six feet deep. In this layer there are relatively few other fish, and little organic decomposition takes place; the incoming fluid is usually clean and rich in oxygen.

THE ADVANTAGE OF CAGE CULTURE: The great single advantage of cage culture is that it permits raising fish in bodies of water that are not otherwise suitable for aquaculture, bodies in which large nets and other methods of harvesting are not feasible.

Public (or large private) waters: Harvesting of fish from public waters is usually restricted to sport fishing methods, and private ponds that cover more than an acre can present formidable difficulties to harvesting the fish with nets. However, such environments are often ideal for cage culture.

Multipurpose ponds: In ponds built to attract wildlife, offer recreational fishing and swimming, or just provide scenic beauty, converting that entire body of water to intensive fish culture may be difficult and would certainly compromise other uses. However, with cages, you could easily produce several hundred pounds of fish without hampering your ability to enjoy the pond in other ways. Also, the cages may even attract wild fish, and thereby enhance sport fishing.

Ponds with more than one owner: Suppose your land fronts on a private body of water that's shared by a number of owners. Since each family probably has its own ideas about how best to enjoy the pond or lake, it could be difficult to get all the owners to agree on an aquaculture management plan. However, you could keep a few cages floating off your section of the shoreline without interfering with your neighbors' activities.

Very deep ponds: Deep bodies of water such as quarry pits usually aren't as productive as conventional aquaculture sites, but the same sites are often good for cage culture.

Brushy ponds: Some ponds are so full of brush, logs, or other obstacles that harvesting with nets is all but impossible. As long as there are patches of open water, however, such locations can be used for cage farming.

KINDS OF FISH: Although most fishes probably can be raised in cages, experience to date suggests that anyone more interested in production than in experimentation should select from one or more of seven varieties.

CHANNEL CATFISH (*Ictalurus punctatus*): Some people are prejudiced against eating these whiskery fish, claiming that "scavengers" aren't fit table fare, but in the South, folks know better. In fact, the well-developed taste in that area for catfish largely supports this country's principal fish culture industry, which is centered in the lower Mississippi valley. Over 50 million pounds of cultured catfish are sold annually, and perhaps two percent of that total is grown in cages.

The channel catfish is really quite a handsome creature. Young fish, those up to about a foot long and covered with round black spots, were formerly thought to be a distinct species and were known variously as willow cats, lady cats, squealers, or fiddlers. Although the channel cat can now be caught in most of the United States, almost all commercial sources are located in the southern and central states and California.

RAINBOW TROUT (*Salmo Gairdneri*): The American Fisheries Society currently recognizes 14 species of trout as being either native or successfully introduced to North America. Most of these are important as sport fish, but only the rainbow trout is widely grown for food. Rainbows are able to tolerate slightly higher temperatures than most trout, and they seem reasonably content in the crowded circumstances typical of intensive fish culture.

The rainbow is indigenous to the Pacific coast drainage areas of North America but can now be encountered almost anywhere trout of other kinds are found.

BLUEGILL (*Lepomis macrochirus*): The bluegill is

probably the best known of the 11 sunfish species. It's always been widely distributed throughout the United States and southern Canada and is now found almost everywhere. It's better suited to most aquaculture purposes than other types of sunfish, primarily because of its large size and its adaptable feeding habits.

You can distinguish bluegills from related species by glancing at the opercular flap (the small, soft tab on the rear edge of the gill cover). If the flap is short and dark blue, and not edged or spotted with a lighter color, the sunfish is probably a bluegill. Other distinctive characteristics include a dark blotch at the rear of the dorsal fin and sharply pointed pectoral fins.

Commercially available strains of hybrids, which are usually crosses between the bluegill and the green sunfish (*Lepomis cyanellus*), have been the subject of some controversy among aquaculturists. The different hybrids seem to vary in performance, but in general they grow more rapidly than either of the parent species. They are expensive, however, and small-scale growers can't expect to produce their own hybrids.

BLUE TILAPIA (*Tilapia aurea*): The many species of tilapia, originally native to the Near East and Africa but now spread throughout the tropics, are among the world's most important food fishes. When Saint Peter and his companions cast nets into the Sea of Galilee, they were fishing mainly for tilapia, which are sometimes marketed as "Saint Peter's fish." In recent years tilapia have also become important for culture in greenhouses and other heated environments, as well as for seasonal culture in the temperate zones.

The blue tilapia is about as beautiful a fish as you could hope to raise. A male in breeding condition, as he is most of the time, is suffused with iridescent blue, particularly around the head, and his fins are edged with brilliant crimson. Blue tilapia have won more than a few prizes at aquarium shows.

You can obtain various species of tilapia from aquarium shops, but you'll get a better price and some assurance that you're not purchasing a miniature species if you buy from an aquaculture dealer.

Not only is the tilapia valuable as a food fish, but if a few are kept in a cage with other fish, they reduce the time spent cleaning algae from the inside mesh of the cage.

MIRROR CARP (*Cyprinus carpio*): Though it was originally brought here as a food fish, the common carp isn't very popular in this hemisphere. However, in Europe, Israel, China, Japan, and other countries, it has become the most domesticated of aquaculture species.

In North America, wild carp are found nearly everywhere that there's sufficiently warm water, except in peninsular Florida. Few of the select varieties are available in this country, but it is worth the trouble to look for the mirror, or Israeli, carp, which has only a few large, scattered scales. It's an even more adaptable eater than the wild type, and has a higher height-to-length ra-

tio. If you can't locate carp stock elsewhere, you might want to contact bait dealers, as they sometimes sell small Israeli carp as minnows.

EELS (*Anguilla rostrata*): The American eel is a catadromous fish. Its life cycle reverses that of the anadromous salmon, as eels live in fresh water and spawn at sea. Therefore, the controlled breeding of captive eels is for all practical purposes impossible. However, in many estuaries along our Atlantic coast, young eels, or elvers, can be collected in numbers sufficient to supply eel-culture systems. For this reason, though an occasional large eel will turn up in a body of water hundreds of miles inland, eel culture will probably always be a coastal enterprise.

Furthermore, eels aren't the easiest creatures to keep in cages. The young fish may slip through the mesh, and adults often become adept at crawling up and out through cracks. Their exceptional food qualities, and the fact that they have the lowest percentage of dressing loss of any fish, do make them worth the trouble, though.

BROWN, BLACK, AND YELLOW BULLHEADS (*Ictalurus*): The bullheads, with their large heads, stocky bodies, square tails, and usually sluggish movements, conform more closely to most people's conception of a catfish than does the channel cat itself. While bullheads are native to the eastern two-thirds of the United States, they are now found in almost all parts of the country.

The differences among the three major bullhead species are not easy to distinguish, yet it's very important for the cage culturist to know which type of bullhead is being dealt with. In brief, a yellow bullhead (*Ictalurus natalis*) has whitish or yellowish barbels (whiskers), a long anal fin with 23–28 rays, and small serrations on the inside edge of its pectoral fin's spine. The brown (*Ictalurus nebulosus*) and black (*Ictalurus melas*) bullheads both have black, dark brown, or darkly spotted barbels. The brown bullhead has a medium-length anal fin with 22–24 rays and stout serrations on the interior pectoral fin's spinal edge. The black bullhead has a distinctly short anal fin with 16–22 rays and a smooth, or barely serrated, pectoral fin edge.

OBTAINING FISH: There are three ways to obtain your fish stock: Buy them, catch them, or breed them. You should be able to locate dealers who sell channel catfish, rainbow trout, hybrid sunfish, Israeli carp, and even some of the tilapias. You may also be able to find folks who deal in some of the other species, but don't count on it.

You may well be able to locate free fish for stocking —particularly bluegills and bullheads, which are rapid reproducers that can quietly overpopulate a body of water if they're not kept in check. Many farm pond owners will be glad to relieve their fish population crunch by letting you haul away some of their stunted stock. Such fish will resume normal growth patterns when they're again placed under favorable conditions.

Taking your starting supply from public waters is usually illegal, especially if you're after such prized game fish as trout. Still, it can't hurt to check with a local fishery biologist concerning any unwanted surpluses of bullheads or carp, which can generally be caught with seines, cast nets, or traps baited with liver, fish, or meat offal.

Among the fish discussed here, bullheads, nonhybrid sunfish, and tilapia will readily reproduce in any pond in which they can survive. Channel catfish and carp are a bit more particular about their breeding grounds, but most home growers should be able to get them to reproduce. However, many backyard aquaculturists consider trout too tricky and time-consuming to breed. Breeding hybrid sunfish requires specialized skills, and eels are unlikely to reproduce at all in captivity.

On the other hand, none of these fish will breed in a cage that's kept properly suspended off the bottom. This apparent disadvantage is actually an advantage more often than not, because it lessens the chance of the cage culturist encountering the problem of stunted, overpopulated groups of fish. Growers who own farm ponds can use their ponds as natural hatcheries to produce young with which to stock the cages, then use the containers to raise collections of fish to optimal eating size away from the competition present in the pond at large.

THE CAGE: Once you've gotten access to a body of water and are confident that you'll be able to line up a supply of fish, it's time to build your cage. You could, of course, buy a fish box, but commercial cages often cost three to five times as much as homemade units. Rectangular cages seem to work best. Home growers planning to manage one to six boxes will probably do well with 3′ X 3′ X 6′ structures.

Although you can make the cage walls out of almost any sort of mesh material, nylon webbing—which is sold in hardware stores and is often used to keep leaves out of rain gutters—works well. Flexible nylon mesh is easy to work with, slightly buoyant, long-lived, and chemically inert. Wire, on the other hand, may be less expensive initially, but it's also much heavier than nylon, so extra flotation is needed to compensate for the added weight. Also, it usually has sharp ends that can injure people and fish, and the mesh corrodes in water. There are many sad but true stories about bumper fish crops that fell through rusty cage bottoms at harvesttime.

Whatever the material, though, using the largest mesh capable of preventing new baby fish from escaping will allow good circulation, reduce cleaning labor, and save some money.

The cage will need a rigid top frame made of either treated wood or aluminum tubing. You can frame all of the underwater sides of the cage as well, or you can make a basket cage by simply lashing the sides together with nylon rope or twine. Basket cages are lighter, easier to store, and less expensive than full-frame ones, but they take longer to construct and don't hold their shape as well.

The other three essential cage components are the flotation devices, a top, and a feeding ring. It takes one cubic foot of an ideal flotation material like polystyrene foam to support a 50-cubic-foot full-frame, nylon-web cage. Also, the floats must be attached in such a way that the top of the cage sits at least four inches above the water.

The cage will require a solid top that's hinged or removable, because most fish prefer shade to sunlight. Such a lid will also help deter theft, predation, or high-leaping escapes. The feeding ring is simply a band of fine mesh, such as mosquito netting, that prevents floating feeds from slipping out the sides of the cage. You can stitch a length of this material around the inside of the cage at the water line, construct a floating wood-framed feeding skirt, or cut a hole in the cage's lid and trim that with netting to make a feeding well.

SITING CAGES: The ideal site for a cage will be a spot where the water is about six feet deep. Shallower locations will normally have reduced water circulation, and some deeper spots are subject to turnover, a sudden reversal of water layers that brings oxygen-starved bottom water to the surface. Caged fish that are caught in a turnover may be killed.

Try to choose a site that's exposed to breezes but protected from high waves and motorboat traffic. Consider, too, that if you can set your cage off the end of a dock, you won't have to take a boat out to feed the fish. Should you need to put the enclosures in open water, secure them with at least one anchor fastened at each end of the cage with nylon lines. Always put the cages out and make sure they float properly before stocking them.

STOCKING: A delicate, indeed critical, moment in any aquaculture operation is stocking, the transferring of the captured or purchased fish to their permanent home. You should always transport your stock in large, double plastic bags that are half full of water and have plenty of air inside.

Begin by floating the fish-filled sack in your cage, and checking the water temperatures of the enclosure and of your container. Unless the two temperatures are nearly identical, wait for them to equalize, a process that usually takes from 15 to 45 minutes, but can be speeded up by carefully exchanging small amounts of water between the sack and cage. If you try this, however, be sure you change the water temperature gradually. Too drastic a jump can either kill the fish outright or lower their resistance so much that many will die later on.

When the two temperatures have equalized, submerge the bag, tilt it sideways, and allow a few minutes for the two fluids to mix. Only then should you move the bag to encourage the fish to leave it.

In general, it's best to stock cages when the ambient water temperature is slightly below the range desirable for growth. That would mean introducing trout into 50 to 55°F water, tilapia in 70 to 75° ponds, and the other species discussed here in 60 to 70° water. Consequently, in most cases you'd probably want to stock your cages in the spring.

However, in many areas larger, more vigorous stock is often available in the fall. If stocked then, these fish can be kept through the winter and finished out during the following spring and summer. If you live where hard freezes are not a problem, you can even stock young fish in the fall for overwintering. Remember, though, that fish set out in autumn won't grow appreciably during the cold months.

The cost of purchased fish will depend on their size. Smaller ones are naturally less expensive, but if possible it's best to stock the largest young fish available because they'll outgrow their little kinfolk and will have a higher survival rate.

To figure out how many fish to stock, you have to calculate backward from your anticipated harvest, keeping in mind that the carrying capacity of a cage is the weight, not the number, of fish it will support. As already indicated, you might expect to raise about 200 pounds of fish in a 50-cubic-foot basket. However, since

most cage culture depends upon a growing season of six months or less, you probably won't be able to produce fish that average more than 3/4 pound. One-half pound is an excellent pan size for the majority of species, and it's also an efficient size, since fish grow fastest when they're small. Therefore, if you intend to produce 200 pounds of 1/2-pound fish, you'll want to rear 400 individuals. So, allowing for some mortality, you could stock a 50-cubic-foot cage with about 440 fish.

FEEDING: Fish in cages have very limited access to natural food. The cage culturist is responsible for providing a diet that is complete both quantitatively and nutritionally.

Most American fish culture is based on processed commercial feeds. These are somewhat expensive, but the rations are both effective and convenient, and beginning cage culturists have enough to learn without trying to create their own feeding schemes.

Most ready-made fish food is tailored to the requirements of either channel catfish or rainbow trout, the two major conventional aquaculture crops, and is thus only partially suited to other species. Such feeds also often lack certain trace elements, since pond-raised fish for which foods are created are expected to gather minor

FRAME

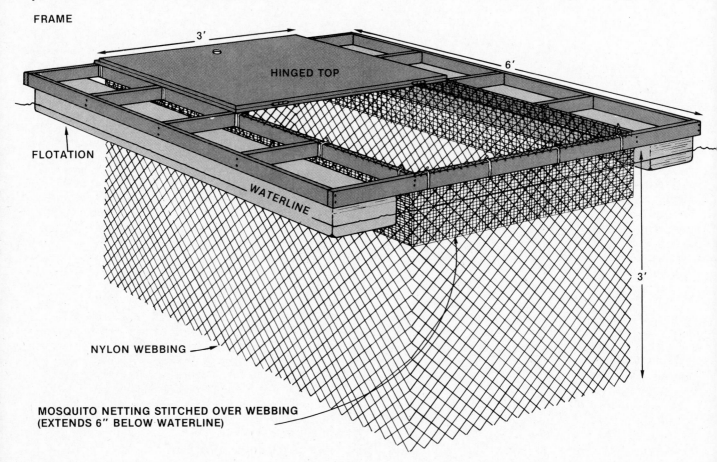

FLOTATION

HINGED TOP

WATERLINE

3'

6'

3'

NYLON WEBBING

MOSQUITO NETTING STITCHED OVER WEBBING
(EXTENDS 6" BELOW WATERLINE)

quantities of natural organisms. However, some manufacturers do offer special cage culture feeds that are nutritionally complete.

The other characteristic essential to any feed used in cages is that it float; sinking rations will be largely lost through the bottom mesh.

Commercial feeds range in size from meal to 3/16-inch pellets. You can pretty well gauge the size you'll need by the mouths of your fish. Since that size will change as your stock grows, and because the feed doesn't store well, you should always buy the smallest convenient quantity at one time, and keep those rations tightly covered.

The best time to feed is usually at dawn, and later in the morning or at dusk are second choices. As a rule, you'll want to give your fish three percent of their total body weight at each feeding, and feed them six days a week. To determine the total weight of your fish, simply catch and weigh a sample periodically, and use this information and the number of fish in the cage to calculate the group's weight.

To gain some idea of the kind of feeding schedule you'll have, make a few calculations using the "end point" method. To illustrate how this works, let's suppose you begin with 200 bullhead fingerlings that weigh a total of 2-1/2 pounds. Assume that you want to raise them to an average of 1/2 pound each, thus yielding 100 pounds of fish. Using the three-percent-weight-a-day feeding rule, you would then give them 0.03 X 2.5 = 0.075 pounds of ration the first day. Furthermore, on the last day before harvest, you'd be feeding 0.03 × 100 = 3 pounds of feed. If you have some idea of when that harvest date will occur—a good time is just after the date your water temperature falls below that needed for optimum growth—you can then count the number of feeding days between stocking and harvesting, and calculate an approximate weekly feed allotment that gradually increases from 0.075 to 3 pounds a day. Be sure, however, to allow for the fact that fish put on weight most rapidly at first, and more slowly as they grow.

NATURAL FEEDS: With the exception of the sunfish, which can be reared on a 100% processed food diet, all the fish mentioned here will eat some commercial feed even though they really don't make good use of it. Of course, all fish will eat available natural foods.

Nocturnal flying insects can be attracted to the space above a cage by a light that costs only a few cents a day to operate. The bugs then drop into the water and become food for the fish in the cage. Although almost any species of fish will eat insects floating on the surface of the water, trout and bluegill—among the fish best suited to cage culture—particularly relish downed bugs. At least one commercially available type of light comes equipped with a fan to pull in the insects and blow them down onto the surface of the water.

Earthworms can also be used to supply caged fish with natural meals. A special feeder can be constructed by simply punching a few holes through a thin block of polystyrene foam. Worms are spread on top of the block, and it is placed on the water in the cage. The worms will crawl down through the holes, and the fish will make a meal of them as they reach the water under the foam block.

Fish are also fond of maggots, and these can be provided for the caged swimmers by mounting a hardware-cloth basket on a pole a few feet above the cage and filling the basket with putrid meat or rotting fish. As the maggots begin to pupate, they'll move away from the meat and fall into the water, where they'll be eaten by the fish. The meat or fish in the basket will need to be replaced weekly.

If you have a source of unwanted fish, meat scraps, or offal, you can use these leavings by grinding, chopping, or boiling them. Any food particles that are so small they might pass through the mesh should be placed in a large container and lowered into the cage.

Although most of the fish discussed will not eat leafy matter, tilapia are quite fond of plants, and Israeli carp will take some. Most soft aquatic plants, comfrey, purslane, carrot tops, and hairy vetch can be used. Serve the vegetation by tying it in bunches and suspending it in the cage.

You may not be able to provide much natural feed, but keep in mind that even an amount totaling less than one percent of your fish's total diet may improve their growth or flavor, or even enable you to switch from a complete commercial feed to a less costly supplemental one. Remember to allow for water content when calculating feeding rates—or ratios—with natural feeds. Commercial products are relatively dry. Insects contain approximately 75% water. Fish, meat, and worms are about 85% water, and green plants contain 90 to 95% water.

MAINTENANCE: Inspect your cages daily. When necessary, clean the mesh so any accumulated algal growth won't inhibit water flow. (A toilet brush mounted on a long handle works fine for this purpose.) You should also examine the fish to see that their feed is being eaten and that they're in good health. If food is being wasted, cut back on the amount, skip a day's serving, or change their diet. If your stock remains off its feed after you've taken the above measures, check the fish for disease.

HARVESTING: Mass harvesting of cage-cultured fish is the simplest process imaginable: Just lift the cage and take out the crop. To catch only a few fish for dinner, you can drive some into a corner with a shallow, square-cornered dip net and scoop them out.

THE PAYOFF: Though the cost of operating a caged fish operation will vary from one area to another, there is little doubt that even a small-scale setup can produce clean, protein-rich meat for a fraction of the amount a person would have to spend for it in the supermarket.

RAISING A BACKYARD DAIRY COW

Just one milk cow contentedly chewing her cud in the lower 40, or even in a small backyard plot, can easily provide a family with all the milk, cheese, and other dairy products it'll ever need. In fact, a cow can actually overwhelm a single household with an overabundance of delicious milk, but the problem of dealing with the excess is just the sort of hassle that most homesteaders hope to face.

What's more, milk and its by-products aren't the only goods that a dairy animal will provide. She'll raise her own calf or calves each year to supply your freezer with meat and will also add her share of material to the compost pile.

PICK THE BEST COW: If there is any single livestock-raising commandment that is of prime importance, it's the rule that you should always pick the very best animal you can find. When you realize that, poor producer or not, you'll have to milk and feed a hungry hay-burner twice a day, seven days a week, for the next 10 to 15 years, it should be evident that you want to start with a good cow.

If you haven't been around dairy cattle much, it's best to have an experienced herder, preferably not a person who's trying to sell you an animal, give you some pointers on making a good buy. As an alternative, you can also learn a good bit about choosing a cow by simply sitting ringside at a local fair or cattle show and matching your discerning eye against that of the judge.

Naturally, the animal you select should be healthy. Look for clear, bright eyes, a shiny coat, a clean, moist muzzle, and normal feces. Also, be sure that the animal has no limps, lumps, or cuts.

A quality cow will look a lot different from a beef-bearing steer. A good milker will appear angular, having prominent shoulder tops and hipbones. Her ribs will show, but they shouldn't stick out. She'll have a large chest area with plenty of room for lungs and heart, and her belly should look as if it could easily hold a 55-gallon drum's worth of food.

A dairy cow's udder is the beast's most important asset. You should learn how to recognize a quality, high-producing udder before you even consider shopping for a cow. In general, the bigger and more capacious the appendage, the better. When you look at the cow from the rear, the udder should fill a large area between her hocks, and when viewed from the side, it should extend well forward in the flank region. Though the udder should be large, it shouldn't be pendulous.

Since you'll probably be the person doing the pail filling, pick an easy milker. Look for a gentle animal, one whose teats just fit your hands (if you plan to hand-milk, as most small-scale cowherds will) and whose milk flows easily into the pail.

In other words, don't buy any cow until you've tried her. There are few more discouraging ways to start your dairy enterprise than to find that you own a cantankerous old hussy who's nearly impossible to milk without first playing rodeo or whose streak canal, the passage in the teat through which the milk flows, is so small you've got to squeeze the life out of her to get a dribble of liquid.

Almost all dairy operators maintain good records that

will show which of the herd are the best producers. Only the offspring of prize animals should be used to start any herd, large or small.

PLAN THE COW SHED WELL: Unless the weather in your area is particularly severe, neither your cows nor their calves will need elaborate shelters. Even folks in northern Wisconsin have been getting along just fine for years with open-ended cattle sheds. Such structures should face south to catch the sun's warming rays and provide 60 square feet of bedded area for each adult and 25 to 35 square feet for each calf. About a ton of bedding is needed each year for each cow.

For most operations with one or two cows, fenced pasture is much more economical than a small enclosed feedlot. Just how much pasture your cow will need during a growing season will depend on the quality of the

fields involved. An acre of top-of-the-line grass may be sufficient for a cow and her calf, but in sparse pastures —such as are found in western Kansas—it may take 40 to 50 acres to support one adult cow.

Most dairy animals are as docile as lambs, so they generally won't turn into fence wreckers unless they're in heat. Any sturdy enclosure about 39 inches high will keep the animals home on your range.

KNOW ABOUT BREEDS: There are five major dairy breeds available in North America: Guernsey,

---

BOTTOM LEFT: Jersey cows give milk that is rich in butterfat and other milk solids. BOTTOM CENTER: Traditionally, Brown Swiss were used as draft animals as well as for meat and milk. BOTTOM RIGHT: Ayrshires are generally large, hardy animals.

Jersey, Brown Swiss, Ayrshire, and Holstein. The following chart shows the approximate composition of each breed's milk:

BREED	FAT (%)	PROTEIN (%)	NONFAT SOLIDS (%)
Ayrshire	4.0	3.5	9.0
Brown Swiss	4.0	3.5	9.0
Guernsey	4.9	3.7	9.4
Holstein	3.6	3.2	8.7
Jersey	5.4	3.8	9.4

There are also several breeds that are considered dual-purpose animals and are raised for both milk and meat. These include the Milking Shorthorn, the Devon, the Dexter, and the Dutch Belted.

Jerseys and Guernseys originated in the English Channel islands between England and France. The farms on such isles were generally divided into many small fields in which the cows were most often chained or tethered to a stake that was moved several times every day. Milkmaids visited the cows right in the fields, rather than bringing the animals in to be milked. Because the milk had to be carried some distance, it proved more practical under the circumstances to have a small cow that gave a limited volume of milk rich in butterfat and other solids than a heavy milker whose output was not as rich. A Guernsey or Jersey typically produces a little less volume than do other major dairy breeds, but the milk—as the chart indicates—contains a higher average percentage of butterfat.

In contrast, Ayrshires originated in Scotland, where herds often had to graze over a considerable acreage to get enough food. As a result, Ayrshires are usually large, hardy animals.

Holsteins, on the other hand, were developed in Holland on very fertile soil with lush grasses. With plenty of feed available to be converted to milk, Holsteins became large-volume producers.

In the early days of the Brown Swiss, Switzerland's farmers needed triple-purpose animals: beasts that could provide both meat and milk and be used for draft purposes. The Brown Swiss is typically a large, thick-muscled animal that also gives a good volume of milk.

The dual-purpose breeds result from efforts to reach a compromise between meat and milk production. Such animals are usually meatier than the other dairy cows, but they generally won't give as much milk as will those that have no other job.

KNOW YOUR MARKET: Assume you've chosen a good-looking animal that appears to be just waiting to turn her spigots on; how much milk should you expect her to give? Dairy operators figure that they need to get 9,000 to 10,000 pounds of milk per cow in a ten-month lactation period in order to break even. That works out to about 30 to 34 pounds, or about four gallons, a day

for 305 days a year. Now around five tons of milk is a lot for most families to drink, and there'll also be a pound or so of cream that you can ladle off the top of the milk jar every morning.

Even if you can't find several friends to share in your excess milk, it can be used as a highly nutritious diet supplement for other animals. For example, ten pounds of milk will be a bellyful for a calf. In fact, depending on how much milk the cow gives, you may be able to feed two or three calves and still have enough left over for your table. What's more, the calves should be weaned when they reach 2-1/2 to 3 months of age, so a family could conceivably have its fill of milk and raise a total of six to nine calves annually in three separate batches.

Extra newborn calves can often be bought for reasonable prices from dairy farm owners who don't want to fool with bull calves. The calves you raise can then be sold as weanlings, and you can pocket the money; or you could turn the beasts out to the back 40 to become meat for your table.

Even if you choose not to feed extra calves, you'll probably have one calf of your own each year that'll eventually end up in the freezer. Don't let anyone tell you that dairy steaks aren't tasty; they're delicious. There just aren't quite as many of them on each animal as there are on beef cattle. However, if you want your cow's offspring to be a little meatier, you can simply breed your cow to a beef bull every year (until it's time to replace her with one of her daughters), and she'll give you a meat-producing beef-dairy cross calf whose fast growth and tasty meat may amaze you.

FEED THE COW CORRECTLY: Cows, as well as sheep and goats, are cud-chewers and have four-chambered (ruminant) stomachs designed for digesting grasses. If all your cow had to do to earn her keep was to raise a calf every year, she'd probably get along just fine on nothing more than pasture and hay. However, you'll be asking her for 10,000 pounds of milk and 400 pounds of butterfat, as well as for that annual calf. This means you'll need to feed the cow plenty of protein in the form of grain and supplements to keep her system running smoothly.

The key to feeding for profit and health, then, is to provide your milkmaker with what she needs when she needs it, realizing that her requirements will vary. During a typical lactation cycle, for instance, a cow will give a tremendous flow of milk for the first one to three months, after which the amount produced each day will decrease gradually until the animal finally dries up. A really good producer will have difficulty eating enough during the first few months of lactation to meet her energy needs, so be sure not to spare the grain or hay at such times.

As the animal's flow decreases, supply her with feed according to the amount of milk she gives each day. For each pound of milk she generates, feed the cow half a pound of 16% protein grain so the final mix of forage and grain contains 12% protein. In addition to the grain, your animal will munch from one to four pounds of forage, depending on the quality of the grass, for every 100 pounds she weighs: A 1,000-pounder will need to eat 10 to 40 pounds of grass and hay a day. Never let a cow's daily grass consumption drop below 10 to 12 pounds, though, or her digestive system won't function properly and you'll end up having to treat a 1,000-pound bellyache.

Your cow will be dry, not giving any milk, during the last two months before she calves, or freshens. For her future health's sake, it's extremely important to keep the expectant cow svelte and supple. Don't let her become obese, but don't allow her to lose weight either. Watch her ribs; they should neither start to stick out obviously nor disappear under a layer of fat.

During her dry period and up to the final week before she's due to calve, your animal should be on a low-calcium diet including such food as nonleguminous hay (prairie hay and timothy, for example), low-calcium grains (corn, wheat, milo, and oats), and a mineral mix without calcium. Once she freshens, of course, you'll want to get her on a high-calcium diet right away: Legume hays, grains such as soybean, cottonseed, and linseed meal, and a mineral supplement that includes calcium will help keep her in good shape after she calves.

In addition to hay or grass and grain, cows have other needs. One healthy dairy animal will need 12 to 15 gallons of fresh, clean water daily. She also must have an accessible salt lick that'll provide this essential ingredient at 1% of her food ration. To provide calcium and other trace minerals that may be lacking in the cow's diet, it's best to use a salt and mineral mix during lactation. Check with a local veterinarian or county extension agent to find out which salt supplements are usually considered necessary in your region: selenium or iodine, for instance. If she's not on green pasture or hay, your cow will also need vitamin A, especially when she's expecting. Add at least 30 mg. of carotene (vitamin A precursor) to her daily ration during the last few months of her pregnancy.

Many of the dairy animal disease problems you've probably heard about such as milk fever and pregnancy toxemia can be prevented simply by using good cow-feeding common sense.

A cow can be a very practical, and relatively easy to care for, addition to almost any homestead. If well chosen, the animals are cost-effective, producing enough meat calves and milk to more than offset the expense of feed, and in many cases, they really become part of the family.

FROM MILK PAIL TO SUPPER TABLE

Raising a healthy dairy cow is by no means all there is to having your own fresh milk for the table. To insure that your homegrown dairy products are tasty and safe to eat or drink, several procedures and guidelines need to be followed.

Before the cow even reaches the milking barn, it's important to make certain the animal doesn't eat anything that might taint the flavor of the milk. During and after the actual milking, it's mandatory to assure that the building, equipment, and the cow herself are scrupulously clean.

In order to avoid otherwise perfectly good milk having an "off" taste, make certain the dairy animal doesn't have access to onions, silage, cabbage, moldy grain, spoiled hay, or any other food that might impart a peculiar flavor to the cow's milk.

The milking area should be spotless, and many dairy operators paint these enclosures white so it's easy to see fly specks, spots of fecal matter, or dirt. Also, strong odors should be kept out of the milking and milk storage areas.

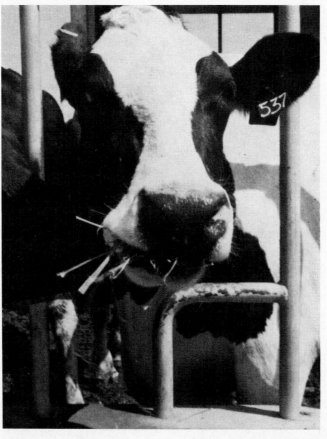

Any equipment used for milking or milk handling, such as pans, pails, strainers, and bottles, should be sterilized, and the people involved in milking or processing the product should always scrub their hands and arms before setting to work.

Make certain that the animal is clean and keep the hair around and above the udder clipped. Immediately prior to milking, clean the udder thoroughly, using a paper towel soaked in a disinfectant solution to wash off any mud and dirt, and throw the towel away afterward. When you've finished with the udder itself, clean each teat in a dip cup filled with fresh disinfectant solution. Both dip cups and disinfectants are available from farm supply or feed stores.

Finally, be sure that the milk itself is clean. Strip the first three or four streams into a black cup and swirl the liquid around. Look for the small chunks or clumps that can indicate mastitis, an inflammation or infection of the mammary gland.

KEEP A READY ROUTINE: There's more than one reason for washing your animals' udders carefully. Milk flow is brought on by the hormone oxytocin, the production of which is stimulated by massaging the udder and performing other premilking routines that the animal is accustomed to, such as the noisy, but familiar, routine of scrubbing the milking pail.

After the stimulation begins, it takes about 45 to 90 seconds to produce a milk flow, and the hormone's effect lasts only eight minutes. The milking process should thus be finished within about eight minutes after you have washed the cow's udder.

When you're done, dip each teat once again in fresh disinfectant. This procedure leaves a drop of solution at the end of the teat canal to help prevent infections.

Dairy animals must be milked at least twice a day, allowing about 12 hours between sessions. If you milked three times a day, you could likely increase production by 10% to 20%, but the additional labor and time involved would have to be weighed against the value of the extra milk.

ABOUT MASTITIS: Mastitis can occur in any dairy animal, and it is caused by a variety of organisms: bacteria, fungi, and possibly viruses. It can be triggered by a seemingly inconsequential bump to the udder, which can lead to inflammation and eventual infection, or by cuts, bruises, cold, dirt, or stress, which also leave the udder vulnerable to the invasion of mastitis-causing microorganisms.

On the other hand, proper milking techniques can help prevent the disease. The cleaner a cow's environment, the less chance there is of introducing mastitis-causing organisms into the udder.

Extra care in the selection of your animals will also help prevent mastitis. A cow with an udder that's carried tightly up against the flank will suffer a lot less udder banging and bruising than will an animal with a pendulous, low-slung bag. The less vulnerable the udder is to being bumped, the less chance there will be for infection to occur.

Severe mastitis can be identified by clumps in the milk, which are actually fibrous masses of infection-fighting white blood cells, but evidence of milder cases isn't always visible. However, a simple procedure called the California mastitis test (CMT) helps bring together any cells which may be present. This makes detection of less advanced cases much easier.

The CMT uses a blue indicator liquid and a white paddle-shaped device that has attached cups. A stream of milk from each teat is collected in a cup, after which a few drops of the indicator fluid are added. The examiner simply swirls the two substances together, then tips the paddle slightly so that the milk slowly runs to one side. If white cells are present, they'll show up as clumps that are easily seen against the blue color.

Another mastitis screening procedure is the somatic cell count (SCC). Performed by the Dairy Herd Improvement Association (DHIA), the test provides a count of the somatic cells—white blood cells and epithelial cells, for example—present in the milk.

An excess of somatic cells in the milk might be an indication of mastitis. However, some epithelial cells are continually sloughed off into the milk produced by any animal, and the normal quantity will vary according to the stage of lactation and the age of the beast. Your herd's DHIA records should help you determine whether an animal's cell count is normal or too high.

A CHECK PROGRAM: There are three steps that should be taken to keep a close watch for mastitis in your dairy animals.

First, every time you milk, swirl the first few streams of milk around in a black cup to check for evident mastitis.

Second, periodically use the California mastitis test to uncover any less obvious cases. A guideline for testing would be to perform the CMT once a month for non-problem herds, once a week for problem herds, and once a day for problem individuals. If your DHIA records provide a somatic cell count, compare your cows to the organization's norms. When an animal scores higher, assume that she's contracted the ailment.

Third, if mastitis has been diagnosed, feel the animal's udder. If it's hot, call the vet immediately. Should the udder feel only normally warm, simply milk the cow out every two or three hours for a total of 72 hours, and discard the milk or, in light cases, feed it to your

A final "teat dip" in a disinfectant solution will help protect against disease-carrying microorganisms.

pigs. Many cases of mastitis can be cured without the use of antibiotics by merely emptying the udder as often as possible and letting the cow's immune system work its own magic. However, if the repeat CMT is still positive after three days, call your vet.

You can increase disease resistance in the udder by giving all cows a two-month layoff between lactations. The vacation will give their milk-producing systems a chance to recuperate and regenerate.

PREPARING MILK FOR CONSUMPTION: What should you do to guarantee that a bucketful of fresh milk will be pure and tasty for meals?

Well, once you've got the liquid into a bottle or pan, cool it as rapidly as possible to 40° Fahrenheit to insure a longer shelf life and better flavor.

After chilling it, you may want to pasteurize the milk. This process will kill most of the disease-carrying bugs that could affect people. There are two ways to go about the task. One is to heat the milk to 165°F for 20 seconds (actually, you just bring it to 165°F and then shut off the burner). The other is to warm the milk to 145°F and hold it at that temperature for 30 minutes. Be sure to use stainless steel pans and to stir the milk constantly with a stainless steel spoon while it's heating. Copper, iron, or chipped enamel pots, and metal (other than stainless steel) thermometers may give the milk an "off" flavor. When the time is up, quickly cool the liquid to 60°F, and store it at 40°F.

Pasteurization and animal testing have greatly reduced the incidence of brucellosis and tuberculosis in this country, but it's still wise to exercise caution. Whether you consume raw or pasteurized milk from your homestead animal, test the cow annually for both diseases.

By maintaining the health of your animals and the sanitation of your milking facilities and equipment, handling the milk properly once it is out of the cow, and following a proper breeding cycle to insure continued production, you and your family should have no trouble being certain of an ample supply of fresh, wholesome milk.

RAISING A HEALTHY FLOCK OF CHICKENS

Chickens can be ideal animals for the beginning homesteader or backyard farmer. More and more people are discovering that raising their own poultry can provide them with all the fresh eggs they could ever want and lots of tasty fried, roasted, or stewed chicken, frequently for a fraction of the commercial cost of these products.

The homegrown meat won't reach your dinner table filled with growth stimulators, hormones, antibiotics, and whatever else goes into mass-produced poultry these days, and the eggs will be fresh, with rich yellow yolks that stand up in the frying pan.

A backyard flock can also provide a good supply of manure for the compost pile or garden, and you can even use your friendly fowl for pest control, especially in the fruit orchard.

Perhaps the most attractive aspect of having chickens, though, is that the birds are really pretty easy to raise. In order to establish your own flock, you'll just have to set aside a bit of space, build a small coop, obtain a few birds, and follow the rules of poultry care.

RECOGNIZE YOUR MARKET: The kind of chickens you select will depend on your purpose in raising them. Today, thanks to the ingenuity and selective breeding efforts of scientists and poultry fanciers, the birds are available in all sizes, shapes, colors, and feather patterns. There are 350 different combinations. Generally speaking, however, chickens can be divided into four main classifications: the egg layers, the meat-makers (broilers), the dual-purpose birds (egg and meat producers), and the exotic or exhibition breeds.

Each general type of fowl is represented by various breeds, and there are several varieties of each breed. The term breed is used to categorize a group of individuals whose characteristics can be passed on to future generations. A variety, on the other hand, is a subclass of the breed that differs from other varieties of that breed, usually by only one characteristic. For example, the buff Orpington and the black Orpington are different varieties of the same breed (Orpington). The differing characteristic in this case is color: One variety is buff, and the other is black.

Egg-laying breeds have been developed specifically for that purpose. A good leghorn (the most common egg-producing breed) will lay 250 to 300 white-shelled breakfast treats a year. But don't expect to use such a bird as a fat fryer or plump roasting hen; these barnyard fowl will barely tip the scales at four pounds, no matter how much you feed them.

Broilers, on the other hand, will often weigh more than eight pounds, and if you keep pouring feed into them, the roosters may reach 17 to 18 pounds. Such tasty grain-peckers can be butchered when they are anywhere from 5 to 24 weeks old, depending on how much meat you want from each bird. In fact, Cornish game hens are nothing more than smallish, five-week-old hens of the Cornish rock "broiler" breed.

The chickens most often found on supermarket fresh meat counters are probably eight-week-old broiler-type birds, either male or female. The roasters that are displayed in a grocery store's frozen food case are birds that are allowed to reach 11 to 15 weeks of age before being butchered.

Dual-purpose breeds fall somewhere between layers and meat producers in size and characteristics. They will lay about 200 to 250 eggs per year and will also grow into fairly hefty birds, weighing five to six pounds when they reach maturity in six months.

Exotic or exhibition birds aren't bred for egg or meat production. These fowl are most often unusually colored chickens, decked out in brilliantly hued costumes of head-to-toe feathers. They're primarily show birds and are exhibited in various competitions.

BUILD A GOOD CHICKEN HOUSE: Like most living creatures, chickens sometimes need a place to get in out of the rain, the wind, and the sun. Besides four walls and a roof, your birds' coop should have a roost for the sleepyheads to doze upon and a secluded place for the hens to sit while laying their eggs.

Chicks will need about half a square foot of indoor floor space per bird until they're about six weeks old. The young birds will also need a brooder—either the hen that hatched them or a heated enclosure—to keep them warm. Adults require three square feet each, but if an outdoor run is provided, this figure can be cut in half.

Every bird should have ten inches of roosting space. A limb that's about two inches in diameter works well as a perch, or you can simply round the edges of a length of 2 X 2 board. Place the roosts 24 inches above the floor, spaced 13 to 15 inches apart.

Hens need nest boxes to hide in while they're laying eggs, so make a number of the simple open-faced shelters, each about 12 inches square with a perch in front, and situate them 24 inches off the floor. Not every hen will need a box; one for every four biddies should be plenty.

As you build your coop, keep in mind that ventilation and sanitation are both extremely important. For that reason, the easier the shelter is to clean, the better. Always keep plenty of fresh, dry litter on the floor; there are a number of good, inexpensive materials that can be used, including sawdust, wood chips, straw, old hay, and leaves.

Several times each year scrub all the roosts, nest boxes, feeders, and waterers with a solution of one tablespoon of chlorine bleach per gallon of water. You'll find your cleaning chores easier if you put a shallow wire-covered pit beneath the roosts. Use a wood frame covered with 1/2-inch wire mesh for the lid. The pit will collect the droppings, which can then go directly into the compost pile.

A portable coop (that is, a shelter on wheels) will enable your poultry to serve more than one function. With a movable house, it's easy to transport the chickens to a fresh pasture every week or so. On each site, the birds will scratch and dig, and eat many of the pests that are getting ready to attack your garden. Then, after feasting on greens and bugs, the hens will deposit a layer of fresh fertilizer. In essence the birds act as miniature farm implements, removing weeds, turning the earth, killing the bugs, and fertilizing the soil.

If the space is available, you can let your chickens run the range. By choosing their fare every day, free-roaming birds are able to balance their own diets. Giving them the run of some pastureland is easier on your budget than having to purchase all their food, but most range chickens need to have their diets supplemented with commercial feed containing 5% to 15% protein.

Furthermore, unconfined chickens can take daily dust baths, which will help keep the birds free of mites. One word of caution, though: Roamers can be active and aggressive garden destroyers. They love succulent, newly emerged seedlings, so either fence their pasture in or fence the birds out of the garden.

While you're building enclosures, you'll need to provide some kind of protection from predators. Make your range fencing and the coop ratproof and strong enough to keep out roaming dogs, raccoons, coyotes, and other predators. A two-foot-wide band of small-mesh welded wire, secured to the lower portion of the chicken-wire fence and extending at least six inches underground, should do the job.

KNOW WHAT NORMAL LOOKS AND FEELS LIKE: A healthy, normal chicken is bright-eyed, alert, and active. In contrast, a sick bird will have dull, expressionless eyes and will sit with its head drooping and its feathers fluffed out. A hen that's broody (one that either is trying to hatch eggs or thinks she is) will often look about the same as a bird that's ill, and it'll take a little time to learn how to distinguish between a chicken that is actually sick and one that is merely broody.

BUY ONLY THE BEST: There are several ways to purchase chickens, and your situation will probably determine how you choose to start your flock.

Most folks get started by buying day-old chicks and raising them at home. The babies can be bought in batches of 25, and you can purchase sexed chickens, all roosters or all hens, depending on whether you want meat or eggs. If you don't particularly care about the gender of the birds, you can buy straight runs, which are sold just as they come out of the eggs, with about an even mix of males and females.

Sexed chicks will cost around twice as much as do straight runs, but as with other animals, prices will vary from area to area and from breed to breed.

If you'd prefer not to raise the chicks yourself, it's possible to purchase older birds that'll be ready to lay eggs a few weeks after you receive them. These pullets, as they're called, are usually from 18 to 20 weeks old and will cost five or six times as much as will straight-run chicks.

It might also be worth your while to purchase older hens from other poultry raisers. The older biddies won't cost much, because they will probably be past their

dual-purpose chicks. When they reach 20 to 24 weeks of age, you can butcher the roosters and expect the hens to begin laying.

The following spring, buy a replacement batch of day-old dual-purpose babies and begin again.

During the second and each succeeding year, when the time comes to kill and dress out your 20- to 24-week-old roosters, you can butcher the previous season's hens (for stewing purposes) as well. By the time you've put the roosters and old hens into your freezer, the new young biddies will be about to begin their laying duties.

A good hen in peak egg production will lay about once every 30 hours. She'll produce best, however, when she's exposed to 14 hours of sunlight every day. In the fall, when the sunshine hours decrease and egg production consequently tapers off, you can keep the hens producing by setting up an inexpensive light timer and keeping the coop bright for the recommended 14 hours per day.

All in all, keeping a backyard flock of chickens can be a very rewarding experience. You'll be treated to fresh, wholesome food and the opportunity to watch the fascinating social interaction of your birds. And if you keep a rooster around (it isn't necessary to do so to get eggs, but having one of the old boys in the coop does seem to lend an air of completeness to the flock), you will be treated to the early morning crowing chorus that has wakened people for centuries.

egg-laying prime and therefore won't be considered very valuable.

BE AWARE OF THE CHICKENS' CYCLES: An egg-laying chicken has only one year of peak egg production. After that she'll molt and stop producing. In about six to eight weeks the hen will regrow her plumage and begin to lay again but will produce at least 10% fewer eggs than during her first laying season. The fact that a nonproducing chicken will cost almost as much time and money as will a good layer will probably prompt you to consider managing your flock in the following manner:

In the spring, purchase a straight-run batch of day-old

AN EGG CANDLER YOU CAN MAKE

"Don't count your chickens before they hatch" is one proverb poultry raisers learn to take literally. The frustrating and time-wasting experience of trying to hatch an unfertilized egg under a hen or in an incubator can be avoided with a homemade candler that allows you to see inside unhatched eggs. Not only can infertile eggs be distinguished from fertile ones, but the freshness and purity of those infertile eggs can be checked.

CANDLER CONSTRUCTION: The main component of this little lantern is a metal can with a lid. A coffee can or any similar canister with a tight-fitting lid will do. To make the candler, position an ordinary light fixture inside the can, punch a few mounting holes in the container's bottom, and secure the fixture with a couple of small bolts and nuts. Make one other opening in the bottom of the canister for the light's electric cord. On the free end of this wire, attach an electrical plug, and then add an in-line switch to the cord.

To make a hole for illuminating the eggs, cut a 1-1/2-inch-diameter hole in the container's lid. A 2-1/4-inch-diameter cork gasket glued around that opening prevents an egg from cracking if it accidentally bumps the can while being examined. If you have a hard time finding cork gasket material, either felt or rubber can be used for this part.

Four legs attached to the side of the candler allow horizontal viewing. These are easily made by cutting two six-inch-long strips from thin sheet metal and bending each strip to form a pair of legs. Secure them to the can's side with sheet metal screws or pop rivets.

Punch a few holes in the container's sides for ventilation, and coat the outside with high-temperature auto engine paint as a finish. When the paint's thorough-ly dry, screw in a 40-watt light bulb, plug the device in, and darken the room. With that, you're ready to start candling eggs.

GLOWING REPORTS: It's best to test the fertility of white eggs around the fourth day after they've been laid. Dark ones, on the other hand, give the most accurate results after about a week. Any dirt on the shells should be gently brushed, not washed, away. To check for signs of fertility, carefully place an egg's wide end to the candler opening so that the entire oval is illuminated. In a fertile, hatchable egg there will be a fine network of veins running out from a dark center. "Clears," those with no visible embryonic development, are ones that were never fertilized, while the few with small blood spots could be either fertilized eggs in which the embryo has died or infertile eggs that have simply had some veins rupture.

Candling can also be used to check the quality of eggs going to market or to the kitchen. Here again, the oval is held with its broad end to the light opening. However, in this case, the egg is given a few quick turns so that the contents rotate within the shell to promote fuller viewing. A fresh egg will have an air space 1/8 inch or less in depth and a yolk that's free of foreign particles, blood rings, large spots, and other defects. You probably won't want to sell the eggs with blood spots, as most buyers consider them unsightly, but if you merely remove the specks with the tip of a knife, they'll do just fine for your own table.

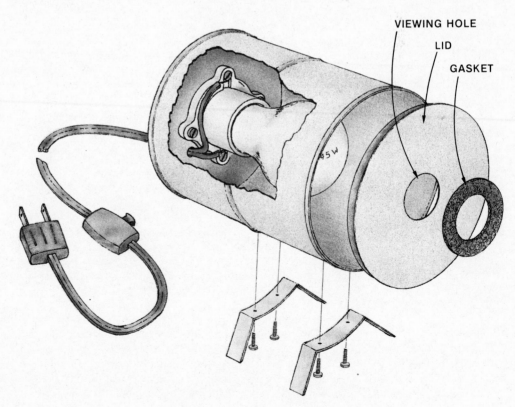

VIEWING HOLE

LID

GASKET

DO'S AND DON'TS OF RAISING HEALTHY RABBITS

Even if your backyard is no bigger than about 30 square feet, you can produce 200 pounds of homegrown meat every year by raising rabbits.

Domestic rabbit meat is a tasty, amazingly versatile food. Its flavor is often compared to that of chicken, and like the barnyard fowl, rabbit is good fried, baked, stewed, cooked in casseroles, and prepared in many other ways. The mammal's firm, fine-grained flesh actually makes for more healthful eating than does the bird's, and in fact, rabbit has more protein, less fat, and fewer calories per pound than some more popular meats.

Rabbits are a wise choice for the small livestock fancier for other reasons, too: They are quite easy to raise, feed, and care for. They're also quiet, an important consideration for folks who are rearing animals in an urban area.

People getting into caretaking a batch of the furry beasts will want to keep their livestock as healthy and productive as possible. There are several matters a person needs to consider in setting up and maintaining a rabbit-raising operation.

RECOGNIZE YOUR MARKET: Obviously, the main reason for raising your own rabbits is to produce meat. So before getting started in your venture, you should know just how much food you can expect to get. A good doe will yield four to five litters with six to nine youngsters a batch per year. Each of the young animals should reach a weight of 4 to 4-1/2 pounds at the standard butchering age of eight to ten weeks. At that age they should dress out to between 2 and 2-1/2 pounds. Therefore, a single doe can contribute 60 pounds or more of meat for your larder in one year, which isn't a bad output from one 10- or 12-pound animal. What's more, unlike a steer, which yields all its 500 freezer-filling pounds at one time, your rabbit meat will be produced in meal-sized portions throughout most of the year.

You won't need to throw out your rabbits' innards, either. Slice the kidneys in half, deep-fry the segments, and serve them as hors d'oeuvres. Rabbit liver can be cooked and chopped up into a tasty sandwich spread, or fried with mushrooms and bacon. Even the remaining viscera from your butchered fryers can be utilized: It makes a tasty treat for dogs or pigs.

Rabbits produce more than meat, too. You can, for instance, shovel their high-quality manure straight onto a vegetable plot. Rabbit manure has more nitrogen and phosphorus than does horse, cow, or pig manure, and it won't burn plants, as chicken droppings will.

You could also set up a ground-level bin under your elevated rabbit hutches and start a worm farm in the collected droppings. Many rabbit producers have successfully combined bunny and earthworm raising operations. Furthermore, the rabbits' pelts make excellent hats, collars, and mittens.

Always remember, though, that you are the real market for the bounty your bunnies produce. Sure, you might eventually want to try your hand at commercial breeding, but no one should undertake such an enterprise without enough experience to understand fully the labor, costs, and marketing possibilities involved.

BUILD A GOOD HOUSE: Domestic rabbits don't need a lot of space to hop around in, but if they're to be as healthy and productive as possible, the animals will need some room in their cages. Each doe or buck should have a hutch that's at least 3 feet long, 2-1/2 feet deep, and 1-1/2 or 2 feet high. You can construct the sides and top of a rabbit hutch out of small-gauge chicken wire, but be sure to use only sturdy and easy-on-the-furry-feet 1/2" X 1" galvanized hardware wire for the cage floor. The entire box can be framed on the outside with wood or metal, but note that rabbits will chew on any exposed wooden members they can reach. It should be constructed so that it stands well off the ground.

Your hutch will also need a door about 14 inches square, which is large enough to place the nesting box through and to let you reach every part of the cage's interior. You can build the portal from a piece of welded wire and should hinge the door to swing inward.

Rabbits tolerate adverse weather and harsh climates fairly well, but you should construct a sloped hutch roof to shed snow and rain, and in areas where harsh winter gusts occur, build some form of windbreak. The animals actually suffer more in hot weather than they do in cold, though. Prolonged exposure to heat can be fatal to your animals, so be sure the rabbitry is positioned so it'll get adequate shade during sweltering midsummer days.

Along with a good hutch, you should supply your rabbits with a feeder, a waterer, and a nesting box. The food container can be nothing more than a heavy earthen crock or a coffee can fastened to the side of the cage. On the other hand, you might prefer to buy one of the commercial automatic feeders that attach to the outside of the hutch and are therefore difficult for the rabbits to contaminate.

A waterer can be as plain as a frequently cleaned and replenished dish, or as elaborate as a commercial drip waterer. You can construct a homemade automatic device by suspending a filled and inverted bottle over a watering pan. Just make sure the jug's lid is slightly under the pan's water level.

Finally, each doe will need a nesting box to use when she kindles, or gives birth. This maternity ward can be built out of wood and should measure about 20 inches long by one foot wide by one foot high. Also, fasten a six-inch-wide wood strip across the bottom of its otherwise open front end to keep the newborns from rolling out. Leave the top partly open to allow ventilation.

KNOW WHAT TO LOOK FOR: When you begin to look for your starter rabbits (most rabbit breeders start out with two does and one buck), you'll soon learn that the long-eared animals come in many different breeds and sizes. However, most rabbit raisers across the country agree that the midsize (10 to 12 pounds) New Zealand White and California varieties make about the best backyard livestock.

You'll want to be certain that any animal you buy is

healthy, so examine each rabbit closely before making a purchase. The inside of the animal's ears should not have the dry scabs that are caused by ear mites; its hocks and feet should be free of sore spots; its nose shouldn't be wet, runny, or crusty; and its droppings should be firm and round. If the animal looks fit in these and other obvious respects (does should have eight or more nipples, for instance), you can be pretty sure you've found a healthy one.

Also, never lift a rabbit by its ears. Always pick it up by gently grasping a handful of skin at the scruff of its neck and at the same time, placing a supporting hand under its bottom.

CHOOSE THE BEST ANIMALS: Many of the individual traits that go into producing plenty of meaty rabbits for your table are passed on from one generation to the next, so be sure to buy superior specimens. Purchase only bucks and does with excellent production records or youngsters bred from such prolific propagators. In addition, you can tell a lot about what sort of offspring your breeding stock will produce by examining the potential parents. Most of a rabbit's meat comes from its hind legs, so gently squeeze the rear thighs to judge how plump and meaty those areas are. Give a squeeze test to the back between the animal's pelvis and ribs as well. This loin muscle section should be long, wide, and firm.

CULLING: It's an easy matter to remove the poor producers, negligent mothers, and seriously uncooperative breeders from your rabbit herd: Simply butcher and eat them. Even the most productive parents will decline after five or six years, so your older animals should also be regularly culled.

FEED THEM CORRECTLY: Water is the single most important element in a rabbit's diet. A doe and her litter will consume a full gallon each day, so keep plenty of clean water in the hutches at all times.

A nesting box for rabbits should be sturdy, clean, and well-ventilated. The does will use the unit when they kindle, or give birth.

When it comes to selecting solid food, you should be aware that protein is the most critical food ingredient in assuring superior growth and production. Adult rabbits require a diet with at least 12% of the valuable foodstuff, while nursing mothers and growing youngsters need a 20% protein ration. A rabbit on a protein-deficient diet will grow more slowly, and if it's a doe, she may bear fewer young and produce less milk.

Most rabbit raisers rely on commercial feed, which provides plenty of vital protein and a completely balanced diet as well. Putting together a do-it-yourself rabbit feed that includes all the correct amounts of digestible nutrients, protein, minerals, vitamins, and sheer food energy but doesn't contain poisonous weeds, molds, or other toxins is simply too difficult a task for the average person.

You can, of course, supplement your critters' meals with an occasional helping of root crops, green vegetables, and bits of hay, though you should note that greens will give young bunnies a severe case of diarrhea. Keep in mind that any time you add such a treat to your rabbits' ration, you will undoubtedly be decreasing the percentage of protein in the animals' overall diet.

Baby rabbits should be given free access to all the feed they can eat to help them grow as quickly as possible, but don't overfeed your adults, because obesity is one of the most prevalent causes of infertility in both male and female rabbits. An adult buck or "dry" doe should be fed about three to six ounces of pellets a day, a pregnant female needs five to ten ounces daily, and nursing mothers may require as much as 20 ounces. It's best to tape ration sheets right to your feeders so you know how much food each animal should get.

One last note about rabbits' eating habits: You may have occasion to notice that the critters are coprophagous (in other words they eat their own fecal matter). This "recycling" process is a necessary part of the animals' digestive cycle·that provides, among other essentials, niacin and riboflavin, so don't interpret the habit as a sign of ill health. On the other hand, don't worry if you never see coprophagy, either, because rabbits tend to engage in this and most other feeding practices at night. They are able to maintain this habit even in wire-bottomed cages.

BE AWARE OF YOUR ANIMALS' CYCLES: All rabbit raisers should pay close attention to their animals' reproductive life patterns. Mature rabbits can breed year round. Does actually don't ovulate until ten hours after they're bred, so every mating union should be a fertile one, providing neither animal is overweight and the buck has not been exposed to too much hot weather. As with many animals, excess heat causes short-term sterility in male rabbits.

You can tell whether your doe is pregnant by giving her a checkup two weeks after her mating. At that time, place the animal on a table, restrain her with a one-handed scruff-of-the-neck grasp, and palpate her belly with the other hand: Squeeze gently and slide your hand from the lower rib cage back and up to the pelvic region, feeling carefully for any marble-sized placentas.

A small or young rabbit can be lifted by its loin area, and a grown rabbit should be held by its neck and bottom, never by its ears. A female can be identified by its slitlike genital area, while a buck is characterized by a rounded reproductive region.

A doe usually gives birth 30 to 32 days following conception, so place the nesting box in the animal's hutch no later than 27 days after her mating. You'll be able to wean the fast-growing youngsters within two months after their birth. The doe can be rebred before this separation, but be sure to give her a good two weeks' rest between the end of caring for her past litter and the birth of the next offspring.

KEEP MEANINGFUL RECORDS: If you can imagine the difficulty you'll face in trying to keep track of when to wean and when to mate and when one doe is due to kindle and which of your rabbits came from which doe, and in doing all this while those busy rabbits are multiplying faster than electronic calculators, you'll readily understand the need for keeping accurate records. Without the information they'll contain, it's impossible to tell which rabbits are the most, and which the least, productive.

You can design your own buck and doe breeding forms or use ready-made record-keeping charts. If your flock starts getting really large, you may even want to tattoo each rabbit's ear for identification.

CARING FOR THE YOUNGSTERS: Newborns don't need much human attention because their mother will take care of everything except providing the nest box: That's your job. Be sure to give the nursery a good supply of clean straw or wood shavings—three or four inches' worth in summer and twice that amount during the winter. Then put the box in the hutch three or four days before the doe is due but not any earlier

than that because she may turn her delivery room into a toilet. The mother will then contribute some of her own fur to the nest to make the home even more comfortable for the expected youngsters.

The day after the rabbits are born, check the box and remove any dead newborn. After the little ones are three or four weeks old, remove the nest box itself and let the new residents get used to the hutch. Before the portable nursery is brought back for a new batch of youngsters, it must be thoroughly emptied, cleaned, and disinfected.

HELP YOUR ANIMALS AVOID BECOMING DISEASED: If you buy and raise good rabbits, feed them correctly, and keep your rabbitry clean, you'll avoid 99-44/100% of all rabbit disease problems.

However, there are a couple of persistent health bugaboos that may require particular attention. For example, ear mites, which hide in the crevices of your hutch and love to nibble the insides of rabbit ears, are often a problem. You can control these pests by putting a few drops of mineral or olive oil into your rabbits' ears once every six weeks or so.

In addition, the rough wire floor of the hutch can sometimes produce sores, scabs, and even inflammation on the animals' feet, especially their hocks. You can help remedy that problem by placing flat 6″ X 10″ boards over part of the cage bottom away from the animals' favorite toilet corners so the rabbits can rest their weary toes.

Once you've tried raising these prolific animals, you'll be surprised that more folks don't do likewise.

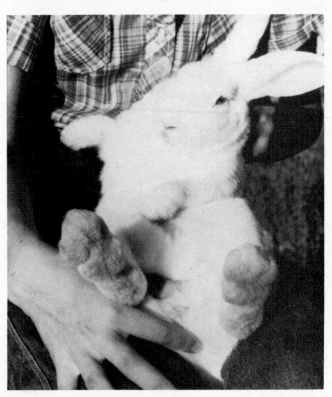

BASICS FOR THE BACKYARD BEEKEEPER

The picture of serene individuals calmly tending the "little golden folk" in their beehives presents a rare and heartwarming example of how people can work in cooperation with the natural world. However, although experienced beekeepers may lyrically praise the sweetness of both their labors and their harvests, most people find the idea of actually taking care of a hive intimidating, even if it means having a personal supply of a nutritious sweetener.

Folks are often frightened by the mere thought of tending to a colony of 30,000 to 80,000 stinger-laden and venom-carrying flying insects. Those who do feel inclined to learn this seemingly mysterious art find that many beekeeping how-to guides plunge into such bewildering barrages of complicated explanations that the books actually add to the readers' muddlement.

Well, in spite of the facts that bees do have stingers, that many texts do seem, at first, to be almost unintelligible, and that no beginner can become an expert and serene beekeeper in a single honey season, it is quite possible for an interested novice to learn to work with bees and to harvest honey.

As long as there are flowers that bear nectar in your area, you can become a beekeeper and successfully manage one or more hives to produce all the fresh, unadulterated honey you and your friends can use. This holds true even if you live in the middle of a large city. In fact, many urban beekeepers maintain hives on apartment house roofs or in attics. Before getting into beekeeping in a city or anywhere else, however, you should check state and local ordinances.

STINGS: Many people don't have beehives simply because they're afraid of being stung. That concern is not unfounded; if you keep bees, you will get stung. Many times you'll visit them and not receive a single poke, and other days you may acquire one or two light "tip" stings that don't even swell. Then again, odds are that someday you'll make a careless mistake, such as working with insects under unfavorable weather conditions, and get severely stung.

However, getting stung is not a disaster. It hurts, but most beekeepers soon build up an immunity to the venom itself and eventually suffer no aftereffects from such incidents. A minority of people, though, are especially allergic to bee stings, and their sensitivity may increase with time. Such folks should not, of course, even attempt to keep bees.

In addition, there's a technique that can be used to greatly reduce the amount of venom absorbed from occasional stings. Simply use a fingernail or some other thin-edged object to scrape the stinger out immediately; otherwise, its venom sack will continue to pump poison into the flesh for a minute or more. Don't try to grab the stinger with your fingers as many people do, or you'll squeeze even more venom into your system.

That beekeeper's trick will greatly reduce the damage inflicted by stings. But of course the goal is to get stung as little as possible while tending hives, and the following tips should greatly reduce the number of stings you receive.

First, wear a snug, beetight veil and light-colored clothing: White coveralls are excellent for beekeeping, blue jeans are poor. Eliminate any entrance spaces between your garments and skin by tucking your pants legs into your socks and by wrapping rubber bands around your shirt sleeves. Do not wear wool. And consider not wearing protective gloves. During the first few months you may feel more comfortable if you do don them, but eventually you'll probably find that it's easier to work a hive without crushing bees when you're bare-handed.

Second, do not wear clothes that have previously received stings. When bees strike, they release a banana-scented pheromone to alert their comrades and entice other bees to sting the same area. So wearing garments that are still scented with that alarm odor is literally asking to be stung.

Third, always use a smoker. The portable bellows/firebox combination, a standard piece of beekeeping equipment, enables the beekeeper to puff plumes of smoke into the beehive. For some reason, perhaps because bees believe they're getting ready to flee a forest fire, they engorge themselves with honey whenever they smell smoke and become much less aggressive toward intruders. A smoker is also useful for temporarily covering up the scent of pheromone if you do get stung.

Fourth, whenever possible, visit the bees on a warm, sunny, windless day when plenty of nectar-bearing flowers are in bloom—or as beekeepers say, when there's a honey flow. On such occasions many of the insects will be out working in the fields, and the stay-at-homes will be so busy with their own labors that they'll hardly notice your presence.

Fifth, don't block the hive entrance with your body. Tend the bee house from the side or back.

Finally, try to make all your movements calm, even, and efficient. Don't alarm the insects by moving jerkily or hastily or try their patience by taking more time than you should. Such poise may not come naturally at first, but with experience the skills involved and demeanor will soon improve. Also, if at all possible, it's best to get some experience working with other beekeepers; a lot of their self-assurance will rub off on you.

THE HIVE—PARTS AND MEMBERS: Before you can begin beekeeping, you need to know something about the equipment and community you'll be working with. The design of the modern beehive, devised in 1851, incorporated two vital features that are considered standard today: movable, interchangeable frames and uniform "bee space."

The fact that all the interior parts can be easily taken out and moved about is what makes precise and nondestructive manipulation of the hive possible. Since all the internal pieces of equipment are separated by the 5/16-inch spaces that bees naturally prefer as passageways, the insects usually won't be tempted to close off their "halls" by sticking the hive parts together with extra comb or bee glue (propolis).

The basic parts of the bees' home are a hive stand, a bottom board, inner and outer top covers, and open

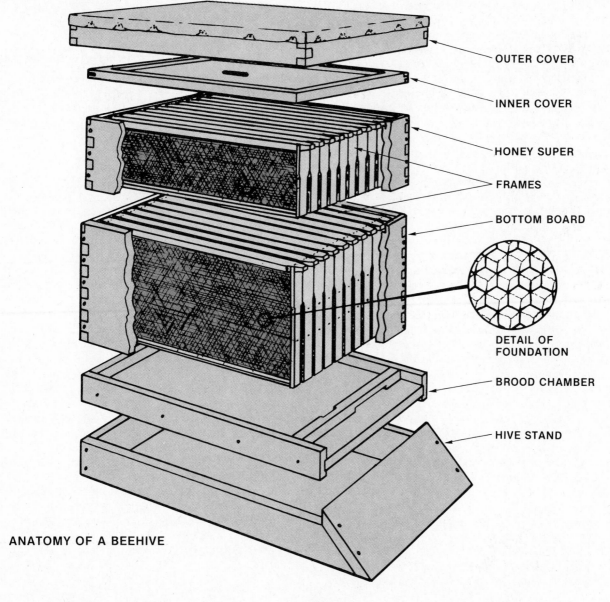

OUTER COVER

INNER COVER

HONEY SUPER

FRAMES

BOTTOM BOARD

DETAIL OF
FOUNDATION

BROOD CHAMBER

HIVE STAND

ANATOMY OF A BEEHIVE

boxes, or supers, that make up the body of the hive. Inside every one of the bee-housing boxes are eight to ten frames, with each of these removable rectangles containing a thin sheet of beeswax imprinted with hexagons the size of a worker bee cell. Such foundation sheets give the bees ordered starting points for drawing out either egg or honey cells.

The main hive body, or brood chamber—sometimes called a deep super—is 9-5/8 inches high and is used to house the queen and her eggs (brood). Many beekeepers like to keep two brood chambers on each hive.

The shorter boxes, or shallow supers—most frequently referred to simply as supers—are only 5-3/4 inches tall. They're stacked on top of the brood chamber(s) and used primarily for storing honey.

The membership of a hive colony includes one queen bee, thousands of worker bees, and a random—but in the most productive hives, small—number of drone bees. The queen, the longest-lived member of the colony, resembles a worker bee but has an enlarged abdomen. After a few youthful mating flights, she spends the rest of her life, which may be as long as seven years, in the hive performing one function: laying eggs—more than 1,500 a day during the peak of each season.

The worker bees are all females that lack fully developed reproductive organs. These industrious insects run the hive: They feed and clean up after the queen; they gather honey, pollen, and water; they keep the internal temperature of the hive constant (they can both cool and heat their enclosed environment); they feed the larvae; and they build all the honey and brood comb.

In contrast, the drones—large, indolent male bees—do no useful work. They simply eat honey while waiting around for an opportunity to mate with a young queen (their sole purpose in life).

Bees can be obtained in three different ways: by mail-order, by buying a working hive from a local beekeeper, or by catching a wild swarm.

Catching a swarm isn't really as difficult as you might imagine. Usually seen hanging from tree limbs, posts, or shrubs, the tight, homeless clusters of bees tend to be remarkably mild-mannered. Still, anyone who's never handled bees before or doesn't want to depend on the chance of finding a swarm may prefer to start out by purchasing bees.

It's often possible to buy a strong established colony from a local beekeeper. Such a working community should contain about 50,000 bees along with a complete hive. And if subsequent weather and honey flows permit, you ought to be able to harvest 50 to 100 pounds of honey your first season.

Many states require that such purchases be examined by a bee inspector, who can be contacted through the county agricultural extension service. The examiner will inspect the colony for signs of highly contagious bee diseases, such as American foulbrood. If you don't have an inspector look into your hive, you should have read

enough to be able to spot problems yourself, and should ask the seller to go through the hive in your presence.

Some beginners start their colonies with mail-ordered packages of bees, and this is surely the safest way to be sure you're buying the kind of bees you want. (There are several varieties of *Apis mellifera*, but the vast majority are variants of the "Italian" strain.)

If you choose to go the package route, however, you should place your order as early in the year as possible, because most bee suppliers become quite busy in the warm months. The package, which will be shipped four to six weeks before the first spring bloom, will contain a healthy, mated young queen, two or three pounds of worker bees, a can of syrup for the insects to eat en route, and complete instructions for both installing the colony in the hive and feeding its members until the first honey flow. This method costs less initially than buying a working hive, but since you'll be starting out with a small nucleus, your new bee community may not make any honey beyond its own wintering food needs during the first year.

COMB OR LIQUID: After your bees are in place and prospering, you should consider adding your first honey super to the hive. But before you can take this

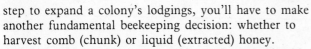

FAR UPPER LEFT: Using a hive tool to pry out a super frame. FAR LOWER LEFT: Honey is ready to harvest. ABOVE LEFT: Before opening the hive, an apiarist blows smoke through the hole in the lid. ABOVE RIGHT: A bee-covered frame is carefully lifted from the hive.

step to expand a colony's lodgings, you'll have to make another fundamental beekeeping decision: whether to harvest comb (chunk) or liquid (extracted) honey.

Chunk honey is produced in frames that contain thin, chewable foundation. The foundation used for honey that is to be extracted must be thicker and reinforced with either preset or hand-inserted wires so that it will be sturdy enough to withstand the pressure of the honey extractor that spins the viscous liquid out of its combs.

Beginners will probably encounter less trouble and expense starting off using comb foundations. By doing so, they'll be able to harvest the honey by simply cutting it, comb and all, out of the frames. Then, liquid honey can be separated from the yield by smashing all the comb cells with a kraut chopper or a beater from an electric mixer and letting the honey drain out through a small-mesh screen lined with cheesecloth.

Heating and then cooling the leftover comb shards in a double boiler will yield some more honey. This will be topped by a solid layer of yellow beeswax. Don't throw that substance out! You can either use it for making wonderful candles or save it until you accumulate enough to sell to bee supply companies, other beekeepers, or craft shops.

Because bees use a lot of honey and energy while building their combs, you can harvest about 50% more honey from your hive if you extract the sweetener and reinstall the intact cells in the hive instead of cutting the combs out altogether. Ah, but there's a rub: The smallest hand-cranked extractors cost more than all the other combined start-up expenses for a single-hive operation.

However, if you want the increased yield possible with extracted honey without the full expense of purchasing the necessary machine, you might be able to share the purchase cost of an extractor with some other small-scale beekeepers, or you may be able to pay—with honey—a nearby commercial apiarist to do your comb/honey separating.

A VISIT TO YOUR HIVE: To give you a better feel for what it'll be like to tend a flock of insect livestock, imagine that it's a sunny day in June. Wildflowers are blooming like crazy, the hive seems to be prospering—a honey super was added two weeks ago—and you're a mite curious as to just how well those bees are doing. In short, it's a perfect day to inspect the apiary.

Having donned beetight garments and started a steady

fume-producing flame in the smoker, approach the hive from the side and watch for a moment. Yep, there's a good honey flow on. Plenty of bees are flying in and out of the wooden home . . . and the ones coming back are so laden with nectar, which will be converted to honey inside the hive, that they almost droop their way through the air.

Put the tip of the smoker in the mouth of the hive's low entrance and puff a couple of clouds into the brood chamber. The bees near the entrance will buzz around a bit, but soon most of them will go into the hive.

A minute later, lift off the hive's outer cover and blow smoke down the narrow hole in the inner lid. Wait for a short time after this, then using the hive tool, an inexpensive crowbar implement that's an indispensable beekeeper's aid, pry the inner cover's corners loose and lift that thin top off.

Using your hive tool as a lever, carefully pry up one corner of a spare frame until you can grab the wooden rack's top edge with one hand. Then pry up the opposite top corner, grab that end, too, and pulling slowly so you don't crush any workers, lift the entire bee-covered frame out of the hive. Some of the cells you examine are capped with white beeswax (indicating the presence of ready-to-harvest honey). Most of the hexagonal units, though, are unsealed and contain clearly visible honey. Since such ambrosia needs further curing by the bees, this indicates it's not yet time to make the first harvest.

After carefully replacing the frame, give the entire super a few puffs with the smoker and then start prying that honey-holding box free from the brood chamber. Even though the super may have been on the hive only a short while, the bees will have already stuck it tightly to the brood box, and you have to free all four corners carefully with your hive tool and then slowly twist the upper story sideways to break the gummy seals.

When not laden with honey, the super's not very heavy (if full, it would weigh at least 40 pounds), so you'll be able to lift it off easily and set it on the overturned outer cover. You then grab the smoker again and give the bees at the top of the brood chamber a few brief puffs.

One by one, now, pull out a few separate frames from the central hive room. Except for the less occupied outer racks, each frame you examine is, as some beekeepers say, "slam full of brood." A large semicircle of dark convex cappings will cover much of the surface, some cells will contain uncapped white larvae, and honey or pollen will be stored in the frames' corners.

You may not happen to spot the queen as you forage through the chamber, but rest assured that since the colony is so full of fine brood, the hive is obviously healthy and "queen-right." Don't bother the bees by needlessly searching for her but carefully reassemble the hive and head back home.

Returning to the scene a week later, you'll find the honey crop is 80% sealed and ready to harvest. You could leave a "one-way bee escape"—a gateway that lets bees out but not in—under the super, walk off, and reap insect-free racks in a day or so. But if you've just got too much of a hankering for some homegrown honey to wait, pull out the sweet-filled frames one by one and simply sweep all the bees off them with a soft-bristled brush and take the golden gatherings home.

BEEKEEPING'S VITAL SEASON: Every beekeeping season has its annual tasks. Summer work includes jobs such as adding supers and harvesting the honey. Fall is the time to make sure your bees have all their winter stores built up, and before winter hits, you need to add some hardware cloth to your hives' entrances to keep out mice, and start assembling gear for next year.

But the most crucial beekeeping season is surely the spring. Having made it through the winter on their own supplies and being ready to begin foraging anew, many colonies are then faced with a few change-of-season weeks when no harvestable flowers have yet bloomed. If the nectar-gatherers don't have enough extra stores to see themselves through this period, you'll need to provide some sugar or honey syrup and perhaps some pollen or pollen substitute. Otherwise, the bees may have survived the winter only to starve in the spring!

The warming weather after a long winter brings yet another threat to the colony's productivity: swarming. In the wild, bee colonies reproduce annually by division. Many of the workers and the old queen emerge from the hive and fly off to find a new home. If your bees swarm, a new "replacement" queen and some workers will be left behind to carry on. But much of your best winged livestock will have flown the coop, so the hive will probably not produce a good honey crop that season.

Although you can take some hive-saving steps, you won't prevent all swarms from occurring. You might, however, balance your losses with gains, since spring is also the season to catch stray runaway clusters and thus increase the number of hives in your apiary.

The danger of swarming, and the quality and number of bees that do desert the hive in such instances, decreases as spring turns to summer. As an old nursery rhyme notes: "A swarm in May is worth a load of hay. A swarm in June is worth a silver spoon. But a swarm in July isn't worth a fly."

SWEET REWARDS: If you take up beekeeping and manage your honeymakers with care, you'll have the pleasure of learning about one of nature's most intriguing phenomena. The intricate patterns of bee behavior provide continual discoveries to the most experienced apiarist.

Although there's commitment and labor required of the beekeeper, as the colony's caretaker you'll probably feel humble when you compare your efforts to those of your partners. As long-time beekeeper Richard Taylor has artfully phrased it: "The truly monumental work of apiculture is always done by the bees themselves."

A RUNDOWN ON THE BREEDS OF SHEEP

Sheep can make an excellent livestock addition to the small farm or homestead, and selecting the appropriate breed is vital to anyone considering raising the animals. Several important considerations need to be taken into account, such as whether the beasts are being raised mainly for their wool or for the meat they produce. There are breeds that are primarily meat producers; there are some that produce fine wool and others that yield a fleece of not so fine a grade but still useful for coarser cloth; and there are those that can be raised for both wool and meat.

Increased interest in homesteading and in homespun apparel and furnishings has caused a lot of people to begin raising sheep, and they are finding them to be practical livestock for the small farm and a source of easily handled, unusual wools. And whether a person wants animals for meat or wool, a backyard flock can be one of the most economical components of a self-reliant homestead.

The breeds listed here include some of the most popular, as well as a few not so popular, types of sheep in the United States. This is only an overview, and people who are considering acquiring a flock should make a thorough study of the breeds that seem most appropriate to their purpose before making a purchase.

CLASSIFICATION: Sheep can be grouped in any of several ways: by their suitability as meat producers, by the length or quality of their wool, by their facial color, or by their adaptation to altitudes. The most useful grouping is classification by wool grades. The latest method of classification by wool grade uses the micron (just under 1/25,000 inch) as a standard, and then rates wool by the average diameter of the fibers in a given lot: The finer the wool, the smaller the micron number.

The micron system appears to be more technically accurate than its predecessors, and there is some effort being made to establish it as the standard for describing wools in the United States. Few people, however, have a "feel" for micron measurement, so the sheep listed here are simply categorized as having fine, medium, or long wool.

FINE-WOOLED BREEDS: The fine-wooled breeds in the U.S. include the American Merino, Delaine Merino, Rambouillet, and Debouillet. Like the Spanish Merino from which they're all descended, these varieties are noted for fine, tightly crimped wool that has a heavy, greasy covering called yolk. When refined, this combination of secretions from the sebaceous and sweat glands becomes the smooth, oily product we call lanolin.

In recent years the meat-producing capabilities of these breeds have been improved, but if putting lamb chops on the table is your aim, there are better meat types available. On the other hand, ewes of the fine-wooled types will often breed out of season, a definite advantage for the owner who's interested in maximum productivity.

No other breed has contributed more to the development of other sheep types than has the Merino. Early examples of this breed had thick wrinkles along their entire bodies, a characteristic that breeders later discovered produced wool of inferior quality. Called "type A," these sheep are rarely seen today, having given way to the less wrinkled varieties known as "type B" and to the virtually wrinkle-free "type C," or Delaine Merinos.

All the Merinos are hardy and long-lived, and possess a strong flocking instinct. Their fleece is extremely fine and therefore difficult for any but an experienced spinner to manage, but it does yield yarns of very high quality.

The Rambouillet, a direct descendant of the Spanish Merino, is the largest of the fine-wooled breeds. The animals are commonly used in crossbreeding programs, and it's been estimated that at least 50% of all the sheep in the United States have some Rambouillet blood in their background. The Debouillet, for example, is a Delaine/Rambouillet cross.

Rambouillets are considered dual-purpose (meat and wool) sheep. They have superior long, dense, fine wool that's very popular for spinning. Most rams of the breed sport large spiral horns, though some strains are polled (hornless).

MEDIUM-WOOLED BREEDS: The most popular medium-wooled breeds include the Cheviot and North Country Cheviot, Montadale, Dorset, Tunis, Hampshire, Oxford, Shropshire, Suffolk, and Southdown. The last five examples in this list are sometimes called the "Down" breeds, a reference to the hills and downs of southern England where they originated.

All the medium-wooled sheep were developed for meat, and their fleece is rated somewhere between the extreme fineness and density of the Merino and the coarseness and open quality typical of the long-wooled varieties of sheep. Most of these breeds have dark faces and dark legs.

The smallest and oldest of the Down types, the Southdown is said to produce the finest mutton of any sheep. Its compact, wide, deep body was used as the foundation stock for all other Down breeds. The young reach market weight quickly, but the ewes, which are just average milkers, are not prolific. Southdown wool is relatively short and can be used to make a fine yarn.

The original Shropshires had a wool "cap" extending down to the muzzle, but because this contributed to an ailment known as wool blindness, breeders have worked to develop a clean-faced variety. Long-lived, hardy, and prolific, Shropshires have the heaviest fleece of the mutton types, but the wool tends to be short and varies in quality from fine to medium grade.

Oxfords, the largest of the medium-wooled sheep, are the result of crossing Hampshires and Cotswolds in the mid-1800's. Oxford lambs weigh 9 to 12 pounds at birth and reach market weight early.

A very popular breed used extensively for crossbreeding is the Hampshire, which is a heavy milker and often produces twins. The lambs are born dark and gradually turn white, retaining dark legs and faces. Because of their large size (they're second only to the Oxford among the Downs), Hampshires need good pasture and feed, and won't thrive if left to forage on poor ground. The ewes sometimes experience lambing problems because of the large head and shoulders typical of the young ones.

The thin, black-faced, black-legged look indicative of the Suffolk strain can be seen in many of the crossbred sheep raised on the western ranges in this country. Unlike the Hampshires, Suffolk lambs have small heads and shoulders and give little trouble at lambing time. Members of the breed are active foragers, too, and their meat has less fat and a finer texture than does that of most other medium-wooled breeds.

Both the rams and ewes of the original Dorset breed had massive horns. Recently, however, a polled strain has been developed. Dorsets will breed out of season, are noted milkers, and are active, thrifty foragers.

The Cheviot, with its distinctive white face, erect ears, Roman nose, and small size, is easy to identify. This hardy breed originated in the rugged hills of Scotland and is quite suitable for small farms. Cheviots produce a medium-grade fleece which is prized by many spinners because it doesn't need carding.

Larger than the original Cheviot, the North Country Cheviot strain is also calmer in temperament. The fleece of this interesting breed is of medium grade and excellent for spinning.

Montadales originated in America in 1932 and are the result of crossbreeding Cheviots and Columbias. They are an attractive and hardy dual-purpose, intermediate-size sheep with good medium fleece.

Easily recognized by its red or tan face and pendulous ears, the Tunis originated in North Africa. Like some other desert sheep, it has fatty tissue in its tail and can call on that stored energy when forced to go without food for extended periods. Popular in the South, the Tunis was nearly wiped out during the Civil War but staged a comeback in the late 1890's. It's once again growing in popularity.

LONG-WOOLED BREEDS: The long-wooled breeds—Cotswold, Border Leicester, Lincoln, and Rom-

ney, for example—were developed primarily for mutton. They are typically the largest sheep, and 225- to 350-pound rams and 175- to 275-pound ewes are common among them. Their wool is generally very long, open, and coarse, and it's frequently used in carpets, wall hangings, and outerwear. Heavy rains may cause the fleece to part and allow the sheep to get wet to the skin. When that happens, the wool is undamaged, but the animals sometimes become ill as a result of their drenching. These strains tend to mature slowly and are likely to become fatty, but their large size often makes them desirable for crossbreeding.

One of the oldest breeds, the Cotswold has a tuft of hair on its forehead and long, lustrous, naturally curly wool that many spinners find pleasant to work with.

Developed in the country along the border between England and Scotland, the Border Leicester has the erect ears and Roman nose of the Cheviot and wool averaging between 8 and 12 inches long. The fleece is coarse and has considerable luster.

The Lincolns are the heavyweights of sheepdom and also grow the heaviest fleece (up to 30 pounds from one ram), which is usually from 10 to 15 inches long. The wool is lustrous, long-wearing, and difficult to card. These animals are somewhat sluggish and slow to mature, but when used for crossbreeding, they add size and staple (a term for fiber length and diameter).

In full fleece Romneys are noted for their beautiful faces and coats. Unlike that of some other long-fleeced varieties, their wool is relatively fine, dense, and much

North Country Cheviot

Jacob

Scottish Blackface

Suffolk

Merino

Karakul

desired by handspinners because it doesn't need carding. Romneys are quiet, particularly resistant to foot problems, and known for high milk production.

Breeds such as the Columbia, Corriedale, and Targhee are the result of attempts to produce larger ewes that'll yield more wool and heavier market lambs than do other types. Their fleece is usually of medium to fine quality, and many such breeds have adapted well to western United States range conditions.

The Columbia was developed from a Lincoln/Rambouillet cross in the early 1900's. It's a tight-flocking, dual-purpose sheep that does well on range or farm.

A New Zealand breed resulting from a cross between Lincoln and Merino sheep, Corriedales generally produce more pounds of wool and lamb per pound of ewe body weight than any other range type. They're fairly prolific, adequate milkers, and tight herders that produce wool noted for its brightness, softness, distinct crimp, and ease of handling. Their fleece can be worked without carding.

The Targhee, so called after the national forest of the same name, is an American breed developed in Idaho around 1926. These sheep are prolific (often having twins or triplets), large, and resistant to both internal parasites and hoof problems.

OTHER BREEDS TO PONDER: The Scottish Highland (or Scottish Blackface) is a very old breed and is one of the most common sheep in Britain today. Members of this breed tend to be small, horned, and oddly mottled with black on their faces and legs. Highland fleece is 15 to 18 inches long and quite springy. It's used to make carpets, tweeds, and mattress stuffing. The sheep also produce excellent mutton.

Multiple births are the Finnsheep's claim to fame. The ewes may have litters of anywhere from three to seven lambs. Finnsheep are fine-boned and medium-sized, and they produce a very lustrous, light fleece.

The Karakul is the only true black sheep, and all the other dark types are mutations of various white breeds. Karakuls are the source of broadtail, Persian lamb, and half-Persian furs, terms that refer to the pelts of lambs at various stages of growth. Adult Karakul sheep have long, coarse outer hair with a fine undercoat. Usually born black, they do lighten in color as they age, and may turn to any of the various shades of brown, blue, gray, or even white.

The Navajo is quite possibly a descendant of the Spanish Jacob (or Piebald) sheep. The breed hasn't been standardized and therefore occurs in a wide range of sizes, shapes, and colors, and with a varying number of horns: The rams may have from one to four.

The Barbados Blackbellies are hair sheep with practically no wool. A long cape around the neck and shoulders does have fibers that can be spun, however. Barbados are used in crossbreeding to add hardiness, multiple births, and—important for handspinners—color variety. The sheep will also breed out of season.

A HOW-TO LOOK AT RAISING GOATS

Raising goats for milk can help the homestead budget stay in balance, but there are several things a person should know before becoming a small-scale goatherd. Selecting and buying stock, providing shelter for the animals, and maintaining a healthy herd are vital areas where the tips of experienced goat raisers can keep the beginner from stumbling into any of several easily avoided pitfalls.

FOR BEGINNERS:
Though some people feel it's best for novices to buy only one or two young female goats, you'll end up with a better herd by starting out with five or six. Three or maybe four

goats are a practical number for a person to milk twice a day. Working any fewer than three animals means the time spent setting up to milk—cleaning utensils, hauling grain and hay, and so forth—really isn't economically used. On the other hand, milking five or more goats can leave the owner exhausted by the time the task is done.

With a starter herd of five or six doelings, you can select the three best producers of that first year to keep and still have a couple of young does to sell that'll bring a premium because they're "in milk" and have their kids at their sides. Then you can keep the very best of the unsold female kids until the next year to see how she turns out. If she looks as if she'll be a better milkmaker than another animal in the herd, keep her. If not, sell the doe to someone who is less critical.

However, it's easy to become trapped in the creeping spiral of goat inflation. "Goatflation" occurs when an owner starts out with one or two animals, fully intending to limit the herd size to that number but not realizing that the kids will be too cute ever to sell. Well, that kindhearted goatherd just naturally keeps the youngsters. The third year is a replay of the same scenario: The owner soon has eight to ten milking does, all too "valuable" to sell or cull. And so it goes, until the goat fancier has so many animals to take care of that there's time for little else.

The key, then, is to decide how many goats you want to milk, and no matter what, to stick to that maximum number by selling every excess milker. Be firm with yourself, because once you get rid of the ones that don't measure up to your standards, you'll be tempted to keep the rest, even if you still have too many.

SHARING THE WEALTH: Now that you've decided on the perfect herd size and have sworn to keep absolutely no more than a certain number of milkers, there's one more task to be taken care of before starting off on a buying spree: rounding up some folks who like goat's milk. The problem with dairy goats is that they're prolific producers. Just keeping one nanny will give you a gallon of milk per day—enough to leave most families awash in goat's milk.

Many goat owners have spent a lot of time and effort devising ways to use all that excess liquid. Some owners have even tried selling their dairy products to friends or neighbors. At present there are very few licensed commercial operations in the country that are financially successful at peddling goat's milk or other products. This fact, sad but true, should tell you there's a rather limited future in the sale of goat's milk.

One way to distribute your milk is to your own household and another family or two. Ideally, these other folks will be more than just customers; they'll also be willing to take their turn at getting their farm fresh milk right from the source. After all, you may not mind milking, but you very well might get tired of performing the ritual twice a day, every day of the week.

That's why swapping works well: Friends get free milk in exchange for milking your nannies once or twice a week, which gives you a nice break from the chore.

BUYING TIPS: If possible, when it comes time to pick a goat, buy a youngster about four to six months of age. By this time the doeling should have outgrown her gangly teenaged appearance, so by looking at her body size and type, you can get a fairly good idea of what kind of producer she'll be. She should weigh 60 pounds or so and be ready to breed that first fall. If she's too small (generally under 60 pounds) or too young, don't buy her. Look for an unbred doeling, because then you'll be able to select the buck to which she's going to be bred.

A second goat-shopping choice would be to head out in the spring and look for a promising kid. True, you'll know better what an older animal is going to look like as an adult, but for that very reason a tyke should be less expensive.

With only rare exceptions, don't shop for an adult doe. Purchasing a full-fledged milkmaker is too much like buying a used car: There's a good chance you'll end up with someone else's problems, plus you'll have to pay a lot more for a grown-up than for a younger girl. Bear in mind that most livestock owners rarely, if ever, get rid of their best and most trouble-free producers.

Furthermore, buy only registered animals with American Dairy Goat Association (ADGA) papers, not grade, unregistered young goats. Of course, you can expect to pay more initially for a purebred youngster, but it more than makes up the difference when you're able to sell her offspring at registered prices.

Also, it's a good idea to buy the breed that's most common in your area. By sticking with the most popular variety, you'll find a receptive market for the offspring you'll be selling later on.

SELECTING AN ANIMAL: Being able to choose a fine dairy goat is especially important, because unlike a feeder pig or calf you'll butcher down the line, you'll be living with your decision (and her offspring) for many years to come. The best way to learn what a decent goat looks like is to attend some judgings at local goat shows or at a county fair. Spend enough time there looking at good examples until the image of an ideal goat is firmly established in your mind.

In addition to knowing a good goat's general physical attributes, you should pay attention to specific crucial qualities.

Size is the most important characteristic in determining how much milk the animal will produce over her lifetime. The rule here is the bigger the frame, the better. Look for a long, tall doeling with a deep, widespread chest. The prospect's belly should look like the cross section of a barrel. However, be careful not to confuse size with heft; the creature under consideration should be big but refined—not coarse and thick-boned.

This lean, angular look is an elusive quality that livestock owners refer to as "dairy character." In general, the more of this trait that a beast carries on a large body, the more milk she'll produce over her lifetime.

After determining that a prospective purchase is big and well formed, look at her teeth and legs. To have a long and fruitful life, the doe will need to eat and to

carry herself to the feeding trough—hence the need for structurally sound teeth and legs. The animal's lower incisors should touch squarely on the upper dental pad, not in front of or behind it. Her legs should appear to drop straight down from her body when she's viewed from the front and the back, and her forward and rear pinnings should have the correct angle at the hock, hip, shoulder, and pasterns.

A healthy udder will be firmly attached to a doe's belly by broad rear and fore ligaments. It should also be symmetrical and evenly divided from side to side, with a firmly attached median ligament. And the teats need to be properly shaped. They should be hand size rather than huge or pendulous. Teats of the proper size are easier to milk, leave more room for the milk-producing part of the udder, and are less prone to mastitis. The milk canals (the passages through which the liquid passes) need to be large enough to allow milking with an easy, rhythmic squeezing of the fingers.

Admittedly, udder evaluation is a little difficult when you're sizing up a doeling that's never been milked. However, you can get a better idea of how that animal's udder will probably turn out by checking its mother's apparatus.

Actually, you should evaluate both of the prospect's parents if possible. Once you've given a doe a thorough once-over, you'll have pretty good grounds for guessing how her babies will look when they grow up. Remember to pay special attention to the mother's size, her undercarriage, her teeth, and her mammary system.

Even more important than a mother goat's appearance, though, are her milk-production records. How much milk does she yield annually, and how many kids does she usually have at one time? Pay particular attention to the animal's length of lactation as well as to the overall pounds of liquid produced. You'll want a doe that's going to keep you in milk throughout her entire ten-month lactation spell, not one that pumps out a lot of milk for four or five months and then dries right up.

HOME, SWEET HOME: Where to keep your newly acquired charges turns out to be less complicated than many would-be goat owners want to believe. A simple three-sided shed that keeps out the wind and the rain and offers about 15 square feet of bedding space for each adult goat is the best kind of shelter. The open side of the shed should be aimed south to catch the sun's warming and cleansing rays. Enclosing a goat barn or adding heat to it increases the chance for bacteria to grow and flourish. Bacterial pneumonia, in fact, is quite prevalent among kids kept in stuffy barns. So the most desirable approach is to keep the shelter simple and draft-free, yet well ventilated.

Choosing the right kind of fencing for your goat pen is every bit as simple as erecting the right kind of shed. The best kind of fence for goats is one made out of commercially available stock panels. Slippery caprine Houdinis can wiggle through welded wire fences and can squeeze under or through electric strands, and some goats have even learned how to take advantage of the timed pulses to make a shock-free escape.

In contrast, goats can lean or stand against stock panels without beating them down or pushing them over, and the sectioned barricades are tall enough to contain all but the most rambunctious breeding buck. The only disadvantage of such fencing is its cost, but since nothing else quite does the job, stock panels are worth the expense.

BRING ON THE KIDS: Rather than keeping a buck around the homestead for breeding purposes, it's usually better to get together with half a dozen or so other nanny owners in your community and pool all of your resources to buy one exemplary buck that can serve all of your does. Then see if you can't talk one of those other goat lovers into boarding (with the expenses shared by everyone, of course) "old whisker face" on his or her farm. Naturally, you'll have to go to the trouble of hauling your does over to this benevolent neighbor's barn at breeding time.

If you can't find someone magnanimous enough to care for a collectively owned buck, consider utilizing artificial insemination (AI). This method is well suited to goat raising and is the best and least expensive way to upgrade your herd. Semen from some of the top breeders in the country is available for as little as $5 to $25 a unit. Unfortunately, it's sometimes hard to catch the females in heat, but you'll have to in order to use artificial insemination. In fact, some gals won't come into season unless there's a male goat on the premises. However, you can fool them. During the fall breeding period, take an old rag and wipe it on a buck's head where the horns should be and along its hocks. Then hang the dripping-with-maleness cloth where the does can smell it. In 48 to 72 hours, your ladies should be in heat.

MILKING: To avoid the risk of having unwanted barnyard fumes taint your fresh milk and to allow yourself more comfort, you might want to milk your does in an area that's separate from their pens.

Milking stands, easy-to-construct goat restrainers, can be placed almost anywhere, and they can turn a potentially back-straining job into an easy sit-on-a-stool task. Since milking time rolls around twice a day, that's quite a plus.

Don't worry about how your animals might take to using one of these stands. If you make sure there's always plenty of food in the bin for them to snack on, the does will just hop right up and munch away peacefully while you do the milking. As a bonus, such a structure can serve the purpose of holding your animals when you need to trim their hooves, vaccinate them, or perform any other unpleasant chore for which they might otherwise be unwilling to stand still.

Before milking, clean each doe's udder with a fresh paper towel saturated in disinfectant. Then direct the first few streams of milk into a black strip cup to check for the stringy material or cheesecake chunks that are signs of mastitis, an inflammation of the mammary glands. If the milk is okay, continue to work, straining the liquid through a clean cheesecloth into a sanitized metal container. In place of cheesecloth, some sources advise using tin or stainless steel strainers that are specifically made for your pail, or even disposable strainers. When you're finished milking, but before you send that little mama back to her pen, dip each of her teats in a specially prepared solution to help protect her against mastitis.

With that done, pour the milk into sterilized glass containers with lids, and place the covered jars in a refrigerator. To insure that the milk stays fresh as long as possible, some folks place the containers in an ice bath before refrigerating them. If put directly into the icebox, unpasteurized milk will remain fresh-tasting for at least three days. Simply date each jar, and when day number three rolls around, give the old milk to the pigs or dispose of it otherwise.

Are you wondering what you'll do with your regular and sizable supply of nice, fresh goat's milk before day number three? Well, it can be used to produce delicious yogurts, custards, and ricotta cheese. Goat's milk also adds a delicate sweetness to almost any bakery or candy recipe.

KID CARE: Of course, the production of milk is triggered by pregnancy, which means that come spring you'll probably have some youngsters to care for. However, that extra work can be quite worthwhile, because if the mamas give birth to a good crop of quality kids, selling them could yield enough money to feed your milkers for a year. With this in mind, then, you'll want to do everything possible to make sure that your valuable kids remain robust and healthy.

Start your kid-care program by seeing to it that each youngster gets a healthy dose of colostrum, the mother's first nutrient-rich and antibody-laden milk, within the first 12 hours after birth. From then on, the little guys and gals will need to have their mother's milk fed to them three times a day, from a soda bottle or similar container fitted with a special lamb's nipple. Of course, you could let them nurse from the doe herself, but if you do, you'll probably find that they're much harder to wean. Besides, almost any kid will take to a bottle with no problem, as long as its mother is nearby to provide company and reassurance.

During the first week, feed your young animals 6 to 8 ounces of milk three times a day and then increase the dosage to 10 to 12 ounces. Be careful not to overfeed, though. Once the kids are about two weeks old and while they're still nursing, you can help them start to develop their rumens, that is, their adult stomachs, by providing them with access to tasty grains such as cracked corn and rolled oats, and fresh, leafy hay. Be sure, also, to put a new section of hay in their midst daily and to change the grain regularly to accommodate any particularly fastidious eaters.

In addition to maintaining an appropriate feeding schedule for your kids, you'll need to see to it that the youngsters have ample pen space and adequate shelter. Though stock panels are effective goat fencing, during your kids' first month you can make do by simply putting up a 32-inch hog stock-panel fence, which you can easily step over. Also, you can save yourself a little more money if, instead of building sheds for the kids, you house them in old 4' X 8' wooden packing crates equipped with lots of regularly changed straw bedding.

The young goats can all be penned together on one lot until they're ready to be weaned at three to four months. Then move them onto another section of ground. However, do not put your juveniles in with the adults until the youngsters reach breeding age—six to eight months old. Also keep in mind that next year's kids shouldn't be kept on the same terrain as were this season's. In fact, you should wait at least three years before using the same ground for goat turf again. By rotating the kid lots in this manner and keeping the offspring away from the grown-ups, you can all but eliminate the goat-killing disease coccidiosis. As a further precaution against this disease, burn the packing crate sheds as soon as the kids have outgrown them.

If you've decided not to board a buck, you can slaughter all the male kids immediately after birth or within six months after they're fattened up. Perhaps this sounds harsh, but adding chevon to the freezer is one good way to fight the rising tide of goatflation.

THE THREE PRIME FEEDING PERIODS:

There are three nutritionally critical periods in a goat's life: a kid's first few months, a mother's first two months of lactation, and a doe's dry months. If you maintain adequate records so you'll be prepared for such periods before they come around, and feed your animals according to their needs during each of these times, you should be able to keep your critters pretty healthy.

During the initial months of lactation, a doe will produce the maximum amount of milk she's capable of. Therefore, in order to fuel her internal factory sufficiently, she has to eat the best grain and hay available. Generally, you can figure that a lactating female should get about one-third to one-half pound of grain for each pound of milk she yields in a day. However, when she's at her peak, it can be nearly impossible to satisfy all her energy requirements. If that seems to be the case, just be sure that during this time you give her the best grain and hay (preferably alfalfa) you can afford, and that you allow her plenty of time to be able to eat as much of her food as she can pack away.

The grain mix should be from 16% to 18% protein if it's fed along with a low-protein hay (such as timothy or prairie hay). But should you be feeding a high-energy hay (like alfalfa), you'll be able to get by with a grain that's only 12% to 15% protein. You can figure that an average milker will need about 1,000 pounds of hay a year and roughly 1,000 pounds of grain. This should work out to be approximately 1/2 pound of grain for each of the 2,000 pounds of milk she gives. Better producers will, naturally, need additional feed.

The third dietary prime time in a goat's life occurs during the two months prior to kidding. You can do a lot to insure that your doe has an easy delivery, healthy babies, and a problem-free lactation just by keeping her in good flesh without letting her get downright fat and by making sure her calcium intake is low during this period. A pregnant doe will put on kid pounds, but watch her ribs right behind her shoulders. She shouldn't put on so much fat that they disappear. In general, if you feed a doe a couple of pounds of grain each day and all the hay she wants, her developing babies will stay healthy and her figure will remain fit and trim.

Then, in order to keep your mother-to-be's calcium intake in line, simply feed her a mineral mix that doesn't contain that substance. Also, feed her only a low-calcium, nonleguminous hay, such as timothy or prairie hay. After the kids arrive, switch to a mix that does have calcium in it and put her on a better quality hay.

Always keep in mind that goats need lots of water and exercise. One doe can drink as much as two to five gallons on a cool day, so make sure there's plenty of fresh water available to your herd at all times. You might also want to take your does for an out-of-pen stroll, preferably every day. However, even the trek from the yard to the milking area is better than no exercise at all.

MEDICAL ASPECTS: Now that your goats are eating well and are getting a lot of exercise, it's time to attend to their medical needs.

Kids need *Clostridium perfringens* C and D plus tetanus toxoid when they reach six to eight weeks of age, followed by a repeat dose of each a month later. Furthermore, adult animals need an annual booster of both these vaccinations 30 days prior to kidding.

Goats must be wormed in the spring and fall, or more often if the herd is confined to a small area. If you use a variety of anthelmintics (worm medicines), the parasites will be less likely to develop a resistance to any one substance. The easiest wormers to administer are those that are available in paste form. Boluses are nearly impossible to get down a goat's gullet, and wormers that are added to the feed are often ignored.

A vitamin E/selenium injection should be given to a doe 30 days before she's due to kid if you live in a region typified by a selenium deficiency. The youngsters should receive a shot when they're three weeks old.

No matter how proficient a backyard doctor you are, you should still take advantage of the knowledge and experience of a veterinarian once a year. This can help pinpoint existing or potential problems, and the vet can assist you in setting up a good health care program for your animals.

PICKING THE RIGHT GOAT FOR MILK

Solomon said, "Thou shalt have goat's milk enough for thy food, for the good of thy household, and for the maintenance of thy maidens" . . . a statement that, besides extolling the beverage-producing attributes of these caprine creatures, goes to show that the generous beasts have been domesticated for a long time! However, a modern goat enthusiast might wish to add to Solomon's wisdom, noting that—over and above its ability to produce healthful dairy products—the "poor man's cow" can be a pretty danged amusing and lovable animal to have around.

Furthermore, the milkers are exceptionally easy to keep, each requiring only half (or less) the barn space that the "competitor" cow needs, and they're able to forage nutrients from practically barren land if necessary. Sadly, goats are often taken for granted and looked upon as mere "lawn mowers." Yet, like many other animals, if they're treated with care and affection, these lively and temperamental characters can provide any homestead with plenty of milk and cheese, and a great deal of pleasure.

Perhaps this "goat fieldbook" will help you decide which of the common breeds might best serve your family.

FRENCH ALPINE: French Alpines attain a minimum height of 30 inches and a weight of about 135 pounds. One of the hardiest of all goat breeds, they are very ruggedly built and can be any of an almost endless variety of color combinations. "Alps" will sometimes produce as much as 5,000 pounds of milk per lactation period (37 to 48 weeks long).

TOGGENBURG: Toggenburgs hail originally from the Toggenburg Valley in the Swiss Alps. They're small (about 26 inches and 120 pounds), sturdy, vigorous goats, and in spite of their size, the animals can produce 3,500 pounds of milk in a lactation period.

LA MANCHA: La Manchas are a recently developed American goat, derived from a cross between a Spanish breed and other varieties. They reach a minimum height of 28 inches and a weight of about 130 pounds, and in one lactation period are able to produce close to 2,500 pounds of milk. Their most outstanding physical characteristic is ears so small that they appear to be almost nonexistent.

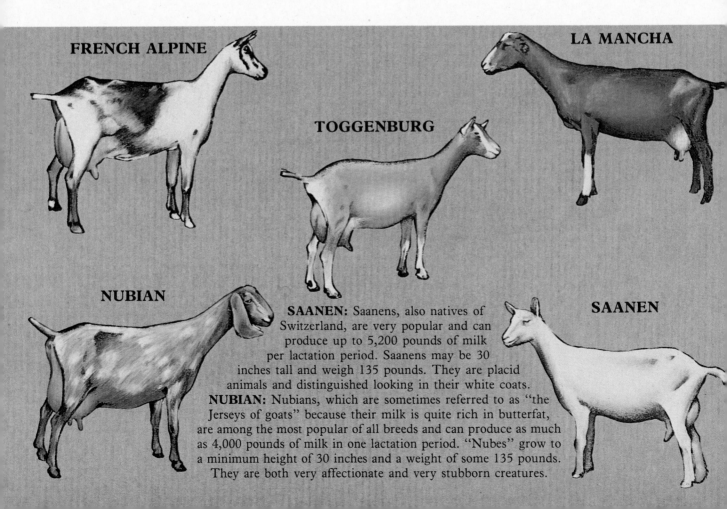

FRENCH ALPINE

LA MANCHA

TOGGENBURG

NUBIAN

SAANEN

SAANEN: Saanens, also natives of Switzerland, are very popular and can produce up to 5,200 pounds of milk per lactation period. Saanens may be 30 inches tall and weigh 135 pounds. They are placid animals and distinguished looking in their white coats.

NUBIAN: Nubians, which are sometimes referred to as "the Jerseys of goats" because their milk is quite rich in butterfat, are among the most popular of all breeds and can produce as much as 4,000 pounds of milk in one lactation period. "Nubes" grow to a minimum height of 30 inches and a weight of some 135 pounds. They are both very affectionate and very stubborn creatures.

AN ICE-FREE SOLAR WATERING TROUGH

Getting up early on bitterly cold mornings to chop through a thick layer of ice on the cattle's watering trough makes the economic advantages of raising livestock wane in the face of the unpleasant task. Commercial automatically heated troughs are expensive, but it's not an enormous task to build a solar-heated unit that will take the bite out of winter waterings.

All it takes to furnish cattle (or other livestock) with a drinkable supply of water throughout the colder months is to construct a small solar greenhouse over their watering trough. Nothing elaborate is necessary in the way of materials, measurements need not be exact, and only a few tools are required. If you have the trough, a supply of water, and an automatic valve, it's easy to build an A-frame structure with a heat sink. The south-facing slanted side of the A-frame must be glazed, and the trough should project from under one side of the frame. In the waterer shown, the cattle drink from the south end of the trough, but if conditions allow, the trough should project from the north-facing side of the A-frame, as there would be less chance of the glazing being broken by the cattle.

The trough can be anything from an old bathtub to an oblong galvanized watering trough, but it should be situated with its length on a north-south axis. If an old bathtub is used, the drain hole should be permanently plugged. To keep the tank full, a livestock-tank float valve needs to be installed and connected to the feed line, which should be buried deep enough to prevent its freezing.

The next step is to place a railroad tie or other heavy timber about three feet out on either side of the tank and parallel to its long dimension. Between the timbers and the sides of the tank, cover the ground with rocks or some other dense material to absorb heat when the sun shines. This warmth will be released throughout the night, keeping the water in the trough from freezing during the coldest hours.

To make the A-frame, nail a 2 X 6 to either end of each railroad tie, angled so that two boards and the tie form a triangle. Spike each pair of 2 X 6's together at their apex, and connect the two triangular frames by nailing several 2 X 4's across the side that will not be glazed. When positioning this structure, make sure that about ten inches of the trough projects beyond it into the feedlot.

The south face of the A-frame can be glazed with discarded windows, plexiglass, or clear plastic sheeting with framing provided as necessary. Fill in any open spaces between the sheeting and the ground, or around the trough, with sheathing or polystyrene foam panels. It's a good idea to stretch plastic sheeting over the top of the sheltered part of the trough.

Next, frame in the triangular sides of the shed, allowing for a small doorway so you can get to the trough for cleaning and maintenance. When all this is done, use some plywood to sheathe the sides and the back.

The inside of the structure, except for the glazed area, needs to be insulated, and this can be done with either foil-faced fiberglass insulation or rigid foam insulation board, though the rigid board is better because it won't absorb water the way the fibrous material will. The inside surface of the insulation, whatever material is used, should be painted black so the structure will absorb all the heat it can. After that, build and hang the door, and turn on the water.

Though this setup should work well and keep the water from freezing throughout the winter, there are at least two refinements that might be made. All the seams can be caulked to keep the wind from blowing away the heat you gain from the sun, and an electric line can be run to the greenhouse so a heater can be put inside to provide warmth during extended cloudy spells.

If the trough must project from the south-facing panel, it may be necessary to erect a gridwork of steel bars between the drinking section of the tub and the glazed portion to keep thirsty, pushing cattle from breaking the panel.

In addition to providing livestock with unfrozen water to quench their thirst, this type of structure can serve as a hothouse or as a fine place to store tools. It can also make a warm, windproof shelter from which to observe your stock.

HOW TO RAISE HEALTHY PIGS

If you'd like to enjoy pork that costs only pennies a pound and tastes far better than the plastic-wrapped meat available in the supermarket, consider raising your own pigs. Just one of the chunky animals can produce a great deal of premium, inexpensive meat for a home-steading family, and the beasts can be fattened on a diet that consists of little more than garden by-products and kitchen leftovers.

If you begin, as many folks do, with already weaned piglets, you'll avoid the task of hog breeding and find that simply rearing the animals is downright easy.

YOUR MARKET: You should be aware right from the start that the best marketplace for your homegrown pork will be your own dinner table. However, if you eventually harvest more meat than you can use, many folks will be willing to buy or trade for some of the sur-plus pork, but there's a world of difference between bar-tering off a little extra bacon and competing in the commercial pig-raising business.

A four- to eight-week-old piglet should weigh any-where from 20 to 50 pounds. If you care for the animal for about five months, or until it weighs 200 to 220 pounds, the butchering-size hog will yield approximately 135 pounds of meat products consisting of roughly 24 pounds of ham, 20 pounds of bacon, 17 pounds of pork roast, 16 pounds of picnic shoulder, 7 pounds of pork chops, 8 pounds of sausage, 7 pounds of miscellaneous cuts, 5 pounds of salt pork, and 31 pounds of lard.

It's best not to raise your animal beyond the prime butchering weight of 200 to 220 pounds, because at that size the hog has reached the optimum stage of growth. As a pig grows beyond that weight, additional gains will be expensive in terms of the feed required and will con-sist of little more than extra fat.

In addition to providing food for your table, each porker you raise to maturity will produce a large supply of manure (about 1.6 pounds per 100 pounds of pig per day) for your garden. However, because of local ordi-nances against the ever-present odor associated with pig manure, this can be a drawback for some would-be swine raisers.

BUILD YOUR ANIMAL HOUSE WELL: There's only one really difficult chore associated with raising weaned piglets: keeping the young animals at home.

Restricting a small swine may sound like a simple enough task, but every pig sports a snout that's perfect-ly designed for assaulting barricades. Any fence you build will have to be strung tighter than the fifth string of a banjo, especially where the barrier is closest to the ground, if you expect to keep your stock from prying their way out.

You can construct a taut welded-wire fence, a sturdy wooden enclosure, or a two-stranded electric fence con-sisting of a bottom cable six to eight inches above the turf with a second line eight inches above that. None of your restrainers will need to be more than 32 inches tall, though, because pigs can't jump very high. You might also want to dig a trench under your barricade and fill that ditch with old logs or rocks to discourage any of the beasts from tunneling out of the pen.

In addition to fencing, you'll need to construct a shelter for the animals and provide them with a way to cool themselves off. Just about any three-sided, roofed house will protect your livestock from storms and winter winds. However, since pigs don't pant very effectively and don't sweat at all, you'll need to be absolutely cer-tain each animal has 15 to 20 square feet of shade with the shadow-casting object located at least four feet off the ground. It's also wise to provide a mud wallow or a sprayer so that any overheated pig can cool off during especially sultry weather.

BUY THE BEST ANIMALS: If you're not going to try to raise the finest-quality pigs available, you'd be better off as far as both your time and your wallet are concerned not to rear any swine at all. It may take a lit-tle practice before you can recognize a premium porker when you see one, but you can gain any needed instruc-tion by attending county fairs or local livestock shows and listening closely when the judges explain why they select one hog specimen over another.

Once you learn how to pick out the best looking pigs in a litter, do so. Never buy the runts of a piglet crop even if the price sounds like a bargain deal. Too many runts never grow worth a hoot.

You'll probably find that the best time to acquire a young barrow or gilt is at the beginning of your gar-den's growing season. You'll have plenty of leftover crop pickings for the hog around then, and in most cases, you can expect to end up with a ready-to-eat adult pig by fall or early winter. This, conveniently enough, is the time of year that provides the best butch-ering weather.

FEED YOUR ANIMALS WELL: Water is the most important food you can give to your swine. A fattening pig will drink as much as three gallons of liquid a day, and the beasts will consume a lot of solid food, as well. Fortunately, since they will pack away almost anything, including vegetables, fruits, milk, meat scraps, spoiled eggs, garden clippings, weeds, and more, they can pretty well balance their diets by themselves.

Still, a 160-pound shoat can handle around 50 pounds

of this food a day, so you'll probably need to supplement its diet with grain or a commercial ration containing 20% to 25% protein. The grain also helps the pig reduce paunchiness and produce firmer, leaner pork. In addition, you may want to keep a steady supply of vitamin and mineral supplements available.

HELP YOUR ANIMALS PREVENT THEIR OWN DISEASE: Pigs are extremely hardy beasts, as demonstrated by their ability to revert rapidly to the feral state, but like all animals they can get sick. A good vaccination program will, however, prevent most illnesses: Check with your local veterinarian so you can inoculate against the diseases prevalent in your region.

Since the snout-nosed beasts are continually rooting around in their own manure, pigs have a never-ending opportunity to acquire internal parasites. They need to be wormed every four to six weeks with the anthelmintic your vet recommends for your locale.

External parasites like the anemia-causing hog louse can also be debilitating, so periodically apply a spray, a dust, or a pour-on insecticide to ward off the bloodsucking pests.

BREEDING PIGS: Though raising weaned feeder pigs is less demanding, a number of folks will want to set up a year-round breeding operation. If you're thinking of going whole hog with your own swine-raising ef-

forts, you should know right off the bat that rearing newborn piglets is a somewhat involved and risky undertaking. In fact, from 30% to 40% of the baby swine born in the hog-breeding business in this country die shortly after birth.

However, a small-scale homesteader can provide more individual caretaking than can most large enterprises, so you should be able to save almost all your curly-tailed youngsters and successfully raise an average of 16 hogs per sow each year. All it takes to achieve the goal is a lot of tender loving care and some knowledge.

MATING THE SOW: A gilt (a young female hog) should reach sexual maturity at five or six months of age and be receptive for two or three days of each subsequent 21-day cycle. You can be sure that a sow's in estrus (heat) if the female has a swollen vulva. She also may have a slight mucuslike or bloody vaginal discharge, act restless, urinate frequently, twitch her tail, hold her ground when you press down on her hindquarters, or try to "ride" other sows.

You should mate gilts on their first day of heat and older sows on the second day. Both young and old sows should receive a second mating 24 hours after their first. As for the male, an 8- to 12-month-old boar can usually service 12 females in pasture, or he can be "handmated" (matched individually in a barn) with 24 gilts or sows. A yearling or older boar can service 50 sows in stalls or 35 to 40 pasturing females.

PREPARING FOR THE BIG DAY: The gestation period for your pregnant sow will be approximately 113 days, or as an old saying goes, "three months, three weeks, and three days." However, there are some important preparations to be made before that magic moment of birth arrives.

For one thing, you should take steps to help keep disease from striking those fragile newborns. So be sure to worm each sow and spray her for lice about two weeks before her due date. You should also immunize an expectant mother against erysipelas to strengthen both the sow's and offspring's resistance to this most common, and usually fatal, swine disease. Likewise, good sanitation is a vital part of preventive health care, so thoroughly clean the farrowing pen and keep it clean. Wash the pregnant sow with a mild detergent and warm water before you pen her up for delivery.

THE FARROWING PEN: Another important pre-farrowing job is building a proper birthing nest. Little piglets need a very warm environment. The baby porkers will thrive at 80° to 90°F, suffer at 60° to 70°, and die if the mercury dips to around 50°. The youngsters' mother, on the other hand, probably has three to five solid inches of lard insulation around her middle, so she's more likely to suffer from overheating!

The different temperature needs of a sow and her piglets can create quite a problem. While the little pigs will try to cuddle up against the mother to stay warm, the parent will just as likely be trying to cool off by continually standing up and sitting down. And every time the mother settles back down, she runs the risk of landing on and possibly killing one of the piglets.

To avoid such a calamity, the farrowing pen should incorporate a separate heat source for the piglets. With their own source of warmth, they won't need to scramble up to their mother. Most folks use electric or gas-powered heat lamps for this purpose, although a few innovative individuals have taken to building solar-heated farrowing pens.

Your pen should also have some piglet guard rails that stand 8 to 10 inches off the floor and extend 8 to 12 inches out from the farrowing pen walls. By crawling under the rails, the little ones can curl up and sleep safely in their own heated spot, and scramble out to the mother only at mealtime.

THE FARROWING: A few days before the piglets are due, you'll want to move the expectant sow into her new quarters so she can adjust to the changed surroundings. Be sure, though, to let her out for two 10- to 15-minute periods of exercise every day that she's in the farrowing pen. This helps the beast ward off constipation and nervous stress.

Around that same time, you'll need to gather together all your nursery items such as iodine, clean rags, and plenty of bedding. Also, keep a pitchfork or shovel around so you can keep the farrowing area clean.

You'll know that the sow is ready to bear her young when she gets restless and tries to make a nest in her farrowing pen. Once the mother actually starts giving birth, you can help events proceed smoothly by talking to the sow reassuringly, or if you feel foolish conversing with a pig, by giving her a small portion of laxative bran meal. As each baby is born, dry the new arrival with clean rags before it hits the ground, if possible.

COUNTERCLOCKWISE STARTING LEFT: Happy, healthy hogs are the result of . . . an abundance of food and water . . . good stock (learn to recognize premium porkers by attending pig shows) . . . shelter to provide shade . . . and a program of dousing for ticks and lice.

176

Also, coat the piglets' navels with iodine by either spraying the disinfectant on each youngster's severed cord or by firmly placing the tot over a wide-mouthed bottle of iodine—so that its naval cord hangs down into the container—and then deftly turning both bottle and pig upside down.

While the mother undergoes her birth throes, it's probably best to keep the newborn piglets in a heated corner or box, away from her. Once they're all born and you've disposed of the afterbirth, make sure each newcomer has the chance to nurse and obtain some of its mother's precious colostrum. This first milk is high in nutrients, vitamins, minerals, and antibodies. You might even milk some extra colostrum from the sow to store in ice cube trays in case you later encounter a mother who won't allow her piglets to nurse.

Finally, after you've cleaned out the soiled bedding and made sure that both the new mother and her piglets are comfortable, you can go back to bed and try to make yourself comfortable. Don't expect to get much sleep, though, because farrowing inevitably finishes just in time for you to begin your morning chores.

INFANT CARE: A sow's milk is naturally deficient in iron, so one of your first piglet caretaking tasks will be recharging the newborns' supply of that mineral. If your youngsters are starting out life on a dirt-floored pen, or if you provide a boxed supply of soil in the nursery, the little ones may get all the iron they need by rooting in the earth. However, if like most folks you choose to raise the piglets in a more sanitary environment, you'll need to give your one- to three-day-old animals either an injection of 150 to 200 milligrams of iron or a feed that contains about 36 milligrams of iron per pound.

Though the piglets' main diet from birth until they're weaned at four to eight weeks of age will be their mother's milk, beginning in the first week, you should also provide the youngsters with an at-hand supply of feed, given to them in a creep feeder so that the sow can't get at the goodies. The feed should contain at least 18% protein and all the essential amino acids, vitamins, and minerals.

Most pig raisers will want to remove the tips of their piglets' eight needle teeth on the same day the young hogs receive the iron supplements. The tips of the teeth are simply nipped off with wire cutters or with special tooth clippers designed for the purpose. If left unclipped, the little pigs can use their tusklike biters to hurt other youngsters or accidentally harm their mother's teats.

Any males that are not going to be raised for breeding stock should also be castrated while young to prevent uncontrolled mating and to keep their meat from developing an "off," or "boarish," flavor and odor. If you perform this operation when the piglets are around two weeks of age, the task will be relatively easy and nontraumatic for the young animal.

Raising pigs from scratch definitely takes more commitment, work, and know-how than simply fattening up some purchased weaned piglets. Along with careful handling of the mating, the farrowing, and the infants' upbringing, you'll need to keep complete records of each sow's productivity and the weights of her piglets when weaned. These records will enable you to cull the poor producers from your herd and promote overall breeding efficiency. You should also keep track of vaccination and worming dates and all other medications used.

All in all, though, breeding your own pigs can provide you with the opportunity to start a worthwhile homestead stock-raising business. Converting those healthy piglets into full-size freezer fillers will take you one step closer to self-sufficiency.

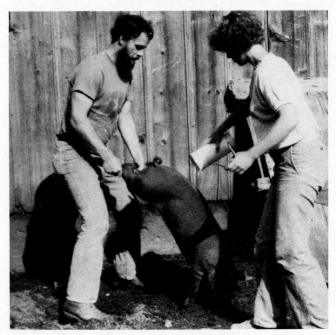

A FARM BUILDING MADE OF STACKWOOD

Homestead livestock can often be allowed to roam in a fenced pasture or be tethered in a field so the animals can graze, but when the air grows chilly or it becomes too hot in the open, a shelter for them becomes a necessity. In a limited operation, a barn that serves only to house animals calls for too much of an investment in a single-purpose building, and the combination post-and-beam and stackwood structure here is a good example of an economically built multipurpose farm building.

From the very beginnings of this do-it-all outbuilding, it was apparent to the builders that the entire structure would probably never be devoted to housing only one kind of animal and that not only would space be needed to house several different breeds of animals at a time, but storage would be required for a variety of feeds and equipment. This projection proved true, as the building has housed beasts ranging from horses to rabbits and has even served as a milk-processing center. At one time, hay, wheat, buckwheat, and straw were all stored in the loft.

Given the basic construction techniques used in this building, it's a small matter to alter the layout to suit the needs of a particular homestead.

THE STRUCTURE: At 32' X 45', the barn is larger than the average outbuilding but considerably smaller than a full-scale dairy barn. Furthermore, the structure's 10-inch-deep, 24-inch-wide footings offer the possibility of dividing the ground floor into stalls as small as 10' X 10'. The interior could easily be left more open, though the posts, which are an integral part of the load-bearing structure, must be positioned as shown.

The 45-foot back wall and one 32-foot end wall are earth-bermed and made of 12-inch concrete block, mortared and laid to a height of ten feet. To withstand the pressure of backfilling, one core of every second block was reinforced with two lengths of No. 4 rebar and filled with concrete. Before the backhoe pushed the earth against the walls, the builders tarred the exterior of the block surface and laid on 15-pound felt and 4-mil polyethylene. In addition, they placed 4-inch-diameter plastic drain tile over a 4-inch-thick bed of gravel against the footers, and poured another eight inches of rock over the ABS pipe to prevent it from becoming plugged with mud.

Both 3" X 6" and 6" X 6" rough-sawed oak, hemlock pine, and white pine posts make up the second-story support framework, and angle braces are used to connect the posts to concrete block stands built up from the footers. The connecting beams are also 6" X 6" rough-sawed timbers, and are supported by both the 6" X 6" posts and the 3" X 6" boards that brace the gates. The beams are tied to the posts with 1/4" X 6" X 18" steel plates and 1/2" bolts as well as by bolted 3" X 6" diagonal beams. Longer 3" X 6" diagonals also span the boxed-in sections at the open end of the building to add strength.

Sills were built on the 6 X 6 beams by nailing two 2 X 8's together, and then toenailing the double boards on edge on top of the timbers. A pressure-treated 2 X 8 sill was then tied to the crest of the block wall to level things up for the addition of 2 X 8 floor joists on 16-inch centers.

Laying down the rough-cut one-inch flooring on the framework presented quite a challenge, since few of the boards were of the same width. To insure that the spacing would work out correctly, the crew started laying the lumber in the center of the floor and worked to the edges across the 32-foot dimension. After every two feet of outward progress, the builders dropped a chalk line along the 45-foot dimension and ripped along the entire length to correct irregularities in width.

In order to get the greatest possible use from the loft, the roof was built as a free span, thereby eliminating the need for interior roof-support posts. The 2 X 6 rafters were tied into the flooring and sills with spikes, and plates were wedged between them to provide additional support. The span itself is a self-supporting angled arch that consists of a 12-in-10 pitch proceeding up from the loft floor, and a 3-in-12 pitch finishing to the roof peak. A vent runs the length of the peak to help keep the loft from overheating or retaining too much moisture. The roofing material is galvanized metal, laid over 1 X 4 nailers running perpendicular to the rafters. The result is a truly spacious loft 13 feet tall at its highest point.

FINISHING TOUCHES: The construction crew closed in the ends of the loft with standard framing on 24-inch centers, using purlins 24 inches apart. Then the same one-inch rough-cut lumber that made up the flooring was applied to the framing as siding. Generous double doors are centered in each end, but as a result of the earth berming, one loft door is at ground level to make bringing hay or other bulky, heavy material into the upper level easier. The other is at second-story height to facilitate loading material from the loft into a truck or wagon. A 16" X 72" tapered gable-end vent sits above each pair of doors and assures proper ventilation of the space.

To ease the job of getting feed downstairs to the barn's hungry clientele, a 29" X 30" trapdoor was cut into one corner of the loft floor, and the appropriate

cripples were then added from below. While bales of hay can be simply dropped through the opening, a ladder allows access from above to the feed room below.

The walls of the feed storage room and the milk room (as well as the partitions between stalls) are formed from stackwood set between the post-and-beam framing. The logs for the cordwood partitions were cut to 12-inch lengths at the site, and then carefully mortared into the spaces between the timbers. The stackwood walls enhance the building's appearance, and as they're constructed of firewood-length logs, there's no question that building them was inexpensive.

THE PRICE TAG: About 5,000 board feet of lumber went into the barn, but 3,800 feet of it came from trees cut to make room for the structure. Thus the bulk of the lumber was obtained for no more than the cutting fee charged by a local sawmill.

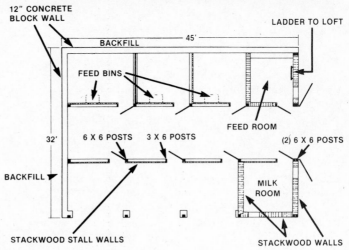

179

FARMYARD MANURE USED AS FERTILIZER

Livestock animals in the United States produce as much as two billion tons of manure a year with a fertilizer value alone of close to $10 billion. And that figure doesn't even take into account the worth of the approximately 500 million tons of humus-building organic matter that's also contained in the excrement.

Unfortunately, a lot of the agricultural value of manure is lost or wasted by either careless handling and storage or inefficient distribution. However, with proper management, it's possible to put back into the soil about 70% of the nitrogen, 75% of the phosphorus, and 80% of the potassium found in livestock feed.

A HISTORICAL PERSPECTIVE: Farmers have known about the earth-enriching potential of manure for nearly as long as people have known about agriculture. Probably the oldest surviving reference to the use of animal leavings in horticulture is found in Mesopotamian clay tablets dating back to about 2000 B.C. Somewhat later, Marcus Terentius Varro, a Roman scholar and writer of the first century B.C., noted that he considered thrush leavings to be the most potent of all manures. Later still, in the first century A.D., Lucius Columella concurred with his predecessor about the superior quality of the songbird's droppings. In his book *De Re Rustica* (On Farming), Columella went on to note the excellence of pigeon and chicken manure also.

Today, gardening experts generally agree that of all the widely available animal wastes, those of poultry are the richest. But these modern-day commentators often differ about which manure is second best: Some say horse, while others claim cow.

RICH OR POOR, HOT OR COLD: Before taking a closer look at which natural fertilizer does rate next after poultry droppings, it's important to understand just what distinguishes a fine "brand" of manure from an ordinary one. Basically, a potent variety will be rich (high in nutrients) and hot (quick to decay). The economic value of a particular kind will depend upon the amount of nitrogen it contains (phosphorus and potassium content are important too) and upon the fermentation it's undergone.

The nitrogen found in a specific animal's waste will vary with the beast's diet, age, and workload. For example, since seeds are generally high in nitrogen and grasses are low, grain eaters tend to produce richer manure than hay munchers do. And mature beasts, whose bodies are fully grown and thus require fewer nutrients, excrete more nitrogen than rapidly growing youngsters do. Finally, livestock that's raised for meat will require less nitrogen than will animals reared for milk, so steer dung, for instance, is more potent than droppings from dairy cows.

Because nitrogen promotes the growth of some of the bacteria responsible for the decomposition process, it's also important in determining how hot a manure is. The amount of liquid in the waste also affects the speed with which the material rots: Too much or too little fluid can inhibit fermentation and cause manure to be "cold."

Since cow and pig wastes are both relatively low in nitrogen and high in water content (containing about 30% to 40% liquid), they're considered to be cold manures. On the other hand, horse leavings, with about the same percentage of nitrogen, are classified as hot because they're only 20% fluid. Sheep and hen manures are also hot: Sheep dung is almost one-third liquid, but it's extremely high in nitrogen, and chicken droppings contain almost no water but are rich enough in nitrogen to counter that dryness.

RATING LIVESTOCK'S PRODUCT: Table 1 provides information concerning how much waste different animals produce in a year, and what percentage of nitrogen, phosphorus, and potassium can be found in each of these manures. The amount of nitrogen varies quite a bit (from a low of 0.3% in cow dung to a high of 1.6% in hen droppings), while the phosphorus content remains about the same (0.1% to 0.4%) for all of the animals—except hens, whose droppings contain as much as 1.5%. Nor does potassium vary a great deal; it tends to be 0.4% to 0.6% in the dung of all the animals except sheep, which produce manure with up to 1.0% potassium.

Of the five barnyard beasts analyzed, pigs, excreting 15 to 18 tons of manure a year per 1,000 pounds of live weight, are the most enthusiastic wastemakers; hens, producing only 4 to 5 tons per 1,000 pounds, are the daintiest. The amount of dung manufactured, however, doesn't always have much to do with how useful it is. Pound against pound, for instance, the porcine product is only half as rich as chicken droppings.

THE BASIC PRINCIPLES OF MANURE MANAGEMENT: In order to get the most fertilizer value out of manure, it's important to understand what happens to the substance during the various stages of fermentation and handling. Fig. 1 shows an extreme (but not, unfortunately, uncommon) example of what might occur in the nitrogen cycle of waste on a farm where livestock spend half their time in the barn and the other half in pasture, and where the barnyard manure is poorly managed.

For every 100 pounds of nitrogen in feed, about 20 pounds will stay with the animal and the other 80 pounds will be excreted. In this example, half will fall on the barn floor and half in the field. About 30 pounds of the nitrogen in the pasture-dropped manure goes back to the soil, while the rest is lost to the atmosphere in the form of ammonia or free nitrogen. At the barn, 20 pounds of the nutrient is lost through leaching and volatilization, because of sloppy storage.

Further losses result when the mismanaged barnyard waste is spread on the top of the garden rather than being worked into the soil. This procedure accounts for the disappearance of another 10 pounds of nitrogen. The result is that only 40 of the original 100 pounds of nitrogen are actually returned to the soil.

Since (as noted above) about 20% of the nitrogen an animal ingests stays with the creature, the waste must be handled carefully in order to get use out of as much of the other 80% as possible. Here are four ways in which soil nutrients can escape, and some suggestions for stopping them from doing so.

The urine of most animals can contain from one-half to two-thirds of the total amount of giveaway nitrogen, and about 60 to 80% of the available potassium. In pasture, of course, this liquid just soaks into the soil, so there's no significant loss there. To save urine in the barn, however, use bedding to absorb it. Then, when the straw or other matter is wet, heap it all into storage piles.

Scattering occurs when waste is dropped carelessly in the barnyard or on uncultivated ground (such as woodlots). To prevent nutrient depletion through scattering, shovel up any barnyard "mishaps" into a managed pile, and fence animals out of uncultivated areas.

Leaching is nutrient loss resulting from percolation of rainwater through manure or from surface-water runoff. The best way to prevent leaching is either to work fresh dung immediately into soil where it's needed or to store it in covered, watertight pits. If you keep the material

in the open, heap it on a level or a slightly concave surface with a clay or concrete base to prevent seepage of juices into the soil. Make your manure pile high enough so that rain can't soak through it, and slightly concave on top to catch water. Then cover it with a thin layer of sawdust or topsoil if you plan to let it stay around for a while.

As animal waste ferments, gaseous ammonia and, under certain circumstances, free nitrogen can form and escape into the atmosphere. The best way to prevent these losses is, again, to add a protective layer of topsoil or sawdust to the manure pile.

RAW, ROTTED, OR COMPOSTED: Manure can be incorporated into soil when it's in one of three stages: fresh, rotted (partially composted), or fully composted. If worked into the ground when raw, animal waste is least likely to lose any of its valuable nutrients, but it's also very heavy to handle in its uncomposted form and is sometimes too rich to be useful to plants. In fact, some fresh droppings (those of horses and chickens, for example) are so rich in raw nitrogen that they can burn tender young vegetation. Therefore, it's a good idea, if possible, to store manure and let it ferment for several months prior to using it. You could also plow the material into your garden in the fall, so that it'll have time to compost before the next spring's planting.

Rotted manure will be about half its original weight . . . which means—in turn—that its nutrients are more concentrated: A ton of rotted excrement is about twice as rich as a ton of fresh droppings. Fully composted manure is only one-eighth its original weight, and therefore eight times as rich. However, complete composting of animal waste is an expensive and time-consuming process.

TABLE 1 NUTRIENT CONTENT AND PRODUCTION OF SELECTED MANURES						
ANIMAL	NITROGEN (%)	PHOSPHORUS (%)	POTASSIUM (%)	LIQUID (%)	TONS/YR. PER 1,000 LB. LIVE WEIGHT	TONS/YR. PER ANIMAL
HORSE	0.4-0.7	0.1-0.3	0.4-0.6	18-20	8-12	same
DAIRY CATTLE	0.3-0.6	0.1-0.2	0.4-0.5	30	12-15	same
BEEF CATTLE	0.7	0.2-0.3	0.4	30	8.5	same
PIG	0.5-0.6	0.1-0.4	0.1-0.5	40	15-18	3
SHEEP	0.6-1.4	0.2-0.3	0.2-1.0	33-35	6-10	0.6
HEN	1.1-1.6	0.4-1.5	0.4-0.8	0	4-5	0.07

SPREAD IT AROUND: Before you reach for the shovel and the hoe, eager to put your barnyard manure to work, there are a few last-minute questions you ought to know the answers to. How do animal fertilizers compare with manufactured ones? How fast does manure release nutrients into the soil? And how much animal-produced plant food will various crops need?

To begin with, you can assume that a ton of manure is roughly equivalent to 100 pounds of packaged fertilizer. For example, one ton of fresh horse or steer leavings with bedding contains about ten pounds of nitrogen, five pounds of phosphorus, and ten pounds of potassium, which is more or less equal to the same nutrients found in 100 pounds of commercially made 10-5-10 soil supplement. On the other hand, 2,000 pounds of dairy cow or pig excrement contains slightly less of these, while the same amount of poultry droppings has the equivalent of about 100 pounds of 25-15-10 fertilizer. And keeping in mind that rotted waste is twice as potent as raw, one ton of fermented equine or bovine manure is comparable to 100 pounds of 20-10-20.

As to the rate at which chemicals are released into the soil, the general rule is that most manures let go about

TABLE 2 ROTTED MANURE NEEDED TO SUPPLY 100 POUNDS NITROGEN/ACRE							
YEAR	AMOUNT (TONS/ACRE)	TOTAL N (LB.)	LB. OF NITROGEN AVAILABLE				
			YEAR 1	YEAR 2	YEAR 3	YEAR 4	YEAR 5
1	10	200	100	50	25	12.5	6.25
2	5	100		50	25	12.5	6.25
3	5	100			50	25.0	12.50
4	5	100				50.0	25.00
5	5	100					50.00
TOTAL AVAILABLE			100	100	100	100.0	100.00

half their nutrients during the first year, around 25% the next, close to 12.5% the third, and so on. Two exceptions, both of which release the bulk of their nutrients within the initial 12 months, are cow dung (75%) and hen droppings (about 90%).

Table 2 gives an idea of how much rotted waste needs to be added to an acre of land each year in order to keep the soil supplied with 100 pounds of nitrogen. As you can see, ten tons of partially composted manure is needed the first year, and only five tons per acre are required during each of the next four years. The reason is that nitrogen is released slowly, so part of the earlier application will be available in succeeding years.

The amount of manure that needs to be added to soil will also depend upon the crop being grown. For instance, hay and pasture grass need only one to three tons of rotted waste per acre, and legumes require only 1/2 to 1-1/2 tons. Corn, on the other hand, requires six to ten tons, and leafy green vegetables like five to fifteen tons per acre.

However, be careful. Too much manure can prove harmful. The application of more than six tons of fresh poultry droppings to an acre of sandy soil, for example, has been known to increase nitrates dangerously in groundwater, and the addition of more than five tons an acre of any rotted manure on land maintaining hay or cereal crops can cause "lodging" (the matting of the grasses on the ground because the stalks have been weakened by too much nitrogen).

All things considered, though, animal waste is about the most economical and natural fertilizer there is.

FIG. 1 NITROGEN LOSSES WITH POOR MANAGEMENT

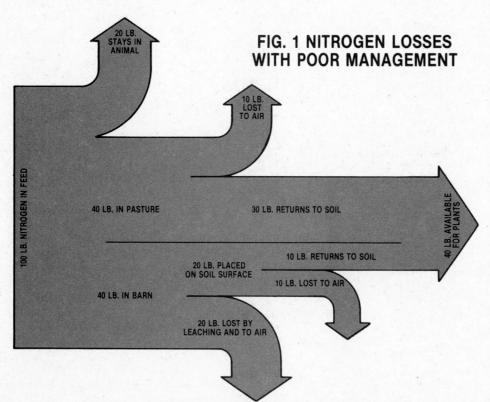

100 LB. NITROGEN IN FEED

20 LB. STAYS IN ANIMAL

10 LB. LOST TO AIR

40 LB. IN PASTURE — 30 LB. RETURNS TO SOIL

20 LB. PLACED ON SOIL SURFACE — 10 LB. RETURNS TO SOIL — 10 LB. LOST TO AIR

40 LB. IN BARN

20 LB. LOST BY LEACHING AND TO AIR

40 LB. AVAILABLE FOR PLANTS

FEEDING THE FAMILY DOGS FOR FREE

A place in the country doesn't seem complete without a few animals roaming about, but the cost of maintaining pets or livestock can be discouraging. In the isolated bush country of central Alaska, nearly everyone has at least one dog. Two sisters there who keep a sled team of eight huskies were accustomed to spending well over $20, including freight charges, for a 50-pound bag of commercial dog food. The expense, coupled with the complexities of shipping in premixed dry food, inspired these dog owners to create a simpler, less expensive way to feed nutritious meals to their canine crew.

The basic ingredient in the resulting low-cost dog dinners is fish, which are plentiful in a nearby lake. If you can't feed your kennel of hounds from a similar source, you may be able to buy large quantities of inexpensive bottom fish from local commercial fishermen.

During the summer, the dog team's owners use gill nets (such nets are illegal in many areas, so be sure to check local game laws before netting fish) to bring up an abundant harvest of whitefish, pike, burbot, and suckers each day. When winter arrives, they first have to chop holes in the lake—a tedious, tiring job—but the nets can then be left in the water for up to a week without any spoilage of the catch. If their haul is larger than the dogs' daily ration, they dry and store the surplus for use during the spring and fall, when erratic ice movement makes netting unsafe.

A FINE KETTLE OF FISH: The fish are usually cooked whole—heads, guts, scales, and all—to provide the dogs with hearty, wholesome meals. If fish is cooked long enough, the bones become soft and easy to chew, posing little danger to canine gullets.

A cereal supplement of rice or oatmeal can be used to fill out a skimpy netful and will also add extra nutrients on those days when the animals are needed to work long hours and haul particularly heavy loads, or when the temperature is extremely cold. Under such conditions, a husky may need extra calories just to maintain its body weight, so it's sometimes necessary to mix a half-cup of lard per animal into the food.

Game birds and other small trapped or hunted animals can be added to the kettle. (Inexpensive meat trimmings that are sometimes available from the grocery store are equally beneficial). In Alaska's interior, the hare population fluctuates regularly, but the sisters can usually snare several large rabbits a day during the peak season, and then stew up one hare, plus a little lard and oatmeal for each dog.

Scraps provide an additional range of possible ingredients for the dogs' dinner menu. Such leftovers as old potatoes, stale bread, cold zucchini, moldy cheese, and carrot tops are never turned down. The dogs even seem to enjoy the chickweed and lamb's-quarters that the cooks occasionally add to the pot when the fish ration is getting scarce. Dogs are not natural vegetarians; therefore, plant matter—much of which the animals can't digest—should be used to make up only a small part of their total diet.

These ladies cook their concoction for canines in the sawed-off bottom half of a 55-gallon drum, which is hung from a wooden tripod over an open fire in the summer and set on top of their woodstove during the colder months. Once the food is in the pot, they pour in two or three gallons of water. Whenever oatmeal or rice is included in the mix, however, it's a good idea to add more water than usual and to stir the stew often, since grains tend to stick to the kettle and burn quite easily.

When the sisters are cooking outside, they build a large fire with driftwood found along the lakeshore. As the flames grow under the pot, the homecooked hash comes to a boil, simmers for about half an hour, and then cools slowly while the fire burns down. It's important to cook fish and game completely, in order to kill any parasites that may be present. The food will be ready when the bones are soft, the meat crumbles easily into small chunks, and the whole mixture has a thick, mushy consistency.

DINNER IS SERVED: Even these hardworking dogs are fed only once a day in portions according to each eager eater's weight. After an active day on the trail, the dogs are always hungry, and their individual reactions to the sight and smell of a steaming pan of fish are predictable and entertaining. One may joyfully hurl his bulk into the air when he sees dinner approaching. Another, who is alert and high-strung, whines and dances impatiently at the end of his chain, waiting with increasing anxiety until his pan is set before him. Some stand and stare intently at the pot, their eyes growing wider and wider, until they're allowed to attack their portions.

Almost any dog, whether it's a husky, a malamute, or a plain old garden-variety mutt, would thrive on a diet of fish, meat, and vegetable stew. This nutritious, well-balanced combination is a great way to feed your tail-waggers economically, and the extra effort will be well rewarded as you see your crew dig eagerly into the tasty mush. As long as you can net or inexpensively buy fish in bulk quantities, you're in luck—and so are the four-legged friends that pull your sled, herd your sheep, or just patrol your homestead acres.

HEALTHFUL HOME COOKING FOR YOUR CAT

If you feel that your cat or kitten deserves better nourishment than affordable commercial cat foods can offer, you can match top-of-the-line kitty dinners in quality and appeal by cooking for your favorite feline. Nutritious homemade meals needn't be either complicated or expensive.

A nutritionally complete diet for a cat breaks down into several main groups: *proteins* (liver, egg, fish, chicken, and beef) with their own fats and oils; *starches* (wheat gluten, soy flour, and modified starches); and various *vitamin supplements*.

You can include all the essential food groups in your cat's home-cooked dinners and still create an economical alternative to canned or dried pet food from the store. Your first step, ironically, should be a visit to the meat counter of the supermarket. A number of free or low-priced ingredients may be available to you there.

Large fish often arrive whole, but they are sold in fillets, steaks, or other dressed forms. Heads, tails, and bones, along with all the meat attached to such pieces, are thrown away. Most butchers will insist on your taking the castoffs at no charge.

Pork liver is among the least expensive of meats, followed by pork kidney and chicken gizzards and hearts. All organ meats are rich in nutrients, and the flavors seem universally to attract cats, so buying a variety of these fresh meats to use in main dishes for your pet is a cost-effective expenditure.

As cooking for your cat becomes part of your kitchen routine, you'll no doubt develop menus, variations, and methods of your own, but until then, even the pickiest feline gourmet can enjoy these cat-tested recipes.

A FISHY FEAST: Fish is the messiest ingredient to handle but quite easy to make into a feline feast. Put it in a pot, cover it with water, and let it cook to a jellied mass filled with chunks of bone. With tongs, remove the largest sections of skeleton and discard them, but leave in the little soft ones. Put the broth through a food grinder while it's still hot and easy to pour.

While a serving of *les petits os de poisson en gelée* cools, add a handful of wheat germ. If this fishy dish is a hit, package it in meal-size quantities and store a supply in the freezer.

ABATTIS EN RAGOUT: To make this treat (which could also be called giblets in broth), boil any combination of chicken gizzards, hearts, and livers until they're tender, and serve them whole with a little warm broth. When you make a large quantity, chill and freeze the giblets right in the liquid, so that they won't dry out.

FOIS DE COCHON AUX OEUFS: You can save time and energy consumption by making this pork liver and egg dish when you're using the oven for something else. Just put the meat in a foil-covered pan with a little water, and bake it until the liver is pink in the center. Slice or grind it, and serve with a raw egg mixed in.

TARTELETTE DE ROGNON À LA KITTY: To prepare a healthful kidney pie for your cat, sauté pork or beef kidney in a little rendered fat or vegetable oil, then chop or grind it up. Mix the meat with wheat germ or egg, or both.

LA SOUPE DE POISSONS DU CHAT: It's easy to make a fine fish chowder for your cat. Simply cook four pounds of fish heads and scraps to a mush, and then remove the large bones. Grind up everything that's left, and stir in 1/2 cup of powdered milk, 1 cup of grain products (anything from stale rye bread crumbs to oatmeal), and up to 1/2 cup of such ingredients as cheese rinds, chopped outer vegetable leaves, cooked carrots, macaroni and cheese, chicken rice soup, or whatever other healthful odds and ends you have. Mix well and freeze the concoction in one-meal portions.

Other leftovers that can be added to the cat's food are cottage cheese, cooked rice, pasta, baby cereal, and almost any vegetable or grain product. If you feel that a vitamin supplement is needed to provide your pet with those "boosters" contained in commercial cat food, most pet stores carry a variety of cat vitamins.

A cost analysis will show that even when using only purchased meats at regular prices, you can prepare cat dinners that will cost less than half as much as the store-bought variety, and those meals consist of nutritious food without fillers, emulsifiers, or artificial coloring. Your pussycat will be purrfectly delighted!

184

CUTTING
ENERGY COSTS

PROTESTING THE HIGH COST OF ENERGY

Energy is one of the most useful things we buy on a regular basis, but it's also expensive. The cost of operating water pumps, furnaces, stoves, water heaters, freezers, televisions, and other power-consuming devices is often so high that many people—as a protest—are finding ways to do without commercially produced energy.

Not all the steps taken by one couple who went on the warpath against high utility bills are suitable for everyone, but their method of systematically reducing their dependence on outside sources lowered their power and gas bills substantially.

Their protest began in a small way when they turned off the pilot light on their gas range. Not using the continuously burning flame resulted in a meager but satisfying reduction in their utility bill, but that small savings convinced the couple they could cut back a great deal more without sacrificing comfort. They decided to take a hard look at the items around their homestead that were heavy electricity users.

Their first scheme was to decrease the use of the electric water pump. A pipe was run from the well to the kitchen sink, where it was connected to an old-fashioned, hand-operated pitcher pump mounted on the countertop. For a second time a utility bill dropped, and the electric pump, which had run almost constantly, was quiet, coming on for the most part only when the toilet—the next target—was flushed.

Every time the commode was flushed, it not only sent about five gallons of water hurtling down the drain, but also triggered the electric pump to replace that amount of water in the home's pressure tank. The couple had a functional outhouse that was being used for nothing but storage, so after removing the shovels, rakes, and other paraphernalia that were housed there, they put the little brown building back into the service for which it was intended. The electrical bill took another dip, but the disk in the meter still spun at a rapid rate.

The couple next turned to that recreational electricity gobbler, the television, though they had some misgivings about doing without it. Like many families, they tended to turn on the box each evening and stare at a succession of programs, often mediocre. They began by being more selective in their viewing—and by being firm and honest with themselves, found that very few of the offerings were worth the power needed to run the set.

Reading and conversing soon replaced watching television, and while they were enjoying the rediscovery of these pleasant pastimes, the electric bill plunged still further.

About the same time, they also resolved to remove the electric water heater and replace it with a more economical gas model. They didn't realize just how successful this maneuver was until the next monthly bill arrived and with it a form letter pointing out the severe penalties for tampering with the power company's meters and equipment! The couple accepted this as a tribute to their tenacity and overall diligence, and that night they celebrated their feat with a romantic candlelight dinner.

It was clear that their consumption of electricity had hit rock bottom when the following month a huge orange truck from the electric company pulled into the drive. With tears of laughter, they watched the repairman saunter up to the house with a new meter tucked under his arm!

At that point it occurred to them that it would be great fun if the new meter read even lower than the one that had just been removed, so they moved against the lone remaining energy gobbler, a 15-cubic-foot freezer.

Upon considering the matter, the couple realized the machine had been running year-round regardless of whether it was full or all but empty. The solution was easy: About mid-April, when all of the prior season's garden produce had been consumed, they pulled the plug and cleaned the unit. And there it sat, harmless, until the next fall's harvest. Again, they watched the meter slow down.

While they were pleased with the results of their confrontation with the galloping electrons, there was still the overuse of natural gas to contend with.

The largest gas consumer was their circulating heater, so they simply moved it to the rarely heated workshop attached to the house. A picturesque woodburning stove, which added nostalgic charm to the room, was installed in its place. What's more, with its chromed top removed, the woodstove's flat cast-iron surface provided an ideal place to cook.

As they learned to prepare food on the woodstove, the gas range remained nearly idle, and whenever the couple felt like cutting their gas usage still more, they'd heat bathwater on top of the woodstove, running the gas flame under the water heater less and less.

So, in a simple step-by-step manner, they reduced the staggering cost of running their homestead. The process also provided them with benefits they'd never dreamed of. For example, they find the sound of wood splitting beneath the ax on a frosty morning is very soul-satisfying, as is the comforting sight of the ever-growing pile of free fuel stacked up against a cold winter. They feel healthier because of the added exercise, and they have learned to savor the joys of living a much simpler life.

GENERATING POWER FROM THE WIND

The electric bill is a large part of the average family's monthly household expenses, and an investment of even several hundred dollars to reduce that bill will quickly repay itself. Anyone living where there is a relatively constant source of wind can take a substantial bite out of the power bill by installing a windplant to generate at least part of the electricity used in the home for lights and appliances.

A home generating system needs to be designed to meet the requirements of the area and the household it serves, as a man named Marshall Price found when he designed and built his own windplant, which has been meeting most of his electrical needs for more than nine years. The investment Price made in time and money has long since been returned in lower power bills and the satisfaction of having his own independent system.

MAKE DO, AND MAKE IT WORK: Price's story really began after he and his family built their residence on the shore of Lake Erie about 15 years ago. The constant breeze blowing off the water served as an ever-present reminder that free energy was going begging, but it wasn't until Price started collecting information on wind machines that he finally found the answer to the problem that had been keeping him from building his own plant: the need for information concerning the design and fabrication of the wooden blades. Once he'd uncovered that information, the rest, for the most part, was a matter of locating parts and fitting them together so they'd be compatible with one another and with the nature of the lakeside breezes.

"One thing about wind, it's darned unpredictable," says Price. "It can be blowing nicely at a steady 18 miles per hour, and then all of a sudden it whips up to 30 knots without as much as a 'how do you do.' On top of that, it changes direction just as erratically . . . and that can play the devil with your equipment. A rotor spinning at 200 RPM or so and scribing a 12-foot diameter circle has tremendous inertia and doesn't take easily to being reoriented."

It was critical to plan for these contingencies before beginning the construction of his plant. He first located an ambulance alternator that was capable of putting out 147 amps at about 15 volts (about 2,200 watts) in a very strong breeze. After reconditioning this component, the do-it-yourselfer started working on a governor system that would allow his three six-foot-long blades to feather by pivoting on their mounts when wind speeds got dangerously high. When feathered, the blades are less effective as airfoils, and this keeps the rotor's RPM within safe limits.

According to Price, this hub-mounted control setup is similar to the type Marcellus Jacobs used on his well-known wind machines. "I'd read stories about Jacobs, and I wanted to know how his governor worked. Well, I finally located a copy of a drawing from an old service manual, studied it, and then built my own version. It acts on centrifugal force and uses lead weights, linkages, and springs to control the blades' pitch. I knew I wanted a top speed of about 230 RPM on the power shaft, so I just used the trial-and-error method to set up the governor correctly. During the winter I made a little testing stand in the basement and mounted the hub on it. Then I drove the unit with a belt connected to my garden tractor's engine, took RPM readings off the hub using a tachometer, and experimented with the governor until I got it right. I've been using it ever since, and by gosh it works."

If the alternator is to generate usable electricity, it must spin a good deal faster than 230 RPM, so Price set about making a gearbox that would step up the driving speed considerably. To accomplish this, he just welded a housing out of 1/4-inch steel plate and mounted two salvaged Chevrolet gearsets inside. The 8.2-to-1 ratio thus created means that for every one turn the power shaft on the hub makes, the alternator shaft spins 8.2 times, or at about 1,800 RPM in near-gale (36 MPH) winds.

The power shaft itself was recycled from an old Datsun. "I bought the whole car for $10, then sold the body to a junkyard for $15. That left me with the entire drivetrain and with a profit of $5. I stripped out the swing arms from the independent rear suspension, used one—bearings and all—for the windplant, and kept the other as a spare."

Having taken care of governing the high-speed performance of his generator, Price had to consider control at low RPM. Specifically, he used a centrifugally activated microswitch to energize the alternator's field windings when the shaft speed reached approximately 750 RPM. Translated, that means that the alternator doesn't start charging until the breezes reach seven or eight MPH. Below 750 RPM, the alternator is ineffective anyway, so there's little use in allowing battery power to drain into the field circuit when the breeze isn't strong enough.

Finally, to protect his equipment from inevitable heavy blows, Price hinged and loaded the windplant's tail frame so it could be turned to parallel the plane of the blades. A small cable winch mounted at the base of the tower keeps the tail perpendicular to the rotor path under normal conditions, making maximum use of the wind, but when that cable is released, the vane swings to one side, and the tips—rather than the faces—of the blades are then presented to the breeze. This protects the rotor against overspinning.

This method of restraint is commonly used in up-wind-type machines, but in this case, Price again took a tip from the Jacobs design and set the tail springs so they'd shut down the windplant if the cable broke, rather than open it to the full force of a storm. Price also points out that he can take advantage of his machine even in strong winds, simply by unwinding the winch partially and allowing his blades to face the breeze at an angle, so they'll spill off a good deal of wind yet will continue to turn rapidly enough to generate power.

HANDMADE REDWOOD BLADES: Obviously, a knack for foraging, coupled with the ability to understand the potential of each "junk" component, aided Price immeasurably in bringing his project to completion. However, he knew from the start that he'd have to fashion the blades from scratch.

"I went and handpicked three straight-grained redwood 2 X 8's from the lumberyard, then cut and shaped them according to the specifications I wanted. Because a windplant blade is driven by the wind, its contour must differ from that of a standard propeller if it's going to work correctly. After I'd formed and sanded the wood, I protected it with fiberglass resin and matting, coating it evenly to maintain proper balance at speed, then roughed up the glass lightly and gave each blade a second coat," Price said.

"Now those redwood airfoils aren't just bolted to the hub. Each spar coming off the governor pinions is seated on a 7/8-inch-diameter cold-rolled steel spike that extends a full 20 inches into a socket that's been bored into the end of the blade. Furthermore, these internal spines are pinned through the wooden shoulders, and I've also got the blades sandwiched on the outside with 6" X 6" metal plates. This way, I can have my feathering feature as a governor, and still feel comfortable about the integrity of those redwood blades at higher wind speeds."

THE WEAK LINK: After fabricating the blades and working out the best method of mounting them, Price had only to erect a tower and place the plant atop it. Since the source of wind is generally from the lakeside quadrants and thus doesn't suffer interference from trees or hills, it wasn't necessary to build a fancy pivot or to rely upon altitude to catch the best breezes. Price simply sank a length of well casing into a concrete footer, leaving about 18 feet of the casing projecting above

the base. Then he mounted the generator and gearbox on a frame and set that into the tower so it would pivot on a vertical axis. Double-aught copper cables purchased at scrap prices from the local power company, and installed with plenty of slack to allow for yaw, carry electricity to the battery bank.

According to Price, energy storage is the weak link in his system. "There's absolutely no problem at all in making the power; that's the easy part. If I need more juice, all I have to do is build another windplant, or several if I want to set up a full-scale wind farm. But decent storage, something that's affordable and can still take the abuse of constant charge and discharge, is hard to come by."

Price could have avoided the storage problem by generating alternating current and then either using it on a separate line or feeding it back into the utility grid, but he decided against both those options because he wanted a system that would allow him to be somewhat independent of the power companies and that would be

working even when the wind failed to blow.

As his setup stands, the outsized alternator generates alternating current, which is rectified to direct current through diodes and is then stored in a mixed bank of batteries composed of two-volt and six-volt components. The batteries are wired in a combination series/parallel circuit to achieve 12 volts total. Power from the batteries is fed through an inverter that converts the storable DC back into AC for use throughout most of the house.

Price doesn't use a voltage regulator on his system, because when the batteries are depleted, they require a good three days of steady wind to even approach the overcharging point. In fact, he simply uses his appliances as indicators of his storage bank's state of charge: "I can tell by the way the lights burn. If they're too bright, I know I'm getting 13 volts instead of my usual 12 to 12.5, so I shut down the plant. On the other hand, if the batteries are low, the picture on my color TV gets distorted in the upper right corner, and that tells me it's time to crank the tail out straight again. A few years back, we had a nine-day spell without any appreciable breeze, and the cells were able to handle that, so I'm not too worried about my storage capacity."

Of course, batteries do lose their effectiveness, especially when they've seen a good deal of service. But Price stresses the importance of maintaining a cost-effective approach to buying and replacing these essential pieces of equipment.

A SOUND INVESTMENT: This brings us to the all-important bottom line: Has Price's investment both of dollars and of time been reasonably rewarded? Interestingly enough, he admits that at first his main objective was simply to have one windpowered light source over his reading chair. As he made improvements in his plant and added more lights, he boosted his storage capacity. Seeing that the generator kept up with his power usage easily, he installed the inverter and then tied other appliances, including the color TV, into the line. Eventually, he reached the point at which everything in his house except the dishwasher, the washing machine, and the refrigerator was powered by the wind.

At one point, Price had installed a resistive heating element in his furnace boiler to make supplemental hot water when the battery bank was fully charged. A switch allowed him to divert power directly from the windplant to the element, which required no power regulation. This permitted him to make even further use of available winds, because he never had to shut his generator down. That simple load-management system, though effective, was dismantled when Price replaced his leaky boiler tank with a new model.

In summary, Price is an example of someone who, with the help of his welding and metal-shop skills, turned a few hundred dollars' worth of scrap parts into the equivalent of a several-thousand-dollar investment—one that demands little more than an annual checkup and a battery replacement effort every so many years. It doesn't take a very sharp pencil to make sense of economics like that.

6-FOOT REDWOOD BLADES

METAL SHOULDER PLATES

POWER SHAFT (INPUT)

STEP-UP GEARBOX

POWER SHAFT (OUTPUT)

HUB W/INTERNAL GOVERNOR

FLEXIBLE COUPLING

AMBULANCE ALTERNATOR

FOLDING TAIL FRAME

MOUNTING BED

LOLLY PIVOT

POWER CABLES

TAIL VANE

WELL CASING TOWER

MAKING THE MOVE TO HEATING WITH WOOD

Rapidly rising prices tagged onto the sources of energy conventionally used in this country for home heating inspired a large number of people during the past 15 years to seek alternatives to paying the utility companies' rates. Some turned to solar heating systems, which often require major remodeling, and even larger numbers turned to the space heater of bygone days, the woodstove.

However, turning to wood as a source of home heat requires a great deal more than just turning up a thermostat or flicking a switch, and those who made the move to using the renewable energy source from the forests found themselves needing to learn about not only ash removal and chimney cleaning but also woodlore in general.

Making the shift to wood heating several years ago, a couple in northwestern Wisconsin found there was a great deal to learn and a lot of work involved, but they also got a great deal of pleasure from their newfound heating method.

When they bought their Wisconsin farm, they found the toolshed filled with quaint memorabilia: a two-man saw, a six-pound maul with rough-hewn handle, a rusted Swede saw, several wedges, and a sizable double-bitted ax. They hung the items on the toolshed wall as museum pieces and proceeded to install an oil furnace and forced-air heat in the house.

For the next five years they continued using the oil furnace and paying the fuel bills that might be expected in an old, not-so-airtight farmhouse.

About the time that snow flurries began blowing in from Canada, their son developed allergies related to fumes from their oil heating system. Although they have come to know and love wood heat as an efficient source of warmth for their house, they were chagrined at making the initial switch in October, which meant a lot of scrambling before winter set in.

The couple started by stoking up the old country home's fireplace and a small woodburning stove in the kitchen. There was enough dead wood out in the pasture to feed both without their having to face the task of cutting down a tree, but the stove's fire would burn out in the middle of the night, and the fireplace, with its serious heat loss, was no match for the winter wind.

Then they cried for help in their local paper and located a big, secondhand woodburning heater for $50. With it and the aid of a neighboring old-timer, they not only survived but also enjoyed their initial winter of heating with wood.

The heart of their system, the heater, is located in the center of the kitchen where it provides the family with atmosphere, a handy meeting spot, and warmth. It's a great help if you want to take some of the stiffness out of your hands and feet after a frigid taste of the outdoors or if you just need to stop yourself from shaking on a chilly morning. The couple's sons use the stove to dry their mittens, and it's ideal for keeping food and cocoa warm.

The special warmth of wood heat permeates the house and gives a sense of accomplishment, because the owners have personally completed the cycle of finding, cutting, and splitting their own logs and providing warmth for both family and home.

The crackling of the fire in the stove is in itself a basically cozy sound. The steady, subtle murmur of burning logs casts a comfortable feeling around the kitchen and encourages long, lazy daydreams when you tilt back in the old rocker with your stockinged feet stretched out toward the warmth.

An airtight firebox and a well-designed draft system are essential if a stove is to be efficient, and an ash door helps in cleaning the woodburner. In the couple's stove, air for combustion enters the heater's firebox at the top, is warmed by the blaze as it passes through a downdraft stack, and is then distributed evenly along the length of the burning logs by an intake manifold. An automatic thermostat, with which to dial the degree of heat wanted, opens and closes the damper at the top of the downdraft stack to admit just enough air to maintain the desired level of combustion.

The Wisconsin couple found their stove to be highly effective even on the days when temperatures dropped to 30°F below zero and the wind came up to give a chill factor equivalent to 60° below. The family conserved fuel by putting blankets over the kitchen doorways and kept more comfortable than their nearby had their oil burners' thermostats set on high and still couldn't get really warm unless they stood in front of their kitchen ovens. That's the real advantage of a woodstove over modern heat: You can get close to the source and toast comfortably, yet still have warmth evenly distributed to the rest of the house.

Anyone using a woodburner should be aware of the inflammable wastes that can build up in the chimney. A roaring flame could ignite the creosote in the flue and possibly trigger a serious house fire.

Although the chance of such a flare-up is remote, it's wise to be conscious of the hazard. Some old-timers prefer to close the air intake and let any chimney blaze burn itself out, while others keep a large bag of salt handy to dump down the flue to extinguish the flames.

The best answer to the problem of chimney fires, of course, lies in preventing the buildup of inflammable residue in the first place. Just look down your flue now and then and clean off the creosote with an appropriate cleaning tool.

If this sounds terribly complicated or dangerous, it's not. Any kind of equipment should be kept clean and in good operating condition, and doing the same for your chimney will lessen the chances of its catching fire.

A close look at your home's water pipes is also in order if the house has wood heat. Any line that runs along an outside wall can be wrapped with insulation to protect it from freezing. If you leave the house for any length of time, it's most important to have a dependable friend drop in and reload your heater. The better models hold 100 pounds of wood at one filling and will burn up to 18 hours unattended. If you plan to be gone several days or more, it's best to drain the water pipes.

Last winter gave the homesteaders an education in fuel gathering, and before graduating, they'd mangled three axes, one chain-saw bar, and a six-pound maul. Their mistakes were their teachers, and when the temperature plummets to the below-zero mark and stays there, a student learns fast.

Spring and fall are the best times to cut fuel, as there are no bugs, no weeds, no burrs, no prickly heat. If possible, the wood should be left out to dry for a season.

Which timber makes the best fuel? The hardwoods are denser than softwoods, and oak, birch, and maple are generally the favorites. Elm is good, too, but it's tough to split. The Wisconsin homesteaders were lucky enough to have their own stand of oak on their property, the same stand from which their house and barn were built before the turn of the century.

191

It's handy to have your own source of fuel, but it's not a necessity. A little scouting around can turn up many possibilities: neighbors who want a tree taken down, telephone and electric company prunings, outlying farmers or county dump locations with groves to be cleared, or new construction sites where you might be paid to haul away timber.

To handle the wood, nearly any old-timer will tell you, "First thing you need is a chain saw, and don't buy a used one. Get it new, so there won't be any mysteries about how it's been treated." Chain saws, you see, have to be coddled. They dislike sand and dirt and need regular cleaning and maintenance checks.

When you begin to use your new tool, remember that its power-packed cutting action deserves a lot of respect. Work slowly, and follow the good and sensible precautions listed in any good chain-saw handbook. Many old-timers say that two woodsmen should always work together, with one clearing twigs and branches from the ground to give the other open space to do his sawing.

When attacking a tree, make certain your chain saw is properly oiled and filled with gas. Then give an eye to which way the tree leans and gauge your cuts to let it fall in that direction. If the tree is straight and doesn't lean, check which side holds the most, and the heaviest, branches. Unlike the tall pines, thick oaks with massive limbs won't give you much cooperation if you decide to go against their natural inclination. Whenever possible, let the branch weight of a tree be your guide to where it's going to fall.

Your initial cut into the trunk itself should be horizontal and should continue about halfway through. It should be made on the side toward which you want the tree to fall. Next, saw diagonally downward to the deepest point of the first cut.

Make your third and final cut opposite and slightly above the first. When the tree begins to fall, remove the saw from the cut and step well away. However, if the blade wedges in the wood, forget it. Get out of the way. When the great mass crashes to the ground, the branches act as springs and can cause the trunk to kick back.

Begin trimming your fallen tree by cutting away the small branches. Cut the bigger limbs and the trunk into convenient lengths for your stove or heater.

Thick chunks of wood are a little more difficult than smaller pieces, but they can be handled. First, examine the face of the wood for any existing cracks that might serve as splitting guides. Then, with a maul, start swinging away at the center. Sometimes the piece splits open quickly; other times, it won't.

Wedges are excellent tools for a woodsman. If a log refuses to be split with an ax or maul, place a wedge along the grain and drive it in with the maul's flat end or a sledgehammer. You may have to use two, or even three, wedges on a stubborn chunk.

What about kindling? Automatic heaters that burn all night don't need it. In fact, one fire built at the begin-

ning of the season can be kept alive all winter. If you're using a fireplace or smaller woodstove, gather your small fuel early and keep it from getting damp. The drier the sticks are, the easier it is to get a fire going on a chilly morning.

Dry twigs make good kindling, but for a real tried-and-true fire starter, split some of your logs two or three times, let the pieces dry well, and split them again into thin strips. Another first-class kindling source is the log trimmings pile at a local lumber mill. Some operations give trimmings away, while others charge a small amount for a pickup truck load.

Does all this sound like a lot of work? It is, but it's labor of a very satisfying kind. Starting the day with 15 minutes of ax work on the woodpile helps keep a person in shape and the woodbox full. Ax swinging is a safe, nontoxic tranquilizer, and it's a surefire way to get lots of fresh air into your lungs in a hurry.

Perhaps it's those moments between ax swings, however, that are the most valuable benefit of all. Many of us have forgotten the delight of examining in close focus the small things around us, and the chopping of wood offers its practitioner a chance to pause and look.

While resting between blows, it's easy to find oneself counting the rings in a large oak, watching a squirrel scamper down a branch, comparing the bark of a hickory to that of a birch, or examining the way a branch grows from a tree's main trunk.

Smells, too, take on a new importance when you heat with wood. The job makes you get outside in the snow in spite of yourself, and you find that you love it. When you're sawing or splitting fuel, the outdoors has a fragrance all its own, a fresh, clear sharpness leavened with the pungent scent of inner wood newly opened. Inside the house, the soft odor of burning logs greets you like incense and wraps you with warmth and comfort.

Using a woodburning stove for heat may require a bit of work, but not really much more than the labor a person has to perform in order to be able to pay a staggeringly high fuel or electric bill. The difference is that the labor involved is direct; it is a personal involvement in the human need for shelter and warmth.

HEAT A HOME WITH ONE WOODSTOVE

Heating with wood can be a real asset for a home-steading family, but it often has the shortcoming of providing a great deal of warmth in one area of a house while other sections of the same dwelling remain cold.

One couple, when planning to build their own house in Maine, were determined to sacrifice neither space nor comfort in coping with the long, bitter winters. They were also convinced, though many longtime residents tried to discourage them, that they could heat all 1,360 square feet of their home with one woodburning stove.

HERE'S HOW: They attacked the problem of designing and building an energy-efficient yet spacious house from many different angles. Among the factors considered most carefully were sheltering the structure from the wind, building materials, the number of windows, achieving adequate air circulation inside, what stove to buy, and where to install the woodburner.

WIND PROTECTION: Because they'd been warned repeatedly about Maine's stiff winter gales, the couple wanted to build their home where it would have as much protection from the wind as possible. However, they didn't want to put the building near a windbreak that would block either the view or the sun's warming rays. Ultimately, they cleared a small site in the midst of an evergreen-and-hardwood forest and built the dwelling so that it would be surrounded by timber on the east, west, and north.

The air around the house is considerably warmer than the air on fully cleared sites nearby, and even on particularly gusty days, the trees successfully block the wind at the site.

DESIGN AND CONSTRUCTION: The home is a single-story structure and rests on a gravel base that extends to the depth of the region's frost line. The family protects the dwelling's 16-inch crawl space from winter winds by wrapping the entire base of the house with polyethylene plastic sheeting and then packing snow against the plastic after the first good storm of the season.

Four- to six-inch-thick cedar logs planed on one side and rough on the other serve as the structure's primary building material. These timbers provide a durable and attractive wall, and since cedar is a very porous wood, they furnish several inches of insulation too.

The hip roof with four sloping sides that meet at a ridgepole is insulated with three-inch polystyrene plastic foam boards nailed to one-inch sheathing. This arrangement probably doesn't prevent heat loss as well as would a conventional roof with three to six inches of rolled fiberglass, but it seems to work well enough, while allowing the family to enjoy an open ceiling.

WINDOWS: To give the sun every possible opportunity to enter the house, three homemade skylights and as many windows as the budget could stand were installed. Thus, the home receives passive solar heat during the day. At night, all the windows—which are double-paned—are covered with heavy, insulated curtains to keep the stored warmth from radiating back out into the cold darkness.

On chilly, overcast days when the family doesn't want to draw the curtains but does want to keep heat from escaping through the windows, they pull down special shades. These blinds were fashioned from a thin, lightweight, metallized plastic sheeting of the type that's often carried in survival kits by skiers and backpackers. They can be rolled up or down and allow some sunlight to enter the house while letting little heat escape.

AIR CIRCULATION: In order to allow air to circulate as freely as possible inside the house, and to avoid having the cold corners so common to homes in the north, the builders decided to limit the number of floor-to-ceiling walls. Where partitions seemed necessary for reasons of privacy, they put up fencelike room dividers instead. Thus, the two baths and bedrooms, the study, the art studio, and the utility area are separated from each other and from the rest of the house by seven-foot-tall partitions built of weathered pine boards, cedar slabs, or perforated fiberboard. The kitchen, dining room, and living room share the same open area and are separated only by the placement of furniture and rugs.

The space above each of the fenced-off rooms is completely unenclosed. The only areas of the house that are covered with ceilings are the clothes closet, to protect its contents from settling dust, and the pantry. This room is completely insulated from the rest of the house to maintain the steady, cool temperature that is ideal for the storage of food.

THE WARM FLOOR: The heart of the air circulation system, and perhaps the single most important factor in the successful heating of the house, is the enclosed, insulated air space under the floor through which warm room air is blown.

When the house was under construction, a false floor consisting of one-inch lumber, chicken wire, and three inches of commercial fiberglass insulation was nailed to the underside of the structure's main eight-inch support beams. A single layer of aluminum foil was placed shiny side up over the insulation and that was covered with a layer of polyethylene sheeting. The wooden floor people

VENT
BED-ROOM | STUDIO | PANTRY | STUDY
BATH | BATH | KITCHEN
PLYWOOD COLUMNS ABOVE FLOOR FANS | CLOSET | CHIMNEY
UTILITY | STOVE
BEDROOM | LIVING ROOM | DINING ROOM
VENT

walk on is almost 13 inches above the polyethylene, since it rests upon eight-inch joists.

Warm air is drawn under the floor and through the insulated air space beneath by a pair of inexpensive, kitchen-type exhaust fans set into the floorboards between two joists and on either side of the house's center support beam. An eight-foot-tall plywood column stands over each fan, so the blowers draw warm air down from the building's open ceiling and through the columns, and direct it under the floorboards. The air is then vented back into the house through four two-inch-wide, six-foot-long openings set into the floor near the structure's corners. This creates a continuous flow of warmth from the highest, and warmest, parts of the house, down under the floor, and back up through the coolest parts, the corners.

ANOTHER FAN: In addition to the two fans in the floor, which run almost continuously throughout the winter, a 14-inch exhaust fan was placed above the divider that separates the bedroom from the utility room. This blower is tilted slightly toward the floor, so that when it operates, it pushes warm air down into the bedroom.

When the bedroom fan is running, which is just on the chilliest days, not only is the bedroom's temperature increased, but the whole house becomes cozier.

THE HEATER: The woodstove sits right in the center of the house, next to a simple chimney built of eight-inch flue tiles surrounded by mortared C-shaped concrete chimney blocks. This is only a few feet away from the pair of plywood columns that conceal the floor-mounted exhaust fans. Thus, the two fans are able to draw into the floor the warm air that collects directly over the stove. The woodburner's fire blazes all the time during the winter, although on clear days the sun provides the house with a great deal of warmth. At night the stove is packed with as much wood as it will hold, and the front vent and the flue are closed almost all the way, leaving just enough draft to keep the fire alive. This way, the house temperature automatically drops to about 50°F overnight. In the morning the vents are reopened, and the fire quickly flares up again, thereby raising the building's temperature to somewhere between 65°F and 70°F.

Chief among the points in favor of this heating system are simplicity, economy, and reliability. No part of the setup can break down except the fans, and even if they should malfunction, or stop because of a power failure, the stove will still put out enough heat to keep the family reasonably warm. Since the homeowners aren't dependent on maintenance men or fuel oil deliveries, they needn't fear an interruption of service due to foul-ups in those departments or to increases in labor or petroleum costs.

In short, a relatively large and comfortable house can be simply and inexpensively heated, even in Maine, with a single woodburning stove.

USING WOOD TO PREHEAT WATER

You've installed a woodstove to help cut your dependence on the gas or electric utility companies, but the meter still seems to spin too fast and the monthly bill is still higher than you would like it to be. What do you do next? It might be to decrease the amount of work your hot water heater has to do. Consider the story of how one man cut his utility costs by simply putting a tank next to his woodstove to preheat some of the water his household used.

A RADIANT IDEA: While working in his basement, this homeowner noticed that the water heater was giving off, and therefore wasting, a surprising amount of warmth. He patched that heat leak by wrapping the tank in a blanket of insulation, but he kept thinking that there must be more he could do to reduce the gadget's appetite for electricity. When he pictured the woodstove upstairs, quietly producing plenty of comfortable, economical heat, it occurred to him that perhaps those low-cost calories could preheat the family's water: Maybe the incoming liquid could be piped to a storage tank set beside the log burner and then channeled to the water heater in the basement. He figured that by lowering the number of degrees the water had to be heated—the temperature difference between the cold and hot water in his home was a considerable 68°F—he'd reduce the amount of time the water heater was actually on, and thus cut electricity costs.

The following spring, he scavenged for a suitable used storage container but eventually gave up when the best he could find was a heater that had rusted inside. So, splurging a bit, he bought a new 40-gallon, glass-lined model for just under $100. Before wrestling it into place upright beside his woodburner, he gave the tank a coat of high-heat-tolerant black paint.

To this homeowner's dismay, the addition stood much higher than the stove and looked very cumbersome and unattractive. The solution, obviously, was to lay the tank on its side, but in order to do so, he would need to support it. Without this, the tank would tend to roll, and the weight of 40 gallons of water—about 332 pounds—might warp, and then crack, its glass liner.

After pondering the problem awhile, the homeowner decided that the obvious solution involved building a concrete base that would be contoured to fit the tank. Before starting the project, though, he had to put an extra brace between the floor joists in the space where the base would rest, to accommodate the additional weight that the water, cement, and container would impose.

When that was done, a rectangular form was built for the base, using pieces of scrap eight-inch-wide lumber. The box was filled to within three inches of its top with mixed concrete. After brushing the lower surface of the tank with oil so it wouldn't stick, the man positioned the cylinder and pushed it partway into the mix. Once the concrete had set, he lifted the tank and lined the perfectly indented base with a sheet of plastic to allow it to cure.

After a week, the homeowner stripped the wood forms from the hard block and set the tank in place, locating both components so that the vessel would rest about two inches from the woodstove.

Installing the plumbing came next, and because much of the new tubing would be exposed to intense heat, galvanized pipe was used to connect the tank to the existing PVC system with special plastic-to-steel couplings.

Such a setup is really very simple, and anyone with a little plumbing experience should be able to install a similar one using the accompanying diagram as a guide. Do be sure to connect the cold-water line to the lower portion of the tank, so that already-warmed water won't be cooled by the incoming liquid, and to position the hot-water outlet pipe at the top to set up a natural circulation out of the tank and into the conventional heater. Also, don't forget to install a pressure-relief valve on the outlet pipe, and it's a good idea to run a length of pipe from the valve to a small basin to catch any water that might escape if the relief mechanism opens.

The three line valves in the system are essential, too, and be certain to place them as they are in the illustration, so that when you want to use the preheating tank, you can simply open valves 1 and 2, and close No. 3. Shutting the tank down at the onset of the summer months will then be a matter of reversing the process.

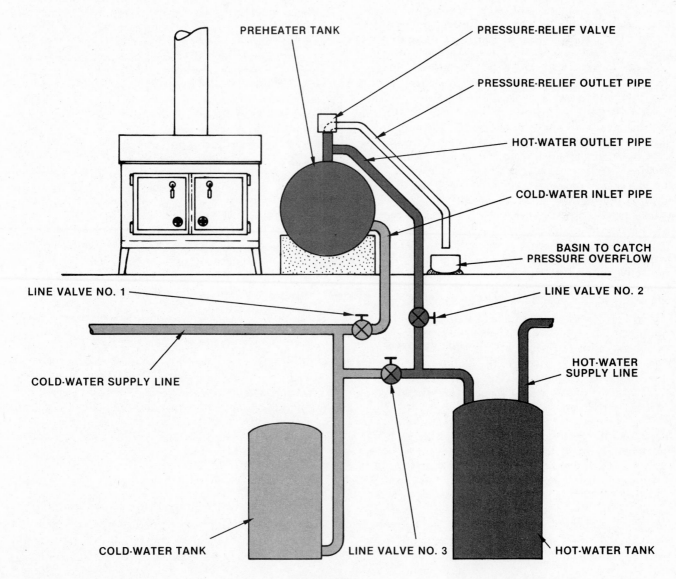

HEAT YOUR HOME WITH NEWSPAPER LOGS

Heating with a woodstove may help keep the winter chill outside the door, but feeding the log-eater can turn into a grueling chore taking a day or more each week for cutting, splitting, and hauling wood. Buying cordwood for fuel often costs as much as heating by other means, and spending all that money defeats at least part of the purpose of having a woodstove in the first place. Fortunately, there is an alternative to both cutting wood and buying it: rolled newspaper logs.

The main necessity when taking the rolled log route is an ample supply of old newspapers, and locating these is really easy. The first step is to approach your friends and ask them to save their daily papers for you. Then arrange to pick these up on a regular, year-round basis.

If you can't obtain enough fodder for your furnace by this method, you might try contacting scout troops, 4-H clubs, churches, or high school clubs to see if the members are interested in collecting papers to sell to you at scrap prices. You can also make this offer to children in your neighborhood.

ROLLING THE LOGS: To create firewood out of those stacks of newspapers, all you need is some wire and some time. First, get a spool of No. 24 wire, cut off a two-foot strand, and lay the metal strand on a table or some other flat surface. Place about a 20-page unfolded but unopened section of newspaper over the wire. Next, place a three-inch-thick stack of still-folded sections on the half of the 20-page section nearest you and begin rolling the pile into as tight a cylinder as possible. The unfolded section serves to keep the bundle together so that when you're finished rolling, you can bring the wire around the log and twist its ends together at the top. With a little practice, it should take practically no time at all to make a log.

There are commercially made log rolling machines for those who prefer not to roll their newspapers by hand. These handcranked devices resemble large-scale cigarette rolling machines and are supposed to be faster and to make tighter logs than those created solely by hand.

WHAT NOT TO DO: While some people recommend soaking the logs in water so they will burn longer after they dry, others report that it takes so long for the thick rolls of newspaper to dry out that they might as well be permanent household ornaments.

Soaking the logs in kerosene to make them burn better and longer is another suggestion, but the cost of the vats of kerosene needed for this defeats the whole purpose of reducing the cost of woodstove heating.

Avoid using old magazines or colored newspaper supplements. Glossy magazine paper is covered with a thin coating of clay that causes the pages to smolder rather than burn, and they leave a lot of leafy, black residue. Also, both newspaper inserts and magazine pages often contain lead, and the smoke and the ashes from them will be filled with the toxic heavy metal.

LIGHT A FIRE: Starting a warm blaze with paper logs is no harder than with cordwood. First, fully open the draft and damper on your stove and leave them open until you have strong flames going. Lay two logs side by side with a slight space in between, and rest a third log on top of these. Next, scatter about 40 pages of crumpled paper or small wood scraps around and over the three logs to act as kindling. The air pocket formed between the three logs permits good air circulation, which will help your newpaper logs burn fairly quickly. That's important, because the slower they burn, the more residue is left behind. You may also want to spear your logs with a poker as they burn down, shaking them hard so the ashes on the outer part of each log don't snuff the fire out.

HOW MANY DO YOU NEED? If you've heated with wood in previous winters, you can count on the fact that your stove will go through about the same bulk of paper logs as it did wooden ones.

However, if you've never heated with a woodstove before, the following formulas will give you a comparison between wood heat and other conventional fuels. Review your old fuel bills and total the amount of energy used. Whatever form of heat was used, find the total amount expended and divide that number according to the appropriate formula.

? gallons of oil	÷	115	=
? gallons of LP gas	÷	153	=
? cubic feet of natural gas	÷	14,000	=
? kilowatt hours of electricity	÷	3,080	=

The answer should be approximately the number of cords of paper or wood logs you will need to burn this winter, assuming that your heating needs will remain the same and that you're using an efficient airtight stove. If you use a nonairtight heater, you'll naturally consume more fuel.

The number of logs needed to get through a winter might seem to call for a mountain of newspapers and for a staggering amount of rolling, but it is an activity that can go on year-round, and it's surprising how fast a stack of the newspaper logs can grow. So start recycling those old newspapers and stay toasty warm this winter.

BUILD SOME BEADBOARD SHUTTERS

When the mercury drops to the subfreezing zone, and the winter chill oozes its way inside in any way possible, it suddenly becomes apparent that regardless of how draft-free you've made the roof and walls of your snug little dwelling, a bone-chilling cold can still make its unpleasant presence very well known through that heat-losing culprit, glazing.

Even though your home's portholes may all be covered with storm doors or windows and even though those barriers may use double-strength—or insulated—glass, the fact remains that the panes which bring warmth in during the day can just as easily let it out at night, during a spell of cloudy weather, or because they face north.

Probably the biggest offender in this theft of energy is the sliding glass door typical of many homes and apartments throughout the United States. Fortunately, though, blocking this heat leak is perhaps one of the simplest and least expensive steps you can take to save a few bucks on your heating bill. The same procedure described here would naturally apply to windows you'd like to be able to cover.

All you'll need is a piece of 3/4" X 4' X 8' beadboard for each glass door panel you plan to protect (this cellular polystyrene insulation is available at lumberyards and paneling centers), 36 six-inch-long magnetic strips (these can be salvaged from the self-sealing gaskets in junked refrigerators) to hold each beadboard sheet in place, and a tube of weatherstrip adhesive, which can be purchased at a hardware or auto parts store. It's a good idea to test a small piece of your polystyrene block to see

whether the adhesive affects it, and if disintegration should occur, use some other glue.

The idea is to cover the door panes with the foam-like boards when they're apt to leak out warmth and to remove the opaque panels when the sun is shining and can contribute to heating the home.

To begin the project, simply measure the height and width of each glass door frame—right to the edges—and cut the insulation boards to these dimensions. It's important that you cover not just the glass itself but as much of its aluminum casing as possible, since the metal transfers heat well also. If you have a wood-cased door or window, you should also plan to cover the frame, because the dead-air space formed between the panes and the beadboard adds to the cover's insulative effect.

Once the panels are trimmed to size and snug cut-outs are made for handles, latches, or anything else that would prevent the sheet from fitting flush against the frame, glue the salvaged magnetic strips to the door's framework—six on each side of each large glass pane and three each at the top and bottom, all evenly spaced.

Next, take a soft-leaded pencil and coat the face of each strip with graphite, and position the polystyrene sheet back over the frame so the board picks up the pencil marks at each magnet's location. Using a single-edged razor or a small blade, cut a channel at each smudge spot large enough to allow you to insert and cement in place the remaining 18 magnetic strips to mate with those on the frame. In order for the panel to fit flush against the frame, the channels must be twice as deep as the thickness of a single strip.

Your heat-stopping shutter is now ready to install. If you want to cover the panel with a decorative fabric to jazz it up a bit, be certain the glue you use won't melt the foam, or if you should decide to paint the polystyrene shutters to match your room, use a latex-based product.

That's all there is to it. This winter will find your dwelling more snug than ever because you'll be keeping the warmth inside, where you need it.

ATTRIBUTES OF VARIOUS TYPES OF INSULATION

Holding down the cost of home heating is a serious concern for many homeowners these days. It's generally recognized that it's less expensive in the long run to insulate a house well so it will hold in the warmth, reducing the amount of heat that needs to be generated. Before deciding what material to use, know the attributes of the various types of insulative materials, their suitability for various applications, and the amount that will be needed to block the winter chill effectively.

There are dozens of insulation product choices for installing during new construction and for adding to old structures. Each material has its place, and proper selection will help a homeowner obtain the most effective thermal barriers for the least amount of money.

CLASSES AND TYPES: Insulants generally fall into one of three categories: batts and blankets, which fit into a home's wood framing; loose fill, which is blown or poured between joists in a ceiling or into closed wall spaces; and rigid board, which can serve as sheathing material. Batts are distinct from blankets in that they have no facing, while the latter have either a paper material for stapling to studs or a foil layer for securing the blankets and reflecting radiant heat.

EFFECTIVENESS: The importance of the thermal resistance, or R-value, of a particular insulating material is most evident in situations where there is a limited amount of space to fill with the insulant. Within a stud wall, for example, 3-1/2 inches of fiberglass will give a finished R-value of about 13, while filling the same space with polyurethane foam could produce a rating of about R-26. However, the cost of all that polyurethane would be quite high compared to the fiberglass. In locations where space isn't at a premium, as in attics, it will generally be more practical to stack up less costly materials to a greater depth.

DENSITY: The amount of insulation that can be placed in a given location will sometimes be limited by the weight the material will add to the building. Loose-fill insulants such as vermiculite and perlite can be quite heavy, and in an attic space where the insulation is resting atop the ceiling, loads over three pounds per square foot may cause the ceiling to sag.

MOISTURE PERMEABILITY: Some insulants let water vapor pass through easily, while others are effective vapor barriers. However, the latter quality can prove to be either an advantage or a disadvantage. For example, if you have walls insulated with fiberglass that doesn't, itself, have a vapor barrier, and if you are considering adding an inch of polystyrene while replacing the siding on your house, watch out. That impermeable rigid board will prevent the walls from breathing, and the fiberglass may become waterlogged with trapped condensation. You'd be better off putting the polystyrene on the inside, though it would have to be covered for fire protection. In either instance, the added R-value of the board would be particularly effective; it would insulate the studs, which provide direct conductive paths between the inside and outside walls.

MOISTURE ABSORPTION: Compared with air, water does an excellent job of conducting heat, and when the air spaces in an insulant become filled with water, the effectiveness of the insulation deteriorates significantly. For this reason, insulation that absorbs water should never be used below ground level. Furthermore, it's important to protect insulants from water vapor that may penetrate a building's shell and then condense upon reaching the colder areas. Even if the material doesn't absorb the water, the liquid may form conductive paths and cause the insulant (particularly a low-density material) to become compressed and ineffective.

COMBUSTIBILITY AND SMOKE TOXICITY: Many common forms of insulation are combustible and should be separated from a home's interior by a barrier. Some materials release a large amount of carbon monoxide when they're exposed to flames, and that gas can prove a serious life threat long before a fire actually engulfs a home.

COST FACTORS: Because the price of insulation varies by region, distributor, dealer, and season, actual prices are not listed in the accompanying chart. Instead, the different materials are rated on a scale of one to five (least to most expensive) according to their average cost per unit of R-value. Before buying insulation, price different types at several building supply stores. When purchasing a good deal of material, be sure to inquire about a quantity discount.

Determining how much insulation to install for effective heat retention in a home depends on where the dwelling is located. In general, the greater the number of heating degree-days in the area, the higher the R-value should be. An insulation recommendations map divides the United States into six zones and gives the Farmers Home Administration (FmHA) and Mineral Insulation Manufacturers Association (MIMA) suggested standards for each zone. Anyone building new housing should insulate the structure to meet these guidelines, and owners of established dwellings should consider adding insulation if the building doesn't meet the standards.

Whether installed in a new building or added to an existing structure, insulation is an investment that can provide a cost-effective return through lower fuel bills.

FARMERS HOME
ADMINISTRATION/MINERAL INSULATION
MANUFACTURERS RECOMMENDATIONS

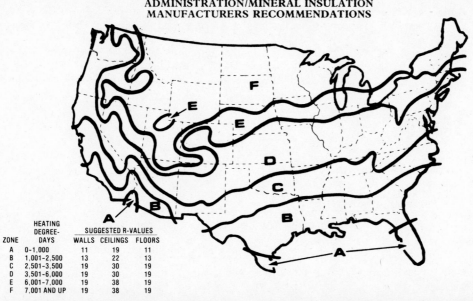

ZONE	HEATING DEGREE-DAYS	SUGGESTED R-VALUES		
		WALLS	CEILINGS	FLOORS
A	0-1,000	11	19	11
B	1,001-2,500	13	22	13
C	2,501-3,500	19	30	19
D	3,501-6,000	19	30	19
E	6,001-7,000	19	38	19
F	7,001 AND UP	19	38	19

ILLUSTRATION COURTESY OF MIMA

CLASS AND TYPE	R-VALUE/IN.	DENSITY (LB./FT.³)	MOISTURE PERMEABILITY	MOISTURE ABSORPTION	COMBUSTIBLE?	SMOKE TOXICITY	COST FACTOR	TYPICAL APPLICATIONS
BATT AND BLANKET								
fiberglass	3.2	1.0	high	low	binders and paper backing	low	2	New construction: walls, attic, floors. Retrofit: attic, floors.
rock wool	3.2	2.5	high	low	binders and paper backing	low	2	New construction: walls, attic, floors. Retrofit: attic, floors.
LOOSE FILL								
cellulose	3.4	2.6	high	varies	yes	carbon monoxide	1	Retrofit: blown into attics and walls; poured into attics.
fiberglass	2.2	0.6	high	low	binders	low	2	New construction: blown into attics. Retrofit: blown into attics and walls.
rock wool	2.9	1.5	high	low	binders	low	2	New construction: blown into attics. Retrofit: blown into attics and walls.
perlite	3.7-2.5	2-11	high	low	no	none	4	New construction: inside concrete block. Retrofit: attics and crawl-space floors.
polystyrene beads	3.8	0.8	medium	medium	yes	carbon monoxide	3	Retrofit: attic fill; windows.
vermiculite	3.0-2.4	4-10	high	low	no	none	4	New construction: inside concrete block; mixed in concrete. Retrofit: attic fill.
RIGID BOARD								
polyisocyanurate	7.0	2.0	medium, low if faced	low	yes	carbon monoxide	5	New construction: solar collectors, sheathing, floors.
polystyrene, expanded	4.0	1.0	medium	medium	yes	carbon monoxide	3	New construction: above-grade concealed sheathing.
polystyrene, extruded	5.0	1.8	low	low	yes	carbon monoxide	4	New construction: above- or below-grade concealed sheathing and floors.
polyurethane	7.0	2.0	medium	low	yes	carbon monoxide	5	New construction: above-grade sheathing; foamed in place.

THERMAL SHADES TO COVER WINDOWS

Thermal window shades can reduce heat loss through and around windows by acting as barriers to drafts and moisture. Ready-made shades are costly, but you can make comparable window coverings that are handsome, efficient, and inexpensive.

There are three different approaches you can use in assembling a window shade, depending upon your sewing skills and the materials you have available. Any of these will be practical for covering window units up to 4' X 8'. Excluding the time spent in acquiring materials, a single shade should take less than three hours to complete.

THE PRELIMINARIES: Begin by measuring the inner dimensions of the window to be covered, adding two to three inches to the resulting figures to provide for seam allowances. With this information, you can now buy the amount of fabric you'll need.

Up to a point, you'll have the same shopping list for any of the thermal shade designs. A pretty, chintzlike cotton-blend fabric that is already quilted to a layer of polyester filling with a backing of thin cloth is recommended. Such piece goods are customarily used for bedspreads and are readily available, reasonably priced, and easy to handle. By judiciously shopping for materials, you may further reduce the cost of the project. Muslin, for instance, may be used to back some models, and it can be bought by the pound at fabric outlets, as can the quilted cloth described above.

THE VARIOUS OPTIONS: Before you actually start cutting and stitching, pick out one of the designs listed below and obtain the other components and the sewing notions you'll need to construct your window shade.

Model 1: This option consists of a layer of batting-backed quilted material, a layer of 4-mil polyethylene (a drop cloth or a plastic garbage bag will make an adequate vapor barrier), another layer of polyester batting, and finally, the muslin backing.

Model 2: This window cover consists of a layer of quilted fabric, a polyethylene bubble sheet (the material, which will provide a vapor barrier and an additional air space, is used to wrap items for shipping), and a muslin backing. Enough bubble packing for this project should cost less than a couple of dollars.

Model 3: The third design consists of quilted fiberfill backed by a nonporous reflective material such as that used in the heat-retaining "space blankets" carried by many backpackers. A twin-size space blanket and some Velcro-brand fastening complete the necessary purchases. This is perhaps the least efficient model because it lacks the bulk to thoroughly block air drafts, but it's definitely well suited to applications in which light weight is of primary importance.

In assembling these window shades, do not puncture the vapor barrier, except at the edges where it's necessary to attach the Velcro; otherwise the layer will not offer maximum resistance to moisture and airflow.

CONSTRUCTION TECHNIQUES: After the windows have been measured, the materials for the shade selected, and the pattern pieces cut out, it's time to pay close attention to the assembly of the thermal "sandwich." Place the quilted fabric right side up on a table and then lay the backing layer (either muslin or reflective) directly on top, right side down. Next, add the other components to the top or bottom of the stack. (When you use this method, you can be sure that you won't wind up ripping out seams because you've gotten a wrong side facing inward.)

Once you've added and pinned the polyethylene, batting, packing bubbles, or whatever, thread your sewing machine, using a large needle, and set it for a fairly long stitch (this adjustment will keep the polyethylene and batting from becoming bogged down in the machine's feed dogs). After making absolutely certain that your backing material and quilted fabric are right sides together, sew along the outer edges of your window quilt. You'll probably find yourself taking wide seams to insure catching every layer in the stitching, so it is strongly recommended that you cut the components with large seam allowances (at least one inch).

Continue sewing around three sides of the shade, leaving a generous opening on the fourth edge. Turn the whole bulky package right side out, being careful to square the corners, and then finish up by slip stitching the open edge closed.

PUTTING UP AND SHUTTING OUT: With the sewing done, it's time to attach the Velcro. It's a good idea to separate the nubby Velcro strips from their fuzzy "mates" at the outset, as they tend to tangle at your ankles while you're trying to attach them to the slippery thermal shade.

The following Velcro-application idea works really well, but it does call for quite a few yards of the expensive fastener. Sew the fuzzy side of the tape along the top and halfway down each side on the rear of the shade. Then attach the gripper side of the tape to the remaining edges. Next, staple the corresponding strips of Velcro along the edge of the window frame. This method allows the shade, when not in use, to be folded into either a pillow cover or a child-size sleeping bag, and the technique is so satisfactory and versatile that the cost of the Velcro is justified.

There are, however, other methods of fastening the thermal quilt to the window casing that would consider-ably reduce the cash outlay. One way would be to attach continuous stretches of Velcro only at the corners, with tabs of the material strategically placed along the edges. Another, less flexible, idea calls for attaching cloth casings along the top and bottom edges of the rear of the shade. Thread lath through the casings and then staple or tack through the wood into the window casing.

The Velcro technique described works pretty well, and it looks good because it allows you to place your shade behind even a close-fitting window treatment like shutters.

These shades may admit enough light so that you will feel no need to remove them during the day. Some folks will undoubtedly desire more sunshine, though, and if you've attached the quilts by means of Velcro, you can easily peel them off or reposition the shades at half-mast to let in more light.

Those who decide to leave the coverings constantly in place should be forewarned that moisture may condense on the windows and run down into the wells, although the inclusion of a vapor barrier in the shades alleviates this problem somewhat. The best way to deal with this annoying situation is to check frequently behind the drape, wipe away any condensation, and then replace the shade. Mold may form where moisture has been allowed to collect. In this case prevention is the best cure: Periodically wipe the window surfaces and wells with a rag dipped in diluted liquid chlorine bleach.

THE OUTCOME: There are many steps homeowners can take to cut down on heat loss throughout a house: increasing the insulation in walls, ceilings, and floors; sealing cracks around windows and doors; installing storm windows; wrapping the hot water tank; and so forth. Many of the procedures are not cost-effective for renters or for buyers who will not be living in their home long enough to realize a financial benefit from their investment. Even renters, though, can put a stop to substantial heat loss by using insulated shades in the right places at the right times. In winter, it's best to keep northern windows covered at all times, but to uncover eastern and southern windows to the morning sun. Then lower the shades on those exposures late in the day. Let late afternoon sunshine warm the house through western windows, too.

Properly constructed thermal shades will halt the icy blasts of wind that whiz through cracks and chill your back as you're toasting your toes in front of the fire. Homemade draft stoppers are about a tenth as expensive as ready-made thermal shades, and you can individualize them to add decorative appeal to your rooms.

WALL COVERINGS KEEP IN THE HEAT

"It's not the heat, it's the humidity" is a statement commonly heard from sweltering people during the muggy summer months, and there's a lot of truth in it. Drier air feels cooler, both in summer and winter.

When the moisture content in a house gets too low for comfort in the winter, the occupants counter the chill they feel by turning up the heat, when if the house were properly equipped to retain the moisture in the air, they could be comfortable at a lower, more economical thermostat setting.

In cold weather, a relative humidity of between 40% and 50% is desirable in the house. Unfortunately, most home heating systems lower the natural moisture content in the indoor environment, making the rooms feel cooler and less comfortable.

One way of counteracting the escalating cost of home heating is by deliberately increasing the relative humidity inside the house. There are several ways of doing this, including placing pans of water on radiators, on a woodstove, or near fireplaces. The water evaporates, adding moisture to the air.

However, many contemporary homes, though fully insulated, are not equipped to hold in humidity, and any method used to increase the moisture in the air will be less than fully successful unless some form of vapor

WALL COVERING PROPERTIES, ADHESIVES, AND PRIMER REQUIREMENTS

WALL COVERING	THERMAL VALUE	VAPOR BARRIER	WALL PRIMER REQUIRED	ADHESIVE
Paper	No	No, unless vinyl-laminated	Oil or acrylic primer sealer	Wheat, cellulose, or ready-mix
Vinyl (paper or fabric backing)	No	Yes	Oil or acrylic	Ready-mixed vinyl adhesives
Foil (paper or strippable backings)	Yes	Yes	Oil or acrylic	Ready-mixed vinyl adhesives
Mylar (paper or strippable backings)	Yes	Yes	Oil or acrylic	Ready-mixed vinyl adhesives
Foam-backed vinyls	Yes	Yes	Oil or acrylic	Ready-mixed vinyl adhesives
Foam- and foil-backed textiles	Yes	Yes, if vinyl sheeting on surface*	Oil or acrylic	Ready-mixed vinyl adhesives
PVC-backed burlap	Some	Yes	Oil or acrylic	Ready-mixed vinyl adhesive, clear drying
PVC-backed felt	Some	Yes	Oil or acrylic	Ready-mixed vinyl adhesive, clear drying
Textiles on tracking system	Yes	Yes, if vinyl sheeting on wall surface*	None	None
Nonwovens	Yes, with vinyl coatings	Possibly	Oil or acrylic	Ready-mixed vinyl adhesives
Cork	Yes	Yes, with vinyl sheeting on wall*	None	Special cork adhesive
Wall carpeting (foam backed)	Yes	Yes, with vinyl sheeting on wall*	Oil or acrylic	Special carpet adhesive
Grasscloth (paper or strippable)	No	No	Oil or acrylic	Wheat, cellulose, or ready-mix
Silks	No	No	Oil or acrylic	Wheat or cellulose
Flexwood (wood veneer with fabric backings)	No	Possibly	Special manufacturer's instructions	Special manufacturer's instructions

*Don't use polyethylene sheeting on the interior wall of a heated room if a vapor barrier already exists on the present insulation.

barrier is used to keep the humid air from escaping through the walls to the colder, drier environment outside.

There are several barriers that can be installed between interior and exterior walls during construction, and there is even paint available that will protect against moisture loss. However, perhaps the best choice for protecting an existing home and combining function, beauty, and versatility is one from the large selection of wall coverings on the market. These can be very effective in preventing the loss of humidity, and some of them combine a vapor barrier with heat-reflective or insulative materials. The accompanying chart describes some of the many choices available, and provides information on thermal value, vapor barrier qualities, primer requirements, adhesives, and installation methods.

One of these coverings could be just the thing to help you retain humidity, lower heating costs, and be more comfortable, as well.

METHOD OF INSTALLATION

Directly pasted on surface

Directly pasted on surface

Directly pasted on surface

Directly pasted on surface

Directly pasted on surface

Directly pasted on surface

Directly pasted on surface

Directly pasted on surface

Special tracking system

Directly pasted on surface

Directly pasted on surface or stapled

Directly pasted on surface or stretched

Directly pasted on surface

Directly pasted on surface

Directly pasted on surface

LIMITING THE FLOW OF YOUR SHOWER HEAD

When weather forecasters start intoning warnings about below-average levels of precipitation, and the well begins to send up hollow echoes instead of a steady stream of water, you know it's time to pay attention to your family's water-consumption habits. Whether you live in an area where cutbacks are mandated from time to time, or ever-increasing water bills are simply forcing your household to economize, it's a good idea to conserve this limited resource.

You can significantly affect household use by merely regulating the amount of water that runs down the drain when you shower. If you live in a house that was built recently, your bathroom may already be equipped with a water-saving shower head. For the majority of people who live in somewhat older homes, however, there are reasonably priced brass washers that can be slipped inside a shower attachment to restrict the flow, and there is an even less expensive option you can use to modify your shower head so it will use about 75% less water.

To put together this almost no-cost adapter, first remove the existing shower head, using an adjustable wrench. Pad the jaws so the chrome doesn't get scratched. Then rummage through your workshop odds and ends or visit the local hardware store or a plumbing supply house and find a rubber washer without a hole in the middle, of about the same diameter as the inside of the pipe that connects with the nozzle.

The next step is as tough as this project gets. Using a pair of snips, cut a number of little wedges all the way around the rubber disk, from the outside of the circle and not quite to its center.

Insert the saw-edged washer into the shower head as far as it will go and refasten the whole affair to the connecting waterline. Try out your modification and if the flow is too constricted, disassemble the fitting and deepen the notches in the washer. If the flow has not been reduced enough, however, start over with another washer and remove smaller slices this time.

With a retrofitted shower head, the water flow will be about 25% of what it was before, and the spray will have the same force regardless of how far the faucet handles are turned. So enjoy! Now you can shower twice as long while using only half the water.

CONSTRUCT A SOLAR ENTRY

Imagine a cold, windy midwinter day, and picture yourself basking in the sun on your front steps and enjoying the first daffodil of the season. A solar entry to the front door of your dwelling can turn this make-believe scenario into a reality. For about a hundred dollars' worth of materials—concrete blocks, 2 X 4's, and window sash—you can construct an entranceway that is enclosed in glass and includes a planting bed. No longer will you need to pick your way up ice-rimmed steps and be ushered into your living room by a howling draft.

If your doorway faces south, you can garner extra sunshine for gardening, but regardless of a home's orientation, this air-lock entry can effectively reduce the amount of cold air actually penetrating the interior of your dwelling.

DESIGN: First, build a raised bed of concrete block, which can be made more attractive by facing it with brick or some other veneer. Construct a framework of 2 X 4's (redwood is used in the entry shown here), and space them to correspond to the size of the available sash. Then secure the uprights of the framework in the concrete blocks and fasten the crosspieces to the eaves. Once the glass is put in, the winter air is shut out.

EXTRAS: You might consider making the whole addition detachable. The section of ceiling over the planting beds can be made to swing back under the eaves, and the steps will remain covered. The rest of the glass sash can be removed from the framework and stored.

That way, the biggest part of the entranceway is open to the pleasant weather of spring and summer.

BENEFITS: Daily temperature readings taken before sunrise during the month of January show that the thermal mass provided by the raised planting beds in this sun-powered portico holds the heat quite well. A consistent 10 to 20° temperature difference exists between the inside of the vestibule and the bone-chilling outdoors. (Sealing the joints of the addition and using double-paned glass will make it even more draftproof.)

These readings were taken before the morning sun hit the glass enclosure, but the temperature difference on a bright midafternoon, when the portico is really gathering in the solar heat, can be much more extreme.

Other positive results of glassing in the entranceway include planting areas that never freeze, steps that stay dry, and reduced fuel consumption. Moreover, the greenhouse foyer is an ideal spot for comfortably removing soggy winter outerwear.

Still another benefit that will warm any gardener's heart is the possibility of starting many types of bulbs and seedlings early and conveniently. Around the first of March, whether the bitter cold of winter has ended or not, the solar entry makes a large and effective cold frame. Not only daffodils and crocuses, which are fairly hardy, but carnations, camellias, jasmine, cyclamens, and other flowers as well as a variety of vegetables can survive in this solar entry.

One of the finest features of such an entranceway is the surprisingly minor amount of maintenance it requires: 15 minutes in the spring to take the glass out and 15 more in the fall to install it again. Except for the pleasant responsibility of selecting the next plants to try, that's all there is to it. So consider a solar entry for your home. The benefits are mighty attractive.

CLOTHING AND HOUSEWARES

BRAID A RUG USING SCRAPS

The wool braided rug is traditional and has certainly stood the test of time, but there is another version of this classic that is more practical and less complicated to make. The four-strand braided rug described here can be made from inexpensive synthetic or cotton scraps, making it washable, and the interlocking of the rows of braid eliminates the process of sewing the rug together, as well as giving the rugmaker greater control over the colors.

RIP, SNIP, AND SEW: If you'd like to braid one of these lovely rugs, you'll need a pile of fabric scraps, a pair of scissors, four medium-size safety pins, a needle, and thread. (A sewing machine makes the job of preparing the scraps easier, but you can get by without one—it just takes patience.)

To begin, cut your rags on either the lengthwise or crosswise grain—but never diagonally—to make the longest strips possible. These bands should be two inches wide and anywhere from three to five feet long. (Tear the strips—when you can—to save time, and sew the short pieces together to get the right lengths.)

Next, fold each strip's raw edges into the center, and then refold along the middle of the strips to hide those turned-under edges. If you do have a sewing machine, stitch the folds closed as you go, to make a permanent crease. If you don't own a machine, you will need to baste or iron the folds in place. Each strip will now be four plies thick, which will add strength and durability to the finished rug.

After that task is done, sort the strips by color into bags or boxes. You don't have to fuss too much over the design unless you want to, but even a random pattern will look sharper if a particular color (usually a dark one) is saved for the outer border. A small amount of any hue will be most effective if used in the center of the rug.

PLAN AHEAD: If you wish to make an oval rug, you'll have to decide how big your rug will be before you start it, because those dimensions will indicate how long you need to make the center braid. As a rule of thumb, the length of that braid can be found by subtracting the proposed width of the rug from its length. A 2' X 3' rug, then, will need one foot of center braid, while a 3' X 5' rug will require two feet. A round rug, as you'll see, needs only a few inches of center braid.

Until you get the hang of four-strand braiding, don't attempt a really large rug. A 2' X 3' rug, which is a good size for your first project, requires about three or four pounds of scraps.

BRAID AWAY: To make the center braid, pick three strips of cloth and sew them together at one end. Make sure that each of these pieces is a different length. Continue to vary the lengths as you sew strips onto those that are braided in, because three stitched connections—if too close together—will produce a weak spot in the rug.

While it is certainly possible to do the braiding by yourself, you'll find the going easier if you can persuade someone to hold the sewn ends while you braid (as you would hair) the center piece. With the sewn end held while you work, you'll produce a straighter, more even braid. For an oval rug, make this central "rope" an inch longer than you determined by the length-minus-width formula above, as the end will have to turn back on itself when you begin to work on the next layer of rug. To start a round rug, just braid two or three inches, and fold this center braid over to form a "core."

When you have completed the center braid, sew a fourth cloth strip under the last crossover formed by the original three. This will give you the four strands that are needed for the interlocking method. Then, fasten a safety pin—to use as a "needle"—to the end of each strip.

If you're right-handed, hold the working end of the braid in your left hand (or vice versa for southpaws), and fold back that extra inch so that the four strands lie side by side—to the right of the braid—as shown in Photo A.

Now, imagine that the strips are numbered—one through four—from right to left. Take strip No. 1 and "weave" it over strip No. 2, under strip No. 3, and over strip No. 4. Then, using the safety pin as a needle, pull strip No. 1 through the adjacent loop of the center braid as shown in Photo B. Strip No. 2 (the new "outside" strand) can then be woven over No. 3, under No. 4, over No. 1, and through the next loop of the center braid. (See Photo C.)

This process of weaving the outer strip over, under, and over the other three and then through the succeeding

loop of the adjacent braid will continue (with some variations . . . see below) until the rug is finished. Keep sewing new strips to the unbraided ends as you go—and remember to vary the lengths of these new strips to avoid weakening the rug.

KEEP IT FLAT: Every time you round a corner, your rug will have a tendency to "pucker." To prevent this, just braid more than one strip through each center braid loop as you round these turns. For example, on your first row around the ends of the center braid, you may have to weave through one loop five or six times. When you go around the same spot the next time, though, braiding twice through every other loop might be sufficient. It's nearly impossible to provide strict rules for this, except that fewer of these "extra" passes through one loop will be necessary as the rug grows. Just keep your work on a level surface—so you can see whether the rug stays flat—and braid two or more strips through the same loop more often if the center starts to pucker. If the edges of the rug begin to look frilly, on the other hand, use fewer of these extra "corner" weaves. Expect to make a few mistakes until you get the proper feel for the corners.

Finally, when your rug is the right size, trim each strip to about an inch long, weave each of these tips under a loop, and stitch all of them in place.

That's all there is to it. After exhausting your own supply of old clothes and sewing scraps, scout out what garage sales, thrift shops, remnant counters, and neighbors have to offer. You'll have the satisfaction of recycling often unusable goods into beautiful floor coverings that are easy to make and as durable as any traditional braided rug.

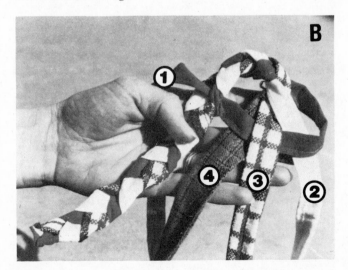

CREATIVE CARPETS FROM CASTOFFS

What's the secret of acquiring beautiful, durable rugs at a fraction of the market price? Recycle scraps of quality carpet into your own attractive designs!

The out-of-pocket expense of your creation will vary somewhat with your method of fabrication and the availability of materials. You can recycle cast-off floor coverings obtained from almost any source—the unworn corners of discarded rugs or samples of discontinued styles—but the best places to find quality material are the trash bins in the back of establishments that specialize in the sale and installation of carpet and other floor coverings. Just visit the alleys at the rear of these shops and cart off what you need, as long as no one objects.

In the salvaging process, the finest carpet costs the same as the poorest—nothing—so go first class and get the longest, deepest, thickest, richest, and most luxurious you can find. Pass up inexpensive shags with one yarn per square inch, because they won't blend well with the better elements of your proposed rug and they'll be worn to the backing before the good pieces in the mosiac even look walked on. Indoor-outdoor carpeting and other rubber- or latex-backed varieties aren't worth your time, either. They're likely to reject the glue you use and are usually not valued highly as floor coverings. Do gather plenty of quality scraps, though, because the job will probably take twice as many remnants as you think, and you never know what color you'll need when you get down to work. (Who can tell? That little piece of rosy fuchsia may be just the thing to liven up a dead spot in your rug!)

At this point, your new carpet has cost you nothing except time, but all you have to show for your efforts is a large box of small scraps. You still have to put the covering on your floor in one piece, somehow. The best method of putting unity and stability into your stock of odds and ends is to glue them to a cloth backing. A large piece of burlap or any sturdy cloth will work.

Glue the carpet scraps in place with a water-soluble white latex cement, which becomes waterproof as it sets. Less expensive adhesives are not as resistant to moisture after they cure. (Be sure to choose an adhesive that's water soluble when fresh, as other thinners can damage your rug or your body.) One gallon of glue will cover about 75 square feet of textile backing.

You'll also need a spatula or palette knife for spreading the glue, a utility knife for cutting, a rolling pin for smoothing seams, and some wet rags. The utility knife (a tool used to open boxes in supermarkets) is almost a necessity for cutting the carpet. Single-edged razor blades might work for a really small job, but they dull very quickly.

You don't have to know a lot about design as such to lay out an attractive rug. Some general rules can be helpful, though.

First, the fewer pieces in your creation, the faster the work will go and the less glue you'll use.

Second, try to plan the pattern so your mistakes won't look like mistakes. For instance, a crooked attempt at a straight line looks more wrong than an equally crooked attempt at a crooked line, and a seam between two pieces of the same color is more obvious than one between completely different patches. That's why a "crazy quilt" is a good first design.

Third, always work from inside to outside and from difficult to easy areas. If part of the rug consists of several small pieces that must be right, do that bit first and then move out from there.

Some recyclers carefully sketch a design on the backing and fill it in, but equally appealing rugs can evolve when you casually arrange the scraps on the burlap and think and fuss and fiddle until a pattern appears.

Start in the center of the intended design or in the middle of the trickiest area, and trim the first piece of scrap to shape. Always cut the carpet carefully, from the back, so that you don't slice off the individual loops of yarn. Then spread glue evenly over the underside of the trimmed section, line it up, and press the patch lightly into place. Cut the second scrap, spread glue on it, brush the pile away from the seam on the first section, and slide the new addition into position, and so on.

Warning: This business gets really messy, and this is where the wet rags come in handy.

Continue around the rug, pressing each newly formed seam with a rolling pin and taking care to keep the loops of yarn brushed away from the seams. Try to get the tightest fit possible as you lay each piece, so that the pile can "fill in." If you do have a few quarter-inch gaps, though, don't worry about them. In the kind of design suggested here, such minor flaws tend to disappear with use.

When you've finished your creation, you'll realize that the medium has other possibilities. How about a bits-and-pieces wall hanging, for example?

One thing that people may ask in regard to your fanciful carpet creations is "Why don't you sell them?" Well, if you made the rugs or hangings specifically to decorate your home, you probably don't want to part with them; however, you may enjoy knowing that similar creations would be popular merchandise. It's a fact: Low-cost recycled carpets can beautify your home and possibly supplement your income, too!

WARM YOUR BED WITH CHERRY PITS

Children in Switzerland have long been accustomed to a certain household ritual on winter evenings: Cherrystone pillows are popped into the kitchen's warming oven, and at bedtime each family member retrieves a pillow on his or her way to bed. The warmers work wonderfully well for taking the chill off cool sheets in unheated bedrooms.

Because many people are heating their homes with wood and trying to rely less on the more expensive fuels required for most central heating systems, the unheated bedroom is no longer a thing of the past. Cherrystone pillows could be the perfect bed and foot warmer. With three times the heating capacity of pebbles, and a much lower conductivity, cherry pits provide steady, soothing warmth for long periods.

The little bed warmers are quite simple to make. The hardest task seems to be remembering to save the cherry pits throughout the year. During the balmy days typical of cherry season, it's easy to forget about those long, cold winter nights. Just collecting the seeds is no easy task, either. In fact, if you're the ambitious sort who plans to make several pillows, you'd do well to contact a cannery. A phenomenal quantity of fruit is required for a usable amount of pits: It takes 30 to 40 pounds of good ripe cherries to supply enough stones to make one pillow!

COLLECT, CLEAN, AND DRY: Cherrystones must be thoroughly cleaned and dried before they can be sewn into pillows. First, pile the pits in a large pan or in the kitchen sink and cover them completely with fresh, cold water. Then rub and squeeze the stones together to loosen any remaining pulp. When that's done, rinse them and repeat the process several times.

Once the cherry seeds look clean, simmer them in a pot of water—stirring occasionally—for about 15 minutes. Then dump the cooked stones into a sinkful of cold water and rub them again. Rinse the cherry pits a few more times (it's absolutely essential to remove all the pulp) before draining and placing them on clean dish towels to dry. You can finish the dehydration process by spreading the pits in one layer across a shallow pan and baking them in a warm oven. Stir them now and then so they'll dry thoroughly. The pits will be evenly colored when "done" and can then be stored indefinitely in jars, plastic bags, or paper sacks until you're ready to make your bed-warmers. (The last are the best choice, because they'll absorb any moisture that may still be present.)

To make the pillow cases, use a sturdy material such as denim, sailcloth, or drapery fabric. (Avoid any kind of synthetic material that might melt when exposed to heat.) Cut two rectangles measuring 8" X 11" or use a single 16" X 11" piece. Put the pieces together face to face—or fold the double-sized rectangle in half—and stitch around the edges, leaving an opening large enough to let you turn the bag right side out. Finally, fill the sack, keeping it loosely packed, with the dried cherrystones and sew up the hole. You're ready for the next nippy night.

To use the bed warmers, begin by heating the pillows in an oven set to a very low temperature, in front of the fireplace, or over the woodstove. Take care with any of these methods that the warmers are not exposed directly to a glowing oven element or an open flame that might ignite the fabric. When the cherrystone cushions are toasty warm, take them immediately to your bedroom and place them in the bed between the cold sheets. By the time you're ready to turn in, your bedding should be just the right temperature.

REHEEL YOUR WORN-OUT SHOES

Are you feeling a little "down at the heels"? Do your old shoes or boots need to be made fit for walking again? If you're dismayed by the high prices and unsatisfactory materials typical of many shoe repair shops, reheel those shoes yourself, by using cast-off automobile tires.

Cobbling heels with tire tread is easy to learn, it doesn't require a lot of expensive tools, and it's a rewarding activity. After all, you're recycling discarded materials into inexpensive and very durable heels.

GETTING ATTIRED: Discarded tires aren't hard to come by, so be a little picky when you choose your new "heels in the rough." Try to find a tire with some tread left on it; old "baldies" are too thin to bother with. Also, if you plan to replace a child's or woman's smaller heels, you might want to look for a used motorcycle tire. They're easier to work with than the automobile variety and are just about as sturdy.

You should be certain that whatever tire you do decide to use is not one of the steel-belted models. Steel-belted tires are nearly impossible to cut through, and even if they could be shaped into heels, sharp wires would project around the edges.

Once you've located a serviceable tire, you'll have to remove the tread. A kitchen knife or jackknife won't be up to this task, so use a good, heavy-handled utility knife with strong, replaceable blades. Just make a cut through the sidewall right under the tread and carefully continue to cut—with your free hand behind the knife blade—all the way around the tire. Do this on both sides of the tread, and it will come away from the sidewalls in a ring. Then slice through this loop, cut off a bit more tread than is needed for a pair of heels, and roll the rest of the material up and store it for later use.

COBBLE IT UP: At this point, you should pry the old heels off your shoes with a sturdy screwdriver (or any substantial flat-tipped lever) and use pliers to remove the nails that remain in the shoe. Then cut the piece of tread in half and trace the outline of each heel support (the built-up place where the heel was attached) on the inside of each piece of tread. If this support is worn down, try to arrange the tread so that its thickest part will cover the worn area, to even things out.

Now, rough-trim the pieces of tread with your knife, but leave about a half inch of extra material all the way around. It'll be much easier to give the heels a final trim after they're nailed to the shoe.

The next step is to hold each roughly trimmed heel against its shoe, tread side out, to see how it fits. While the heel is in place, mark a pencil line on the tread to indicate where the nails will go. (Look at the heels that you took off to get an idea about locations.)

Your choice of nails will, of course, depend upon the shoe that you're reheeling. Be sure to pick a length that'll go deep into the heel support but not all the way through and into your foot. You'll be countersinking the nails, so figure the length accordingly. It's best to avoid small-headed fasteners—like finishing nails—because they could tear right through the tire cord and let the heel pull off.

With the appropriate nails at hand, set each new heel, tread side up, on a board and drive four or five spikes in along each penciled line. Use pliers to hold the nails while you pound—to save wear and tear on your fingers—and just hammer each nail in far enough to get the point through the rubber. You're not supposed to reheel the board!

You'll need a length (14 inches or so) of two-by-four to serve as your cobbler's last. Just stand this board on end and put one of the shoes (upside down, of course) over the plank's upper end. Steady the makeshift last between your knees and set the new heel in place against the bottom of the heel support. Align everything and pound in the nails. When you're done, examine the results and add more nails wherever they seem to be needed. One pair of boots may have 10 nails in the right heel and 11 in the left; that's okay.

With the footwear still on the last, use a nail set to countersink the heads deep into the tread (exposed nail heads will send you sprawling more quickly than any banana peel). Remember that those nailheads are under constant pressure from the rubber that they compress. If the nails begin to creep out in a day or so, just pound them in again. They'll stay put after you've done this once or twice.

After both heels are attached, brace each shoe, toe up, against a board and trim off the overhanging tread. Always work toward the back of the heel. Cut slowly, and try to trim off as much material as possible with each smooth slice. Do the sides of the heels first, and then tackle the trickier rounded backs.

That's about it . . . except to put the shoes on and try them out. If they feel a little funny when you walk, some more trimming—probably at the backs of the heels—is likely to be needed. Don't worry if your first pair looks a little rough-hewn; you'll get better and faster with practice. With a bit of experience, you'll be able to get out the tools, nail on a pair of heels, and put everything away in about 20 minutes.

By using old tires as replacement material for reheeling your shoes, you may find that the heels no longer wear out often enough to give you much practice in this kind of cobbling; after all, you can get a lot of mileage out of such retreads!

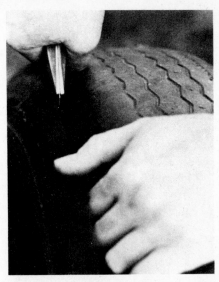

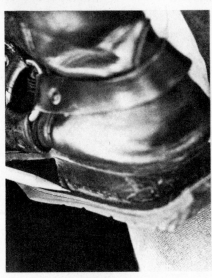

Using a sharp utility knife, cut through the sidewalls, being careful to hold the tire behind the cut you're making. Tread not used right away can be rolled up and saved for a later job. Pry off the old, worn heel and trace the pattern from the boot or shoe onto a piece of tread. Holding the nails with a pair of pliers to save wear and tear on your fingers, use a hammer to start the nails into the tread, driving them just barely through the tire. Place the footwear sole up over the end of a piece of 2 X 4, position the tread where it belongs, and drive the nails home. Set the nail heads below the surface of the heel, and trim the retread to the shape of the heel support.

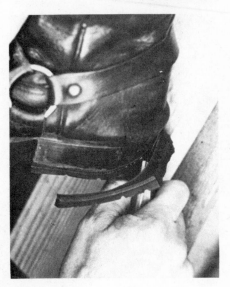

PROJECTS USING CLOTH LEFTOVERS

Fabric scraps are a natural by-product of any sewing project. While some of these bits and pieces are too small or frazzled to use, most of them can be turned into a host of delightful creations with only a little time and effort. If you're a remnant saver, you may already have bagfuls of colored cloth to use "someday, somehow" . . . but if not, there are numerous sources of cloth trimmings available that you can easily tap.

SCOUTING FOR SUPPLIES: Once you alert your friends to the need for fabric scraps, you may never require another source! However, should you need to supplement their offerings, you may want to check local thrift shops or garage and rummage sales for old clothes, nearby factories for rejects or discards, and area fabric stores for remnants.

If your creations are to be for children, look for bright colors, small prints, and interesting textures. The type of weave you choose—knit or woven—will depend upon the particular project. Knits tend to stretch, which affects the shape of the finished item. Tightly woven fabrics, on the other hand, are stable and tend to wear well. The weight of a material is important, too. Heavy corduroy would be hard to sew into the shape of a tiny, rounded toy, and muslin would do much better for a doll's apron than for a stuffed animal. Washability and wearability should also be considered, especially for children's items.

Stuffing is used in many fabric objects, particularly in toys. Old nylons and polyester fiberfill are two types that wash well. Tiny bits of material or even sawdust will also produce good results.

Patterns can be found in books, craft magazines, and even coloring books. Don't be afraid, however, of letting your imagination run free and creating your own designs

CONSTRUCTION BASICS: Begin by sorting through a pile of scraps and selecting the colors, prints, textures, weight, and weave suitable for the pattern you have chosen. Usually it's best to stick with one weight and type of weave in a single item, but special effects can be created by mixing unlike fabrics.

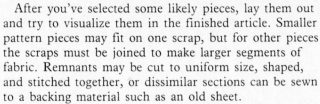

After you've selected some likely pieces, lay them out and try to visualize them in the finished article. Smaller pattern pieces may fit on one scrap, but for other pieces the scraps must be joined to make larger segments of fabric. Remnants may be cut to uniform size, shaped, and stitched together, or dissimilar sections can be sewn to a backing material such as an old sheet.

When pieces aren't stitched directly to a backing, join them (wrong sides out) by hand or machine stitching until you reach the size you require. If you have a particular design or color scheme in mind, take care to sew the scraps together in order. Also remember to keep the grain of the fabric consistent, since pieces sewn on the bias will stretch out of shape. (A doll's cheek, though, can be plumped nicely if it is cut and sewn on the bias.) It's important to backstitch at the beginning and end of each seam to keep it from coming apart.

After you have sewn enough pieces together to fit your pattern, press the seams open. Now you're ready to cut. It's a good idea to cut a backing at the same time to give added strength to clothing and toys. Once you've attached the backing, begin sewing according to the directions given in the pattern.

FABRIC-SCRAP IDEAS: Fabric leftovers can be fashioned into all kinds of playthings to amuse your little ones. Small animals, teddy bears, and dolls are just a few possibilities. Teddy bears—made of fabrics with different patterns and textures—are particularly popular. You can also sew doll clothes by using commercial patterns or your own original ones. The following three projects, a small sampling of the possiblities, can help you get started.

SNAP-TOGETHER CATERPILLAR: This cute cloth critter is easy to make and should delight youngsters of all ages.

First, select a fabric: Felts or knits are good choices. Use pinking shears to cut eight pairs of circles, starting at 3-1/2 inches in diameter and becoming gradually smaller to about one inch. Cut two 1/2-inch circles for eyes and blanket-stitch them to the front of one of the two largest circles. Embroider a mouth, and coat some thread or yarn with wax to make antennae.

Blanket-stitch each pair of circles together, right sides out, and leave an opening for putting in the stuffing. Fill each pair lightly, close up the seam, sew 3/8-inch snaps between segments, and put your caterpillar together.

FINGER PATCHBALL: This plaything is great for infants and little tots because there are lots of places for their tiny fingers to grasp. It can be made in either knits or wovens, and even embroidered velveteens have been used successfully for these delightful toys.

After you've chosen the cloth, cut 12 each of pattern pieces A and B (see Fig. 1). The patchball is made of 12 stuffed triangles, sewn separately and then joined together.

To make one triangle, stitch an A piece to a B piece along the seam line from the X to the Y points on each cutout (Fig. 2, Step 1). Clip the edge of A above point Y to allow some ease, then pull the open side of B over and stitch it to the other half of A, following the seam line from Y to Z (Fig. 2, Step 2). Turn the shell right side out, stuff the triangle, turn the free edges in, and sew them shut.

When all 12 triangles are completed, you can make the ball. First, using a needle and strong thread, sew through point P of each triangle until all 12 shapes are strung together. Draw up the ends of the thread and tie them tightly so that all the triangles are pulled together into the center at one point. Now, choose four adjoining triangles and sew them together at their points XZ. Select one of these joined pieces and sew three new triangles to its remaining point to make another cluster of four. Continue in this manner until all the stuffed triangles have been stitched together in an interconnected series.

PATCHWORK APPAREL: Making pieced-fabric clothing requires patience if you're to do a good job, but the extra effort is well worth it. Take time to select carefully from among your swatches. When you sew them together, match the seams perfectly. Your care

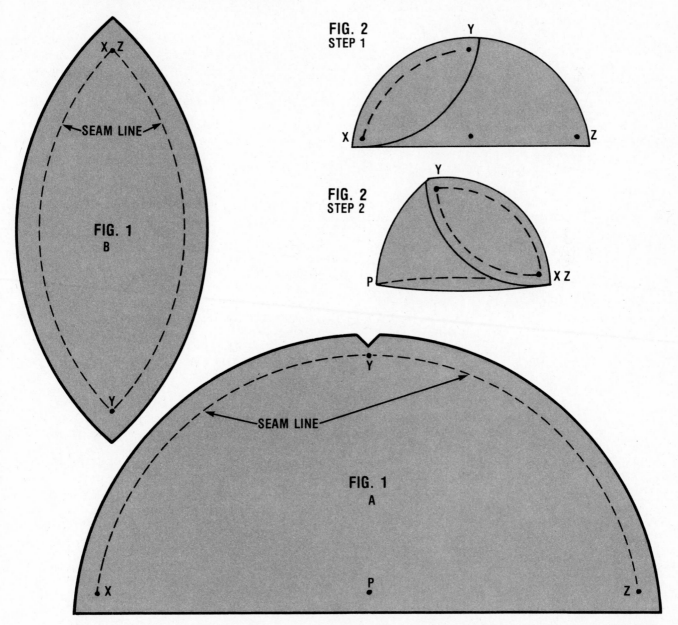

will show! Scraps can be used either as appliqués or for an entire garment. Again, combine enough pieces to fit the pattern you choose. Cut out the pattern, line each section for strength, and construct the garment as directed.

A child's pinafore—made of four-inch squares—is sure to please, especially with an adorable matching bonnet, and adults enjoy patchwork skirts and vests.

Handbags and totes are also very attractive and make great gifts. To create an eye-catching stuffed-square purse, first cut three-inch squares of outer fabric and two-inch squares of lining fabric. Sew each outer piece to a lining piece—wrong sides facing—with pleats on the sides of the outer piece so that it fits the smaller lining square. Leave the fourth side open, stuff lightly, and sew shut. Join the stuffed patchwork squares, right sides together, into two rectangles of the same size and press the seams open. With all right sides facing, stitch a long strip of fabric, five inches wide, (or squares joined together) to three edges of both rectangles to form the ends and bottom of the bag. Turn the whole thing right side out.

To line the handbag, cut pieces the same size as the rectangles and the fabric strip. Assemble the lining and insert it—wrong side out—into the bag. After matching the side seams and temporarily pinning the lining in place, stitch a two-inch binding around the top. Now, attach a fabric or rope handle.

These are but a few suggestions for making fabric-

crafted apparel. All of your cloth creations, whether toys, clothing, or accessories, will turn out especially well if you show care and love at every step of construction. You will be proud of the result, and it will have special appeal for the lucky recipient or prospective customer.

MEND YOUR MOTH-EATEN WOOL SWEATERS

Moths are no respecters of woolen clothing, no matter how special, expensive, or dear to your heart the garment might be. These mischief-makers aren't the only culprits, either: Rips, stains, and snags can spoil the appearance of any sweater. Whatever the mishap, it's almost impossible to locate matching yarn in order to repair the damage, and many a fine woolen knit has been relegated to the rubbish as a result.

Well, it doesn't have to be that way. Stains and holes need not mean the end of a sweater. Indeed, a moth's meal or a flaw can be the start of a new life for your garment.

First of all, don't even try to find perfectly matching yarn. Instead, look for a selection of colorful two- or three-ply hanks of twist (a friend or relative who knits or crochets is an ideal source for these scraps). Next, get yourself a pair of sharp scissors and a tapestry needle with a large eye. Then sit down with your mending tools, the multicolored yarns, and your old sweater, and get ready for a good time!

Begin by patching the hole or stain with one strand of yarn. Go right over the fault, catching or covering the edges with yarn, making a little "button" of color. Now, put a few petals around the little patch (the "lazy daisy" embroidery stitch works well here), and you have a flower! Mend a sweater with daisies galore, or let your imagination run wild and embroider fish, fowl, and a veritable Noah's ark of creatures. Furthermore, there's no need to limit your efforts to depicting flora and fauna: Sailboats, cars, buildings, or office supplies can be worked into attractive thematic patterns. Then again, if you prefer abstract decorations, simply cover the offending spots with squares or rectangles, using a variety of colors for the geometric designs.

While you may never welcome the harm that can come to your favorite sweaters from moths or mishaps, you can feel confident that the injury isn't irreparable and that it's even possible to make a damaged garment more attractive than it was originally.

MAKING LONG JOHNS FROM OLD SWEATERS

There's nothing like a pair of old-fashioned woolen long johns to take the bite out of a cold winter day. A layer of wool next to the skin—even wet wool—is about the best insulation imaginable. Since this material has fibers that lift moisture away from the body, a good pair of "woolies" provides ventilation as well as insulation.

In fact, the only problem with yesterday's answer to the cold is today's inflated economy. It's nearly impossible to find a pair of woolen long johns for under $25, and even the blended cotton or synthetic imitations (which are often anything but warm when they get damp) aren't cheap.

So, how can a person afford to stay cozy and dry while working or playing in the snow? It's easy . . . just make a set of woolen underwear yourself. Even if you haven't had much sewing experience, you can custom-tailor a couple of old sweaters into warm winter underwear in an hour or so, and the necessary materials shouldn't cost more than a couple of dollars, if anything at all!

WOOLGATHERING: First, locate three old woolen sweaters: one for the top portion of the long johns, one for the bottom, and a third that can be cut up to extend the arms and midriff of the other two.

If you don't have any cast-off sweaters around the house, you should be able to find a few at a secondhand clothing store or rummage sale. You can expect to pay a dollar or two per sweater. If the prices are higher than that, keep on looking.

Don't let the appearance of these bargains discourage you. Remember, you're going to make underwear, so a few moth holes won't be a problem unless they're big enough to let in the breeze.

It pays, however, to be a bit fussy about the kind of wool used in your "raw materials." Machine-washable woolen sweaters have an obvious advantage, and if one's skin is sensitive, a soft wool helps avoid that hair-shirt feeling.

TOP TIPS: The undershirt portion of the woolies will require little work. Simply select the snuggest-fitting (but still comfortable) sweater. If it's too loose to fit nicely under clothes, turn the sweater inside out, gather the extra material, seam it on both sides, and then clip away the excess.

BOTTOMS UP: Pick a sweater with long, baggy arms to serve as the legs of the long johns. Have the intended wearer of the underwear put the sweater on—feet first through the sleeves, of course—and you're ready to tailor the long john pants.

Begin by tucking in the sweater neck to take up the excess material in the crotch area and pin the neck closed from front to back. Then remove the garment, run a crotch seam along the pinned line, and trim away the extra material from the inside.

When the first seam is sewn and trimmed, repeat the gathering and pinning process, but this time run your crotch seam from right to left and trim away the excess.

If the underwear bags between the waist and crotch, just fold it in, stitch a yoke seam from right to left across the abdomen, and—again—trim it from the inside. You can repeat this procedure on the backside, if necessary, but be sure to leave a little "sitting down room." If you need to tighten the hips and waist, run a seam up each side or down the middle and repeat the trimming process.

LONGER LONG JOHNS: The sweater arm legs of these long johns may not be long enough for tall folks. To extend the legs, just cut off as much length as is needed from the sleeves of the third sweater and stitch the ends of these tubular pieces to the cuffs of the existing legs.

And, if the undershirt won't stay tucked in when the wearer bends or stretches, you'll need to lengthen the body of that piece. To do this, simply cut the midriff off of the third sweater and stitch it to the waistband of the underwear top.

That's all there is to it. You'll have made some inexpensive, superwarm long johns to help ward off the winter winds. Of course, this homemade underwear may look a little funny, but it's a lot easier to laugh when your teeth aren't chattering!

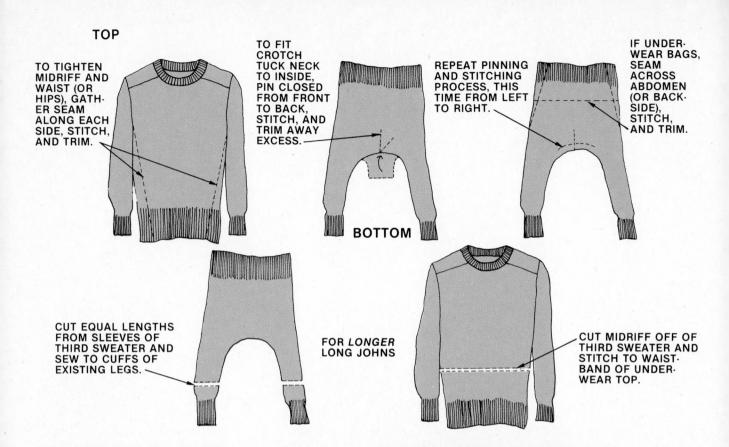

TOP

TO TIGHTEN MIDRIFF AND WAIST (OR HIPS), GATHER SEAM ALONG EACH SIDE, STITCH, AND TRIM.

TO FIT CROTCH TUCK NECK TO INSIDE, PIN CLOSED FROM FRONT TO BACK, STITCH, AND TRIM AWAY EXCESS.

REPEAT PINNING AND STITCHING PROCESS, THIS TIME FROM LEFT TO RIGHT.

IF UNDERWEAR BAGS, SEAM ACROSS ABDOMEN (OR BACKSIDE), STITCH, AND TRIM.

BOTTOM

CUT EQUAL LENGTHS FROM SLEEVES OF THIRD SWEATER AND SEW TO CUFFS OF EXISTING LEGS.

FOR *LONGER* LONG JOHNS

CUT MIDRIFF OFF OF THIRD SWEATER AND STITCH TO WAISTBAND OF UNDERWEAR TOP.

A BABY CARRIER FROM OLD BLUE JEANS

By the time an infant becomes an active, roly-poly dynamo with a few months of age to its credit, most parents are wishing for a practical way to tote the little one around with them and to gently restrain the small adventurer at the same time. A stroller works well in the city, but it's more trouble than it's worth in woods and fields where buggy wheels just won't roll.

You can solve the child-carrying problem in a few hours' time and at no out-of-pocket cost by making a denim baby carrier. The pack is washable, easy to carry, and adjustable. If you sew, you can whip one up by hand or by machine. A machine-stitched verson will take less time and will have stronger seams.

GETTING THE BLUES: Begin the project by locat-

ing two pairs of adult-size jeans that have no worn spots on the backsides. With the rear pockets facing up on your work area (the floor will do), remove the backs of the pants from their fronts. Leave the thick side seams attached to the discarded fronts, and use only the seam-free backs for the project. (See Fig. 1 for detailed cutting instructions.)

Spread the two jean backs out flat and make a T-shaped cut up each crotch (again, as in Fig. 1). Note that the top of one T runs approximately through the center of the pockets, while the other lies only midway between the crotch and the bottom of the pockets.

Flip the denims pockets-down, and fold each of the

four legs in upon themselves to create four-inch-wide "legbelts" (see Fig. 2). If you spray-starch the legs and iron them flat, you'll find it easier to stitch the belts closed (see Fig. 3). Then, using Fig. 3 for reference, go on to double-stitch the two pieces together along the line above the pockets.

At this point you're ready to try the tot-toter on for size. Tie the shorter (bottom) pair of folded legs securely around your waist. Then, with the help of a friend, hold the baby so that the child's stomach is against your back and his or her feet are on either side of the sling seat. Bring the two remaining bands up over your shoulders. By holding these, you can safely support the baby while your friend marks the spot where the shoulder straps meet the seat sling when you and your child are both most comfortable. Once those points are determined, remove the baby and the pack, and sew the straps to the marked spots on the inside of the seat (as in Fig. 4).

Finish the job by folding and hemming the cut edges and snipping off any loose threads. You can take an optional extra step, and that would be to decorate the carrier with patches or embroidery to make it more attractive.

Babies seem to enjoy the closeness and security provided by the sling, and the price is certainly right. So what are you waiting for? Carve up those Calvins, vandalize your Vanderbilts, lacerate some Levis, or offer up your Oshkoshes—your youngster has places to go and people to see!

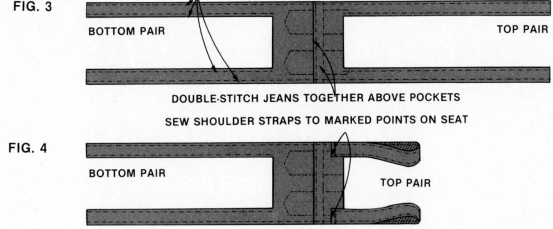

FIG. 1

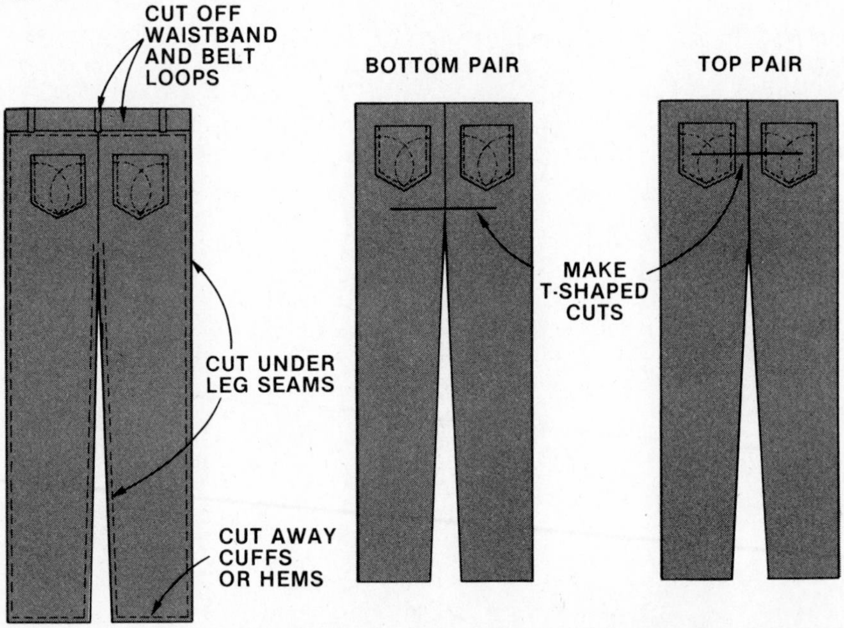

CUT OFF WAISTBAND AND BELT LOOPS

CUT UNDER LEG SEAMS

CUT AWAY CUFFS OR HEMS

BOTTOM PAIR

MAKE T-SHAPED CUTS

TOP PAIR

FIG. 2

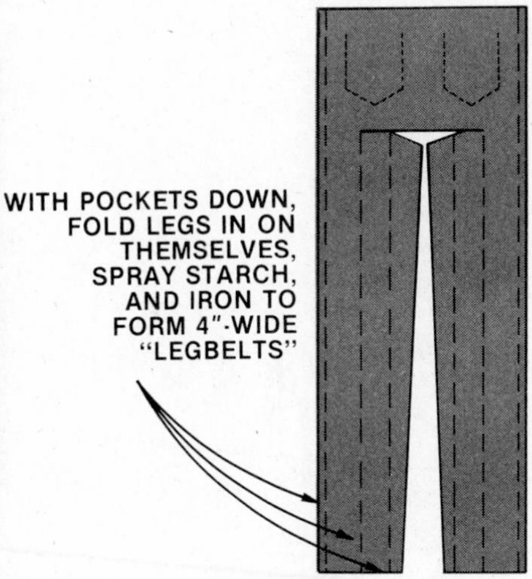

WITH POCKETS DOWN, FOLD LEGS IN ON THEMSELVES, SPRAY STARCH, AND IRON TO FORM 4"-WIDE "LEGBELTS"

STITCH ALONG LENGTH OF EACH FOLDED LEG

FIG. 3

BOTTOM PAIR

TOP PAIR

DOUBLE-STITCH JEANS TOGETHER ABOVE POCKETS

SEW SHOULDER STRAPS TO MARKED POINTS ON SEAT

FIG. 4

BOTTOM PAIR

TOP PAIR

USING REMNANTS TO SEW A SLEEPER

A young couple with a solar heat grabber and a wood-stove found that these alternative methods did a great job of heating their home during the day, but at night when the solar heater was off duty and the woodburner wasn't being stoked, the house could get a mite chilly. Sleeping comfortably during those hours was no problem for the adults, who could pile on more comforters, but their baby, Andy, always kicked off his blankets before morning. In order to keep him securely covered, his mother had to come up with an idea for supplementing the warmth provided by Andy's blanket-sleeper pajamas, which helped but weren't quite enough to keep out the cold night air. The baby now has his own personal sleeping bag made from an old quilt. This cover remains snugly on him with the aid of shoulder fasteners, yet it's roomy enough to accommodate the boy, his heavy-duty pj's, and his tattered "Blankey" (which warms his cheek, but mostly warms his heart).

Because Andy's sleeper sack worked very well and was so easy to make, his mother decided to share her pattern and instructions to help other folks' youngsters stay cozy during the long, cold winter. You'll need an old discarded quilt or heavy blanket and a cotton fabric scrap (measuring 16" X 22"), and you can expect to finish the project in about two hours.

Begin by cutting two rectangles (those used here were 23" X 40") from the old bedcover. (To determine the best size for the rectangles, measure the tot from shoulder to shoulder and from shoulder to toe, and then add another foot or so to each dimension to allow for "kick and grow" room.)

Next, pin the "front top" pattern to one end of a blanket rectangle, and attach the "back top" form (both of them will have to be redrawn to size, of course) to the other rectangle. Draw a line connecting the outer corners of each pattern to the corresponding bottom corners of the rectangles, and cut out the front and back of your sleeper-to-be.

Once that's done, use the lightweight cotton scraps (and the patterns shown) to make the facings. With the right sides of the material touching each other, sew the front and back facings together at the side seams, press open the seams, turn the long, unnotched edge under 1/4 inch, and stitch that edge down.

Again, with the right sides of the "blanket" pieces together, sew the sides and bottom of the bag. Press open the side seams . . . and then turn the sack right side out. Pin the facing onto the top of the sack (with the right sides of the fabric touching) and sew. Then trim the seam so that it measures 1/4 inch, and clip the curves. Now, turn the facing to the inside of the garment, press again, and tack it down at the side seams.

Finally, you'll want to attach fasteners at the shoulders. Heavy-duty snaps seem easier to handle, especially when putting the bag on a sleeping child, but buttons will work also.

With the sleep sack fitted over pajamas, a baby can slumber in snug comfort. And that means that parents sleep better and enjoy fuel savings, as well!

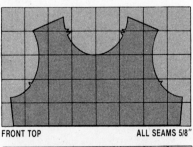

FRONT TOP   ALL SEAMS 5/8"

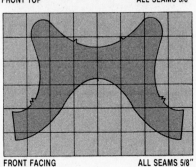

FRONT FACING   ALL SEAMS 5/8"

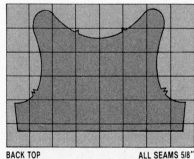

BACK TOP   ALL SEAMS 5/8"

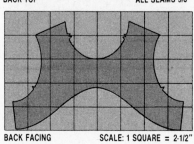

BACK FACING   SCALE: 1 SQUARE = 2-1/2"

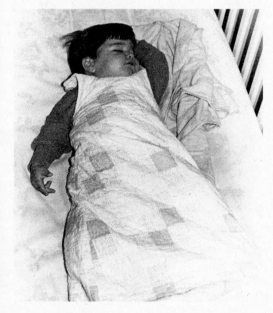

FASHION BABY FOOTWEAR FROM FABRIC

Like any other item of children's apparel, new shoes for Baby can put a crimp in your clothing budget. Such gear is quickly outgrown at the infant stage, and if the little one isn't walking yet, the child's footwear needn't be long-lasting or hard-soled. A sensible and satisfactory alternative to buying expensive leather or vinyl shoes for such a young child is to make fabric moccasins.

To fashion the footwear, you'll need a pencil and a large piece of paper, remnants of a sturdy material such as corduroy or denim (the amount will depend on the size of the child's foot), regular scissors or pinking shears (the latter will prevent fabric from fraying or will create a decorative edge on leather), straight pins, a needle for sewing heavy fabric (you can either stitch by hand or use a machine), thread, a hole-punching implement, and a pair of shoelaces.

First, place the baby's foot on the sheet of paper and trace its outline (make sure to allow for a little toe-wiggling and growing room) to make your pattern for the sole of the moccasin. Then draw the side-piece (as shown in the illustration), making certain that— when curved around one edge of the bottom piece—the upper extends from the middle of the sole's toe to the middle of its heel. This side section must also be high enough to provide for a fold-over cuff.

Now, pin the paper patterns for the sole and the upper to your material and cut, allowing an extra 1/8 inch for the seams as you snip around each piece. To make the second upper, turn over the pattern for the side section and pin it— wrong side up—to your material. Then follow the same cutting directions that you used for the other pieces. Depending upon the thickness of the fabric, you may want to double or triple the sole by sewing

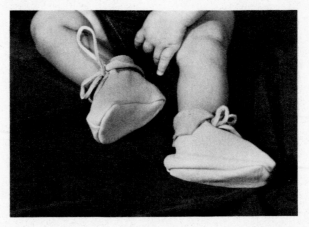

two or three bottoms together into one reinforced piece.

To prepare your pieces for sewing, pin each upper to the sole and pin together the front and back ends of the side sections. If you plan to use decorative stitching— which you'll want to be clearly visible—put wrong sides together. If you'd like to conceal the stitching, pin the right sides together, then when the sewing is completed, you can turn the shoes inside out. (In this case, you may want to cut a couple of foam rubber insoles to protect the baby's feet from the roughness of the inside seams.)

Begin your stitching with the front seam that joins the two uppers, and—as shown in the illustration—proceed from Point A at the toe to Point B, about five-eighths of the way up (you can adjust this distance if it's difficult to slip the shoe on and off the child's foot). Work from front to back, joining one upper at a time to the sole by stitching from A to C, up to (but not through) the 1/8-inch seam allowance where the side-pieces meet at the heel. Finish by sewing up the back seam from C to D. Check to be sure the sole is firmly attached to the uppers at the toe and heel; if not, catch-stitch these points by hand.

You're ready now to punch two holes in each side-piece (as indicated in the drawing) to accommodate a pair of shoelaces. You can either bind the holes with stitching or use an eyelet inserter to prevent fraying. Next, wrap each string around its moccasin along the cuff's fold line and thread it into the back hole and out of the front hole on each side. Turn down the top flaps to hold the ties firmly in place. These homemade shoes will stay securely on Baby's restless feet, warming and protecting them as well as any store-bought bootees could.

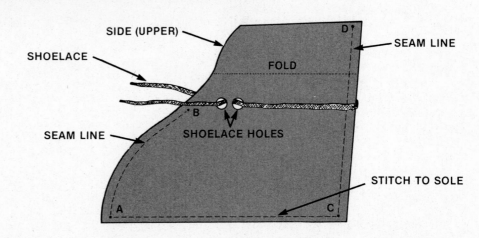

SIDE (UPPER)
SHOELACE
SEAM LINE
FOLD
D
SEAM LINE
B
SHOELACE HOLES
STITCH TO SOLE
A
C

BETTER USES FOR BATTERED FOOTWEAR

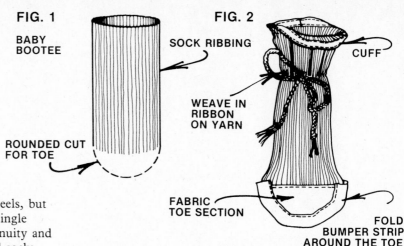

FIG. 1
BABY BOOTEE

SOCK RIBBING

FIG. 2
CUFF

WEAVE IN RIBBON ON YARN

ROUNDED CUT FOR TOE

FABRIC TOE SECTION

FOLD BUMPER STRIP AROUND THE TOE

Holes in socks seem to develop first in the heels, but that's no reason to pitch the pair or even the single stocking that wears out first. With a little ingenuity and a little cutting and sewing, worn or unmatched socks can be recycled into useful articles of clothing that make excellent small gifts or supplement a growing child's rapidly changing wardrobe.

Very little time and no complex skills are needed to recycle the castoff foot coverings. Here are a few ideas.

BOOTEE BASICS: To stitch up a pair of infant foot warmers, you'll need a pair of adult-sized crew socks, a scrap of material, and a bit of ribbon or yarn. Keeping in mind that you'll need to perform each step twice to make a pair of bootees, begin by cutting a sock just below the ribbed section and forming a curved toe as shown in Fig. 1.

Being certain to allow for some overlap when you measure it, cut a strip of fabric one-inch wide and long enough to form a border all around the top of the ribbing. Fold under the raw edges of material and stitch the strip to the inside of the sock, overlapping the fabric where its ends meet. The resulting band folds down to form a cuff as shown in Fig. 2.

With that done, trace the outline of the bootee's toe, add a seam allowance to this curve, and cut a half-circle of fabric to match. With the right side out, stitch this half-round (folding its raw edges under as you go) to the upper layer of sock material.

Cut another inch-wide strip of fabric long enough to encase the toe of the bootee, and secure it in place, being sure to stitch through all the thicknesses of the cloth and the sock. This piece forms a bumper at the tip of the shoe.

Finally, weave a length of ribbon or braided yarn through the ribbed portion of the sock to form a tie just above where the baby's ankle will be.

These bootees not only are warm, but they also have

the capability of growing with the child: As the toddler's foot gets larger, simply move the tie higher.

MITTENS IN MINUTES: If warm hands are what your youngsters are clamoring for, you can easily stitch up enough mittens so there'll always be a dry pair to replace those that soak through in the process of winning snowball fights and such. To tackle this project, you'll need one crew sock, preferably wool, for each mitten, some elastic thread, and if you'd like to embroider the hand wear, a few strands of colorful yarn.

Start by making a curved cut across the sock below the neck at a distance appropriate to the size of your child's hand. Be sure to save the excess material; you'll use some of it later on. Make a slit to accommodate the thumb, starting from the cut end of the sock as shown in Fig. 3.

Though decorations can be added after the hand warmers are finished, this is a good time to embroider

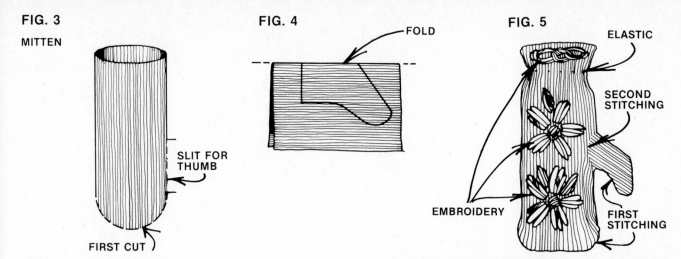

FIG. 3
MITTEN

SLIT FOR
THUMB

FIRST CUT

FIG. 4

FOLD

FIG. 5

ELASTIC

SECOND
STITCHING

EMBROIDERY

FIRST
STITCHING

designs on the main part of the mitten. Make sure that the thumb incision faces right on one mitten and left on the other. A simple, bright design adds an attractive, durable trim.

The next step is to fabricate the thumb. To do so, cut

STITCH A TURTLENECK SHIRT: To whip up a turtleneck shirt, you'll need a pair of crew socks, about half a yard or so of stretchy knit fabric, depending on the child's size, and a pattern. You can purchase the last item, but it's just as simple and far less expensive to trace your own from another shirt of the desired dimensions.

After transferring the pattern to the cloth, cut the knit material into four sections: the front, the back, and two arms. With that done, slice straight across each sock just below the ribbing. Measure three inches up the ribbed section and cut again. This will give you two three-inch-wide pieces to use as cuffs and two larger, top-of-the-sock sections for the collar. Cut the latter pieces so that each is in the form of a flat rectangle rather than a tube.

With the right side of the shirt front and the wrong side of the sock rectangle together, sew the ribbing to the neck of the shirt, stretching the sock material slightly as needed. Repeat the procedure using the other rectangle to form the shirt back, and overcast all the seams to prevent unraveling.

a hooklike section of the appropriate length and width from the leftover sock material as shown in Fig. 4. Then open the thumb up and pin its base to the top of the mitten slit, making certain that the right sides of the fabric are facing each other. Stitch these pieces together, overcast the seam edges to prevent the knitted material from unraveling, and turn the mitten wrong side out to complete the stitching and overcasting. Finally, while the mitten is still inside out, weave in a strip of elastic at the wrist (see Fig. 5) and tie its ends.

Repeat the whole process with the second sock, turn the mittens right side out, and find some cold hands to go inside them.

Next, with right sides facing, stitch the collar together at the side seams to form the actual turtleneck. Turn the garment wrong side out and sew up the shoulder seams (see Fig. 6).

If the shirt material has plenty of give, you can skip this paragraph and go on to the next step. However, if you've used a minimum-stretch fabric, you may want to add an opening at the back of the pullover that will make it easier for the child to put on and take off. To do this, slit the turtleneck down the back and cut a couple of inches on down into the shirt, as shown in Fig. 7. Then fold the right sides of each collar half together,

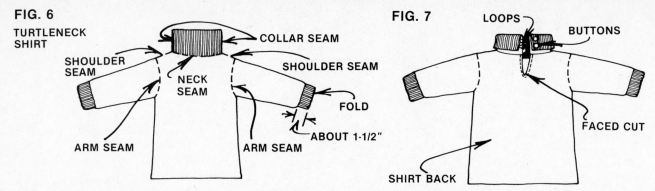

FIG. 6

TURTLENECK SHIRT

COLLAR SEAM

SHOULDER SEAM

SHOULDER SEAM

NECK SEAM

FOLD

ARM SEAM

ARM SEAM

ABOUT 1-1/2"

FIG. 7

LOOPS

BUTTONS

FACED CUT

SHIRT BACK

stitch the ragged edges shut, and turn the right sides out. Next, cut a bias strip of shirt fabric that's approximately one inch wide and four inches long. With the right sides together, stitch this scrap down one side of the cut and up the other. Turn the facing to the inside, tuck the raw edge under, and sew again. Finish this portion of the job by attaching loops and buttons to the collar opening.

Once the neck is completed, turn the garment inside out. With finished sides together, attach the arms to the shirt. Then stitch the side seams and the underarm junctions.

With that out of the way, go on to fold the three-inch sock sections reserved for the cuffs in half and attach them to the arms, making certain that the right sides of the fabric are together. Finally, machine-hem the shirt bottom and overcast any raw edges.

A HANDMADE HEAD-WARMER: Hats are a wintertime must for children, and it's always good to have a few extras on hand.

You'll need one pair of socks and some decorative yarn to make a child-sized stocking cap. Begin by cutting the socks off just below the ribs, as you did when making the turtleneck shirt. Then slit each tube open and sew the resulting rectangles right sides together around the three cut edges, leaving about an inch open at the bottom of the seam on each side. Overcast the seam, turn the cap right side out, flip the one-inch brim up, and hand-stitch its seams closed.

Gather the top of the hat in an X-pattern as shown in Fig. 8, and fasten a yarn pom-pom in place. Use a few

more scraps of yarn to make a pair of braided ties, and then set these fastenings aside for the moment.

Find the foot portions of the socks and cut a half-circle with its diameter on the fold in each one. These will serve as earflaps (see the photo), so adjust their size to the ears in question. Fold each flap with its right side in, put one of the braided ties between the halves so that just its tip protrudes at the centerpoint of the curve, and stitch around the semicircle, leaving a small opening at the end of the seam so that you can turn the earflap right side out. Attach the earmuff to the inside of the hat, just above the fold of the brim.

As a last step, embroider a design on the cap if you like, then tie it to your tot's chilly head.

SCRAP TOGETHER A SCARF: By now you've probably completed quite a collection of children's clothing, but you may be wondering what to do with the unused sock feet that are beginning to pile up. Well, ponder no longer. Simply sew the leftovers into a warm scarf.

To make a child-sized muffler, you'll need the arch sections from at least five pairs of socks. They don't need to match; in fact, a variety of colors makes the scarf more attractive.

Cut the heel and toe from each sock, leaving a tubular section. Turn one of these arch portions wrong side out and pull it over a right-side-out one (see Fig. 9). Sew one end closed, stitching through all thicknesses, overcast the seam, and turn the outer tube right side out again to form two joined scarf links. Repeat this process until all the pieces are attached.

If decoration is desired, you can embroider the end squares as shown in Fig. 9. Then fold the raw edges under, handstitch the end seams shut, and add fringe to complete the scarf.

DESIGN YOUR OWN: There are many other useful items for which old socks can be used: drawstring bags, new feet for old pajamas, cuffs for worn coats, a tube top for summer wear, a cold-weather face mask, pot holders, stuffed draft stoppers, an eyeglass case, a shoe polisher, and a washcloth (possibly filled with bits of soap). In fact, the demand for worn-out socks could become so great that you'll be tempted to give up darning for good.

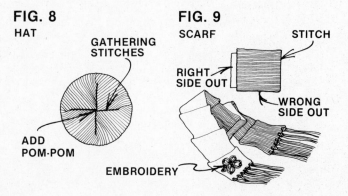

FIG. 8

HAT

GATHERING STITCHES

ADD POM-POM

FIG. 9

SCARF

STITCH

RIGHT SIDE OUT

WRONG SIDE OUT

EMBROIDERY

STITCH A MARVELOUS MONEYSAVING VEST

Avid craftspersons are always on the lookout for bargains. One such handicrafter spied an end-of-summer sale on sleeping-bag mill ends at a discount fabric outlet and immediately began musing about possible projects that would put the remnants to good use. She bought a ten-pound sack of quilted scraps for only a dollar, thinking that the polyester batting inside the nylon shells was worth far more than that and could be used as stuffing in her holiday craft items. Upon closer examination of her find, she discovered that many of the sections were quite large. She realized how wasteful it would be to tear the pieces of material apart and decided instead to make fiberfill vests from them for her husband and herself.

The resulting garments were attractive, ridiculously inexpensive, and warm. The batting serves as a thermal layer that conserves body heat yet adds no appreciable weight or restriction of movement. Stitching together a couple of these snug, lightweight sleeveless jackets could be a good way for you, too, to beat the high cost of ready-made outerwear and the low temperatures of winter. Here's how the creator of the vests shown here achieved her success.

After selecting an appealing pattern for her husband's vest, she chose the largest remnant for the back and used smaller pieces for the front of the waistcoat. (Each section of material was a different color, so she wisely selected hues that complemented each other.) To make the vest's lining, she pieced together nylon stripped from the polyester batting of scraps too small to use otherwise.

Once the fabric was spread out, the pattern pieces were pinned to it, with the quilted stitching that secures the nylon to the batting running horizontally in what would be the outer layer of the finished garment. She cut out the sections and followed the pattern's instructions for sewing the vest. Some heavy-duty fasteners finished the job. She was able to present her husband with a new downlike vest that cost less than $5.00 to make.

She assembled her own jerkin in the same manner, but the pattern for it was a bit simpler, as it had no collar, pockets, or snaps. Since she wanted a brightly colored lining in her vest, a scrap of red plaid flannel left over from an earlier sewing project was used. A few ties to close the front of the vest were fashioned from the same material. The vest cost less than 50¢ (for "her half" of the sleeping-bag mill ends), but even if she had bought the pattern and the flannel, the total cash outlay for her comfy creation would still have been well below the price that such quality garments sell for in sporting goods and department stores.

This seamstress and her husband were so pleased with their vests that she made others to give as gifts. In the quest for additional supplies, she learned that salvage clothing stores and thrift shops are worthwhile hunting grounds, and many large manufacturers of camping gear are glad to give mill-end scraps away! Just look in your phone directory's yellow pages under "Garment Mfg.," "Sleeping Bags—Whol. & Mfrs.," and "Sporting Goods—Whol. & Mfrs." to locate potential sources.

As you become more proficient in the creation of such vests, you would do well to consider fashioning extra thermal wear to sell. Vests aren't the only salable items to be made from sleeping bag scraps; quilts and bootees are profitable possibilities, too.

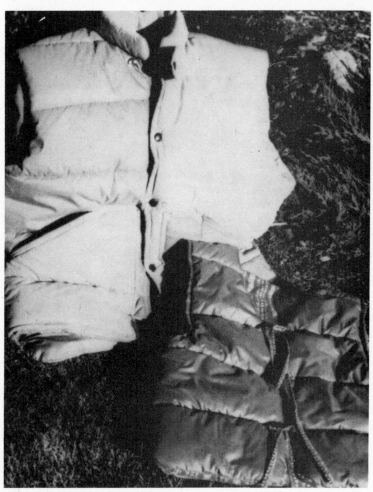

DESIGN HOMESEWN QUIET BOOKS

When Peggy's son, Keith, was one year old, he was the joy of his mother's life, except on those occasions when she had to take him with her to meetings. Alert, active, and noisy, he exhausted (and embarrassed) her until she was ready to fully endorse the old saying that the only quiet youngster is one who's sound asleep!

Fortunately, however, a seamstress friend helped solve her problem by sending Keith a wonderful, homemade birthday present: a charming, ten-page booklet that's chock-full of colorful things to button, zip, tie, stick on, and otherwise play with—quietly. These entertaining quiet books cost only pennies to make, and the idea's merit has been proven by generations of children who have been entertained by such homemade books. After carefully studying her son's book, Peggy tried her hand at making some similar booklets for other children, and although she's not a seamstress, she managed to fashion some very nice ones with little trouble. Here's the format that she used.

GATHER THE BASICS, CUT, AND FOLD: A quiet book consists of ten pages (ten double layers of cloth), each of which is decorated on both sides. The "artwork" is either embroidered or appliquéd on plain fabric, and each page contains at least one activity (tak-ing pieces off or putting them on, lifting flaps, opening and shutting parts of a design, for example). Finally, some kind of closure, such as tie strings, is usually provided to hold the booklet shut when it's not in use.

To make one of these books, you'll need about 1-1/2 yards of 45-inch sturdy fabric—such as denim, duck, or light canvas—with a basic background. You'll also need embroidery thread and needles, some bits and pieces of colorful cloth, scissors, regular needles and thread (your project will be even easier and more durable if you use a sewing machine), a fabric-marking pencil, pins, a little bit of stuffing, some Velcro-brand fastening tape, and lots of notions, including snaps, buckles, buttons, a zipper or two, and perhaps some eyelets and shoelaces. It's a good idea to make a paper facsimile of your booklet before cutting or stitching the fabric, so you'll also need a pad of paper and a pencil.

To prepare the pages, cut ten 10″ X 20″ rectangles from the sturdy cloth, making sure to keep the pieces of uniform size. Fold five of these in half (to 10″ X 10″), each with its right sides together, and iron them to sharpen the creases. Then go on to fold the remaining five pieces in half, each with its wrong sides together, and iron them, as well. Now, match the rectangles as shown in Fig. 1, arranging them into five pairs, right sides exposed. While you have the iron hot, turn under a 1/4-inch hem on all four sides of each rectangle and press it flat, mitering the corners (see Fig. 2).

The center folds will become the spine of the booklet. Each pair of rectangles will be decorated on the right sides of the fabric and then stitched together around the edges, producing a total of four pages, front and back. Finally, all five double-layered rectangles will be sewn together on the center crease to make the finished book-

FIG. 1 MATCHING THE PAGES

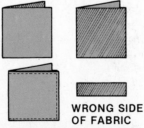

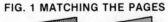

WRONG SIDE OF FABRIC

FIG. 2 MITERING THE CORNERS

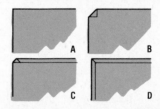

FIG. 3 POSSIBLE DESIGNS FOR YOUR HOMEMADE QUIET BOOK

let of ten leaves for a total of twenty decorated pages. (You can see why a preliminary mock-up would be helpful.)

DESIGN TO PLAY WITH: The first and best sources for quiet book designs are probably your own observations and imagination. For instance, many children have a special interest in a particular subject such as firefighting, boats, animals, or cars. Fascinating "scenes" or figures can be developed using any or all of these favorite themes (see Fig. 3 for some possibililities). Whatever the designs you choose, however, each should involve at least one activity: zipping open an appliquéd suitcase that contains some Velcro-backed stick-on toys, perhaps . . . snapping wheels on and off a truck . . . removing and replacing Velcro-fastened sails on a fleet of boats . . . tying shoelaces in real eyelets on a lightly stuffed, fabric-scrap shoe . . . rearranging stick-on animals in a jungle scene . . . and so on. (A popular page in Keith's book features an apple tree outlined with embroidery thread—green for the leaves and brown for the trunk. Apples made from red knit scraps with Velcro backings are stuck to matching Velcro patches on the tree, and the words "Pick the Apples!" are embroidered directly underneath the tree.)

Once you've chosen your designs, sketch them lightly on the background fabric with a marking pencil if you're going to embroider them, or make paper patterns from which to work if you plan to use appliquéd designs. Be sure to position the artwork-to-be on the right side of the background fabric, then stitch it in place. The pictures can be embroidered or appliquéd, or both. Just keep in mind that the booklet and its parts will receive a lot of handling, so all of the components must be assembled securely. (A sewing machine—especially one that makes zigzag stitches—does a good job with appliqué, and may be suitable for freearm machine embroidery, as well.)

When you've covered each half of each of the 10″ X 20″ rectangles, including those of the front and back covers, you're ready to put the booklet together.

PIN, STITCH, AND GO: The first assembly task will be to make a set of ties (or some other type of closure), perhaps from leftover scraps of fabric. Insert the ends of the ties between the cover rectangle and its matching inside piece (see Fig. 1) and pin them in place. Now pin the two rectangles together and stitch them all the way around, 1/8 inch from the outside edge, catching the tie ends as you do so. For added strength, go over those joinings twice with the machine. Match and stitch the other rectangles in the same way, making sure that all the designs are right side up before you sew.

When you're done, lay the resulting five double-sided rectangles one on top of the other, lining up the center creases. Check to be sure the front and back covers are on the outside where they belong, and sew all five pieces together with a seam down the center crease. (Again, go over this seam two or three times for extra strength.) Finally, check to see that all the removable parts of each design are in place, close the booklet, and tie it up.

Keith's booklet stays safely tucked away until the time rolls around for a meeting, a conference, or a church service. Because the toy is reserved for special occasions, Keith is always fascinated when he gets to play with it. Furthermore, the little quiet book improves his ability to manipulate zippers, shoelaces, buckles, and buttons while encouraging creative silence at appropriate times!

PICK THE APPLES!

PADDED APPLIQUÉ WALL HANGINGS

Maybe you'd like to make good use of those long winter nights that you're now spending curled up by the fire. And maybe you'd also like to recycle some of the attractive scraps of material you've saved over the years. But—and here's the worst "maybe" of all—maybe the sheer logistics of making a quilt have intimidated you enough to keep you from trying it. Well, if that's your situation, perhaps you should try your hand at a padded appliqué wall hanging.

The machine-appliquéd "woodstove" wall hanging shown in the accompanying photos is an original design by Paula Newcomer. Working nights only, she completed the hanging in less than a week, and the total cost for the project was only a few dollars.

DESIGN: The great thing about appliqué is that you don't have to be a Picasso to create stunningly beautiful designs. If there's a particular part of your homestead that you find especially attractive, you can make a simple sketch of it and translate some of that beauty into a highly original piece of folk art. You might want to capture some trees against a sunset, or a portion of the barn and field with a farming implement or two thrown in. Indoor objects such as an old-timey bathtub can be fun to portray, too.

Then again, you don't have to copy real-life objects. You can create your own thematic designs. Bold, simple shapes are the most effective. Highly textured material and the use of underlying padding will eliminate the need for a great amount of detail. If you choose to get fancier, you can add some interesting touches with bits of embroidery here and there.

THE "ROUNDED" LOOK: The most appealing wall hangings have a three-dimensional quality with a depth and richness that ordinary flat appliqué can't match. The secret? Pad each element of the picture as it is applied to the cotton fabric "front" and then pad the entire piece again when you put the backing on. This way, it's possible to get a "rounded" look without having to stitch through five or six layers of batting all at one time.

CRAFT NEEDS: If you do any sewing at all, odds are you already have most of the materials for making padded wall hangings. By dipping into the scrap bag, it's easy to keep costs to a minimum.

Here's a complete list of the tools and materials for making a 31″ X 31″ wall hanging:

TOOLS
[1] A zigzag-type sewing machine
[2] Scissors
[3] Straight pins
[4] Embroidery needles and hoop
[5] A yardstick or ruler
[6] Chalk and/or a pencil and pen

MATERIALS
[1] One 32″ X 32″ sheet of heavy drawing paper (or several smaller sheets taped together)
[2] Two 36″ X 36″ pieces of heavy cotton fabric
[3] Scraps of material
[4] Regular sewing thread
[5] Embroidery floss in a variety of colors
[6] One package of 100% polyester fiber (layer-built batting)
[7] Seam tape (optional)
[8] A 32-inch-long wooden dowel (optional)

HOW TO SELECT FABRICS FOR MACHINE APPLIQUÉ: Appliqué, which began as a way to patch

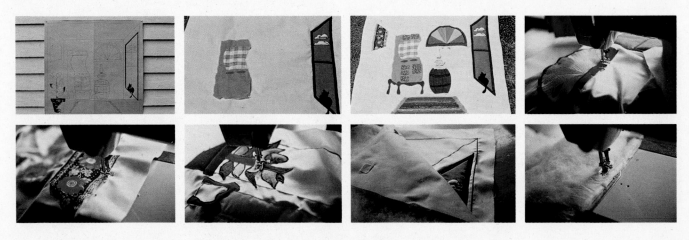

worn clothes, is simply a technique for applying one fabric to another. There are various ways to do this, but the machine-appliqué method is the quickest and easiest.

In machine appliqué, small pieces of material are cut to shape, then zigzag-stitched along their rough edges to a larger piece of cloth. It's essential to use heavy cotton or firm, non-fraying fabrics for this method. By choosing firm fabrics from your scrap bag, you can avoid the laborious finishing and handstitching operations that usually accompany appliqué. If you enjoy handwork, save your talent and efforts for decorative embroidery stitches, where you can get as elaborate as you like.

MACHINE ADJUSTMENTS: Use a fairly wide zigzag stitch (usually four or five on the dial), and place the dial on "satin stitch," which is close to zero on most machines. Be sure to use a medium to heavy machine needle (size 14 to 16) for this kind of multiple-fabric stitching.

THE PATTERN: First make a small sketch of your design, keeping the figures simple. When you've got something you like, redraw the scene on a 32″ X 32″ sheet of paper in actual size, leaving a two-inch border around the artwork. This gives you room for a one-inch

HOW TO MAKE LOOPS ON THE BACK OF YOUR WALL HANGING

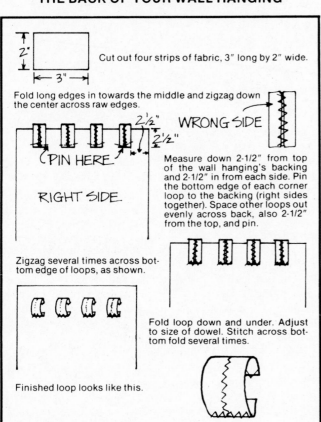

Cut out four strips of fabric, 3″ long by 2″ wide.

Fold long edges in towards the middle and zigzag down the center across raw edges.

Measure down 2-1/2″ from top of the wall hanging's backing and 2-1/2″ in from each side. Pin the bottom edge of each corner loop to the backing (right sides together). Space other loops out evenly across back, also 2-1/2″ from the top, and pin.

Zigzag several times across bottom edge of loops, as shown.

Fold loop down and under. Adjust to size of dowel. Stitch across bottom fold several times.

Finished loop looks like this.

SOME SIMPLE EMBROIDERY STITCHES

BACKSTITCH: This—one of the easiest and most useful of embroidery stitches—can be used to outline shapes and embroider curved lines. It is worked from right to left, as follows: Bring the needle through to the front side of the cloth and make a small stitch backward (i.e., to the right) . . . then bring the needle through again to the left of the first stitch and make *another* backstitch to the start of the first stitch, and so on.

CHAIN STITCH: The chain stitch can help you cover a lot of space quickly . . . and attractively. Just *how* quickly depends on how big you make the "loops". First bring the needle through to the fabric's front side. Next, hold the thread down with your left hand and insert the needle back through the cloth very close to where it first emerged. Then bring the point of the needle up through the cloth a second time in front of your first entry point. Pull the needle through, while you keep the thread under its point so that the next stitch holds it down against the face of the fabric in a loop.

FRENCH KNOTS: Here, each "stitch" resembles a dot or bead. First pull your needle through from the back to your cloth's front side. Next take the working thread in your left hand and wind it two or three times around the needle, close to its point. Then—while you hold the thread taut in the left hand—insert the needle close to where it first emerged. Now either pull the needle through to the back of the cloth and tie off the stitch, or—if you intend to make a series of French knots—bring the needle through to the front of the fabric again in position for the next stitch.

seam allowance and lets you top-stitch one inch in from the outer edge. This sheet is your paper pattern.

The first thing you should do with the pattern is lay it down on your "background" fabric and cut around the pattern to make a 32" X 32" square of material. Do this with both of the 36" X 36" pieces of heavy cotton fabric. These squares will form the front and back of your finished wall hanging.

Next, cut the individual design shapes from your pattern and trace their outlines onto the scraps of fabric that will be used in your finished wall hanging. Use pencil if the fabric is light-colored and chalk when the material is dark. Also, trace the outline of each design element onto the background fabric, again using pencil or chalk as appropriate.

Keep in mind that you'll achieve the best results with bold textures and color combinations.

EMBROIDERY: If you plan to embroider details onto any of the components, leave plenty of room around the edges of each piece as you trace the design onto the fabric so you'll be able to get your embroidery hoop around the work. After you've finished stitching in your decorations, you can cut away the excess material.

Very simple stitches are used on the individual design elements of the "woodstove" wall hanging shown in the accompanying photographs. Chain stitches, for instance, run in alternating colors across the rug, chain stitching makes up the stove's "burners," chain stitching and backstitching are used on the barrel motif, and backstitching and French knots grace the kerosene lamp. (See the accompanying diagrams for information on how to do this embroidery.)

LAYOUT: Spread out one of your 32-inch squares of material, and lay the pieces of your design out on the fabric. If you'll place a 32" X 32" or larger piece of plywood or cardboard beneath the square of cloth, your work will be easily portable for cleanup, and the back of the fabric will stay clean. By all means, experiment with different juxtapositions of design elements and with different types of material; you may discover some particularly striking combinations.

ASSEMBLY: When the layout is satisfactory, you're ready to move to the sewing machine. It's usually easier to apply the larger pieces first, and here's how to prepare the "stuffing" for one of these.

First trace the original paper pattern onto the layered batting. Use a triple thickness of batting for most large pieces, and more for those items that you really want to stand out. You can work with a pen or felt-tip marker here, since you'll want to cut inside the lines and make the batting a fraction of an inch smaller all the way around than the piece of fabric that it will be installed under.

Next, place the batting underneath the corresponding piece of appliqué and hand-baste (close to the edge) through both onto the 32" X 32" fabric front. After you've done several pieces, you'll probably be adept enough to forgo the basting process and to pin the pieces directly onto the square of cloth.

Now you're ready to machine stitch. (If you've never tried this before, it wouldn't be a bad idea to practice on some scraps first before you attempt the real thing.) One advantage of machine appliqué is that you can use contrasting thread around the edges of each piece of fabric, which really helps to define the design. As you zigzag over the raw edge, try to keep the machine moving but don't force the fabric. What you're aiming for is a smooth, even satin stitch. Finish each appliqué by backstitching and clipping the loose ends of the threads.

On smaller pieces such as plant leaves, stitch nearly all the way around the piece, stuff tufts of batting into the leaf to plump it up, and then close up the edge.

FINISHING TOUCHES: After all the design pieces have been appliquéd to the front large square of cloth, it's a good idea to iron your future wall hanging. Press around the edges of the zigzag stitching (on the wrong side only) but never directly on the padded areas.

It's time to put the backing on. Hidden loops through which a dowel may be inserted for hanging the finished piece can be added by sewing them on the backing. First, cut out a 32-inch square of polyester batting. (Some crafters prefer to use three or four layers.) Next, place the front and back pieces of the 32-inch-square fabric together (right side to right side), lay the square of batting on top of the back panel, and pin all three pieces together.

Sew one inch in from the edge and all the way around the square except for a six-inch-long area left open at the center of the bottom edge. If you'll use thin tracing paper or seam tape—or the paper, cut into strips, that comes between the folds of batting—along the seam line between the sewing machine needle and the batting, you won't have problems with the machine's pressure foot catching or tearing the stuffing.

Trim the bottom seam to 1/2 inch and all other seams to 1/4 inch and clip the corners. Then carefully turn the hanging right side out through the six-inch opening and push out the corners. Turn under the six-inch-long open area at the bottom and close it by hand with a simple slip stitch.

Finally, using the satin stitch setting on your machine, topstitch through all thicknesses of the wall covering an inch in from the piece's outer edges. This helps hold the batting tightly in place when the piece is hanging. For the "woodstove" design shown here, the designer topstitched through all thicknesses along the lines that define the "padded room."

There you have it: your own colorful, three-dimensional appliqué wall hanging to brighten up your living space. Who knows, if you really enjoy this craft, you might enjoy making several wall coverings in the same theme and sewing them together to create one smashingly beautiful quilt. And you thought you didn't have time to make quilts!

RECYCLED CLOTHES FOR YOUR CHILDREN

Anyone who has shopped recently for children's clothing knows how dismayingly expensive such apparel has become. Price a five-year-old's outfit: Jeans are about $9.00, shirts are at least $5.00, and socks, shoes, and underwear now sell for as much as comparable adult wear. One change of clothes for a small child can easily cost $25.00. Sewing the clothing yourself would cut that cost, but patterns, fabric, fasteners, thread, and needles are expensive, too. There is a still better way to keep your little ones attractively and economically attired, and that is by turning unwearable adult garments into winsome children's outfits.

WHERE TO GET THE RAW MATERIALS: The neighborhood grapevine is usually effective for letting those in the immediate community know that you would welcome hand-me-downs for recycling. Friends and acquaintances will probably be delighted to accommodate you. If free garments aren't forthcoming from these sources, put an ad in the local shoppers' news. Many people are happy to give away worn-out apparel to anyone who will come by and get it. In all likelihood, you'll be able to accumulate more free clothing than you'll have time to transform.

TWO THINGS TO REMEMBER: You'll get more out of your recycling efforts if you'll [1] think of discarded garments not as wearing apparel but as fabrics and [2] remember that the fabric from several different worn-out items can often be pieced together to produce a finished children's outfit that looks prettier than any of the original garments.

Directions are included here for making tops and pants. Bear in mind, however, that you're by no means limited to just these two kinds of clothes. Once you've learned how to sew a top, for instance, it's no trick to create a dress by lengthening the top, a vest by omitting the sleeves, or a coat by using heavy material for the top and adding buttons. Any number of variations are possible. How diversely you modify or embellish any basic pattern is a matter of using your imagination.

THE BASIC TOP: For this, you'll need [1] an old shirt to use as a pattern, [2] a piece of material at least six inches wider than the "pattern" and at least twice as long (or twice the length you want the top to be plus four inches), and [3] a piece of matching or harmonizing fabric—approximately 15 inches square—to use as facing material. (Your "pattern" must, of course, fit the intended wearer. Don't use a stretchy pullover-type top as a guide, or your finished garment may turn out too small.)

Begin by folding the shirt you intend to use as a pattern in half, sleeve to sleeve. Fold your material in half lengthwise (right side in), then widthwise, as shown in Fig. 1. Lay the pattern on it.

Next, trace around the pattern with chalk, leaving a 3/4-inch seam allowance. For straight sleeves, draw a sleeve line that's parallel to the top of the material (Fig. 1-A), and for flowing or puffed sleeves, draw a diagonal line to the armpit (Fig. 1-B). If the top is for a boy, draw straight sides; otherwise, make the sides flare diagonally outward (Fig. 1).

Cut the shirt material out along the chalk lines. Then using the shirt/pattern as a guide, cut a curve for the neck as shown in Fig. 1. (Assume that the pattern shirt in this illustration has a scoop neck.) Remember that you can always cut more fabric later, but if you cut the neck opening too big, you can't "uncut" it. When you're done, open the material up and have the child try it on to check the size of the neck hole.

Now fold the shirt in half, sleeve to sleeve, right side in (Fig. 2). Cut a rectangular piece of fabric the width of the neck opening plus four inches all the way around. This is your facing: When sewn to the neck, turned under, and pressed, it will give the neck opening

FIG. 1

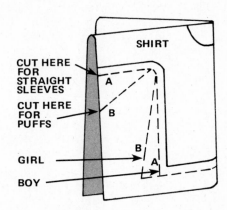

SHIRT

CUT HERE FOR STRAIGHT SLEEVES

CUT HERE FOR PUFFS

A

B

B

A

GIRL

BOY

FIG. 2

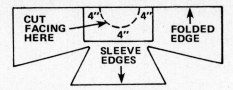

a smooth, finished edge.

Next, fold the facing lengthwise and pin it to the garment (Fig. 2). Trace the neck outline onto the facing and cut it to match the shirt's neck opening. Then remove the pins, open up the garment and facing, and round off the facing's edges with a pair of shears.

At this point, lay the shirt out flat and pin the facing to the top—right side to right side—making sure the neck openings line up. (See Fig. 3.) Sew over the pins

FIG. 3

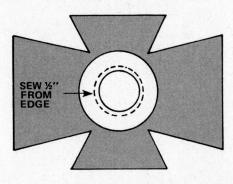

1/2 inch from the edge of the neck opening. (This is the only 1/2-inch seam in the garment. All the others are 3/4-inch seams.) For a stronger seam, double-stitch it.

Finally, remove the pins and clip the curved neck seam almost to the stitching, as shown in Fig. 4. (A curved seam naturally tends to bunch and pucker. Clipping prevents this.)

FIG. 4

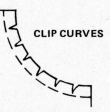

CLIP CURVES

Note: In all drawings in this article, the "right" side of fabric is shaded . . . the "wrong" side, unshaded.

You're ready now to sew the top's sides. Fold the shirt in half at the shoulders, right sides in, and then pin the edges together as shown in Fig. 5 and sew a 3/4-inch seam along the garment's sides. (Sew these seams twice if you want a finished article of clothing that will stand up to hard use.) Clip the underarm seams as you did the neck seam.

To finish the top, you need to [1] hem the sleeves and the bottom of the shirt, [2] turn the entire top right side out, and [3] turn the facing under, press, and hem the facing's ragged edge and/or tack it to the underside of the shirt.

Congratulate yourself: You've just created a "brand-new" child's top for free.

FIG. 5

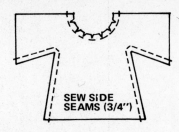

SEW SIDE SEAMS (3/4")

THE SLASH NECK: Rather than sew a scoop neck as previously described, you may prefer to make a neck with a slit opening at the front or back (that is, a slash neck). To do this, proceed according to the directions already given until you're ready to cut the garment's neck opening. Then—with the shirt folded—make a four- to six-inch cut (depending on your child's size) in the material as shown in Fig. 6.

FIG. 6

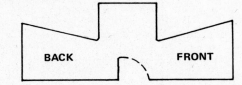

CUT ON TOP FOLD

3" SLIT
2" SLIT

Next, open the garment up and fold it sleeve to sleeve as depicted in Fig. 2. Mark a neck curve in chalk (on the wrong side of the shirt only) to match the neck curve of the shirt you're using as a pattern. Cut a semicircular neck opening in the fabric as shown in Fig. 7. (The curved part of the semicircle faces forward, and the flat part faces the back of the shirt.) On the "wrong" side of the material, mark an F for "front" and a B for "back" in chalk.

FIG. 7

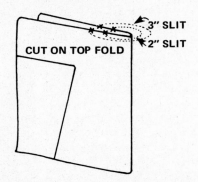

BACK   FRONT

Use a 10" X 16" (for a small child) or 12" X 18" (for an older one) piece of matching or contrasting fabric as facing material and fold it in half lengthwise. For the sake of illustration, assume that you want a back opening (a front opening can be made just as easily). Place the facing material on the folded garment as shown in Fig. 8 and [1] pin the facing to the shirt, [2] cut the neck opening in the facing, using the shirt as a guide, [3] remove the pins, and [4] trim the facing's edges as indicated by the dotted lines in Fig. 8.

Open the facing, lay it wrong side up on a flat sur-

FIG. 8

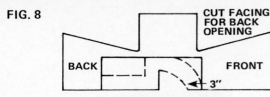

CUT FACING FOR BACK OPENING

BACK   FRONT

3"

FIG. 9

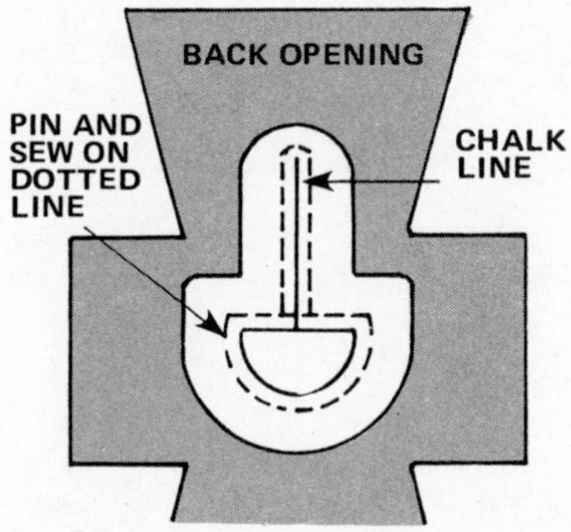

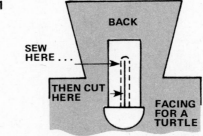

BACK OPENING

PIN AND SEW ON DOTTED LINE

CHALK LINE

face, and draw a chalk line down its center, beginning at, and perpendicular to, the "flat" part of the semicircular neck opening. (See Fig. 9.) Open the garment and lay it out; then spread the facing on the shirt, right side to right side. Pin the two together as shown in Fig. 9, sew over the pins, and then remove the fasteners.

Along the chalk line, make a cut through both garment and facing to within 3/8 inch of the seam. This slit is the shirt's "slash" or opening. All that remains is to clip the seam where the neck opening curves in front, fold the facing to the inside of the shirt, and press. If you wish, you may also sew on buttons, snaps, or hooks and eyes.

To make a front (rather than a back) opening, turn your facing so that most of it goes below the neck curve (as illustrated in Fig. 10) and proceed as previously instructed.

FIG. 10

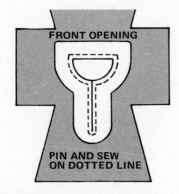

FRONT OPENING

PIN AND SEW ON DOTTED LINE

TRY A TURTLENECK: If you really want to get fancy, you can make a turtleneck for your basic top. Here's how it's done:

First, cut a semicircular neck opening in your garment as shown in Fig. 7. (Remember, the curved part always goes in front.) From scraps, cut a 3" X 8" rectangle of

material to use as the facing. Spread the shirt out flat and lay the facing on it, right side to right side, as illustrated in Fig. 11.

Next, draw a chalk line down the middle of the facing and then [1] pin it down as shown in Fig. 11, [2] sew over the pins, [3] take the fasteners out, and [4] cut along the chalk line to within 3/8 inch of the turn in the seam. Turn the facing to the inside of the garment and press.

FIG. 11

BACK

SEW HERE . . .

THEN CUT HERE

FACING FOR A TURTLE

Now measure the distance around the neck opening. From matching or contrasting scraps of material, cut a strip to this length plus three inches. This will be the turtleneck itself. Make the piece twice the width, plus one inch, that you want the finished neck to be.

Pin the neck strip to the shirt's neck opening—right side to right side, with the shirt right side out, leaving 1-1/2 inches of the turtleneck material extending beyond each edge of the back slit. Sew over the pins and remove them. Then turn the lip of the turtleneck under 1/2 inch, fold the turtleneck itself under, and pin the 1/2-inch fold to the neck seam on the inside of the shirt (Fig. 12). Hem the turtleneck's edge on the seam and remove the pins.

Finally, turn in the 1-1/2-inch turtleneck extensions and hem them in place. Finish off the neck with hooks and eyes, buttons and loops, or snaps. (See Fig. 13.)

FIG. 12

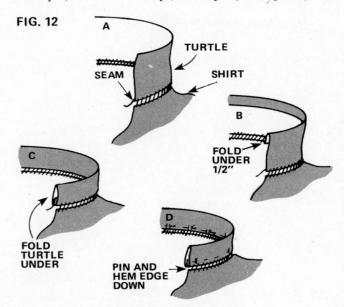

A

TURTLE

SEAM

SHIRT

B

FOLD UNDER 1/2"

C

FOLD TURTLE UNDER

D

PIN AND HEM EDGE DOWN

FIG. 13

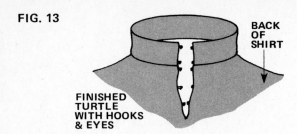

FINISHED
TURTLE
WITH HOOKS
& EYES

BACK
OF
SHIRT

HOW ABOUT SOME PANTS? It's easy to make elastic-waist pants for children of either sex. Adults' outdated slacks can be made into serviceable and stylish pants for youngsters.

First of all, round up a good, roomy pair of children's pants that you can use to make a permanent fabric pattern (so that you won't have to use real pants as a guide every time). For the pattern itself, find some awful material that you can't use for anything else. Fold the pants as shown in Fig. 14, lay them on this fabric, and trace around the pants with chalk, leaving a 3/4-inch seam allowance around the crotch and legs plus four

FIG. 14

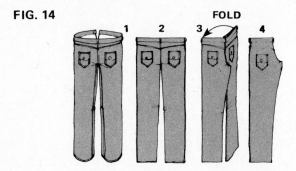

FOLD

1   2   3   4

inches (or more, depending on how fast your child grows) at the bottom of the leg, and four inches above the waist. (See Fig. 15.) Cut along the chalk line, and you've got your pattern.

FIG. 15

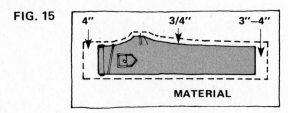

4″   3/4″   3″—4″

MATERIAL

Now obtain a pair of discarded slacks to use as material. (You'll find that one pair of adult pants makes one pair of children's trousers, with some nice scraps left over.) Rip open all the pants' seams and lay the material right side to right side. Place your leg pattern over one double thickness of material, trace around it with chalk, and cut on the chalk line. (Remember: You've already included seam and hem allowances in your pattern, so there's no need to allow for seams again.) Do the same for the other double thickness of material. You should now have four leg-shaped pieces of fabric.

Next, match two of the pieces you've just cut right side to right side. Pin the leg halves together in the manner indicated by the dotted lines in Fig. 16 and sew over the pins. Remove the pins and repeat the procedure with the other two pieces of material.

FIG. 16

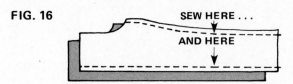

SEW HERE ...

AND HERE

With that done, turn one of the two "leg tubes" right side out and place that tube inside the other tube so that [1] the crotch edges match up and [2] the right side of the inner tube faces the right side of the outer tube. (It's a good idea at this point to study the construction of an existing pair of pants.) Pin the crotch together from the front of the waist to the back.

Before going any further, turn the pants right side out and have your youngster try them on for size. (Be careful, though, unless you've used safety pins to hold the pants together!)

After the pants have been tried on for size (and—if need be—adjusted for a better fit), turn one leg tube into the other as before (right side to right side) and sew over the pins in the crotch area. This is one seam that must be sewn twice or even three times (or reinforced with a strip of fabric), so take your time and do a good job. (Your children are like everyone else's if their pants always rip at the crotch.)

Next, turn both pant legs wrong side out and fold the top edge of the trousers down 1/2 inch. Fold the edge down again—about 1-1/2 inches this time—and pin the first fold to the pants. Hem all but two inches of this edge in place. This creates the casing through which you'll push the elastic waistband.

For the waistband itself, you'll need a piece of elastic that's at least 3/4 inch wide and equal in length to your child's waist measurement plus at least one inch. If you're in the mood to be superthrifty you can recycle the waistband from an old pair of pants instead of buying elastic. If you're using a drawstring instead of elastic, cut the string 18 inches longer than the waist measurement.

Attach a safety pin to one end of the elastic or drawstring and snake it through the casing. When it's halfway around, pin the dangling end of the elastic to the pants near the starting point so you won't lose it later. Continue to work the elastic all the way around and through the opening at the other end of the casing. Overlap the elastic's ends one inch inside the casing and pin it in place.

Once again, have your youngster try the pants on. Adjust the elastic to fit snugly but not tightly. After your young model sheds the pants, tack the casing to the elastic (be sure to penetrate all layers of material), remove the pins, and sew up the two-inch opening in the casing. Now hem the legs to the proper length, and your child's homemade trousers are ready to be playground tested.

TRY MAKING HARLEQUINS: One delightful way to recycle several pairs of slacks at once is to use them to make harlequin pants for your boy or girl. Use blue fabric for the left front and right rear leg pieces, and red material for the right front and left rear pieces. Or make the top half of each leg green and the bottom half brown. The possibilities are many.

OTHER VARIATIONS: As mentioned earlier, it's easy to make a top into a dress: Simply sew additional strips of cloth to the bottom of the garment (Fig. 17). If you cut these strips longer than necessary and then gather them, you can create a pretty ruffle, too.

FIG. 17

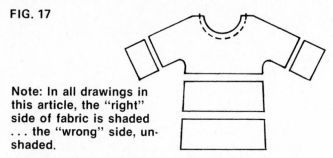

Note: In all drawings in this article, the "right" side of fabric is shaded ... the "wrong" side, unshaded.

By the same token, when your children's legs grow longer than their britches, you can sew strips of fabric to the bottom of each pant leg. (You can lengthen your daughter's pants with add-on ruffles.)

Sleeves can also be made longer. For straight sleeves, simply cut strips of material wide enough to go around the wearer's arm (plus 3-1/2 inches for seams and added comfort) and sew the pieces to the shirt's arms. For puffed sleeves, cut longer strips of fabric and gather them as you pin them to the arms. With a little imagination, you should be able to create dozens of beautiful shoulder, elbow, and/or wrist puff combinations using matching and contrasting materials.

CLOTHES FOR THE TINIEST PEOPLE: Baby clothes are easy to make, too. Try this: Using a one-year size shirt as a pattern, cut a top that's 12 inches longer than the baby. (Recycled blankets make especially cozy tops for wintertime. In spring or summer, use old towels for a durable, washable garment.) Make a facing for the neck opening and sew the side seams as you did for a child's basic top. Then sew a casing at the bottom of the shirt, snake a drawstring through the casing, hem the sleeves, and you have a "sleeping bag" top. Decorate the bag with embroidery, appliqué, and love.

PARTIAL RELIEF FOR SHOPPERS' SHOCK: Recycled clothing won't completely eliminate the high-price woes of shopping for children; unless you are a jack-of-all-trades, there will be items in your children's wardrobes that you can't make. Also, as children grow older and peer pressure to conform grows greater, you will find that your homemade fashions, no matter how professional in appearance, just don't charm your offspring any longer. But until the inevitable occurs (and after it passes, which it will . . .), enjoy and take advantage of the opportunity to be artistic and thrifty in providing quality clothing for your children. They will love sporting your latest creation and will feel very special in their designer togs. A little make-do ingenuity is a marvelous moneysaver.

WOOLEN SOAKERS, NOT PLASTIC PANTS

A young mother on a West Virginia homestead felt that in her environmentally committed life there was no place for nonessential plastic. It seemed right to her that her firstborn should be delivered naturally, thrive on mother's milk, and wear plain cotton diapers. The baby's dresses were fashioned from simple patterns and natural fibers. Everything about this little one seemed part of a larger harmony—everything except the plastic pants that had to be used over her diapers.

The pants themselves weren't that big a problem to be sure. The baby exhibited no allergy to the plastic, as some babies do, and had no greater incidence of diaper rash than is usual, but the plastic pants represented one niggling aspect of life that wouldn't succumb to self-sufficiency. The mother enjoyed the service rendered by the diaper covers and didn't mind the small purchase price, but it bothered her mightily that there was something she needed which she couldn't provide with her own do-it-yourself skills. In her battle against synthetics as a way of life, she felt it would be humiliating to be beaten by a pair of plastic pants!

She reasoned that other mothers at other times must have faced and solved this particular problem in some manner (after all, babies have been around longer than plastic or rubber), but her research kept turning up unsatisfactory solutions: The inner bark of oak trees was used to diaper East Coast Indian papooses, while Eskimo and Canadian Indian babies were swathed in sphagnum moss. Eventually this homestead mother's inquisitiveness uncovered an acceptable idea that had been working for generations: woolen soakers.

Whole generations of healthy farm children had their diapers covered by these short, plain pants crocheted from wool yarn. The lanolin (an oil in sheep's fleece) which remained in the handspun, unprocessed wool made the pants water repellent.

Not everyone raises sheep or has access to homespun wool as this present-day pioneer did, but you can still make soakers if you find the idea appealing. Store-bought woolen yarn will work, too. Just crochet the pants about three times too big and then shrink them down to size. It's important that you use *wool* yarn. It will absorb and hold a certain amount of moisture, whereas synthetic fibers will not. (If your baby is aller-gic to wool, you can substitute Angora goat hair or rabbit fur.)

To make a medium-sized pair of soakers, all you need is a size J crochet hook and four ounces of wool. Cast on 55 stitches and crochet for 6-1/2 inches. Add a second crocheted piece that is 10 stitches wide and 2 inches long. (The crotch area can be crocheted with a small needle to make it "tighter," but then the stitches must be adjusted so that this part of the garment will be as large as it's supposed to be.) Increase 5 stitches on both sides of the second strip and continue crocheting for another 6-1/2 inches. It's then a simple matter to join the sides of the last panel to those of the first. Note that the pants have only two seams. In sewing them together, you may want to use yarn of a different color from the body of the soakers. As the baby grows, you will be able to find the seams easily, ravel them, and add an inch or two all around the crocheted panels. The pants can grow, also.

About a dozen soakers are needed for one child, because wool dries slowly; if you don't have a good supply for changes, the baby will be wet—or without—while laundering takes place.

These woolens should be washed with mild soap in lukewarm water and dried in the sun whenever possible. (The sun will bring out more of the wool's lanolin.) As long as detergents aren't used, the lanolin will never wash completely out of the fibers. The natural water repellency of the soakers can be increased or restored by rubbing some vegetable oil or unscented lanolin into them. (Most drugstores stock lanolin.)

Unlike plastic pants, which often cause rashes, these all-wool soakers keep baby bottoms warm, even when wet, and actually help to prevent diaper rash. No two pairs of these crocheted baby pants will be exactly alike anyway, so get colorful and creative: These homemade diaper huggers can put plastic pants to shame.

HEALTH
AND BEAUTY

COLOR YOUR HAIR NATURALLY

Many people have the urge from time to time to change or enhance the color of their hair, but they are reluctant to pay the price of expensive over-the-counter products and are unwilling to use the harsh chemicals found in most commercial dyes and rinses.

Anyone concerned about the hazards of such ingredients will be glad to learn that you can quickly, safely, and inexpensively achieve results similar to those possible with beauty shop products. Just as others have done for thousands of years, you can change your basic hair color, put new highlights in your locks, or naturally darken gray strands—all with safe herbs.

HOW THEY WORK: Although there are a few especially potent exceptions such as henna and walnut hulls, most herbal dyes act progressively, and they should be used repetitively over a period of time until the desired shade is achieved. While no herb will actually bleach your hair, there are plant-based colorants that will highlight, darken, lighten, or cover the gray.

Despite their versatility, herbal preparations cannot match the strength of commercial products, and unless you decide to dye your curls black, an organic rinse won't cover your hair's present shade. The best idea is to enrich the natural color of your hair and to avoid trying to make drastic changes such as turning blond tresses to a very deep shade or dyeing gray hair darker than it was originally. You should also keep in mind that herbal dyes aren't permanent and will fade unless renewed occasionally.

If you've recently used commercial dyes, color rinses, or straighteners on your hair, you'd be wise to test any herbal mixture before applying it to your head, since chemical residues left your locks make it impossible to predict the outcome of the natural treatment.

To perform the evaluation, save some snips of hair from your next trim or cut a lock from the nape of your neck and prepare a small amount of whatever recipe you intend to try. Following the instructions for that particular mixture, apply it to the sample of hair, rinse the lock thoroughly, and let it dry (in direct sunlight, if possible). Observe the result under strong natural light, and if you want more or less color, simply adjust the number of rinses and/or the timing accordingly. After a couple of trial runs, you should be able to produce the shade you want.

Here are several preparations that should serve as an introduction to herbal hair coloring. Though the possibilities are almost unlimited, these few formulas will allow you to produce some of the most frequently used natural rinses and dyes. No matter what shade your hair, you should be able to find something here that will give you safe, attractive results.

MORE FUN FOR BLONDS: Chamomile is probably the most popular herbal hair colorant among blonds. A weekly rinse with this herb tea will brighten dull tresses and remedy the brown streaking that results from overexposure to the sun.

To prepare a chamomile rinse, steep half a cup of the flowers in a quart of boiling water for half an hour. Strain the mixture and let it cool while you shampoo. Then pour the brew through your towel-dried hair at least 15 times, catching it in a basin between each rinse. Wring out the excess moisture and leave the solution in your hair for a quarter of an hour before rinsing your hair with clear water.

Don't limit your herbal experiments to chamomile, however. Just about any yellow-blossomed flower or herb can be used on blond hair, including calendula (pot marigold), mullein blooms and leaves, yellow broom flowers, saffron, turmeric, and quassia chips.

Lemon is also a time-honored hair lightener. Strained into a quart of water, the juice of two fruits makes an excellent rinse that can be used in the same way as the chamomile preparation. In order to get the most from the treatment's lightening effect, try to dry your hair in the sun after using a lemon rinse.

Another native dye favored by blonds and prepared from rhubarb root will also add attractive honey gold tones to light brown hair. To put those glints in your locks, pour three cups of hot water over four tablespoons of chopped rhubarb root and simmer the concoction for 20 minutes. Strain the liquid and pour it through your freshly shampooed hair 15 or more times. Rinse your hair in clear water, and weather permitting, dry it in the sun to strengthen the effect of the dyeing agent.

A BONUS FOR BRUNETS: For more than 5,000 years, Egyptians have used a dark powder made from the henna shrub to give their hair and beards an auburn tint. Today you can buy henna powder at many herb supply houses and at some health food stores and co-ops. It's known as a safe, healthful dye, and since it coats the cuticle layer of each strand, it'll make your hair feel thicker. However, be warned that henna tends to produce an almost brassy orange-red shade when used alone, so it's best to mix it with a lightening herb like chamomile. Since it is so strong, henna shouldn't be used at all by persons with white, gray, or very light blond hair. Always try a timed test swatch first, too, to insure that you don't end up with an unexpectedly bizarre orange head.

One favorite recipe that can put reddish gold highlights in a dark mane calls for putting one part of powdered chamomile and two parts of powdered henna into a nonmetal bowl and adding enough boiling water to make a thick paste. Then a tablespoon of vinegar is stirred in to help release the plants' colors, and the blend is cooled for a few minutes.

When the paste is lukewarm, put on a pair of rubber gloves (henna can stain your palms and fingernails) and massage it into your clean, wet hair. Comb it in with a wide-toothed comb to insure even distribution of the dye. Next, pile up your hair, fit a plastic bag over it, and wrap a heavy towel around your head to hold in the heat.

You'll need to leave the dye and towel turban in place for anywhere from 30 minutes to two hours: The darker your natural hair is, the longer you'll have to wait for the henna-chamomile to do its work. When the time is up, remove the towel and the bag, and rinse your hair until the water runs clean. Then allow the newly colored tresses to air dry, in the sunshine if possible. Any stains that the dye might leave on your hands or around your hairline can be removed by rubbing them with lemon juice.

Should you prefer a simpler, slower-acting procedure, make a weaker henna solution and use it as you would any of the previous color rinses. Just mix together one tablespoon each of henna, chamomile, and vinegar, and steep them in a quart of boiling water for 15 minutes. Naturally, you should cool and strain the liquid before using it.

Sage is one of the oldest and most effective colorants for use on dark brown or black hair. A rinse made from sage leaves can be used to deepen any brunet shade, and it will also effectively cover gray in dark hair.

A sage rinse can be made by steeping a handful of the dried herb in a quart of boiling water for 30 minutes or more. The longer it steeps, the darker the tint will be. Cool the tea, strain it, and pour it through freshly shampooed hair 15 or more times. Then wait ten minutes before washing the liquid out with clear water. Because a sage rinse is a progressive dye, you'll have to apply it weekly until you produce the shade you want and continue using it once a month to maintain that color.

Tag alder bark is another popular hair-darkening botanical. However, it generally produces a lighter tone than sage, so it's best used to darken blond hair or to cover gray in locks that are light to medium brown. To make a tag alder rinse, simmer an ounce of bark chips in a quart of water for about half an hour. Then cool and strain the solution, and use it exactly as you would the sage rinse.

A very dark, sable-colored dye can be obtained from walnut hulls, but this one is tricky, since the nuts' outer casings tend to stain everything they touch. Because of this, it's a good idea to wear gloves throughout all the

stages of the process and to avoid rubbing the mixture into your scalp. To prepare the dark juice, first crush the hulls in a mortar, cover them with boiling water and a pinch of salt, and let them soak for three days. Then add three cups of boiling water and simmer the hulls in a nonmetal container for five hours, replacing the water as it steams away. Strain off the liquid, place the walnut hulls in a cloth sack, and twist it tightly to wring out all remaining juice. Finally, return the liquid to the pot and reduce it by boiling to about a quarter of its original volume. This will be the base for a rich walnut dye.

Add a teaspoon of ground cloves or allspice to the prepared extract. Allow the dye mixture to steep in the refrigerator for about a week, shaking it periodically during that time. When it's ready for use, strain the liquid through a piece of cheesecloth and pour it at least 15 times through freshly washed hair before rinsing thoroughly.

By experimenting with the formulas contained here, you'll be well on your way to achieving just about any hair shade you'd like without resorting to expensive, unsafe chemical dyes. You'll not only be saving money by using easily gathered materials, but you'll also be protecting the health of your hair.

SUBSTITUTES FOR COMMERCIAL COSMETICS

You may be surprised to learn that there are safe, inexpensive, and readily available substitutes for many of the personal care products that you are accustomed to buying at cosmetics prices. These alternative preparations, many of which are household staples, will not be elaborately or expensively packaged as drugstore toiletries usually are, but such home beauty aids have been demonstrating their usefulness for years.

A VERSATILE ITEM: Common cornstarch is a good substitute for talcum or bath powder, and it's especially valuable to those whose skins are sometimes irritated by the perfumes in commercial products. (In fact, a paste made of cornstarch and mineral oil is often used as a soothing mixture for dry skin.) You might also try patting on a thin layer of cornstarch the next time you need a colorless face powder to take the shine off your nose.

On those hectic days when your schedule calls for a quick dry shampoo, just sprinkle a generous amount of cornstarch into your hair, distribute it evenly, let it soak up the dirt and oil for a few minutes, and then vigorously brush it out.

ANTISEPTICS AND ASTRINGENTS: It's commonly known that hydrogen peroxide is a fine first aid antiseptic for the treatment of minor cuts and abrasions, yet few people realize that this product can also serve as a mouthwash and gargle. Simply mix a teaspoonful in a glass of water and swish.

Rubbing alcohol is another useful product. Indeed, many store-bought astringents (also called toners, tonics, or fresheners) are usually half-and-half mixtures of alcohol and water. Besides saving money, you can reap an added benefit from preparing your own astringent: It's easy to adjust the proportion of water and thus control the solution's drying effect.

Many aftershave lotions are based on astringent formulas, too, so try an alcohol-water blend in place of your usual "bracer." If you prefer a scented astringent, just add one teaspoon of extract (vanilla, peppermint, almond, lemon, or what have you) to a pint of rubbing alcohol before adding the water.

Witch hazel, an alcoholic solution containing extract from the bark of the witch hazel bush, is another household product that can be diluted with an equal amount of water to make a pleasant astringent, or that may be used full strength as an aftershave.

An application of witch hazel will alleviate the pain of bruises, bites, stings, sunburn, and minor scalds: Splash it on freely, cover the area with a soft cloth, and keep the bandage saturated. A witch hazel rub can ease stiff muscles, though several applications may be necessary to bring about the desired results, and if you happen to stray into a patch of poison ivy, just make a paste of witch hazel and baking soda and spread it on the affected areas for quick relief.

Witch hazel can be a boon for tired eyes, too. Soak cotton pads in the cooling fluid and place them on your closed eyelids while taking a ten-minute rest.

For a sweet, clean scent, use it after shampooing as a hair-setting aid.

MULTIPURPOSE OIL: One of the most versatile home cosmetic ingredients is mineral oil. If that lubricant seems too heavy, substitute one of the various vegetable oils: cottonseed, corn, olive, wheat germ, soybean, peanut, sesame, safflower, or whatever you like best.

Any of these can be used to replace a number of the oil-based products probably found in your bathroom. Baby oil, for example, is often no more than mineral oil with added scent, but you'll pay several times more for the leading brand of baby oil than you will for plain mineral oil!

Mineral or vegetable oils can also stand in for high-priced bath oils and skin softeners. If you pour two or three tablespoonfuls into your tub, the beauty aid will float on top of the water and coat you with a fine, velvety film. If you'd prefer the oil and water to mix, simply combine 1/2 teaspoon of clear shampoo with 1/4 cup of mineral or vegetable oil and pour the mixture under the running tap.

Mineral oil can take the place of your cleansing lotion as well. Just smooth it on with your fingertips, wipe it off with cotton, and follow the application with a splash of astringent. It can be an especially gentle but effective eye makeup remover.

Many thrifty folks use vegetable oil to replace expensive hair conditioning treatments. (Mineral oil may affect the color of blond or gray hair.) To do so, just rub a small quantity of the natural lotion through your hair, keep your head wrapped in a very warm, moist towel for 30 minutes, and then shampoo thoroughly. (Another good conditioner, one which combines the well-known benefits of oil and eggs, is mayonnaise. Spoon it directly onto your head, rub it in, wrap as instructed above, and wash the hair well.)

You can even soften whiskers by using mineral oil in place of regular shaving cream! If the oily residue bothers you after you've finished, a mild astringent will readily remove it. Apply a tiny amount of oil to your lips as a combination gloss and moisturizer. To make a lip salve, heat one part beeswax and six parts olive oil and pour the mix into a cleaned-out lipstick container.

Put the tube in the refrigerator to harden the mix.

BENEFICIAL BAKING SODA: Baking soda (also called bicarbonate of soda) is another kitchen standby that can be utilized in any number of ways.

It works well as a tooth powder, used either plain or mixed half-and-half with salt. To make such a cleaner easy to dispense, put a supply in a small salt shaker. Soda also makes an effective mouthwash if you stir a teaspoon of the powder into a glass of water and gargle.

If your area is afflicted with hard water, you'll be glad to know that baking soda is a good substitute for bath salts. Pour two or three teaspoons under the running tap and enjoy.

Baking soda is a fine body deodorant, too. In fact, it's currently a primary ingredient in several commercially formulated deodorants. To apply it, just pour some in a shallow dish and pat it on with a powder puff or a piece of cotton.

To prepare a facial mask for oily skin, combine one tablespoon of baking soda with three tablespoons of unprocessed bran (an abrasive). Add just enough water to make a paste and apply the mixture to your face. Leave it on for 15 minutes, and then wash it off, using either lukewarm water or a weak astringent.

SIMPLIFY FOR QUALITY AND ECONOMY: More and more people have begun to question the wisdom of paying exorbitantly for convenience, gimicky packaging, and excessive promotion. It's a step in the right direction to replace some of the overpriced, specialized preparations in your medicine chest and on your dressing table with a few basic ingredients that work safely and well and have a variety of uses.

NATURE'S OWN SUNTAN PRODUCTS

Most of us are aware that overexposure to the sun's ultraviolet rays can be dangerous, and that a gradual tanning routine is the only commonsense approach to sunbathing.

It's less well-known, however, that you can augment your body's natural sun-protection systems by increasing your consumption of vitamin C and the B vitamins, all of which are depleted when your body is regularly exposed to ultraviolet rays. Summer's delicious harvests of fresh cantaloupe, strawberries, tomatoes, green peppers, broccoli, and collard greens provide excellent sources of vitamin C, as do citrus fruits and juices. Foods rich in B vitamins include eggs, liver, poultry, wheat germ, unrefined cereals, milk, bananas, tuna, salmon, spinach, peas, and dried brewer's yeast.

INEXPENSIVE PROTECTION: Other natural protective aids are readily and economically available from your kitchen, bathroom cupboard, pharmacy, or health food store. When using them, as with all sun-care products, it's best to avoid application in the eye area.

Sesame is the polyunsaturated nut oil that, according to herbalist and natural beauty expert Dian Dincin Buchman, "most fully absorbs the ultraviolet rays of the sun." Ms. Buchman suggests applying sesame seed oil alone as a tanning aid. If you only have access to whole seeds, grind a handful of them in your blender or nut grinder, add a few drops of water to make a milky fluid, and then apply that. One-quarter teaspoon of witch hazel or ethyl alcohol can be used as a preservative, or you can just label the bottle and keep it refrigerated. When swimming, you'll have to reapply the lotion each time you come out of the water, as it will wash off and leave you unprotected.

Ms. Buchman also mentions that a combination of sesame oil, anhydrous lanolin, and water can be used as an effective tanning cream. Simply melt 1/4 cup of lanolin in the top of a double boiler, then immediately blend in 1/4 cup of sesame oil and 3/4 cup of water. This mixture can also be stored in the refrigerator in a clean, labeled container.

Another natural suntan lotion can be made by peeling and mashing one large cucumber, straining the liquid through cheesecloth, and adding one teaspoon each of rose water and glycerin, both of which you can probably buy at your local pharmacy.

For a minty suntan cream that's soothing and helpful while soaking up the sun's rays, drop a handful of fresh mint leaves in a blender containing a couple of tablespoons of water. Add 1/2 cup of sesame or coconut oil, one egg yolk, and one tablespoon each of wheat germ oil and lemon juice. You might want to put in a drop of peppermint oil for extra fragrance before blending the ingredients. Once again, keep this lotion refrigerated.

SUNBURN TREATMENTS: When all precautions fail and you get a whale of a sunburn, there are many effective home remedies that can bring relief. Some folks find that if they break open vitamin E capsules and apply the oil to the skin, the burn will often disappear overnight. The same vitamin packaged in ointment form offers similar results. As alternatives, you might try applying sunflower, safflower, or cottonseed oil, all of which are rich in the healing nutrient.

Herbalists and natural beauty experts also recommend compresses made with tea from comfrey leaves or roots, black tea, or the juice of a grated raw potato for the treatment of painful sunburns. You can also dilute apple cider vinegar with water and pat it on the burned area or use it in a compress. A cloth or bandage that's kept saturated with witch hazel, or with equal parts of vinegar and olive oil, can also be beneficial.

Some additional homemade sunburn remedies include the following: sesame, peanut, corn, or some other vegetable or nut oil mixed with vinegar; a solution of equal parts of witch hazel, olive oil, and glycerin; the gel taken directly from the succulent leaves of the aloe vera plant; a paste made of baking soda or laundry starch and water; a tub bath in water to which a cup of baking soda has been added; lemon juice and yogurt combined to a spreadable consistency; witch hazel mixed with a beaten egg white and honey; plain cucumber slices laid directly on the burn; and mashed cucumber pulp or juice strained through cheesecloth and used either alone or with witch hazel for a cool, soothing compress.

Finally, old-fashioned barley paste is recommended to soothe sunburn discomfort. To make such a paste, grind or blend three ounces of barley and mix the powdered substance with one ounce of raw honey. Blend the ingredients into a smooth paste and add one unbeaten egg white. Rub the concoction gently into the reddened skin and leave it on for several hours, preferably overnight, for slow but sure relief.

OLD-TIME ORGANIC BEAUTY SECRETS

For centuries, the only beauty aids in existence came from herbs, fruits, and vegetables. With the development of the cosmetic industry, an alluring array of prettily packaged chemicals replaced the homegrown compounds used by generations of carefully groomed women. As old-time recipes for beauty preparations have been rediscovered, even consumers who can afford the best commercially available cosmetics are inspecting their kitchen cupboards and gardens for safe and proven ingredients to use in their beauty routines.

Years ago a conscientious mother might have given her daughter the following advice on beauty care:

IN THE MORNING: Mix a handful of oatmeal with enough spring water to make a paste, and put this mixture on your face and neck. When it dries, rinse the paste off with whey, and then with water. Dry your skin with a soft cloth.

AT NIGHT: Rub a mixture of honey and glycerin onto your face; then after a few moments, wipe it off gently with a towel.

ONCE A WEEK: Add a teaspoon of honey to one mashed apple, blend them together, and smooth this mixture onto your face and neck. Leave it in place for half an hour, and then rinse with whey or cold milk.

TO SMOOTH WRINKLES: Apply barley water and a few drops of balm of Gilead (balsam) to your wrinkles every day.

TO BLEACH YOUR SKIN: Rub cucumber slices on your face.

FOR SOFT HANDS: Shake together a half cup of glycerin, a half cup of rose water, and a quarter cup of witch hazel in a jar. Apply this to your hands after they've been in water.

TO HEAL CHAPPED HANDS: Rub them with damp table salt.

FOR BRIGHT HAIR: Add vinegar to the rinse water after washing your hair, or make a rinse of mullein, nettle, sage, or burdock tea.

TO DARKEN GRAY HAIR: Boil an ounce of chamomile or sage in a quart of water for 20 minutes. Rinse your hair with this brew, and use a hairbrush dipped in strong chamomile or sage tea.

TO PREVENT DANDRUFF: Rub a tea made from the leaves and bark of a willow into your scalp. Rinse with a tea made from marshmallows (the pink-flowered perennial).

FOR A RELAXING BATH: Hang a bag of dried comfrey or rosemary in the bath water.

FOR PERFUME: Fill a jar with pressed rose petals (or any sweet-scented flowers), add as much glycerin as the container will hold, and cover it tightly. After three weeks, pour the perfume off into a bottle.

TO MAKE A SACHET: Combine one ounce each of powdered cloves, caraway seeds, nutmeg, mace, and cinnamon with six ounces of dried, powdered orrisroot (the fragrant rootstock of certain European irises). Put the mixture in pretty bags and place them in closets and dresser drawers.

A WORD OF CAUTION: Anyone can be allergic to almost anything, so check out any unfamiliar substance before you rub it all over yourself. To do this, just place a small amount on the tender skin of your inner arm and cover the area with an adhesive bandage. Then wait 24 hours and have a look. If the patch shows redness or any other obvious irritation, that ingredient just isn't for you.

Many lovely mature women say they don't feel a bit older than they did at 16, and often they don't look their age, either. Could strictly adhering to certain organic beauty rituals account for that healthy glow and assurance? Possibly. It's certainly safe to say that natural beauty routines can't hurt, and that's a claim that some cosmetics companies can't make.

RECREATION

RECREATION AT THE COUNTY FAIR

People beginning the homesteading life and leaving the urban bustle behind often find themselves without the diversions they enjoyed before. The annual county fair may well be a replacement for these things—an economical and delightful substitution that the entire family can anticipate and enjoy.

These festive gatherings are held annually in a great many counties across the country. A family's initial experience might vary from a casual visit, to a stop to familiarize themselves with the types of livestock and crops grown in their new area, to entering their children's projects as exhibits. With camping facilities available near the fairgrounds, a visit of several days need not be an expensive proposition, even for families on a scrimp-and-save budget.

A family's initial exposure to the county fair might well come through their children when one of the youngsters becomes involved in 4-H club activities, which usually include preparing exhibits for the fair. Those first entries might be in one or more of several categories such as sewing, canning, crafts, or livestock, and winning a ribbon or two can spur one on to branch out into more activities and to enter other areas of competition.

The fields in which one can enter exhibits are almost unlimited. The prizes won by just one family member can spread fair fever throughout a household, and few people are immune. There's an outlet for everyone's interests, whatever those may be: cooking, canning, crafts, beekeeping, making jams and jellies, raising livestock, growing fruits and vegetables, collecting minerals or arrowheads, sewing, knitting or crocheting, needlepoint, painting, photography, and so on. Preparing for the annual judgings can be a year-round activity, climaxing only when the prizes and premiums are awarded at the fair itself.

However, the fair is more than just a place and an opportunity to display the fruits of a year's labor. There is plenty to do besides setting up exhibits and looking over the competing displays. There are usually how-to demonstrations and workshops on crafts, cooking, canning, and other topics; there are homegrown and home-cooked meals to sample; there are friendly people with similar interests bustling about; and there is usually at least a small carnival with rides, games, hot dogs, and cotton candy.

Quite aside from all the fascination and the fun, a fair can provide an education for the beginning homesteader. It may, for instance, be the place where a person first learns how best to plant and care for produce, simply because of a desire to get in on the fun of entering the prime specimens of the harvest at the fair. Watching the livestock judging has inspired many a family to begin raising chickens, goats, sheep, pigs, or other farm animals.

Getting to the fair can be as easy as loading the family and its exhibits into the truck or car and driving a short distance. But staying a few days will make the outing a real vacation, and camping near the fairgrounds can hold the cost of the venture to the expense of gas, meals, and any gate charges. Moreover, winning a few premiums can very well offset the money spent for these.

Such a homesteader's holiday is an enjoyable, inexpensive, and exciting way to enjoy the company of friendly people, meet new folks, learn more about living, and take a vacation the whole family can enjoy. A few days at the county fair are hard to beat.

FIRESIDE FUN WITH FOLK GAMES

Anyone who grew up on a family farm remembers how the house was often filled with company for an evening meal. Sometimes it was relatives, sometimes friends, neighbors, or acquaintances, but no matter who was there, the evenings could still get pretty dull for the youngsters unless someone thought of playing a good game.

A game! As if by magic the age difference between the grown-ups and children would melt away, and everyone would play together in a spirit of excitement and goodwill. Those times generated lasting good feelings. Years may have passed, but when the common leisure diet of spectator activities starts to rankle and you feel restless and uninspired by the usual entertainment, remember what fun participation can be! Try playing together as a family, just the way you loved to do years ago and invite some kindred souls to share your evening of games and conversation.

BE CHOOSY: The right game is especially important in bad weather when indoor activities must suffice. Really enjoyable fireside games are a type of folk recreation: More cooperative than competitive, they focus on the process rather than on the final outcome or score. All the players participate, and the rewarding interaction just naturally produces smiles, friendly laughter, and a positive feeling about oneself and the others involved. It makes sense to be picky about your pursuits, so always look for games that foster mutual kindness, creativity, and self-respect. The best activities are inclusive and allow folks of all ages and abilities to join in without feeling inept or embarrassed.

Choosing the right game for your group or occasion is only one step; leading it is another. The role of host or hostess is very important: Without at least one person to think about the group as a whole, the action can fall flat. The leader needs to set the tone for the evening's fun, lend encouragement to those who are shy, notice difficulties and attend to them, pay attention to the flow of activity, and be ready to step in with innovations or changes when needed. Remember to be flexible. If a game doesn't seem to be "going over" with the participants, move on to another one.

SELECTED FAVORITES: As with any set of directions, games tend to sound mundane and even tedious when written down. Don't be fooled; they really come alive when actually played. Some favorites described below are mildly competitive (which is fine if the sides are randomly chosen, the spirit is playful, and winning isn't the only goal), while others are of a wholly cooperative nature. All of them can be enjoyable.

Dots and Lines is a two-person game for which you'll need only a piece of paper and two pencils. The paper should be prepared with a grid of 100 dots (10 X 10), and one dot—any will do—in the top row should be crossed out. The players take turns connecting any two side-by-side dots with a straight line. You can draw lines vertically or horizontally. Whenever someone completes (and therefore takes) a square, that player initials the box and is then entitled to draw another line. When the grid has been filled in, the player who has the most boxes wins.

Dictionary (sometimes called "Fictionary"!) requires from four to eight people. You'll need a good dictionary, and each player should have a pencil, several pieces of paper or a pad, and an active imagination.

To start, one person looks through the dictionary until he or she finds a word that's unfamiliar to all the others. Without showing anyone else, that individual writes the definition—or a simplified version of it—on a piece of paper while each of the other players makes up a definition and, keeping it hidden from the others, writes it down. All the "ballots" are then folded, collected, and placed in a hat.

Now, the player who chose the word from the dictionary draws out the papers and reads them aloud, one by one. Each of the other players makes a note of the definition that he or she thinks is correct. A tally is made of the choices, and if you want to keep score (although you may think it's just as much fun to play without scoring), a point may be given to every player who voted for the correct definition, and to any player whose incorrect definition got a vote from someone else (one point for each vote). Needless to say, if you're going to keep score, the player who selected the word in the first place can't vote on the definitions.

Progressive Story is a good game to play while supper's settling. From three to eight people sit in a circle, each with a large sheet of paper and a pencil. To begin, each person starts a story by making up and writing down the answer to the question "When?" One phrase will do. This section is then folded under so it can't be seen, and each paper is passed to the person on the left. Next, each player continues the story by answering the question "Where?" The papers are again folded and passed to the left. Every time the papers are passed, the players answer another question: "Who?", "Did what?", "How?", "Why?", and "What's happened since then?" The real fun comes at the end, after you've passed your last contribution, when each person reads aloud a completed story. The results are delightful and often hilarious! One of the beauties of this game is that it can be played anywhere.

In the Manner of the Word can be played with as few as three or as many as twenty people. One person volunteers to be "It." He or she goes out of earshot while the other players choose a descriptive adverb, such as "smoothly." Upon returning, "It" asks a player to perform some action "in the manner of the (chosen) word": to shake hands, to put on a shoe, etc. "It" then tries to guess the adverb and may ask as many players as necessary to pantomime until "It" guesses correctly. The game is then repeated with another person being "It."

If you have about a dozen people and a long table, you're all set to play Jenkins Up. Half the participants sit on one side of the table and half on the other, making two teams. Each team selects a captain.

One team is called the Spotters, and the other the Passers. The Spotters watch carefully while their opponents pass a quarter secretly from one to another under the table. When there has been plenty of time to pass the quarter, the captain of the Spotters calls out "Jenkins Up!" At this, the Passers close their fists tightly, put their elbows on the table, and in unison thump their elbows three times. On the fourth count, their hands come down hard and flat on the table, concealing the sound of the quarter hitting the tabletop. The captain of the Spotters, in consultation with his or her teammates, can either eliminate hands that don't have the quarter (leaving the hand with the quarter until last), or can "spot" by immediately identifying the hand with the coin. If the captain makes a wrong call, the game is lost, and the original Passers get to pass again. If the Spotters are correct, the game's won, the quarter changes sides, and the office of captain is given to another member of each team. Jenkins Up is particularly good as a leveler, making differences in age and ability unimportant.

Another game that's successful with people of different ages is I'm Thinking of a Word That Rhymes With. . . . Anywhere from eight to thirty people can play this one. All are seated in a circle, with one player as "It." This person thinks of a one-syllable word, such as "plow," and says aloud to the group, "I'm thinking of a word that rhymes with 'cow' " (or any other appropriate rhyme). The group must now identify the secret word, but the guessers are not allowed to speak and must use dramatic action instead.

Any player who wants to guess raises a hand and, when called upon by "It," acts out the word. If "It" recognizes the pantomimed guess as being incorrect, "It" says—for example—"No, it isn't 'sow' " (or whatever). If "It" doesn't recognize what the mime is trying to "say," other players can help the actor with additional dramatizations (confirming in whispers that they've correctly identified the guess) until "It" finally determines the word.

The game has a two-part objective: The players must guess the word "It" has chosen, and "It" must understand the players' guesses. If someone identifies the word correctly, that player becomes "It" for the next round. Of course, if a reasonable length of time has passed and "It" still hasn't guessed the players' actions (or if they haven't guessed the word in question), common sense dictates that the word be revealed aloud and the game be continued with another word!

Actually, there are many similarly enjoyable pastimes based on informal dramatics, from the simple guessing game of Pretend (you're a fairy princess, an auto mechanic, a gardener, or whatever) to Charades with its array of hand signal clues. Of all recreational activities, these games combine some of the most exciting and satisfying elements of cooperative play.

An interesting offshoot of dramatic games, incidentally, is Build a Machine, a group effort which can be enjoyed many times with both children and adults. You'll need about ten people. Draw numbers from a hat or "count off" into groups of three or four. Each group goes off to a separate corner or room and decides on a machine to portray together, using their bodies for the parts. Each machine is then acted out in front of the other groups. Guessing the identity of the machine is as much fun as acting, and a clock will never be just a clock again, once you've been the pendulum!

WINDING UP THE EVENING: One good way to bring the evening to a close is with music. Group singing provides a comfortable transition from games to settling-down time, if you use one of the many action songs from our folk heritage. The rhythmic movement and simple melodic chant keep the group united, while gradually slowing down everyone's level of activity. *Ah, Wooney Cooney*, a folk song game from Africa, is a happy choice for the evening. Let everyone sit in a circle on the floor, sing the following song, and perform the actions described below, with each knee slap timed to the beat.

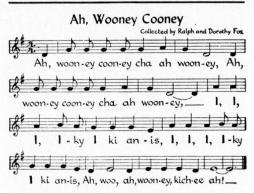

Ah, Wooney Cooney

Collected by Ralph and Dorothy Fox

Ah, woon-ey coon-ey cha ah woon-ey, Ah, woon-ey coon-ey cha ah woon-ey,___ I, I, I, I-ky I ki an-is, I, I, I, I-ky I ki an-is, Ah, woo, ah, woon-ey, kich-ee ah!___

From *Music Makers*, published in 1957 by Cooperative Recreation Service. Used by permission of World Around Songs.

Sit close enough so that each person can touch the knees of the neighbor to each side. The action is repeated over and over throughout each verse.

Actions first time through:
Hands on own knees
Hands on knees of person to left
Hands on own knees
Hands on knees of person to right
(Hands rest on own knees at end of verse)

Actions second time through:
Hands on own knees
Hands crossed on own knees
Hands uncrossed on own knees
Left hand on knees of person to left, right hand on knees of person to right

(Hands rest on own knees at end of verse)
Actions third time through:
Extend left arm forward
Touch left wrist, then left shoulder with right hand, keep right hand on left shoulder
Cross left hand to right shoulder
Extend right arm forward and repeat actions with left hand
(Hands are crossed, touching opposite shoulders, at end of the song)

By the time *Ah, Wooney Cooney* is finished, the mood is quieter, and singing a few more songs will bring the evening to a conclusion. When choosing a song, look for one with repetitions and a simple melody that lends itself to harmony. A variety of tunes to express different moods and perhaps a round or two will bring a comfortable sense of closure to the gathering. Friends can ease on home, and you and your children can slip off to bed.

After such a gathering, participants often feel as if something significant has happened, and indeed it has. Cooperative songs and games have, for the most part, been refined over the years to a beautiful and deeply human simplicity, cutting across centuries and cultures to appeal to something basic in all of us. They are strengthening and positive: Someone may feel beset by problems, but after such activities, that person gains a sense of hope and enthusiasm generated by the spontaneous fun and joy that's been shared. This kind of play with one's fellow humans is pleasurable and nourishing to the spirit, and all participants are able to experience a special sense of triumph.

HOW TO PLAY THE BEAN GAME

During the dark, snowy days of winter, family members can really enjoy playing games with each other. The Bean Game is a favorite indoor diversion.

Start the contest by giving each player ten dry beans (any number is satisfactory, so long as all participants start with the same amount). The object of the game is to see who can acquire the most beans in a given length of time—say, 10 or 15 minutes. The game can also be played till someone gets all the beans, but this can make the game longer and less exciting.

A group may prefer to play the Bean Game while seated around a table, so each cache of seeds can be manipulated undercover. You see, the transfer of treasure takes place in the following manner: Player A holds any number (or all) of his share, in a closed right hand, and shows this fist to player B. Player B must then make a guess as to how many beans are in that fist. If player B guesses correctly, he or she receives the beans in question, but an incorrect guess results in player B giving the number of beans guessed to player A. Regardless of the action, player B then goes on to hold out a fist of beans to player C, and the process is repeated around the table, with the last person turning to player A.

The direction of play can continue the same way until the game ends, or it can be reversed with each round to add variety. The rules are flexible; just be sure to define them before the game begins.

Dried beans can offer more than protein in the way of nourishment: They can readily provide an opportunity for family fun.

PLAY THE FOOTBAG GAME ANYWHERE

Footbags, little leather pouches filled with seeds, can be seen zipping through the air from foot to foot almost anywhere today—in living rooms, town squares, or the checkout lines at the supermarket!

These go-anyplace squashable objects are about the size of racquetballs, but like soccer balls, they're controlled with the foot. The toy was developed in 1972 in Portland, Oregon, by an athlete named John Stalberger to help rehabilitate his injured knee. Footbags quickly became popular across the country.

The popularity of the footbag is due at least in part to its amazing versatility. The bag is small enough to carry in almost any pocket and can provide entertainment for one person or several. As with most games, you can get as serious about playing footbag as your skill and enthusiasm allow. There's even a national association, which boasts a membership of well over 1,000 and sponsors tournaments all across the country.

DO IT YOURSELF: Since the sport has become popular under the name "Hacky Sack," it's now possible to buy "official" (that is, trademarked) Hacky Sack brand footbags in many sporting goods outlets. However, it's an easy enough matter to make your own if you've got about 20 minutes to spare.

First, collect two small pieces of leather. Make sure they're soft, pliable enough to work with, and sturdy enough to hold up to the wear and tear of action. If you have none on hand, inexpensive scraps can usually be obtained from a leather supply shop, an upholstery firm, or even a secondhand store. You'll also need some kind of stuffing such as mung beans or popcorn kernels, a marker, a pair of scissors, some dental floss or heavy carpet thread, a large, sturdy needle, and a pattern.

THE SETUP: Begin by using the pattern to draw two identical outlines on your leather strips, and then cut out the pair of matching pieces. Lay the pieces down, right sides together, with the ends of one peanut-shaped piece lying atop the center of the other. Thread the needle with about 18 inches of doubled floss or thread, and you're ready to begin.

Before you start stitching it's important that you have an idea of how you're going to turn those leather shapes into a pouch. It's easy to visualize the process if you use your hands to form a "demonstration model." Hold up your left hand, palm facing you and fingers pointing right. Now, lay the fingers of your right hand palm down against the thumb of your left. Then slowly cup both hands as if you were making a snowball. This will give you a rough idea of how the two footbag sections will fit together.

SEWING THE BAG: Make your first stitch directly through both layers of leather about 1/8 inch in from the edge at the point where the end of the top piece meets the side of the bottom one. Then go on to seam up the sack, keeping the edges as flush as possible when you roll the leather up into a rounded form. Don't worry if the stitches aren't perfect, but do try to space them fairly evenly, about 1/8 inch apart, and in far enough from the edge of the leather so that they won't cause the material to tear later.

Continue sewing until you're about 1-1/2 inches from completely closing the ball, and leaving the needle and thread attached, turn the pouch right side out. You may need to loosen a few stitches to do this, but they can be tightened back up. Next, smooth out the shape and fill the sack. You'll want to put in enough mung beans, popcorn, or whatever to allow for settling later. However, there's no rule as to how firm the bag should be, so you'll just have to experiment until you determine the fill density that suits you.

IN THE BAG: When your sack is packed, close up the open seam, turning the raw edges under and keeping the stitches as nearly invisible as you can. To finish sewing up the footbag, pull the thread taut and make a large knot as close to the sack as possible. A French knot works well, but any secure tie will do. Then cut the thread, poke the knot into the seam to get it out of sight, and you're done.

Your footbag is ready for action, so if you don't already know what to do with the miniature pigskin, it's time to find out how to play the game.

GETTING INTO THE GAME: The object of most footbag play is simply to keep the little sack in the air, using only legs and feet. The hands and upper body must not touch the ball, even for blocking, and the result is an action-packed activity that really develops eye-foot coordination.

Basically, the game requires five kicks. In order of importance and use, they are the inside and outside kicks, the back kick, the knee kick, and the toe kick. An experienced player should be able to do all the basic kicks with either foot. In each of these maneuvers, you'll soon discover that balance is the most important factor.

The inside kick is used whenever the bag is dropping directly in front of you. To perform it, rotate your ankle and point your toes, then reach out and up with your foot so you can meet the pouch with the arch area.

The outside kick, which is put to use when the sack comes to your right or left, involves turning sideways to the line of flight and sweeping your leg out from your hip and up to meet the little bag with the outside of

your foot. Contact should be made at about knee height.

The back kick is pretty difficult to execute but is called for when the pouch goes over your head. Lean forward for balance and contact the sack behind you with the outside of your foot.

The last two kicks, knee and toe, come into play less often. Use the knee kick, executed by raising your leg and stopping the sack with the top of your thigh, to block a footbag away from your midsection and set it up for either an inside or an outside shot. The toe kick, which is notoriously hard to control, should be reserved for occasions when the pouch is directly in front of you and too low to manage with any other maneuver.

Once you develop some confidence in your ability to control the basic moves, get out with some friends and pass the sack around. Don't worry about rules: Unless you're playing some form of tournament footbag, such as a variation on volleyball called "net-sack," you can pretty much make them up as you go along. Even the number of players is open.

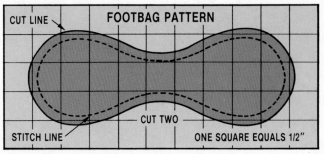

FOOTBAG PATTERN

CUT LINE

CUT TWO

STITCH LINE

ONE SQUARE EQUALS 1/2"

247

CREATE NATURAL OUTDOOR PLAYTHINGS

Most toys produced these days seem outrageously expensive, easily broken, and unnecessarily complicated, but youngsters' reactions to the world around them can provide the inspiration and instruction to create playthings out of free, readily available materials.

A HORSE SWING: For example, while taking a stroll through your woods one day, you might spy a young locust or some other tree with a beautiful curve at its base. The bottom of the trunk would make a sturdy and graceful swing.

To convert the trunk to a swing, first cut it and carry it home. Back at the house, strip off the bark—quite an easy task to do while the wood is green. Then, using a brace fitted with a one-inch bit, bore two parallel holes through the swing-to-be's side, one at each end of the trunk.

Next, saw a pair of one-inch-diameter lengths, each about eight inches longer than the width of the log, from a straight hardwood branch. With the bark removed, blunt the ends. The stubs should fit snugly in the holes with an end protruding on either side of the log. Ropes are then attached to the ends of the crosspieces to suspend the swing.

The hanging horse can be used safely by any child old enough to hold himself or herself in place on it, and the height of the swinging steed can easily be adjusted to suit the length of the young rider's legs by letting out or taking up the rope it hangs by.

BARK PIPELINES: The remainder of the tree used to make the horse swing can be stripped and cut into fenceposts, a process that will produce a pile of curled bark. A four-year-old can construct a water engineering project using these leftovers, and though such a homemade aqueduct might seem just a toy, bark-strip conduits have been used by pioneers and homesteaders for channeling water to a house.

BARK BOATS: Another project using bark will turn the small scraps 2 to 2-1/2 inches wide and 3 to 4 inches long into little Viking ships.

First, use a nail to press holes into the bark at any points where you want to locate masts. The uprights are made from thin sticks whittled to a point on one end. Trapezoid-shaped pieces of paper or big leaves can serve as sails. Just slip them onto the sticks and mount the masts in the nail holes.

When you blow on the little sails, the small bark boats slip prettily across the water, and there are almost always a few exciting capsizings to watch.

A PLAYING PLATFORM: The next time you have to cut down trees near your house, you might leave a little more stump than you ordinarily would. These will make sturdy foundations on which you can build playing platforms.

To make the structure shown in the accompanying photo, it was necessary to set a post in the ground at a point about six feet from two serviceable stumps. Then 2 X 4's were spiked in place running from each stump and the post to form a triangular base. Some old boards were nailed across these two beams, and a small ladder added.

Because this "playform" is shaded by greenery, it has the feel of a tree house. It can be a pretend pirate ship, a goblin's cave, or a knight's castle, but whatever it becomes, this deck will certainly see a lot of use on hot summer days.

BARTER, BARGAINS, AND AUCTIONS

BARGAIN BUYING AT A FARM AUCTION

"Sold!" bellowed the auctioneer, "to the man in the blue jacket for $4.00. And *that*, sir, is one fine bargain."

The item purchased by the guy in the blue shirt *was* a pretty fair buy. For his $4.00 he got a used, but perfectly serviceable, pitchfork—a quality farm tool that would have cost $15 to $18 in a store.

And there's no reason why anyone else couldn't duplicate (or better) this luck. The next time you decide to buy almost any kind of homestead equipment try visiting a local farm auction. You might well latch onto a really first-rate bargain.

If you don't know what you're doing, however, you can drive away from your first farm auction with a truckload of trash, and you might even pay more for a used article than you would to purchase the same item new in a store. Also, there's a real danger of catching "auction fever," an uncontrollable urge to pay too much for something you don't really want or need as a result of getting caught up in the excitement of the moment.

MASTERING THE LINGO: Like most organized activities, auctions have a peculiar set of terms with which the beginner should become acquainted. ("Auction" itself is derived from the Latin word *auctionem*, a process by which Roman soldiers bought captured booty on the battlefield by topping each other's offers for the plunder.) Once you've cracked the code, you'll be able to follow the action with a minimum of fuss.

A *bid* is the amount that you offer to pay for the merchandise, and *increments* are the jumps in price—there's usually a minimum—by which that sum increases. *Opening the bid* refers to the sum at which the offers start, and just how high that initial bid should be is often a source of great debate among auction buffs. Some folks prefer to open low, hoping that buyer interest will be minimal so they can waltz away with the object for a song. Other people—especially those who are really

keen on owning a particular item—will start a little high with the intent of discouraging rival buyers. Still others believe it's best not to bid at all until the action slows down a bit.

A *lot* is a number of pieces that are sold as a unit, such as a set of dishes or a matched pair of chairs. *Knocked down* is the auctioneer's term for "sold": for example, "That table was knocked down at $15." A *reserve* is the lowest price that can be accepted for an article. While most farm auctions will not include a great number of reserve items, an expensive piece of farm machinery or the like may have a reserve price, and a conscientious auctioneer will generally tell you whether that condition exists before the bidding starts. *As is* means that you're buying the object complete with nicks, cracks, burned-out motor, and all.

Many auctions assign *buyer's numbers*. To obtain one, you simply register with the event's secretary, and he or she will give you a card with a number that's recorded each time you "bid in" an item. This simplifies bookkeeping, since the secretary can then run a tab for your purchases, and you can settle up your bill when you leave. Buyer's numbers also provide bidders with a certain anonymity.

HELPFUL HINTS FOR PENNY-PINCHERS: While you're learning "auctionese," you'll also be gaining assurance in your ability to recognize, and bid on, bargains. The following list of tips should help a novice avoid misunderstandings and expensive mistakes.

[1] Read the *sale bills*—which are ads in local newspapers, or fliers that describe the merchandise being offered—before the auction. By doing so, you'll know which things you're interested in and be able to check their retail prices. At the same time, you should note the *terms* of the sale and work out your own financial arrangements. Before you can remove your purchases, many auctions will demand cash, while others will accept checks drawn only on local banks.

[2] Thoroughly inspect any merchandise you want to bid on prior to the opening of the auction. Arrive early enough (or attend the preview day if the goods are exhibited to the public beforehand) to pore over the loot. You should, for example, plug in electrical appliances to see if they work, crank the handles of mechanical items to make sure the gears aren't frozen, and check bureaus or chests for missing or mismatched pulls.

[3] Make a list of the items you want and *stick to it* to avoid compulsive buying. Many auctions place convenient little number stickers on each article or lot, and these are announced as the objects are put up for sale.

Jot down the numbers of any goods you're interested in, with a brief description of each and the *maximum* you're willing to pay for the privilege of owning it.

[4] Find out what an object is worth. If you've done your homework, you won't get so carried away that you pay more for a broken-handled pitchfork than you would for a new one. On the other hand, don't let the fact that an article is used affect your judgement. You can find real bargains in merchandise whose only fault is that its owner no longer needs it.

[5] Know *how* you're bidding. Suppose there are four chairs in a row: Is the auctioneer selling them one at a time or all four at once? If the sale is announced as *one money*, you're bidding on all four chairs. *Times the money* means, on the other hand, that you're bidding the price of one chair, and if the lot is knocked down to you, you'll get all four chairs at *four times* your final bid. *Choice of chairs* means that your winning bid will buy you first pick among the four. (Most auctioneers will then let you—or anyone else in the audience—take any or all of the remaining chairs for the same price, but if there's no interest, the bidding starts anew.)

[6] Be sure you understand the spiel. As a good auctioneer chants in a singsong, he or she is telling you what's being sold and how, plus both the current bid and the price that's being sought. Listen carefully until you're certain you're following the action. It's a shock to find out you bought a hammer for $12.50 when you thought the bid was $2.50.

[7] Stop the show if you have a question. An honest auctioneer won't object.

[8] Secure your goods. As soon as the auctioneer says "sold" and hands over the merchandise, it's *your* responsibility. One of the biggest problems at auctions is thievery. Watch your loot or lock it up.

[9] If you go with friends, stay together and decide—in advance—who'll do the bidding on which items. It can be pretty embarrassing to realize that the "stubborn pest" in the back who keeps topping your offer is your spouse.

[10] Watch your hands. You've likely heard the horror stories about auctiongoers who were waving at friends and suddenly found themselves the proud owners of a moose head. While some such tales are so old they ought to have whiskers, it is probably safest to control your hand movements until an auctioneer becomes familiar with your bidding mannerisms.

[11] Drive a truck. As mentioned before, your new property is your responsibility, and auctions often aren't equipped to hold the merchandise until you can pick it up. If you have plenty of room to stash and transport your goods, you'll also avoid paying hauling charges, which can add considerably to "bargain" prices.

Farm auctions are far more than just sales. They're social gatherings. There's no better place to spend a leisurely day in the country or to get an education in old-time comparative shopping than at a rural auction. And while you're learning, you just may walk away with the "bargain of a lifetime."

With a microphone and a gavel, one of a pair of auctioneers calls for bids and "knocks down" the items when the final offers are reached, while the other keeps a sharp eye out for anyone raising the ante. In addition to offering bargains—such as lovely home furnishings or an old cider press—these competitive sales are social gatherings, often complete with food, beverages, and the company of friendly value hunters.

TRADING YOUR WAY THROUGH A VACATION

We all need a respite now and then, but taking a vacation most often means scrimping and saving to meet the expenses of being away from home. However, by negotiating trades and turning a vacation into an adventure, it's entirely possible to make that break from routine not only pay for itself but be profitable and fun as well.

One Canadian couple who liked to get away from the city to the Okanagan and Similkameen valleys of British Columbia for the summer managed to exchange enough labor and produce to support themselves and their children for an entire three months away from home. The couple had previously made friends with an organic farmer and had arranged to help him with his work in return for a reduced price on produce when harvesttime came. They had also agreed to bring him some seaweed for fertilizer when they came from their home on the coast, where it was freely available to anyone willing to take the time to gather it.

Foraging for seaweed was one of their favorite occupations anyway, so the couple didn't mind at all. They proceeded to harvest a two-ton truckload of storm-shredded kelp, eelgrass, rockweed, and dozens of other varieties of giant algae—all of it seasoned, so to speak, with sand, shell particles, and fine wood debris. After collecting this vegetation, they spread it out to be washed by the rain (fresh seaweed is too salty for use as fertilizer) and dried by the sun. Tending and tedding it like hay, they eventually had a third of a truckload of choice, dry, nutrient-rich fertilizer to take to their farming friend.

When the couple, their six-year-old son, and three-year-old daughter arrived at the farm in mid-July, they found their friend way behind in his hoeing. The grass, pigweed, and nightshade were choking his soybeans, squash, corn, and tomatoes so badly that he couldn't keep up with it by himself. He immediately offered them a credit of $4.00 per hour to hoe his fields for him. This was all the excuse they needed to pick up their tools and get to work.

After gently prodding their friend with "How long have we been hoeing so far?" and "What d'ya think the kids' work is worth?", the couple came right out and asked whether they could swap the whole family's efforts for produce. Further bargaining resulted in a deal that was satisfactory all the way around: The family would hoe a certain part of their friend's fields in early summer and be paid in September with twenty 40-pound boxes of tomatoes.

Then came the question of the seaweed. "What do you figure all that fertilizer's worth?" the farmer asked.

"Well, Hank," said the husband, "we've put so much love and labor into the weed that it's beyond price, so we'll just have to give it to you."

The farmer pulled his beard and chuckled. "You know, that's exactly how I feel about my vegetables. So while you're here, you just take all the fresh vegetables you can eat."

In this way, the land-tiller got quality fertilizer for the farm, and the couple wound up with as many onions, new red potatoes, cucumbers, kohlrabi, and ears of sweet corn as they could eat.

Next, while they were camped out at their friend's, they discovered eight damaged fruit ladders ranging from 8 to 18 feet long, just lying in the grass, left over from the time when the farm had been an orchard. After a quick huddle with the farmer, they had another deal on their hands. Using the tools, scraps of lumber, and other odd hardware that they had on hand, it took the couple only a day to put all the ladders back into prime condition. Then the farmer selected four for himself, and the couple got the others. They were most useful, too, for from that day on, whenever they negotiated deals with orchard owners to pick fruit, they could always say, "We have our own ladders and buckets." And they'd get the job.

Both families liked to dry fruits and vegetables, and it just so happened that the farmer had a plastic-covered dome that warmed up fast when it was set out in the sun. So the vacationers arranged a third deal: Their friend would provide screening, a staple gun, and free access to his private junk lumber pile, and they would construct eight drying racks covered with fine fiberglass screening. Then everyone would share the use of these frames.

Well, they built the racks and dried some cherries on them, but when all was said and done, the couple didn't feel that they had really come out even on the exchange. As luck would have it, this imbalance was corrected at a later date.

The couple and their children stayed at the farm for another week before moving on, but their swapping experiences didn't end then. After untold hours of work in different orchards, they ended up with 1,200 pounds of cherries and 1,000 pounds of apricots and peaches to take home as a supplement to the cash wages they were sometimes paid.

Another time, as they were uneventfully driving along at three o'clock in the morning, the tractor-trailer truck just ahead began to rain 50-pound sacks of chicken feed along the freeway. They salvaged $20 worth of the split sacks and finally located a homesteading family that could use the feed. However, the homesteaders' hens weren't laying many eggs at the time, and their goats weren't giving much milk, so the travelers gave them the feed anyway, with the promise of something interesting in return at a later date.

After a summer of traveling and trading, the family returned in mid-September to their friend's farm, only to find him in a bit of a quandary: He was burdened with a field of luscious, ripe, organically-grown tomatoes for which he had no buyers. The local market was glutted, and those tomatoes wouldn't sell at even a few cents a pound. Yet, two hundred miles away, over the mountains, lay the city of Vancouver, British Columbia, where people were paying ten times as much per pound for tomatoes of poor quality shipped all the way from Mexico.

The couple's two-ton truck was just sitting idle, and both they and the farmer were interested in turning a handsome profit. So, after they all spent the next three days picking and packing tomatoes, the husband started for the coast with nearly 4,000 pounds of perfect fruit and high expectations.

Ten days later, he returned. It had been one of those disastrous treks where people don't keep all of their promises and containers unaccountably collapse; where opening hours and ferry ticket-takers and food co-op buyers all seem to conspire against you; where nothing goes as planned. The husband had sold tomatoes, traded tomatoes, dumped them on friends' doorsteps, thrown away rotten ones, and he had even taken the time to return home and can 400 pounds of the pulpy fruit. When he returned, he gave the farmer enough cash to cover the value of the goods that had survived the journey. Still, the family had not only failed to make wages on the deal; they'd actually lost money. Their friend had accepted the risk of this venture along with them, however, and he compensated them for their loss with 800 pounds of acorn squash on the vine.

During the husband's absence, the wife and children had begun drying and bottling the twenty 40-pound crates of tomatoes they received as part of their July hoeing swap. So they all continued to work on the fruit for more than a week, cutting off tops and bottoms of the juice-filled tomatoes to cook and bottle as sauce, and slicing the meaty centers into thin wheels, which after four days on the drying racks became tissue-thin slivers of potent flavor. It was then that the drying-racks swap finally balanced out.

By the time they'd finished with the tomatoes, it was early October and grape-picking season, so they bade farewell again to their friend on the farm and headed for a vineyard. They found a promising one, and the owner allowed them to camp on his property in exchange for helping him harvest grapes. In addition, they were allowed to keep a pound of grapes for every 15 pounds they harvested.

Grape picking is interesting work. You get to eat a lot of the sugary-tart little fruits (which slows you down), you quickly develop purple hands, and occasionally you snip your fingers with the shears or get bitten by one of the mice that seem to savor grapes, too.

The "vacationers" continued to barter for things they needed. They discovered that the vineyard owner had quite a number of large, sturdy plastic crates. Designed to either stack or nest, and invaluable for shipping wine grapes, they were now cracked and useless. But the husband mended ten of them with an electric drill and scraps of thin wire. The owner was so pleased that he gave them five of the handy containers as payment for the work.

About this time, they decided that they'd picked more than enough. They already had more squash, bottled tomatoes, fresh tomatoes, corn, onions, cull plums, and cull apples than they knew what to do with, and some of the grapes they'd harvested for themselves were wilting. So, borrowing the owner's grape press, the family pressed 500 pounds of muscats and gave the mash (the pulp left over from the pressing) to the vineyard owner for "second wine."

In the meantime, though, the family found that they had picked $9.00 worth of grapes more than they'd earned, and they couldn't pay for them. The owner at first agreed that they could make this up the following year, but before the group left he came beaming to their truck to say that the muscat mash they'd given him was well worth the overrun. Thus, the accounts were balanced after all.

As the family departed the Similkameen Valley in their weary and heavily burdened truck, they found it necessary to make another swap. A friend had driven their car out to the valley for them, but he was no longer around to drive it back. This meant they had two vehicles—the car and the two-ton truck—to take home, but since the wife didn't drive, they had just one driver. Fortunately, they soon met a lady hitchhiker who readily agreed to drive the auto back in return for the free transportation.

Yet another exchange occurred when they stopped overnight at a hostel. There they happily traded plums, tomatoes, and one crate of grapes for their supper and breakfast.

And finally, upon arriving home, they still had an abundance of grapes and squash that could be traded for other produce, magazines and books, or any number of other items or services.

"What a summer of hard work!" their friends exclaim when told about the trip. Well, it *was* hard. But it was also a fun-filled adventure. They returned healthy and fit, and they had their children right there with them all the time. The whole family had made many friends and had experienced firsthand the tremendous effort and care that it took to produce the food they enjoyed in such abundance.

STRIKE BARGAINS THROUGH BARTERING

For kids, bartering has always been a prime way to acquire the enviable, treasured things of life. What child hasn't traded his mother's chocolate chip cookies for his best friend's mother's homemade ice cream? Or a favorite toy for a half-dead frog, a cat's-eye boulder marble, *and* a broken slingshot? Now that's a real deal! Bartering may have been abandoned as baby stuff when you entered the preadolescent world of high finance, where lucrative lawn-mowing jobs paid actual, instant, no-dickering-about-it dollars. From then on, the importance of the green stuff probably exerted a powerful influence on your life, endowing you with the attendant stresses, tensions, and headaches that go with surviving in a cash-oriented society. However, the ravages of recession and inflation have forced many urban and suburban people back to the land in an effort to reduce their living expenses, and a number of farmers are reverting to yesteryear's methods, including bartering their goods and services for those that others can provide.

For the past few years, one such farmer has moved considerably away from paying exclusively with cash to bartering frequently and cleverly for many of the essentials and nonessentials of life on his 150-acre farm. By using the bartering process, he has been able to channel most of his cash flow back into the farming operation. His need for ready cash for a multitude of food items and small services has diminished, and the fun of bartering has relieved some of the everyday financial pressures associated with running a business.

Anyone can barter; it's a learned way of thinking. This man started bartering with two acres of strawberries that he planted to sell on a pick-your-own basis. A neighbor lady who lived on a dairy farm spied them, and the two struck a bargain. For every four cases of his strawberries, her family would manure one acre of his land. This exchange cut his fertilizer bill in half. Later he bartered strawberries for other foodstuffs and for such services as tailoring, knife sharpening, equipment repair, and seasonal promotion spots on the radio. He even traded strawberries for the glass used in a new greenhouse on his property. That was the start of his produce business.

The barterer expanded the operation by putting in melons, and there was the inevitable surplus. Another farming neighbor wanted the waste to supplement his hogs' diet and offered in return to dress a pig at butchering time for the melon grower's freezer. Later, the same farmer agreed to roast the pig to be served at a harvest dinner—if he could invite a set number of his friends. The greenhouse owner furnished the side dishes and derived a fair amount of free publicity for his fruit farm by inviting people who were in positions to spread the word about his booming business ventures.

On another occasion, the bartering entrepreneur hosted a party for 300 guests by swapping various types of publicity. The chamber of commerce in a nearby town approached him about using his farm as the scene of a party for television, radio, and newspaper personalities from across the state, with the purpose of obtaining publicity for area attractions. The money provided for the party by the chamber of commerce was enough to cover only the meat and drinks. The host proceeded to use his main commodity in bartering for the affair: the provision of publicity. For example, he contacted a friend who owned a local restaurant and asked that the chef there cook the three steamship rounds of beef (provided by the chamber of commerce) over a hurriedly dug pit at the farm. In return, the restaurateur would get a sign on the skewer, promoting his business. Next, the barterer called a tent rental company and offered similar advertising in exchange for a large open tent. A square dance group and band were offered free food and television coverage of their performance at the event. The dauntless barterer did the same for a skydiving club that added some unplanned sensationalism when one of the divers landed wrong and broke his leg. (The swap arranger claims that he was hoping the others would do likewise, as that would have generated three times the excitement and publicity, but the parachutists weren't in the mood for crippling experiences.) A beer distributor and long-time friend was persuaded to contribute the fireworks for the mere privilege of setting them off. (Appealing to a person's sense of adventure is important in the bartering business.)

Bartering on many levels has cut the labor costs for this farm by nearly 50%. By offering a package of $1.50 an hour and all the vegetables and fruit their families want, the owner is able to attract a crew of teenagers who give him all the help he can use. One worker who comes out during harvesttime trades a whole day's labor in return for melons, and a neighbor cans an entire winter supply of fruits and vegetables for the owner in return for the produce she needs to put up for her own family.

The farm has 50 acres of woods, which have been a gold mine for bartering. With the returning popularity of woodstoves and furnaces and the increased use of fireplaces to help cut heating bills, wood has been in great demand, and it can be traded for almost anything. The next-door neighbor who has hogs traded another pig for permission to cut from the woodlot. With the

254

extra pork, the owner bartered with the dairy farmer for a side of beef for the freezer and traded garden produce and melons for eggs and milk.

An average family can successfully employ similar bartering techniques on as little as two or three acres by planting cash crops. An acre of produce and a half acre of fruit trees can provide a family with enough surplus to do a great deal of trading.

Good types of produce to raise for barter are pickling cucumbers, tomatoes in quantities for canning, green peppers, and green beans. Homegrown melons have a special appeal because commercially grown varieties are usually picked green, to ripen during shipping, and therefore are less flavorful. Many kinds of berries are also especially sought-after commodities while they're in season.

Services can be bartered also, especially in urban areas. Any specialty, skill, or hobby you have constitutes a commodity. One might barter culinary or sewing talents for baby-sitting or hairdressing expertise. Woodworking skills can be exchanged for produce or labor of another kind. If you own a welder and can use it with facility,

dition of the homegrown foods.

The law of averages dictates that some swaps won't work out as well as you would like. Not all of the deals engineered by the enterprising barterer featured here have rewarded him with the desired results: to wit, the case of the red union suit.

A department store asked him to model for their newspaper ad touting a new shipment of red union suits, the ones that come complete with a rear trapdoor. The model alleges that the mid-February wind was as cold as a well-digger's destination when he posed in front of a blockhouse in the park, and the trapdoor outfit offered precious little protection. For completing his end of the bargain, he got a plug in the ad (for his farm) and two sets of the scarlet long johns.

After spending a month recovering from pneumonia, this big-time barterer had to admit that he could have easily bought a dozen union suits and the ad space for much less than he paid in doctors' bills. He offers these words of caution to beginning barterers: Be careful what you bargain for. You just may get that—and more!

you may find yourself turning away trades for lack of time. The things that can be bartered are endless. All it takes to succeed are imagination and effort. And as more and more people become interested, trading networks can be established in neighborhoods and rural areas for the benefit of everyone involved.

You may find that the quality of services and goods received in barter will be better than that of commercially purchased vendibles. It's a pleasantly curious thing, too. For instance, if you barter produce, you will notice that most people will readily barter for fresh produce at a higher value than they would pay at a supermarket, because of the assured quality and good con-

Despite that caveat, bartering can also provide important intangibles. There's something about a swap in which both parties come out well satisfied that is very special. The goodwill generated by such a transaction can have far-reaching consequences. As other people learn that there is someone nearby with a willingness to barter, they will begin to approach you about working out a deal. And everybody has something to trade. Use your imagination and above all, be flexible. No swap is exactly like any other. Enjoy your interactions with other people. Approached in the proper spirit, this age-old practice can give you both a great deal of pleasure and many of the material benefits you desire.

Other Books Published By
THE MOTHER EARTH NEWS, Inc.

MOTHER'S HOMEBUILDING & SHELTER GUIDE
by the editors and staff of THE MOTHER EARTH NEWS®
64162 $12.95

**MOTHER'S ENERGY EFFICIENCY BOOK:
HEAT, LIGHT, POWER**
by the editors and staff of THE MOTHER EARTH NEWS®
81151 $14.95

MOTHER'S 101 WORKSHOP PROJECTS
by the editors and staff of THE MOTHER EARTH NEWS®
66232 $14.95

LIVING ON LESS
by the editors and staff of THE MOTHER EARTH NEWS®
70104 $14.95

*THE FRESH FOODS COUNTRY COOKBOOK
by the editors and staff of THE MOTHER EARTH NEWS®
74199 $14.95

UPRISINGS: THE WHOLE GRAIN BAKERS' BOOK
by the Cooperative Whole Grain Educational Association
74198 $12.95

WHIRLIGIGS: DESIGN AND CONSTRUCTION
by Anders S. Lunde
66189 $6.95

*MORE WHIRLIGIGS: LARGE-SCALE & ANIMATED FIGURES
by Anders S. Lunde
66239 $9.95

**CLOTH MARIONETTES: SEWING, STRINGING, STAGING
by Lucy and Grace Morton
66240 $8.95

POLE BUILDING: A STEP BY STEP GUIDE
by Norm Ecker, Sr. and Jeff Flanders
64130 $4.95

*Available September 1984
**Available October 1984

These books are available in bookstores or from THE MOTHER EARTH NEWS, Inc.,
105 Stoney Mountain Road, Hendersonville, North Carolina 28791.
When ordering from the publisher, please enclose $1.50
shipping and handling on one or two books, $2.00 on three or more books.